# THE NEW WORLD
# OF NEGRO AMERICANS

BY HAROLD R. ISAACS

The Tragedy of the Chinese Revolution
No Peace For Asia
Scratches On Our Minds: American Images
of China and India
Emergent Americans: A Report on Crossroads Africa
The New World of Negro Americans

*Pamphlets*

Two-Thirds of the World
Africa, New Crises in the Making

*As Editor*

New Cycle in Asia

*As Contributor*

As We See Russia
South Asia in the World Today

# THE

# NEW WORLD OF

# NEGRO AMERICANS

## HAROLD R. ISAACS

*A Study from the Center for International Studies,
Massachusetts Institute of Technology*

**THE JOHN DAY COMPANY, NEW YORK**

My interest in any man is objectively in his manhood and subjectively in my own manhood.
—Frederick Douglass

# CONTENTS

———————— ✿ ————————

Introduction                                          ix

## I. NEGROES AND THE WORLD

   1. The Peril to the Republic              3
   2. The Sins of the Fathers                22
   3. The Peculiar Consonance                32
   4. Wind At Their Backs                    50

## II. NEGROES AND THEMSELVES

   1. Out from Behind the Veil               57
   2. A Name To Go By                         62
   3. Black, Stand Back                       72
   4. Souls So Dead                           97

## III. NEGROES AND AFRICA

   1. The Hazy Presence                      105
   2. "Back to Africa"                        114
   3. The Heart of the Matter                155
   4. Rejecters, Inquirers, Affirmers        173
   5. Du Bois and Africa                     195

6. Five Writers and Their Ancestors                231
7. Something New Out of Africa                      288

IV. NEGROES AND AMERICA

1. The Keeping of the Dream                         325
2. The Losing of the Dream                          332
3. Toward Somebodiness                              343

Bibliography                                        351

Index                                               359

# INTRODUCTION

⸙

This book is about the impact of world affairs on Negro Americans. It is part of a continuing study of the ways in which all our images and self-images are being pressed into new shapes by the great political changes that have been taking place in the world since the end of the Second World War. This impact is universal, for no one is unaffected by these overturns, the end of the Western colonial empires and Western white domination of the earth, the re-emergence of Asian and African peoples, the creation of scores of new nations, the recasting of roles and relationships across national, cultural, and ethnic lines. At the end of a previous work, *Scratches On Our Minds*, a study of American perceptions of China and India, I stated this large theme in these words:

This is history in the large, a great continental rearrangement, bringing with it a great and wrenching shift in the juxtapositions of cultures and peoples. Western men are being relieved of the comforts and disabilities of being the lords of creation; Asian and African men can no longer merely submit, nor live on the rancors of subjection, nor revitalize their own societies by the ideas or sanctions of their own more distant past. All must move from old ground to new, from old assumptions to new ones, and as they move must constantly refocus their views. They will all be engaged, for some time to come, in more or less painfully revising the images they have of themselves and of each other.

In this revision, all the images and experiences of the past have some part. They are not effaced but are absorbed and rearranged in some new design. Much is relegated to the museums and to the memory and to the contending history books, but the greater part remains to bedevil the process of change itself . . . All the sounds, old and new, go on in our hearing at the same time, making the great din in which we live . . .

Continuing to sort out some of these sights and sounds, I began in 1957 to examine the impact of world affairs on race attitudes and behavior in the United States. It had become common by then to hear about the effect of American race problems on American standing in the world, but much less common to give heed to the reverse effect, that is, the way in which changes in the world were forcing changes in the American society. The Federal government and various sections of the white population were being affected by this pressure in many ways, but the greatest effect of all was plainly felt among Negroes. A first set of notes on my inquiries was published in the fall of 1958 in the *Public Opinion Quarterly* under the title "World Affairs and U.S. Race Relations: A Note on Little Rock," and that report concluded with this passage:

The profoundly transforming effect of world events on American Negroes in the last two decades is a major theme which stands quite by itself . . . For it is plain that in some form and some degree, the influence of world affairs has come to bear on Negroes at every level of life, North and South. It expresses itself in a great host of changed circumstances, changed attitudes and states of mind, in varying kinds of awareness in Negroes of the links between what has been happening to them and what has been happening elsewhere in the world, the links between the retreat of white domination in Asia and Africa and the retreat of Jim Crow in America. These notions, ideas, and attitudes appear in many different people in many different combinations, shallowly or in depth and in all sorts of contexts. It is hardly possible to brush against any aspect of contemporary Negro experience without coming upon them. Here too a great many questions beckon and I do not propose to pass them by.

During the next three years I put my questions to a great many people and explored these matters most particularly with a panel of 107 Negro individuals. This number includes first, a group of 80 whom I sought out for interviews and conversations in this country, a further group of 16 individuals working and living in several West African countries, and finally, a group of 11 young Negro men and women who also shared with me in lengthy interviews that year their experience in going to West Africa as participants in a student work-camp program.

This was obviously not a cross-section sample of the Negro population but a panel of individuals chosen mainly, in the case of the 80, because of their role as important communicators in the society, and in the case of the others because of their special experience in relation to Africa. Of the group of 80, 65 are leaders or top achievers in their fields as writers, scholars, educators, editors, businessmen, churchmen, key figures in important organizations. Of these, 17 can be said to be nationally prominent in the sense that their names would be known to large sections of the general public and 48 nationally prominent in the sense that they would be quite well known in their respective professional communities and very well known to that part of the Negro public that reads the Negro press or takes an active interest in Negro affairs. The remaining 15 were sought out not because of any prominence or achievement but because they occupied certain positions or places or were representative of certain types, attitudes, or experience that might otherwise not have been reflected in the report. Because of this difference in their various personal histories, some of these individuals often presented profiles of background or personality quite different from those most common in the rest of the panel.

The entire panel included 85 men and 22 women. In the basic group of 80 the ages ranged from just under forty to well over seventy, the older individuals spanning the crowded decades across the generations of two world wars, the younger coming to their maturity during the time of great change since 1955. These were many different and unique individuals out of a great variety of backgrounds, but the most notable achievers among them shared the experience of having striven hard and won much on the strength of their own gifts. Most of them came out of poverty but would now have to be classified as "middle class," that highly elastic American social category which starts at the first economic level above that of want. The more extended interviews ran inevitably to a great deal of autobiography, and from some of the most notable members of the panel I caught many glimpses of a misty gallery of parents who had played a key role in the beginning of each one's struggle to assert himself in a stifling environment. Approximately a quarter of the group had parents who were either without any formal schooling at all or had never gone beyond the elementary grades. At the other end of this spectrum, nearly another quarter of these achieving panelists had achieving parents who had gone to college and in a few cases on to higher professional education—one in dentistry, one in law, and three in medicine—and there was one parent who had earned a Ph.D. back in the 1890's and seems to have been more of an achiever than his son. In between was a large middle group which had finished elementary school or gone through part or all of high school. A good third of the panel had parents who had "middle-class" status; besides the lawyer, the dentist and the physicians, there were ministers, teachers, postal employees or holders of other small government jobs, and two or three were small merchants, a grocer, a florist, and one a construction-job foreman. But the larger number stood well below this level: laborers, sharecroppers, baggagemen and porters, janitors, and some fathers and many mothers who were domestic servants, cooks, laundresses. In a few cases the parental influence was negative—an errant or absent father or, much more rarely, an indifferent mother. But in most of these cases it was powerfully positive: a father with strong ideas or strong emotions who gave an example of coping with adverse circumstance, or a mother who refused to allow her children to stand at her own low threshold of opportunity. I was tempted more than once to turn aside to fill out the stories of some of these parents, for they add depth and great poignancy to the life histories of some of our more remarkable panelists, but I must content myself with simply noting here the dim but crucial parts they played in the small epic of each of these individual lives.

With 55 members of this panel, I had extended interviews

which often ran to a total of four to eight hours spread over two or even three sessions. With some of these individuals I had further sessions and conversations at intervals of months over a period of three years. In three or four cases, I was exploring these matters with old friends who had been contributing to my education for many years and who allowed me to come back again and again with further questions or for more discussion. With 25 members of the panel I had briefer interviews or conversations. But no matter how partial or even fragmentary these discussions were, they were never casual and hardly ever failed to suggest some fresh or different nuance or insight or facet of experience.

All these individuals who so generously shared their time and thought with me obviously have no share at all in responsibility for the limits of my ability to learn from them, or for how I understood or how I have used what I did learn. I am sure that some would disagree with the way I have organized or interpreted this material, and this would be only natural; my only concern is that I have quoted them all accurately and without misrepresentation. I was usually given permission to quote these individuals by name, but I have chosen in all but a few obvious cases—mainly the writers who by their trade place their inner selves in the public domain—not to exercise this privilege in the text but only to identify them here in order to thank them again and to acknowledge my great debt to them all, for this book is based almost entirely on what I learned in these interviews and conversations, and on the further historical or literary searches into which they led me.

The experience through which these individuals are passing is infinitely complex and I certainly do not presume to suggest that I have dealt with it inclusively in these pages. Negroes in America are experiencing a massive shift in their conceptions of their place in the world and in this society, in their view of who and what they are. Obviously all affairs and all history, everything that is in heaven and on earth and in every man's peculiar philosophy will have to come into any effort to see this process whole. Neither scholarly scrutiny alone nor clinical study will suffice to help us see it fully even in any single person's life.

Only novelists, poets, and playwrights are licensed for this kind
of audacity and one of them will no doubt sooner or later trans-
mute some of these great chunks of contemporary history into
the stuff of individual human experience.

My own essay in these pages is more modest. My first effort is
to try to see something of the larger outlines of this matter in
terms of the impact of world affairs on the patterns of racial behavior in the American society; to show how the end of white
supremacy in the world is forcing the end of the white supremacy system in the United States. I suggest that this interaction
between the place of Negroes in the United States and the place
of the United States in the world has been an element in our
history for a long time, and I describe the peculiar consonance
that has existed between the rise and fall of Western white
power and the rise and fall of white racism in America. On a
world scale the race issue as such was finally enveloped in the
rise of nationalism and the collapse of Western empire. In the
United States, the unresolved problem of racism and democracy
has finally merged with the problem of national survival. In
this way we have come to a rather fine historic pass: for our
democratic system to prevail over the totalitarianism that now
threatens us it must finally become, oddly enough, democratic.
This is the burden of the introductory section of this work, "Negroes and the World."

My further principal purpose was to examine the impact of
these changes and paradoxes on Negro Americans and to show
how it is forcing Negroes to reshape all the important ways in
which they have viewed themselves until now. I try to illustrate
this by singling out certain elementary aspects of group identity—name, color and physical characteristics, nationality, and
origins and history—and to explore how these have been shaped
in Negroes by the pressures of the past and in what forms they
now face the reshaping pressures of the present. The first three
of these elements are dealt with in the second section, "Negroes
and Themselves." The last, which involves examining the place
of Africa in the Negro group identity, is treated in the third and
major section, "Negroes and Africa." A concluding section, "Negroes and America," suggests some of the questions about their

identity as a group that await Negroes as they emerge now from the ghetto and are compelled to face in wholly new ways the old issues of alienation, assimilation, and integration.

My thanks to those who participated in this study go in the first place to the 55 individuals with whom I had extended interviews:

James Baldwin, writer
Claude Barnett, American Negro Press, Chicago
Jesse B. Blayton, President, Mutual Federal Savings of Atlanta
Horace Mann Bond, Atlanta University
Sterling Brown, Howard University, Washington, D.C.
Ralph J. Bunche, United Nations
George Carter, Peace Corps, Accra
W. Beverly Carter, Jr., former publisher, Pittsburgh *Courier*
Kenneth B. Clark, City College, New York
Rufus E. Clement, President, Atlanta University
Warren Cochran, YMCA, Atlanta
John A. Davis, American Society of African Culture
John W. Davis, President Emeritus, West Virginia State College
W. E. B. Du Bois, writer
Edward Dudley, Borough President, Manhattan, New York
Ralph Ellison, writer
John Hope Franklin, Brooklyn College, New York
The late E. Franklin Frazier, Howard University, Washington, D.C.
Lester Granger, former Executive Secretary, Urban League
Lorraine Hansberry, writer
James T. Harris, American Society of African Culture
William H. Hastie, U.S. Court of Appeals, Philadelphia
James L. Hicks, Editor, *Amsterdam News*
Jean Blackwell Hutson, Curator, Schomburg Collection, New York
James W. Ivy, Editor, *Crisis*
Mordecai Johnson, Howard University, Washington, D.C.
Rev. Martin Luther King
Hylan Lewis, Health and Welfare Council, Washington, D.C.
Rayford Logan, Howard University, Washington, D.C.
Thurgood Marshall, U.S. Court of Appeals, New York
Benjamin Mays, President, Morehouse College, Atlanta
Loren Miller, NAACP, Los Angeles
L. D. Milton, President, Citizens Trust Company, Atlanta
Henry Moon, NAACP, New York

Pauli Murray, writer
The late Roi Ottley, writer
Frederick D. Patterson, President, Phelps-Stokes Fund
P. L. Prattis, Editor, Pittsburgh *Courier*
Ted R. Poston, New York *Post*
A. Philip Randolph, President, Brotherhood of Sleeping Car Porters
J. Saunders Redding, writer
Ira DeA. Reid, Haverford College, Haverford, Pa.
Jackie Robinson
Rev. James H. Robinson, Operation Crossroads Africa
J. A. Rogers, writer
George Schuyler, Pittsburgh *Courier*
C. A. Scott, Editor, Atlanta *Daily World*
Maida Springer, AFL-CIO, Washington, D.C.
The late Channing Tobias
W. J. Walls, Presiding Bishop, A.M.E. Zion Church, New York
Roy Wilkins, Executive Secretary, NAACP
Franklin H. Williams, Peace Corps, Washington, D.C.
William Worthy, Baltimore, *Afro-American*
Clayton R. Yates, President, Yates & Milton, Atlanta
Whitney Young, Executive Director, Urban League

I am in debt, for briefer interviews and conversations, to:

W. A. Bacote, Atlanta University
Daisy Bates, NAACP, Little Rock, Arkansas
Walter Carrington, Peace Corps, Sierra Leone
C. C. De Joie, Jr., Editor *Louisiana Weekly*, New Orleans, La.
St. Clair Drake, Roosevelt University, Chicago
William T. Fontaine, University of Pennsylvania
Charles G. Gomillion, Tuskegee Institute, Tuskegee, Alabama
The late George E. Haynes, City College, New York
Ruby Hurley, NAACP, Atlanta
Lewis Jones, Tuskegee Institute, Tuskegee, Alabama
Marie Lee, Shalimar International, Inc., New York
Ulysses G. Lee, Jr., Morgan State College, Baltimore, Md.
C. Eric Lincoln, Clark College, Atlanta
Alexander Looby, Nashville, Tenn.
Ernest E. Neal, U.S. Agency for International Development
Pearl Primus, dancer
Hugh H. Smythe, Brooklyn College, New York
Mabel Smythe, Lincoln School, New York

Harold Snell, Department of Labor, Washington, D.C.
Frank Snowden, Howard University, Washington, D.C.
Robert Thompson, Urban League, Atlanta
Preston Valien, Brooklyn College, New York
Dan Watts, Liberation Committee for Africa, New York
George Weaver, Assistant Secretary of Labor, Washington, D.C.
Samuel Westerfield, Treasury Department, Washington, D.C.

I have written elsewhere an account of a group of white and
Negro American students experiencing these new impacts during a summer of work and travel in West Africa (*Emergent
Americans: A Report on Crossroads Africa*, The John Day Company, New York, 1961) but the particular experience in Africa
of the 11 Negroes among the students with whom I shared that
summer's discoveries became part of what has gone into the
present work, and for this I have to acknowledge here a special
debt to: Sylvia Boone, Richard A. English, Richard Hope, Carol
Ann Jackson, Burniss Lewis, Rosalind Robinson, George B.
Smith, Ida Smith, Lynette V. Tucker, Barbara Walker, Yvonne
Williams.

I must finally, without using their names, express my great
thanks to the group of Negro Americans I interviewed in West
Africa.

My many other debts for help in this work can be only briefly
suggested as I make acknowledgment to:

The Center for International Studies and its Director, Max F.
Millikan, for the continuing opportunity to share in its many-sided
effort to probe the great unexplored spaces of human and political
relations, and most particularly to my colleague Ithiel De Sola Pool
for his part in setting up the project that took me to West Africa
in the summer of 1960.

The New World Foundation and its Executive Director, Vernon
Eagle, for the grant that enabled me to initiate this inquiry.

Rayford Logan and the late E. Franklin Frazier of Howard University, John Hope Franklin and Hugh Smythe of Brooklyn College,
George Shepperson and Michael Banton of the University of Edinburgh, Howard H. Bell of Texas Southern University, Langston
Hughes, James Ivy of *Crisis*, Hylan Lewis of the Washington Health
and Welfare Council, Whitney Young of the Urban League, Franklin H. Williams, now of the Peace Corps staff in Washington, for

reading various portions of the manuscript and giving me the opportunity—which I am sure I did not adequately exploit—of benefiting from their criticisms and comments.

Mrs. Dorothy Porter, Curator of the Moreland Collection at Howard University, and Mrs. Jean Blackwell Hutson, Curator of the Schomburg Collection in New York, for their great and courteous assistance.

An expanded family team of editorial collaborators: Viola R. Isaacs, Arnold R. Isaacs, Kathleen M. Taylor, and Deborah S. Isaacs, for their indispensable part in freeing this work of at least a few of its defects and putting the manuscript into presentable form before it reached the publisher's hands.

My colleague Richard W. Hatch, for his careful reading of the manuscript and his many useful corrections and suggestions.

Mrs. Laura Farnsworth, in the earlier stages of this inquiry, and Deirdre Cooney, for a great host of tasks performed with high and lively interest in the work at hand in matters of research, bibliography, checking, culling, maintaining files, carrying on correspondence, and typing.

The editors and publishers of the various journals and publications in which parts of this work appeared in different forms between 1958 and 1962, namely: *Public Opinion Quarterly; The Phylon Quarterly* of Atlanta University; *Race,* Journal of the Institute of Race Relations in London; The *New Yorker; Current; Journal of Human Relations,* published at Central State College, Ohio; *Commentary.* Versions of some of these chapters have been published in mimeographed form as papers presented at meetings of the American Society of African Culture in 1959 and 1960, the Conference on Africa of the United States National Commission for UNESCO in 1961, and the American Orthopsychiatric Association in 1962.

H. R. I.

Cambridge, Massachusetts
September 13, 1962

## PART ONE

---- ❋ ----

# NEGROES
# AND
# THE WORLD

# 1. THE PERIL TO THE REPUBLIC

The white races are but one-third of the population of the globe—
or one of them to two of us—and it cannot much longer continue
that two-thirds will passively submit to the universal domination
of this one-third.

These words were spoken to a convention of free Negroes 108
years ago, in 1854, by Martin R. Delany, a physician, author, and
leading figure among free Negroes in New York.[1]

On February 6, 1866, Charles Sumner of Massachusetts, arguing in the United States Senate for the full grant of civil rights
to the freedmen, summoned up the same world view that Delany
had grasped twelve years earlier and spoke these words:

The population of the earth—embracing Caucasians, Mongolians,
Malays, Africans, and Americans—is about thirteen hundred millions, of whom only three hundred and seventy-five million are
"white men," or little less than one-fourth, so that in claiming exclusive rights for "white men," you degrade nearly three-quarters of
the human family, made in the "image of God" and declared to be
of "one blood" while you sanction a caste offensive to religion, an
oligarchy inconsistent with Republican government, and a monop-
oly which has the whole world as its footstool.
Against this assumption, I protest with mind, soul, and heart. It
is false in religion, false to statesmanship, and false in economy. . . .
You cannot deny these rights without impiety. And so has God
linked the national welfare with national duty, you cannot deny
these rights without peril to the Republic." [2]

[1] Quoted by Howard H. Bell, "Negro Emigration Movement, 1849–1854, A
Phase of Negro Nationalism," *Phylon*, 2nd quarter 1959, p. 141.
[2] Quoted by John A. Davis, *et al.*, "Foreign Reactions to American Racial
Problems," unpub. ms., American Information Committee on Race and Caste
(New York, 1955), p. 5.

It has taken just about a century for events to confirm these remarkably prophetic insights. In the world, the two-thirds *have* stopped passively submitting to the domination of the one-third. In the United States these rights were persistently denied until now and this denial has much to do with the peril in which the Republic now stands.

From the time of the signing of the Emancipation Proclamation until only a few years ago, the American society was able to deny civil and human rights to millions of its members because of their "race" and yet keep on seeing itself as a striving democracy of free men. For nearly three-quarters of a century, it proved possible to sweep this gross contradiction under the national rug. But the circumstances favoring this massive deception and self-deception began to evaporate about twenty-five years ago. As Sumner Welles observed in 1944: "The thesis of white supremacy could only exist so long as the white race actually proved to be supreme." [3] That thesis was built into the superstructure of Western white-world power; it was used to rationalize and justify on racial grounds the Western white man's sovereignty over the whole of the globe. That system of power and sovereignty had been weakening for decades, barely managed to survive the First World War, began to fall apart with the onset of the Second World War, and finally came tumbling down in the years of its aftermath. The empires that white Europe had established in Asia and Africa over some 300 years were almost completely dissolved in the 15 years between 1945 and 1960 and were replaced by some 40 new nation-states. To be sure, life-and-death power over the world remained in the hands of the nuclear superpowers and economic power likewise remained heavily concentrated in Western hands, but this was something quite different from the intimate and direct rulership of Western whites over Asian and African nonwhites which was the substance of imperial political sovereignty. The whole basis of their relationship now had to be revised.

For with the collapse of its underpinning political power, the whole superstructure of Western white supremacy began to

[3] Sumner Welles, *Time of Decision* (New York, 1944), pp. 297–298.

waver and fall. It has been in these years like watching a slow-motion film of the collapsing of a dynamited building: slowly it falls out into the air, parts of it retaining form and structure even as they sink and are gradually obscured by the dust and rubble into which they fall. Because it is slow motion, some can imagine that these slabs of the familiar façade are still standing there in the air and are not falling at all. But this is illusion becoming delusion, for here they are coming down all around us—all the assumptions we made about each other, about ourselves and about other human beings, about our own and other groups and kinds, "races," peoples, cultures. Here, coming apart amid their fallen power props, are all the myths of white superiority and nonwhite inferiority, all the deeply imbedded notions and emotions, all the patterns of long-practiced behavior. All are being displaced and have to be replaced. All that was *given*, in a word, is now being taken away. Whether we will it, or know it, or like it, or not, we are all participants in this great continental rearrangement of power and human relationships. All Western white men have to get rid of the habits of mastery, and all nonwhites the habits of subjection. This is now the common and nearly universal experience. There is hardly a corner of national or international life now that is not touched by it and hardly anyone, white or black or whatever, who is not now faced by its demands.

In Asia and Africa where the colonies have become nation-states, this process of revision in relationship and mutual image can at least begin with a transfer of political power and thus throw around the new confusions a screen of formal new status relationship. The styles of this transfer have varied greatly—the hasty but relatively skillful improvising of the British, the myopic but brief resistance of the Dutch, the myopic and prolonged resistance of the French, the pell-mell panicking of the Belgians—but the result in every case creates a new formal situation. A new state is proclaimed, a new flag raised, a new government established, a new "power" is established, and from here on out at least the externals of behavior are governed by the protocol of diplomacy and the needs of policy. Seemingly in a twinkling, yellow and brown and black men, only yesterday despised and relegated to the orders of inferiority, now take *their* places in the seats of the mighty. They walk the red carpets of privilege, enjoy all the perquisites of sovereignty, are wooed and pressured instead of dominated and, wherever they can, begin to do a little dominating themselves. The old badges of inferiority are torn off, the signs of discrimination and debasement come down, the exclusive places and modes of behavior are abolished; the Queen now dances with the black Prime Minister, and the Duke with the Prime Minister's black wife. To be sure, behind this façade the new situation remains a jumble of old rancors, guilts, and shames, all of which have to be accommodated to the new needs. The shedding of colonial power does not at a stroke relieve the old colonial master of the whole burden of his beliefs about himself, nor Western white people generally of the legacy of what their whole culture taught them for so long about these matters. Similarly, political independence does not at a stroke free either the new nation or its people from *their* legacy of subjection, imposed inferiority, dependence, and self-rejection. But at least now the power of government is in the hands of one's own kind and the most egregious forms of subordination to foreign rulership are forced to disappear. The new national power, no matter how weak, is at least strong enough to put a prohibitive tariff on the return of this kind of foreign domination and under its protection to produce (to resurrect, recreate, or create as the case may be) a new national, cultural or even "racial" identity on which indigenous self-respect can begin to thrive.

In American society, on the other hand, the end of white supremacy has to be signaled not by *separation* but by *integration*. Here there is no simple initial solution like changing the signs at a boundary line and raising a new flag. Here the issue remains locked in the society's unfulfilled promise of democratic pluralism. This promise is perhaps our greatest and most unique virtue and our failure to fulfill it may be our costliest failure, for we have been overtaken by it at last. The gulf between our profession and our practice has become an abyss to whose edge the world has pushed us.

The downfall of the white-supremacy system in the rest of the

world made its survival in the United States suddenly and painfully conspicuous. It became our most exposed feature and in
the swift unfolding of the world's affairs, our most vulnerable
weakness. It was like being caught naked in a glaring spotlight
alone on a great stage in a huge theatre filled with people we
had not known were there. Here we were now, our vulnerability so highly visible that when hundreds of millions of people
all around the world looked in our direction it seemed to be all
that they could see.

This was because the "world" in which we now live is no
longer the dominant white Atlantic world in which most of us
were born. It is a rudely enlarged place that includes Asia and
Africa on a wholly new footing. Most of the millions whose
scrutiny we are now feeling are the nonwhite peoples coming
so dramatically into view with the scars of Western white dominance still heavily marked upon them. These great masses of
Asians and Africans turn out to be, moreover, people whose future has become a critical factor in the American future, not to
say American survival. For the world-power struggle between
the United States and the Soviet Union now turns not only on
the balance of economies or weapons, on systems of production
or control of strategic resources and territories, but also on the
shape of man's political future, the institutions he will choose
or be led to build, the conceptions of freedom or unfreedom he
will embrace or be embraced by in the next few decades. Unless
it is dissolved by resort to the Bombs, the coming shape of
things will be largely decided by the choices made by precisely
these "new" Asian and African peoples. If, as we insist, the
power struggle is not only a confrontation of Bombs and systems
of production, but also a confrontation of fundamentally different ways of relating man to his society, then the nature of
the American democracy itself becomes a critical issue in this
struggle.

The facts are that the American democracy housed slavery for
its first 75 years, then freed the slaves and promised them the
same constitutional rights enjoyed by all citizens, and then pro-
ceeded for nearly another hundred years to deny Negroes those
rights. It comes now into this new revolutionary epoch faced

abruptly with the need to establish new and more mutually respectful relations with the nonwhite peoples of the earth without being able to show that it has given to its own nonwhite citizens even a minimum measure of the dignity and freedom on which it bases its philosophy and its whole case against the totalitarians. The democratic system itself produced no sufficient self-correction of this profound anomaly. Only the slow trickle of cases through the courts gave evidence of any inward capacity for change, and it was hardly moving at all until it was washed over by the great flood of world events.

So the end of white supremacy in the United States is finally being forced by the end of white supremacy in the rest of the world. We now have to abandon racist practices because we simply can no longer afford to cling to them, any more than we can cling to the idea that there is any security left in continental isolation. No doubt it would have been far better to have reached this point through the working out of the democratic belief in the equality of rights of all citizens or the Christian belief in human brotherhood. It may be that the democratic process works not only as slowly but also as mysteriously as Providence is reputed to do. Nevertheless, both isolationism and racism have had to be blasted out of their deeply imbedded places in American life and history by nothing less than the great world explosions of our time, the technological and political explosions that have transformed all human affairs in this century. Isolationism could not survive the scientific advances that made the globe itself the smallest viable unit of political and social change. White supremacy in America cannot survive the political overturns that have brought to an end the Western white man's sovereignty over the rest of the world. It may be possible to imagine white racist systems persisting in an isolation protected by Super-Bombs. But such systems, even assuming they could survive in a hopelessly hostile world environment, could not remain even nominally democratic. This is what makes the persistence of isolationists and racists among us so perilous and their grip on crucial sections of our national life a drag that threatens to carry us all down with them as they disappear.

There is a certain awesome, almost Biblical irony in the way things have worked out. It is not really very much of an exaggeration to say that as matters stand now, "democrats" must finally become democratic (and "Christians" Christian) or die.

## Interaction at Little Rock

The intimate interaction between surviving American racism and American relations with the world became steadily more visible and more continuous year after year following the Second World War. Every racial episode in the United States was instantly reported around the globe and reaction came bouncing back like radar signals from almost every direction. At each eruption the Federal government was galvanized, its spokesmen forced to keep on finding the words with which to counter these hostile and damaging views of what America is and what it does. The record of this interaction has become a fat file indeed. A study of foreign press comment on American race issues, covering only certain countries for the period 1949 to 1954, filled nearly a thousand pages of typescript.[4] It would take many times that number again even for bare summaries of the world press, radio, and television coverage of all that has happened since then. The news files have bulged year after year with names of persons that became familiar everywhere and of places suddenly ringed on the whole world's maps. In 1955 it was the murder of Emmett Till in Mississippi. Beginning that same year and carrying over into 1956, the whole world watched walking Negroes boycott the buses in Montgomery. That year it was also the case of Autherine Lucy's attempt to enter the University of Alabama and the dynamiting of the high school by segregationists at Clinton, Tennessee. The echoes of these events had barely begun to die away when the first major battle over enforcement of the school desegregation decision erupted at Little Rock in 1957 in circumstances that carried awareness of American race issues into the world's most obscure places and finally caused the whole American nation to feel the heat of the world's new interest in its most private affairs.

4 Davis, *et al.*, *op. cit.*

This came about when Orval Faubus, the governor of Arkansas, placed a detachment of National Guardsmen around Central High School in Little Rock to prevent nine Negro students from entering in accordance with a court-approved desegregation plan. After three weeks of intensive legal and political maneuvering, a Federal court ordered Faubus to end his defiance of Federal authority. He ordered his guardsmen away from the school and at the same time virtually invited a mob to take their place. The next morning, Monday, September 23, a mob outside the school broke through a feeble police line and attacked several Negro newspapermen and others. The next day President Eisenhower sent in a unit of airborne troops to enforce the Federal court's orders. Under the protection of Federal soldiers, the nine Negro youngsters entered the school and continued attending it for the rest of the year, although under constant needling and sneak attacks from a small band of white racists while the fearful or ambivalent white majority looked the other way whenever it passed. The fight for this token integration in Little Rock had a long way to go—a whole year followed in which the school did not open at all—but the nerves of the nine young Negroes held out and the Federal will ultimately prevailed. It did not do so, however, until the name "Little Rock" had indelibly entered all the world's languages as the principal international symbol for American racism. It became the handiest and clearest of all imprecations for hostile demonstrators to throw at visiting American dignitaries from Caracas to Tokyo, and an American traveler can even to this day hardly go anywhere in the world without being asked about it.

The issue was dramatized with such peculiar force at Little Rock mainly because the defiance of the Arkansas governor made it the most dramatic clash of Federal and state authority in the United States since the Civil War. But it was also because of the pictures that went around the world of armed soldiers, grimacing hoodlums, jeering and screaming women and teenagers, all bearing down on a single Negro girl facing them, books in her arms, with a mien of incomparable courage and dignity as she tried to go past them into school. These pictures stabbed at people from newspapers and television screens across the country and around the world, touching all who saw them with shame and anger.[5]

In Little Rock itself, a town hitherto without renown or notoriety, people suddenly found themselves in the world's eye, having to answer the questions and face the cameras of some two dozen European and Asian correspondents and a small army of American reporters and photographers. They all heard every day of the massive national and international reaction to what was going on in their city. They had to react, each in his own way, when Moscow radio mockingly included Little Rock in the daily itineraries it issued for the passage of Sputnik I. It had taken the Russian conquest of space to push Little Rock off the world's front pages and the Russians chose this way of getting it back there. Mail from all over the world descended on the local press, on local clergymen, on Governor Faubus, on the superintendent of schools, and most of all on the nine Negro youngsters whose entry into Central High School was the heart of the whole affair.

Local people of goodwill who were called "moderates" (which appeared to mean that the amount of determination behind their goodwill was extremely moderate) were mortally embarrassed under all this scrutiny but found themselves impotent to respond to it. A leading Baptist clergyman in town who served

[5] One of the most famous and most widely published of these showed Elizabeth Eckford, one of the Negro girls, facing a burly guardsman, and the faces of the crowd, especially the face of one girl contorted with a cry of hate. The Sunday after this picture was published, it reappeared as an advertisement in the Arkansas *Gazette* in Little Rock, with the caption: WHEN HATE IS UNLEASHED AND BIGOTRY FINDS A VOICE, GOD HELP US ALL! And in small type under it: THIS AD PAID FOR BY DAVIS FITZHUGH, RT. 1, AUGUSTA, ARKANSAS. Sometime later I drove the 75 miles from Little Rock to Augusta to find out what part world affairs had played, if any, in Fitzhugh's response. I found him a well-to-do farmer of an old Confederate family whose mother had gone to the Sorbonne in 1902, had taken her sons to live for awhile in the North (while she got herself a law degree) and had given them every chance to travel. Davis Fitzhugh met his wife-to-be, an English girl, in Chile. When war came, he resigned as mayor of Augusta to go into the Army. He went into Germany to set up local administration behind the advancing troops. "I tried to find out from people how they could stand by and see Jews persecuted and murdered. They'd say they felt guilty, but didn't know what they could do; that it was dangerous to do anything. This is something like the feeling I feel here now, something of the same evil spirit, the same inability to act."

on his church's foreign missions board showed me newspapers sent to him by missionaries from the Philippines, Ghana, Nigeria, and Argentina, and described a meeting of the board of Richmond at which communications on this matter from all over the world were reviewed.[6] The segregationists, seemingly impermeable to the world's reaction, were nevertheless strongly defensive about it. "Why just this week," said Governor Faubus in an interview I had with him, "I had a visitor from India who told me that a million and a half people were killed in India in racial troubles. If we want India as an ally, we're not going to question the Indians about *their* minority problems. The Communists don't question the Indians about theirs, but they do question ours. I think it's all exaggerated." But to the Negroes in Little Rock, and mostly to the nine young people in Central High School, the world's response came as a dazzlingly unexpected support for their stand. Each of the nine was swamped in mail from well-wishers in countries they had never heard of or had to look for on the map to locate. One of the girls told me: "I take letters with me to school; they make you feel good, people sharing things with you. I read them in school." Another said: "I read a letter every morning before I go to school, and it makes me feel good all day, and I read one when I come back. It lifts my spirits."

When President Eisenhower went on television and radio to explain why he had sent troops to Little Rock, he spoke of the constitutional issue which had been forced, but he also laid heavy stress on all of the foreign effects of the episode. He called Faubus' action a "tremendous disservice . . . to the nation in the eyes of the world." He said:

[6] "One of our missionaries," he told me, "is just back from Nigeria, and she said her hardest job was going to be to explain how the Christian community can be Christian and do what it did in Little Rock." How, I asked, did the congregation take this statement? He jerked his head back, aghast with surprise. "Why, she didn't say that from the pulpit!" he cried. To whom then, I asked, a little puzzled. "Only to us, privately, the ones she knows. Why she knows how people feel, she's Southern. I would say J—— has been quite discreet and gone as far as she could go. She's been speaking all over the South. But she doesn't say right out that people here have made our task difficult. She does it more subtly . . ."

At a time when we face grave situations abroad because of the hatred that Communism bears toward a system of government based on human rights, it would be difficult to exaggerate the harm that is being done to the prestige and influence and indeed to the safety of our nation and the world. Our enemies are gloating over this incident and using it everywhere to misrepresent our whole nation. We are portrayed as a violator of those standards of conduct which the peoples of the world united to proclaim in the Charter of the United Nations.

The President urged the people of Little Rock and Arkansas to cease their defiance so that the Federal troops could be withdrawn. "Thus will be restored," he concluded, "the image of America and all its parts, as one nation, indivisible, with liberty and justice for all." [7]

The struggle against American racism had not begun at Little Rock and it did not end there. In 1944, Professor Rayford Logan had written that American racism had "become our Number One domestic failure and our Number One international handicap." [8] The national and international file on the subject has fattened ever since, from month to month and year to year. What happened at Little Rock in 1957 was that this fact of life was carried at last to the high peak from which it finally became naked and visible to all. After Little Rock, hardly anyone could fail to know that American racism had become part of the world's business and was therefore now part of American's business with the world.

## The Fattening File

It is obvious that this world-wide interest in American racism can be sorted out and traced in its different parts to a complex of motives and that we have to confront it with something more than simpleminded dismay. Some of it has come out of the cynical use of the issue as a weapon in the power struggle by a Communist foe who has far outdone us in devising and imposing

[7] *The New York Times,* Sept. 25, 1957.
[8] Rayford W. Logan, ed., *What the Negro Wants* (Chapel Hill, N.C., 1944), p. 1.

systems of unfreedom on great masses of human beings. From Western Europe it has come often out of the rancors of dependence on the great new power on whom all had to lean for sustenance and survival, and out of a certain gleeful malice, too, over the exposure of American self-righteousness. Coming from Germans, Frenchmen, Italians, Spaniards, and Portuguese, this indignation was surely also most often a way for these various Europeans to project upon the United States their own assorted guilts.

Different sets of motes and beams could no doubt also be sorted out in the ex-subject countries of Asia and Africa. There is hardly one that does not have imbedded in its own culture some counterpart system of exclusions and taboos which antedates the coming of Western imperialism. But the fact remains that it was Western white power, not any of *their* powers, that dominated the world for three centuries; Western white mythology, not any of *their* mythologies, which shaped the patterns of human relationships on such a massive scale for such a long time. It was Western white power bolstered by its racial mythologies that brought on all the countering emotions and reassertions of nationalism, and was finally brought crashing down by the revolutions of these years. It was, finally, the United States, as both heir and repository of surviving Western power in the world, that had to come to account now for its own surviving white-supremacy system and found itself so deeply vulnerable in the face of all the new forces and emotions unloosed in a swiftly changing world.

So the file grew after Little Rock, with episodes in America and reactions around the world multiplying and becoming familiar parts of each year's experience. In 1958 it was the lynching of Mack Parker in Poplarville, Mississippi. The same year a Negro named James Wilson who had been sentenced to death in Alabama for the theft of $1.95 drew so great a surge of international attention (including an inquiry through diplomatic channels from Kwame Nkrumah, then Prime Minister of the new state of Ghana) that Secretary of State John Foster Dulles felt compelled officially to inform the Governor of Alabama about this "world-wide concern," and when the governor moved a few weeks later to commute the sentence, he said he did so to put an end to the "international hullabaloo" over the case. This was also the period of the closing of schools and the rise and fall of "massive resistance" to school desegregation in Virginia. In 1959 the world saw on its screens the snarling faces of white women on a New Orleans street screaming at children entering an elementary school ordered desegregated by the courts. The global audience was also hearing about the attempt to abolish Macon County in Alabama to keep the Negroes of Tuskegee from voting effectively. In 1960 the center of the stage was taken by the sit-ins, the spectacular action started by Negro students in the South that raised the whole struggle for civil rights from the legal plane to a broad assault on the whole pattern of customary behavior; a technique that spread to wade-ins at the beaches, kneel-ins at churches, and into 1961 with the "freedom rides" on interstate buses to compel desegregation at bus terminals bringing on brutal acts of violence by hoodlums and arrests of hundreds for breaching the segregated peace of places like Birmingham, Alabama, and Jackson, Mississippi. In 1962 came the demonstrations in Albany, Georgia, and the second and greater confrontation of force when Federal troops were sent to Oxford, Mississippi, to enforce the court-ordered admission of James Meredith to the state university after two persons had been killed in a collision between racist rioters and United States marshals on the university campus.

The record of these years is dotted with the testimony of successive directors of the United States Information Agency on the extent and impact of the world-wide coverage given to all these episodes. Edward R. Murrow, reporting on international response to the dynamiting and burning of a bus carrying Freedom Riders in Alabama in May 1961, told a Congressional committee that European, Asian, and African press reaction ranged along "a scale from immediate horror and disgust to longer-range concern that American world policy was being seriously compromised." The incidents, Murrow said, "have damaged America's reputation as a defender of individual rights and have provided America's detractors with the obvious usable material." In Communist China, for example, he said, the press "bore down hard on the theme that rampant racism has 'exposed' the savage nature of American freedom and democracy." [9]

## Diplomatic Embarrassments

Another fat file has accumulated on incidents involving diplomats and other traveling guests of the government caught up in the mesh of American racial discrimination. The common experience of rebuff and insult for nonwhites in all parts of the United States suddenly became the source of acute diplomatic embarrassment when some of these nonwhites turned out to be ambassadors or even simply citizens of the new Asian or African states. Negro Americans have had to go through the galling experience of reading day after day about embarrassed apologies and explanations made to foreign nonwhites for acts of discrimination which remain part of the normal lot of nonwhite Americans. In the earlier 1950's the new states were still largely Asian, thus a dark-skinned man refused service at the airport restaurant at Houston, Texas, in 1955 turned out to be the Ambassador from India, and diplomatic channels overflowed with official regrets for days. Shortly thereafter the greater number of these diplomats and traveling notables were black men from Africa, and the difficulties multiplied. The first in the long series of incidents on Route 40 on the way to Washington occurred when a dark-skinned man, refused service at a Howard Johnson restaurant at Dover, Delaware, in 1957, turned out to be the Finance Minister of Ghana. In that case President Eisenhower invited the minister to breakfast at the White House to make amends. By 1961 the number of new African states had risen to about 30, and as their representatives began to arrive, travel, set up offices and homes, the Kennedy Administration found itself caught in a swarm of these incidents.

Because this is such a peculiarly direct form of the new interaction between American racism and American foreign policy problems, it seems worth dwelling here for a brief space on some examples of the recent record. Consider the items of only four weeks in the summer of 1961. The Freedom Rides into Alabama

[9] *The New York Times*, June 25, 1961.

and Mississippi were still making major headlines when refusal of service to a diplomat from Sierra Leone at Hagerstown, Maryland, brought a personal apology from President Kennedy at the White House and on June 23, 1961, Hagerstown's top 200 citizens turned out for a reception in his honor, held, said the *Times*, "to repair a breach in the delicate tapestry of international relations." The attendance at this function of 30 Negro couples made it "the first such mixed event here in the memory of citizens." [10] On July 11 the governor of Maryland had to apologize to no fewer than four new African ambassadors who had been refused restaurant service along Route 40, one of them while en route to present his credentials to President Kennedy. On July 13 *The New York Times* published a column-long dispatch from Moscow quoting a jeering account from the Soviet press of "how the most democratic country of the world" treated African diplomats while "they hypocritically swear friendship for the peoples of Africa." In a message to 200 Maryland civic leaders who were invited to a special luncheon in order to hear it, President Kennedy appealed for "an immediate end" to segregation in restaurants, motels, and hotels in Maryland. "He cited incidents against African envoys as a sore spot affecting relations with Africa," said the report, "but he stressed that the problem of discrimination against the envoys could not be separated from discrimination against all Negroes." [11] The State Department sent a representative to a hearing of the Maryland State Legislature to argue for a bill barring this kind of discrimination, but the Maryland legislators remained unmoved. Such a bill started moving through their reluctant hands and after being stripped of most of its effectiveness it was eventually defeated.[12]

Even more nettling across these same seasons were the housing difficulties of newly arriving African diplomats in Washington and New York. Both the State Department and the United States Mission to the United Nations appointed special officers for the

[10] *Ibid.* June 24, 1961.
[11] *Ibid.* Sept. 26, 1961.
[12] *Ibid.* Mar. 11, 1962. In spring, 1963, the Maryland legislature passed a public accommodations bill requiring restaurants and hotels to serve Negroes. Twelve counties are exempted, but Baltimore city and 11 counties including all of Route 40 are covered.

purpose of dealing directly with real-estate interests to try to solve the problem. In Washington, the State Department brought a group of realtors to a closed meeting where Undersecretary of State Chester Bowles told them that discrimination against Africans in the capital had created "an unhappy, explosive and dangerous situation." Harris Wofford, special White House assistant on civil rights, told them that "there is no subject on which the President feels more deeply than this one." They were also told that the head of one new African nation "had refused to visit this country because of discrimination his ambassador had experienced there." [13] In a letter to Attorney General Robert Kennedy, Secretary Rusk said:

Many of these difficulties are never officially drawn to the attention of the State Department, but the hurt and the resentment are nevertheless lasting. On occasion, difficulties are of such a gross character as to call for investigation and official apologies which, however, cannot correct the wrong. . . . Apart from the embarrassment created in our relations with countries whose representatives and nationals are concerned—and far more important than any such embarrassment—this sort of incident gives the picture of a United States where racial discrimination is accepted practice, where equal respect for the dignity of human beings is not accorded.[14]

At the bottom of the same column of *The New York Times* (June 2) reporting Mr. Rusk's letter appeared an Associated Press dispatch from Rapid City, North Dakota, with the heading: AFRICAN ENGINEER SNUBBED IN DAKOTA. A Guinean highway engineer, on a tour sponsored by the United States Government, had been denied service in a Rapid City restaurant. The mayor of the city—as has become almost required in these incidents—promptly apologized and invited the engineer to his home. Later in the summer two Nigerian students who were refused lodgings at a motel in Illinois were invited to lunch at the executive mansion in Springfield by the governor of the state.[15]

13 *Ibid.* July 7, 1961.
14 Dept. of State Bulletin, June 19, 1961.
15 *The New York Times*, Aug. 11, 1961.

Still another fat folder in this continuously growing file is filled with the warning or worried statements made by Americans in high places on the damage that surviving racism does to the nation. We have heard words to this effect from virtually every important government or political figure in or near the summits of American life during the last two decades, from Wendell Willkie to Harry Truman,[16] Dean Acheson and Thomas E. Dewey through Dwight Eisenhower, Adlai Stevenson and Richard Nixon to John F. Kennedy, Robert Kennedy and Dean Rusk. As we have moved down through these years and these events, these statements have tended to become more urgent and more distinctly related to specific action. Thus to a meeting of Negroes called at the State Department to discuss the hiring of more high-level Negro personnel, Secretary of State Rusk said:

The biggest single burden that we carry on our backs in our foreign relations in the 1960's is the problem of racial discrimination here at home. There is just no question about it.[17]

In a speech to law students in Georgia, Attorney General Robert Kennedy—who had just sent United States marshals into Alabama to protect Freedom Riders from racist hoodlums left unhindered by the local police—underlined the government's new and greater determination to protect the civil rights of all citizens, and added:

We just can't afford another Little Rock or another New Orleans. For on this generation of Americans falls the full burden of proving to the world that we really mean it when we say all men are created free and are equal before the law.[18]

The Kennedys in Washington have had to make personal demonstrations to underscore their hard sense of the new needs

[16] "The support of desperate populations of battle-ravaged countries must be won for this free way of life . . . Our case for democracy must be as strong as we can make it. It should rest on practical evidence that we have been able to put our own house in order. For these compelling reasons, we can no longer afford the luxury of a leisurely attack upon prejudice and discrimination." President Truman in an address to the NAACP conference, *ibid.* June 30, 1947.

[17] New York *Amsterdam News*, Aug. 26, 1961.

[18] *The New York Times*, May 7, 1961.

of policy. When it came to public notice for the first time that the elite Metropolitan Club did not admit Negroes and would not admit African ambassadors, even as guests for a single meal, Robert Kennedy publicly resigned his membership. Later in 1961 President Kennedy's proposed membership in the equally elite Cosmos Club was withdrawn when the club refused to admit Carl Rowan, Assistant Secretary of State for Public Affairs, who is a Negro. Indeed with the increasing appearances of Negro appointees in higher-level posts in the Kennedy Administration, the hazards of discrimination had come to include by early 1962 not only the danger of insulting some Very Important Person who happened to be African, but equally a Very Important Person who happened to be an American Negro. This happened when Carl Rowan, again, in January 1962 was refused service at the Memphis Airport restaurant and when George Weaver, Assistant Secretary of Labor, was refused a room at a downtown hotel in Houston.[19] There was no reason not to assume that before long a Negro so slighted might be a member of the President's Cabinet or a justice of the United States Supreme Court. These were ironic outcomes, whether for white dignitaries caught with their previous indifference or their hypocrisies showing, or for Negroes, from most of whom the society still largely withholds the grant of ordinary rights and decencies and for most of whom the needed apologies, explanations, and corrections have not yet been made. Nevertheless these episodes showed how far the old patterns of established practice had fallen out of fit with the new realities. The interaction between what was happening to nonwhites in the world and what was happening to them in the United States had clearly begun to reach the point of closure. The old devices of deception and self-deception could no longer work; ignoring the matter was no longer possible. Negroes would no longer submit; whites could no longer impose. The whole system had to be changed.

Maybe American democracy, pursuing its own glacial course, would have come finally to the greater fulfillment of its promises. This we will now never know. We will not know how far

---

[19] Three months after this incident all the downtown hotels in Houston integrated their room and restaurant facilities. *Ibid.* April 11, 1962.

and how fast the American society would have moved itself, what new shapes of freedom it would have brought into being out of the stuff of its own making. We can only muse now on what might have happened in these years if the total world scene had not so drastically altered and brought American white supremacy so abruptly and so painfully into the full view of a world in which white supremacy had ceased to be the accepted order of things.

# 2. THE SINS OF THE FATHERS

It is only partly true to say that American racism has become more visible to the world; it is perhaps truer to say that more of the world has become more visible to Americans. The enlargement of the "world" to include Asia, Africa, and Latin America is "new," and so is the American vulnerability on the issue of race. But the Asian and African image of Americans as racists is not new, not new at all. We are in fact cast here in the role of the third and fourth generations and this may be, in a way, the main point of the whole story.

Americans were seen from Europe for more than a century very largely as democrats and egalitarians, coarse or crude or bold and beckoning, depending on the bias of the viewer. The beckoning view governed through all the years of the great European migrations to America, at least until eastern and southern Europeans began running into the American Anglo-Saxonism that closed the gates of the promised land. But beyond Europe the image of Americans as democrats was blurred, as by a double exposure, by images of Americans as racists. Indeed over much of this same period of time Asians and Africans who came into contact with America and Americans had to struggle to sort out these blurred images and the conflicting experiences and emotions they produced. The imagination of many an Asian and African was kindled during the years of the peak of European empire by the discovery of classic American anti-colonialism and the ideas and credos attached to the names of Jefferson and Lincoln. But on the one hand their expectations of American political support against their European masters were almost always sorely disappointed. On the other hand, those who looked for the American magic in America itself sometimes found it, but rarely without being rasped and bloodied at the same time by the sharp edges of American racialism.

22

This experience is part of a long history of which few Americans were ever aware while it was happening and which is even less known to Americans now. Yet this is the history that accounts for a great deal of the confusion and ambivalence that surround the images of America now held in so much of the world. It underpins much of the hostility that so many Americans now so unhappily feel directed at them in so many places.

By the stereotypes, Americans like to think that they are people who have always acted like democrats devoted to the proposition that all men are created equal with equal opportunity to pursue their happiness. For many it comes as a rude shock now to discover that this is not so and has not been so to a considerable extent in the past. The uncomfortable truth is that the nonwhite in the American society was simply not included in the democratic self-image. The driving force of conscience that went into the abolition of slavery was largely dissipated after abolition was brought about. For most of the century after Emancipation the nonwhite in American society was, as Ralph Ellison and other writers have reminded us, the *invisible* man. What the American society inflicted upon him was somehow assumed not to count in the weighing of democratic or egalitarian merit. That the "world" was "European" and "white" helped maintain this self-deception; it was, after all, a vital part of the system that ruled the earth. Having a "free" and "democratic" society was not contradicted by the unfreedom of the nonwhite, who could simply be ignored. It is only now that he can no longer be ignored that the image begins to be overtaken by the reality and the past that was forgotten or never known suddenly becomes acutely relevant. The American who thinks he does not deserve today's slings of fortune has not only failed to "see" the race issue in his own lifetime but does not know enough of his history to know what a burden it has bequeathed to him of the sins of his fathers.

The central stuff of this history is of course the story of the Negro in America, but it is also related to the experience of other nonwhites in this society. There is a notion still strongly held even now, for example, that there has never been anything —or hardly anything—but benevolent goodwill in all past American relations with the Chinese. But when a Chinese Communist writer now writes of "the savage nature of American freedom and democracy" he need not only be conforming to the current patterns of Communist demonology. He is also drawing on sources that go deep into the past of Chinese experience with Americans both in China and in the United States.[1] In China, Americans for more than a century mixed their benevolent professions and activities with all the features of European dominance, including gunboat diplomacy, armed intervention, treaty port discrimination, and attitudes at best of paternalistic superiority and at worst of sneering contempt. In the United States, Chinese were among the major victims of American bigotry in its most brutal forms of mob action, pillage, and lynching in California and other Western states and territories during the last quarter of the last century, and of other forms of debasement and discrimination in the country as a whole over a much longer period; some of it, indeed, lasting until now. Riding with the wave of bigotry and mob action, the Congress in 1882 passed the Chinese Exclusion Act which for the first time set up racial and ethnic barriers to immigration and citizenship in the land of the free. The society was no longer "open" to the Chinese from the outside any more than it was "open" to the Negro inside. It is hardly ever recalled now that the first antiforeign boycott organized in China was started in 1905 specifically against the United States as a protest against American exclusion and brutal treatment of Chinese in America. The Chinese Exclusion Act remained the law of the land until the late date of 1943. That year the United States finally signed a new treaty relinquishing its extraterritorial rights (which had held Americans above Chinese law in China for a century) and at home passed a new law allowing 105 Chinese immigrants to enter the country each year. It was not until 1946 that in addition to the Chinese, the Japanese, Indians, and other assorted lesser breeds regained the right to enter this country as immigrants and to become naturalized citizens.

[1] For a fuller treatment, see Harold R. Isaacs, *Scratches On Our Minds; American Images of China and India* (New York, 1958), pp. 109–124.

Sometimes the systematic humiliation of nonwhites in the American society would erupt into larger public notice—as when the great Indian poet Rabindranath Tagore, who came to this country in 1929 for a lecture tour, was insulted by an immigration official and left abruptly without fulfilling his engagements. "As a representative of all Asiatic people," said Tagore, "I could not remain under the shadow of such insults." [2] But through most of these years and decades, these facts of American life remained part of the customary behavior, sometimes deplored but most of the time—like the systematic debasement of the Negro—simply ignored, hardly ever noticed as a contradiction of American democratic professions and certainly never seen as a factor in American foreign relations. Yet more than 50 years ago Chinese were boycotting Americans for their racism; more than 40 years ago the treatment of Japanese in the United States became an issue in the slowly accumulating tension between the two countries; some 30 years ago Indians who were just beginning to acquire limited legislative powers in Indian provinces tried to use these powers to impose restrictions on Americans in India in retaliation for restrictions suffered by Indians in America.

Asian and African awareness of American racism came not only from the experience of Asians and Africans in the United States but from many other sources as well. In the first place, the British and French, dealing with burgeoning nationalist movements in their colonies in the decades between the two world wars, were not backward about disseminating information about the plight of the Negro or other nonwhites in the United States. Classic American anticolonialism, the Declaration of Independence, and the Revolutionary War for Independence formed part of a historic tradition which the British and French colonialists had great need to conceal or discredit. Information about American racism had a strong corrective effect, they felt, on colonial subjects who might seek a model for themselves in the anticolonialist American democracy. Hence American racial episodes were given full attention by the British and French news

[2] *Ibid.*, p. 285.

agencies serving their colonial press and by teachers in such schools as they provided.[3]

The Communists, of course, had been exploiting the facts of American racism for many years. In the 1930's they mounted an intensive international propaganda campaign around the issue of the Scottsboro Case, which they made into a world-wide *cause célèbre*. This case involved the trial and death sentences imposed on nine youthful Negroes accused of rape. This was in the time of the rise of Hitler when the whole world was being made conscious in a fresh way of the meaning and nature of racism. It was also the period of the so-called "People's Fronts" when the Communists achieved their maximum penetration of other radical political movements. In their "united-front" movements with socialists and others in Europe and, more particularly, with some nationalist movements in Asia they made major use of the facts and images of American racism. Although manipulated for purposes of Communist propaganda, there was relatively little need even for inveterate falsifiers to falsify the facts. Since they were linked to so much known experience and fell on such fertile soil, they had maximum effect.

In Asia the soil was fertile for the growth of negative views of the American democracy, for reasons that included American racism but also much larger matters. Here again we come upon that profoundly damaging dualism in the nature of the American impact. Asian nationalism was in no small degree inspired by the history and credo of the American democracy while virtually never finding an ally in the actuality of American power. This was true during the imperialist epoch of the century preceding the First World War. It became even more damagingly true thereafter. The generation of Asian nationalists who took power in the 1940's grew up in the years after 1918, and those were the years in which all nationalist-minded Asians discovered

[3] During a 1960 journey to West Africa, a group of young Americans who went to Guinea, for example, found young Guineans intent upon testing the impression that Americans would not physically touch a nonwhite, not even to shake hands. They had gotten this idea, they said, from French teachers in their primary schools. See my *Emergent Americans; A Report on Crossroads Africa* (New York, 1961).

that *their* part of the world had not been made "safe for democracy"; that the Wilsonian doctrine of self-determination had never been meant to apply to them; that Wilson had not come to Versailles to preside over the end of the British and French colonial empires. On the contrary, Wilson was even ready to accede to Japan's demand for special rights of occupation in Shantung, a province of China. It was, ironically enough, in outraged protest against this American betrayal of China's nationalist interests that the great student movement of 1919 arose, opening the modern revolutionary epoch in China's history. The Japanese had also proposed at Versailles a "racial-equality amendment" to the Covenant of the League of Nations. It was a move aimed directly at discriminatory legislation affecting Japanese residents in California. The bind in which this caught the American President was an ironically apt illustration of the historic gap between American profession and American practice on this cardinal matter. The interplay on this issue was complicated but in the end the Japanese proposal was killed by British and American opposition. When an extremely mild version of it finally came to a vote in the League of Nations Commission, President Wilson abstained and it fell to him as chairman to declare that the Covenant which was going to make the world safe for democracy could not include even a pious promise that every state would assure "equal and just treatment" for alien nationals within its borders. The irony of the priorities at work here are underlined by a historian: "The Japanese accepted defeat on the race issue, but they stood firm on their imperialist demands in China and here. . . . Great Britain and the United States yielded to the Japanese substantially all that they desired." [4]

In the decade of the 1920's, partly in rebound from the failure of the hopes raised by Wilsonian rhetoric, Asian nationalism came heavily under the influence and aura of Russian Bolshevism and Marxist ideology. Nothing in American behavior at

---

[4] Seth P. Tillman, *Anglo-American Relations at the Paris Peace Conference of 1919* (Princeton, 1961), p. 304. See also A. Whitney Griswold, *The Far Eastern Policy of the United States* (New York, 1938), pp. 248–253.

this time countered the view that Americans were primarily to be identified with the European imperialists and were racists at home to boot. Hence by the 1930's throughout Asia, whether in China, India, Indochina, or the East Indies, or indeed wherever the nationalist fight was being fought, there were puzzled and even wistful views about American democracy and also a great deal of information and much strong feeling about American racism. And many of the obscure nationalists of that time are the men of power in these countries today.

These same nationalists—and their sons—had still another source for their images of American racism in Japanese propaganda during the Second World War. The Japanese had long smarted under the contemptuous American laws and practices which lumped *them* with Negroes, Chinese, and other assorted "undesirables" as objects of legal and customary discrimination. When they embarked in the 1930's on their own drive to become the master race of Asia, Western racism, and especially American racism, became a key target of their propaganda. Although their central slogan, "Asia for the Asiatics," clearly meant "Asia for the Japanese," they went to some trouble to identify themselves to other Asian peoples as Asian brothers with a common cause to make against all Western white men, and after Pearl Harbor, especially against the Americans. They not only recognized the United States as their prime foe from the beginning, but they also knew that American democratic doctrines and professions were still—despite everything the Americans themselves did to discredit them—the themes they had to discredit and defeat in order to win nationalist allies. In the areas they conquered and occupied between 1942 and 1945, they conducted unremitting propaganda on this theme. Walter White (who felt that "rising wind" some fifteen years sooner than Harold Macmillan did) reported in 1945:

With considerable effectiveness, the Japanese by radio and other means have industriously spread in the Pacific stories of lynchings, of segregation and discrimination against the Negro in the American Army, and of race riots in Detroit, Philadelphia, and other American cities. To each of these recitals has been appended the statement that such treatment of a colored minority in the United

States is certain to be that given to brown and yellow people in the Pacific if the Allies, instead of the Japanese, win the war.[5]

This propaganda, capping all the previous sources of information on the same subject, certainly helped shape the images of the United States held by many of the younger Indonesian and Burmese nationalists who for part of that time joined hands with the Japanese and who became, soon after the war's end, part of the new ruling groups in their countries. The notable thing about this history is that as strong as the American racist image had become, the American democratic image was still so strong that almost all the nationalist revolutions that were made over the face of southern Asia in the aftermath of the Second World War were still made in the American spirit or at least in American terms, explicitly borrowing in their manifestoes and declarations the doctrine that all men are created equal and that the object of their revolutions was to create governments of, by, and for the people. The survival of American racism in the postwar era not only undermined the position of the United States in these new republics; it sapped the vitality of the American idea itself.

In the United States the Japanese had long carried on a special campaign of propaganda aimed at American Negroes and had made a sustained effort to exploit the anger and disaffection of Negroes for the benefit of the Japanese cause.[6] The Japanese had for a long time aroused ambivalent emotions in nonwhites elsewhere in the world—their victory over the Russians in 1905 was the first major defeat inflicted by nonwhites on whites in the modern epoch and was felt as such throughout the colonial world subject to Western white dominance. As late as 1940, even

[5] Walter White, *A Rising Wind* (New York, 1945), p. 148. Another example: "In January, 1942, a Negro was brutally beaten in a small town in Mississippi. Within forty-eight hours, German and Japanese radios were broadcasting the incident. The sordid details were relayed to the Dutch East Indies and India to break resistance against the Japanese just before the fall of Java. Here was clear evidence, the Axis claimed, of how democracies treated the colored races." Cited by R. H. Brisbane, Jr., "The Rise of Protest Movements Among Negroes Since 1900," unpub. thesis, Harvard University, 1949, p. 261.

[6] A detailed account of this effort will be found in Roi Ottley's *New World A-Coming* (Boston, 1943), ch. 22, "Made in Japan."

a writer like W. E. B. Du Bois was having trouble choosing between the images of the Japanese as the nonwhite challengers to the hated white world and as imperialist freebooters who were trying to replace the white man's power in Asia with their own. Among American Negroes, even after Pearl Harbor, there were certain bitterly tangled feelings on the subject.[7] The Japanese effort to subvert Negroes to their cause got nowhere; Negroes doggedly went on to try to make sure this time that the struggle against German and Japanese master-racism would put an end to master-racism at home. It is now twenty years later and they are still fighting that fight. It has been a long, long time, and it seems worth noting that Elijah Muhammad, leader of the race-chauvinist "Black Muslims," whose recent rapid growth as a movement among Negroes is a reflection of their despair and discouragement in the struggle, was jailed in 1942 for impeding the draft by teaching his Negro followers that their true interest lay in the victory of their racial kin, the Japanese.[8]

Across these same decades, finally, awareness of American racism came also to Africa, as it did to Asia, by many different paths, some of which we have already mentioned. It came through the British and French news channels, which kept so much from Africans but did not conceal from them that the American democracy was undemocratic for black men, and, with somewhat less obvious effect, also through the Communist propaganda network. This network was always a very thin affair in Africa itself, but George Padmore, the West Indian writer and revolutionist who became Kwame Nkrumah's mentor in Nkrumah's poststudent days in London, spent the first decades of his political career as principal organizer and propagandist for Negro and African affairs for the Communist International. Padmore became a disillusioned anti-Stalinist when he found that the Communists regarded black men and the race issue

---

[7] A distinguished professor at Howard University remembers being asked by a government official about the effectiveness of Japanese propaganda among Negroes. He replied by telling the official about the white officer who used the term "yellow bastards" in his pep talks to the Howard R.O.T.C. contingent. This did not make Negroes feel more patriotic, he pointed out. "You know," he told the official levelly, "many of us are yellow bastards, second and third generation."

[8] C. Eric Lincoln, *The Black Muslims in America* (Boston, 1961), pp. 26, 188.

merely as tools in their power drive. As a strong nationalist and anti-Communist Marxist, Padmore also became a major influence on many young Africans studying in England, and his view of the black man's problem in the world certainly included a strong view of the black man's position in the United States.

The most direct image of American racism was acquired, of course, by those Africans who came to the United States for schooling—a thin trickle over the years moving mainly along channels of the missionary movement, but gradually increasing in numbers. In the 1930's, African students in the United States included Kwame Nkrumah, now President of Ghana, and Nnamdi Azikiwe, now Nigeria's first African Governor General, and there have been many others since who have returned to become leading men of power in their various countries. At the present time there are some 2,000 African students in the United States, each one acquiring by his own daily experience his own image of the American society. This is never an unmixed image, but hardly ever is it likely to exclude the feature of American racialism.

In sum, the image of a racist America may seem dismayingly "new" to Americans who had simply never noticed it before, but it is an image that has been in the making for a long, long time. It is not "new" to Asians and Africans, and most certainly not "new" to Negro Americans. What is "new" is that white Americans now have to know and care a lot more about what these nonwhite Asians, Africans, and Americans think.

# 3. THE PECULIAR CONSONANCE

Actually there has almost always been a peculiar and fateful consonance between the position of the Negro in America and the position of the American nation in the world; always a link between the history of the Negro here and the history of many other peoples far away.

It was in North America that the act of enslavement of African black men by Western white Christians made its deepest and most fateful impact and had its longest-lasting consequences. For Negro slavery was at the heart of the shaping, the rending, and the reshaping of the American society. It was, in James Conant's phrase, the "congenital defect" with which the American Republic was born. It built into the American experience from the outset the deceptions and self-deceptions of which the Negro was the constantly visible symbol and reminder. It led to a bloody war that was fought to determine the structure of the American union, and during that war it was finally abolished. But white supremacy in new forms was reimposed almost at once on the freed slaves. Chattels no longer and formally admitted to the rights of citizens by Constitutional amendment, Negroes were in fact denied rights of all kinds as citizens and as men and within twenty years after the end of the Civil War were once again totally subject to the white majority of the nation. It is here in the closing decades of the nineteenth century that Professor Rayford Logan has located the nadir of the position of the Negro in America.[1]

But the nadir for the Negro in America was also the apex for the white man in the world. As Professor Logan and others have pointed out, these were precisely the peak decades of the European imperialist epoch. By every device of military, economic,

[1] Rayford W. Logan, *The Negro in American Life and Thought; The Nadir 1877–1901* (New York, 1954).

political, and psychological dominance, the paramountcy of
Western white men over the earth was the most fully established,
and among Western white men the primacy of the English. It
was after the opening of the Suez Canal in 1870 that European
empire entered its most flourishing and profitable years in Asia,
completing its last conquests there and bringing China to the
edge of total dismemberment. In these years also, Africa was
scrambled for and, at the Berlin Conference of the Powers in
1884, divided up among them. The whole "world" accepted
without question that same year the fixing of the Greenwich
meridian as the base point for calculating all the earth's time;
there was no confusion anywhere over what the Near East was
near to, or the Far East far from. It was in this time also, finally,
that the Darwinian view of the survival of the fittest in nature
was put to their own uses by Western men. Racist theories were
built into a pseudoscience to serve as a major prop and justification for Western white men's rule of the world and all its people.
The works of Bagehot, Spencer, T. H. Huxley and others fixed
not merely the white man but the Anglo-Saxon white man forever at the pinnacle of human development.

These ideas were eagerly seized upon across the Atlantic
where, as Richard Hofstadter has remarked, American life already looked like "a vast human caricature of the Darwinian
struggle." [2] The United States played its own uniquely equivocal
role in all this history. While still tangled in the contradictions
between Christianity and slavery at home, America's churches
had joined in the effort to Christianize the world and had done
so by joining in the established system of imposed Western
power. Committed by their history and their national credo to
regard colonialism as equivalent to original sin, Americans held
themselves as aloof as they could from actual acts of conquest
while, as in China, seeing to it that they shared in the plunder
after the fact. At home after the Civil War came the resubjec-
tion of the Negroes in the South and the loosing of lynch mobs
on the Chinese in the West and finally, in the century's closing
years, America's own imperialist adventures carried out in the

2 Richard Hofstadter, *Social Darwinism in American Thought* (Boston, 1955),
p. 44.

Caribbean and the far Pacific.[3] At the time that the Negro in America reached the nadir, white Americans were doing their utmost to share in the best of all possible worlds in which Western white mastery was just about as total as it was ever going to be. To the British school of racial theorists, America contributed a whole school of its own to proclaim and defend the God-given gift of Anglo-Saxon supremacy.[4] Still unknown and unheard, a counterspokesman for the nonwhite had also appeared. In 1900 a young American Negro scholar, W. E. B. Du Bois, addressed a conference on race in London. His theme: "The problem of the twentieth century is the problem of the color line—the relation of the darker to the lighter races of men in Asia and Africa, in America, and the islands of the sea." [5] There was, to be sure, much more than race involved in this history, but when the first successful challenge to Western supremacy in Asia came in the form of Japan's defiance and defeat of Russia in 1904–1905, it was—as we have remarked—seen everywhere in the nonwhite world as the first successful counterblow against white domination.

The Japanese were intent upon winning a place in the company of the imperialist powers hitherto reserved for Western white nations only; the war with Russia was over the "right" to violate China. Nevertheless their victory was also the first by a nonwhite nation over a white nation in a whole historic epoch, and it stirred the entire colonial world. It marked for all who could see it the beginning of the end of the myth of Western white invincibility. Its effects can be traced in the early histories of the men and the movements that eventually displaced Western rule in every part of Asia. The first yielding of Britain to new pressures in India came with the reforms of 1907. Indonesian nationalism dates its beginnings from these same years. In China the revived revolutionary forces, sparked in important degree by students who flocked to Japan after 1905 (including a young man named Chiang Kai-shek), gathered enough strength

3 Isaacs, *Scratches on Our Minds*, pp. 125–126.
4 Hofstadter, *op. cit.*, ch. 9, "Racism and Imperialism."
5 W. E. B. Du Bois, *The Souls of Black Folk* (New York, 1953), p. 13, (original publication Chicago, 1903).

to topple the Manchu Dynasty in 1911. The United States, itself so newly emergent as a world power, intimately felt this clash of force in Asia—the peace treaty between Japan and Russia was signed in Portsmouth, New Hampshire, under the aegis of Theodore Roosevelt.

If these events were a portent for the makers of American world power, they were no less so, however dimly seen, for the Negro Americans who lay prostrate under white power at home. Among Negroes, as among the Chinese, Indians, and other subjects of Western white empire, the impact of Japan's victory made itself felt, as an editorial in T. Thomas Fortune's *New York Age* showed:

Of probably greater significance than anyone is aware is the fact that it is to an off-color race that a white race is suing for peace. It has long been said that no dark race can look a white race in the face and live. The Japanese dared look in the face of the Russian; and the events remind us of the denouement of Goldsmith's "Tale of a Mad Dog"—the white man 'twas who died. The ultimate effect of this startling victory we cannot at present estimate.[6]

The same great turning in human affairs signaled by the stirring of nationalist movements in Asia after Japan's victory in the Tsushima Strait was marked by Negroes in the United States with the launching of the "Niagara movement" in 1906 by Du Bois and others and the founding three years later of the NAACP. It was the beginning of the climb up from the nadir.

## Tides of Two Wars

Actually the Japanese push into the great game of power politics heightened and multiplied the irrepressible rivalries

[6] *New York Age*, Aug. 10, 1905. A letter-writer to the *Age* exultantly claimed kinship to the Japanese, whom he called "Asian Negroes." He wrote: "All along, the average white man has looked with contemptuous or pitying eyes upon the 'darker races' of the world, and our Anglo-Saxon writers have classed them as inferior to the white races. But these darker races, the Asian Negroes, have done stunts which have made them to be respected by the white Russian whose constant territorial encroachments threatened the national existence of this, the most progressive Asian wing of the Negro race, the Japanese." *New York Age*, June 22, 1905.

which were beginning to tear the whole system apart. These erupted into the war of 1914–1918, opening great fissures in the world-power structure. The enormous bloodletting; the massive movement of men across much of the earth; the summoning up of the great moving ideas of democracy, freedom, and self-determination as the "reason," the "meaning," and the "purpose" of the war; the quakelike blow of the revolution in Russia and the tidal wave of ideas out of Marx and socialism—all this shook the whole house the West had built. The victors in that war did not dream of liquidating any empires except those of the defeated foe, but many of their own imperial subjects already had different ideas. Colonial revolts filled the decade of the 1920's from Morocco across the world to China. The house shook but it did not topple. The French won the Riff war; the French and British together—though viciously infighting each other—kept the Arab crescent they had seized from fallen Turkey. The British held on against Gandhi and the Congress movement in India through successive crises of power in 1921 and 1931. The Dutch put down an insurrection in Indonesia in 1927, and the French did likewise in Indochina. The greatest of the nationalist revolutions of this period rose in China in 1925–1927, nearly driving Western foreign power into the China Sea. Partly because of the special role played in these events by the new power of Soviet Russia, the Chinese nationalist movement also aborted, managing to weaken but not to break the Western hold on Chinese political and economic life.

In country after country across the globe the same process repeated itself in the postwar decade. Western power was weakened but remained strong enough to stand; the new forces of nationalist reassertion in the colonies were stronger but not yet strong enough to prevail. Indeed, in countering them, the British could still use their Indian forces and the French their Senegalese. The façade of power stood intact, patched here and there by reforms and concessions, but the system had been drained of its vitality. The economic depression of 1930 became a world economic crisis and the whole structure stumbled again toward its fall. Internal convulsions seized it; Japan in China, Italy in Ethiopia, and Germany in Europe set out to take the power

prizes for themselves and in the process brought the whole system crashing down. In this view, then, the events of the epoch
of the First World War were like a massive rehearsal; what had
sounded like the chords of doom in 1914 turned out to be but
an opening movement, summing up but still only heralding the
great crashing climaxes to come. All that had been left unresolved by the first great war exploded into the second greater
world war. The whole catastrophic process repeated itself on a
scale magnified many times. But this time the war sucked away
the surviving power of the West to maintain its power over other
nations and peoples in the world. This time in the aftermath nationalist forces moved in to push away what the war had left of
empire's battered walls. This brought on a great new tangle of
events and rearrangements, but at least one fact stood clear: the
white man was ceasing to walk the earth as master, and what was
already a new fact in Asia and Africa barely a decade after the
war's end had to become inescapably the new fact also in the
United States.

Between American Negroes and the Asian and African colonial subjects of Europe there are a host of important similarities
and differences. But the ideas and practices of the white-supremacy system to which they were all subjected was part of the common history of Europe and America, rooted in common notions
and mythologies, linked by a common politics of power, and
subject to a common fate. Hence the great tides running against
white supremacy in the world have run by much the same timetable of ebb and flow against white supremacy in the United
States. In the same way that it shook but did not shatter the
colonial system, the First World War produced pressures that
strained but did not break the bonds of second-class citizenship
for Negroes in the United States. Like the nationalists in the
colonies, Negroes in America pushed against the bars that held
them. Like the colonial empires, the American white-supremacy
system was jarred—only much less so—and managed to stand and
wait for another generation's challenge.

Still, the First World War ushered in all the beginnings of
major change for Negroes in American life. Here too there was

a massive rehearsal in almost every particular of the history that was going to repeat itself on a larger and more conclusive scale a generation later. Thus the conflict in Europe and the American entry into the war in 1917 brought on the first great migrations; the war's needs for labor drew nearly a million Negroes out of the rural South, largely to the major cities of the North.[7] In this way began for these great numbers all the changes in economic status, education, aspiration, and way of life that come within a single generation after the move from farm to city. At the same time some 400,000 Negroes went into the armed services. They served under rigid and humiliating conditions of segregation, but they were swept nevertheless out of the old grooves of life to new environments; 50,000 of them to service abroad, and all of them to the great unsettlement of new experience. The Negro too was not going to go so readily back to the "farm" now that he had seen "gay" Paree. Like colonial subjects around the world, Negroes felt themselves directly addressed by the great phrases of the time that were summoned up—by none more eloquently than by Woodrow Wilson—to give meaning to what was happening. To make the world safe for democracy; to realize self-determination—these were purposes that Negroes in America had no difficulty whatever in making peculiarly their own. When Negroes responded to the opportunities the times offered them or simply tried to do their duty as citizens of a nation at war, the great gulf between these lofty goals and the American reality was again harshly exposed by a series of lynchings and race riots in the first months of American involvement in the war. To President Wilson, who studiously looked the other way, Professor Kelly Miller of Howard University addressed an open letter in August 1917 with these prophetically challenging words:

MR. PRESIDENT, you express the voice of the American people in the great world conflict which involves practically the entire human race. You are the accepted spokesman of world democracy. You

[7] The Negro populations of New York, Chicago, Philadelphia, and Detroit alone, rose by 750,000 between 1910 and 1920. See E. Franklin Frazier, *The Negro in the United States* (New York, 1949), p. 191.

have sounded forth the trumpet of democratization of the nations, which shall never call retreat. But Mr. President, a chain is no stronger than its weakest link. A doctrine that breaks down at home is not fit to be propagated abroad. One is reminded of the pious slaveholder who became so deeply impressed with the plea for foreign mission that he sold one of his slaves to contribute liberally to the cause. Why democratize the nations of the earth if it leads them to delight in the burning of human beings after the manner of Springfield, Waco, Memphis, and East St. Louis, while the nation looks helplessly on? . . . The outrages complained of against the Belgians become merciful performances by gruesome comparison. Our frantic wail against the barbarity of Turk against Armenian, German upon Belgian, Russian upon Jew are made of no effect . . . Every high-minded American must be touched with a tinge of shame when he contemplates that his rallying cry for the liberation of humanity is made a delusion and a snare by these racial barbarities . . .

When you speak of the democratization of the world and the liberation of mankind, you are setting up a standard to which the whole world must rise in the ages to come, despite its attitude at the present time. It may be far from the purpose of our present-day statesmen to admit the Negro into this democracy on terms of equality with the rest. But in spite of the purpose of this statesmanship, this must be the ultimate goal of human democracy. A democracy of race or class is no democracy at all. It is with projected imagination that the Negro will endure until these high-sounding phrases have borne their full fruition.[8]

Like the emergent nationalists in the colonies, Negroes in America nursed the half hope that the great themes of wartime propaganda would somehow get translated into reality when the fighting was done. There was the same restlessness and greater aggressiveness, especially among the returning soldiers, the same strong impulse to make over the old order of things. This was met in America, as in the colonies, by the repulse of brute force. The process of "putting the Negro back in his place" began in what James Weldon Johnson called the "red summer" of 1919 with more than 70 lynchings, 10 of them of

[8] Kelly Miller, "The Disgrace of Democracy, an Open Letter to President Woodrow Wilson, August 4, 1917," in V. F. Calverton, ed., *Anthology of American Negro Literature* (New York, 1929), pp. 363–378.

Negroes still in uniform. It continued through 25 race riots during the first postwar year, a veritable race war erupting from Longview, Texas, to Chicago to Omaha to Washington, D.C.[9] This was a time of American racism running amok, of Claude McKay's famous poem: "If we must die, let it not be like hogs . . ."—of the Ku Klux Klan riding again. There was shock, shame, and horror among good people in the population, but it was not strong enough to affect the outcome and could not and did not even summon up enough support for the National Association for the Advancement of Colored People's campaign for Federal antilynching legislation to budge a stolid Congress. White supremacy remained supreme.

Over the next decade the small band of fighters in the NAACP continued to seek redress and change through the courts and through Congress, but the great white world looked the other way, out of indifference; and so did a large part of the Negro population, out of despair. This became the time of the Negro Bohemia in Harlem, the "Renaissance," and the "New Negro," a movement that produced many minor and several major writers. It gave itself over in part to a romantic glorification of African primitivism; but it also began the great task of re-establishing and relocating the modern Negro in the American literary universe. While the artistic and intellectual elite busied itself in this way, large Negro masses—hundreds of thousands, some said millions—were giving ear to Marcus Garvey, a West Indian Moses who rose to call them back to race pride and back to a misty African haven where, he said, the black man could stand on his own ground and become master of himself. Both of these movements—to which we shall have occasion to return for a closer look later in these pages—fell apart: the Garvey movement bequeathing its dream seekers to Father Divine and other such cults; the "Renaissance" of the 1920's dissolving in the onset of the depression and the turn to political radicalism in the 1930's. Like all the other unsettled issues of relationship between whites and nonwhites in the world and, indeed, along with all the unresolved issues of a world society

9 John Hope Franklin, *From Slavery to Freedom* (New York, 1947), chs. 24 and 25.

in crisis, this particular problem of the place of the Negro in American life dragged on into a new decade and into the hands of a new generation.

This generation came up amid the convulsions and the larger despairs of the great despression. Negroes were at the bottom of the social and economic ladder, and they suffered most from the ravages of the crisis. The New Deal won Negro allegiances, but more for its social welfare and philanthropic aspects than for any hope it offered of a basic change in the conditions of Negro life. Through the Congress of Industrial Organizations, industrial unionism held forth a much greater promise, but it delivered on it most slowly, and has not delivered adequately to Negroes to this day. The depression years sapped hopes and energies. The Communists managed to siphon off the radical impulses of a small urban intellectual fringe, but these were soon dissipated in disillusionment and discouragement. The older Negro leadership retained its vigor in the person of A. Philip Randolph, who successfully organized the sleeping-car porters and established a beachhead for Negroes in organized labor. But elsewhere it gave way to a certain despair. W. E. B. Du Bois, who had made himself the first tribune of the fight for civil rights in his work as editor of *Crisis* from 1910 to 1933, now veered between a befuddled radicalism and a reversion to a program for self-segregation among Negroes. He saw this as a refuge in which Negroes could try to survive a prolonged period in which they could hope for no improvement in their status in the white American world. In 1939 a group of prominent leaders of Negro education in the South offered to settle for "separate but equal" treatment if only the "equal" could be made a little more equal than it was. It was another nadir for the Negro in America.

The onset of the Second World War changed all this. Everything that had begun to happen a generation earlier began to happen all over again, only now on a much, much larger scale. The migrations from South to North, from country to city, from agriculture into industry, were this time twice as massive and spread widely over the entire country from coast to coast. Now more than a million Negroes went into the armed forces and were sent not only to Europe but to all ends of the earth—to Africa, Australia, India, Burma, China, and the islands of the Pacific. When this war began, the white society still initially hoped to keep Negroes "in their place." The barriers against their entry into skilled occupations were still there and the system of segregation in the armed forces was intact. But the pressures on this system were now far stronger; the barriers much harder to keep up. Moreover the issues this time were so explicit, so clear, so commanding, that not even the most cynical defenders of the old order could quite get around them. When Roosevelt and Churchill set forth their great phrases in the Altantic Charter of 1941, any mental reservations about not presiding over the liquidation of old empires this time had, as events showed, the character of pious hopes.

For by a truly awesome irony, the issues of racism and democracy came stamped high and hard on all the circumstances that brought on the power collision of the Second World War. The world had produced, among other things, Hitlerism. Hitler reflected the failure of the earlier war to settle any of Europe's problems, but his special brand of superwhite super-Aryan superracism fixed one of the fundamental issues over which the contending powers were forced to fight their war. In this way it fell to the Jews, subject for longer than any other peoples to a great variety of master "races," to make the great blood sacrifice that finally brought Western white racist practice face to face with the great Western Christian and democratic profession. One pauses at the glimpse of this new edge of the Jewish story, not quite sure how far one might follow it or where it might lead. But this much can surely be said: In summoning up the strength to meet the challenge of Hitler with *his* totalitarianism and *his* racism, the Western nations lost their surviving capacity to preserve their own systems of total power in the colonies, their own brands of racism. This time there would be no survival of at least these parts of the old order.

This conviction steadily took hold not only among Asian and African nationalists but equally among Negro Americans. The Negro's stake in this confrontation of master-racisms was explicit and unmistakable, and from the outset Negro spokesmen linked the nation's struggle abroad with their struggle at home. "How can we fight for democracy in Burma," thundered Philip Randolph to a March-on-Washington rally in New York in 1941, "when we don't have democracy in Birmingham?" In a 1944 article, Roy Wilkins, then editor of *Crisis,* magazine of the NAACP, called the new war the "second act" to 1914–1918, only this time, he went on, it was:

... on a broader stage, and the actors spoke plain words from behind little makeup. The villains talked of "master races," of force, of the insignificance of the individual, of the might and power of the state, of the necessity of conquest and slavery. These were things that 13,000,000 American Negroes, even though "educated" in Mississippi, could understand easily. If they had any difficulty with the words "racism" and "totalitarianism," Hitler resolved their fogginess by speaking plainly of Negroes as half-apes. They knew where they stood.

Well, Hitler had made himself plain—what about those who opposed Der Fuehrer? What were they going to say? Britain's rule of her colonies is not exactly a secret to the dark people of the world ... What would the rulers of India, the overlords of Kenya, the collaborators with Smuts of South Africa, the guardians of white Australia, say to Berchtesgarden? And America, bursting, as always with indignation, what would she with her Dixie, say to the Wilhelmstrasse, the Krupps, and the Wehrmacht? [10]

In the course of the war itself, the issues of colonialism and racism were kept barely out of view as force was mustered to win the military decisions. The western Europeans thought they would be returning to their colonies. Among Americans, the system of segregation and discrimination survived in and out of the armed forces, though not without heavy tension, conflict, and bitterness. It was at the war's end that these irrepressible issues again forced themselves into view. In his book *A Rising Wind,* published in 1945, Walter White ended his recital of the wartime struggle for racial equality in the American system with these warning words:

[10] Roy Wilkins, "The Negro Wants Full Equality," Logan, ed., *What the Negro Wants,* pp. 113–114.

The question is posed bluntly: Can the United States, Britain, and other "white" nations any longer afford, in enlightened self-interest, racial superiority? . . . The storm signals are unmistakable. A wind *is* rising [that] blows all over the world. Whether that wind develops into a hurricane is a decision which we must make now.[11]

The winds have been rising steadily ever since. We moved on from the war into the stormy new era of atomic fission, Russian power, and the liquidation of the colonial empires. American racism had to begin to yield at last to the new requirements of American survival.

## New World A-Coming

The coming together of all these pressures over these twenty-five years did in fact force the beginning of considerable change in the position of Negro citizens in the American society. By the beginning of 1962 the change was not yet great enough to justify the glow of self-congratulation among some whites, but it was greater than had seemed possible only a short while before. The conflicts and episodes that commanded so much world attention in this time became more and more the direct result of the onset of change. The worst clashes marked the places where the widest holes were driven through the wall of enforced inferiority and systematic discrimination. The real *news* in all the clamor that filled the world's air about American racism during the 1950's was the fact that the established racist system in the country had finally come under direct and frontal attack—by the Federal courts and the Federal government, by some aroused white citizens in some churches and other institutions, and most of all by Negroes themselves. The pictures of American racists that flashed onto the world's screens were a shocking revelation of what this society still harbored, but they were in every case pictures of snarling people driven into the corners of a hopeless defense. This was not always plainly seen, partly because some of those watching the United States from abroad on this issue were not concerned with its dynamics but with their own need

11 White, *A Rising Wind,* pp. 154–155.

to attack the United States for other reasons, and partly because at home the pace of change that seemed so swift to so many whites was still so unconscionably slow from the standpoint of Negroes. Still the change was underway, the direction clear and irreversible, the outcome inevitable. The only question was whether enough change was coming swiftly enough to meet the needs of the new situation.

The changes have come out of the great blind pressures doing their work, the great migrations, the shift of millions from South to North and from country to city—by 1961 there were six million Negroes living in the 25 largest cities of the country, five million of them in the 10 largest—and the tangible and intangible consequences of the steady movement of greater and greater numbers into places where their votes began to count and into the higher levels of skill and education from which they had been excluded for so long. One major consequence has been the great new visibility of Negroes in places where they simply had not been *seen* before except as menials. They had pushed out everywhere beyond the old ghetto boundaries and they appeared downtown and uptown and in new roles and places, at desks in shops and offices, in government posts at steadily rising levels, in political and judicial positions of increasing eminence. The practices of exclusion which were in effect right up until the 1950's in hotels and restaurants and similar public places in the North as well as the South had largely disappeared in northern cities by 1960. The sit-in movement launched by Negro students in 1960 began the process of breaking these barriers down in the South as well; within a year sit-in pressure had opened lunch counters in variety and drugstores in 112 Southern and border cities and communities; boycotts and economic pressure had begun to force department stores and similar establishments to drop all discriminatory practices; and by 1962 in some Southern cities the big downtown hotels had also begun to give way.

Desegregation and removal of barriers of discrimination have been greatest in this decade in the Federal establishment itself. Desegregation of the armed forces was ordered by President Truman in 1948, and although it had been opposed by Chief of Staff General Eisenhower in public testimony before the

Senate Armed Services Committee that year, it was largely carried through (partly under direct battlefield necessities early in the Korean War) by President Eisenhower after 1952. The capital city itself was still a Jim-Crow town in all its public aspects when the Eisenhower Administration began. Under pressure of Negro protest and court action and under mounting diplomatic embarrassment, the capital of the American democracy was finally democratized. Ironically, it was the discovery of unenforced statutes dating from the Reconstruction era which finally provided the legal basis for forcing hotels, restaurants, and other such facilities in Washington to be open to all regardless of race, color, or previous condition of servitude. Legislation on civil rights adopted by Congress in 1957 and 1960 was limited in scope but was the first such legislation passed since 1875 and gave the Federal government some measure of greater scope to move against state actions which denied civil rights to citizens, especially in the sphere of voting rights. The levers of executive action in this field, sluggishly operated by President Eisenhower, were pulled down much more frequently and energetically under President Kennedy. Although government action on civil rights remained subject to checks and compromises, especially with the segregationists in Congress, more pressure was in fact brought by executive action on the surviving racist pattern than ever before. Here again, it was no longer a matter of things getting done, but of enough things getting done fast enough.

The most notable changes of this time were brought about by the Federal courts. Some thirty years of persevering legal action, initiated by Charles Houston as attorney for the NAACP, led finally to a series of historic Supreme Court actions, beginning with decisions against segregation in higher education in the 1930's, through the outlawing of the white primary in 1944, and reaching a climax in the school desegregation decision of 1954. By 1962 the Federal courts had struck down in virtually all parts of the public domain the state and local laws that provided for segregation and thereby deprived citizens of their rights. In the late 1950's the changing shape of things began to be reflected in new legislation by many state governments. By 1961, 19 states had adopted fair-employment laws, 28 states and the District of

Columbia had laws prohibiting discrimination in places of public accommodation, and 17 states and cities had new laws aimed at discrimination in housing.

Enforcement of these new edicts and laws was uneven and remained for the most part painfully and dangerously slow. Seven years after the school decision, only 7 percent of the eligible Negro children in the Southern states were in desegregated schools. "Massive resistance" had given way in most places to "token" compliance, but there were still three states in which no compliance had taken place at all and where die-hard segregationists were preparing to take their states out of public education altogether rather than yield.[12] The same pattern was repeated in other spheres. Negro voting power had vastly increased in these years, largely owing to the great population shifts, and was, indeed, credited with decisive impact where the margins were narrow, as in the presidential election of 1960. But in the South, despite new Federal legislation and much more Federal pressure for enforcement, there were still, according to the Civil Rights Commission report for 1961, some 100 counties in eight Southern states where Negroes were still "prevented—by outright discrimination or by fear of physical violence or economic reprisal—from exercising the right to vote." [13] The breaking down of the barriers to Negro employment at higher levels in industry began when Philip Randolph's mobilization for a March-on-Washington in 1941 led directly to President Roosevelt's famous Executive Order 8802, signed in June of that year, creating the Fair Employment Practices Commission. Since then, although through constant pressure and struggle the patterns of Negro employment have been altered, they have remained heavily subject to the built-in handicaps of low starting points and the continuing resistance of many employers and unions. The impact of even a relatively minor recession in the economy, as in 1960, showed how meager and fragile the gains were. Negroes were hit twice as hard as all others by layoffs. Again quoting the Civil Rights Commission's 1961 report, they were still largely "confined to the least skilled, worst paid, most

---

[12] 1961 Commission on Civil Rights Report (Washington, D.C.), v. 1, p. 6.
[13] Ibid., v. 1, p. 5.

insecure occupations," and were still "most vulnerable to cyclical and structural employment." [14]

There have been changes, then, many kinds of change. By one kind of timetable the measure of change that did take place in these twenty-odd years could seem—to take words used in many of the conversations and interviews conducted in the course of this study:

Rapid, great, impressive, significant, remarkable, tremendous, extraordinary, revolutionary.

By another kind of timetable, it could and did seem:

Slow, far too slow, too gradual, extremely piecemeal, very late, almost too late.

But swift or slow, timely or late, the changes are taking place. Whether they are broad enough and deep enough and coming fast enough may be in question. As Roy Wilkins said late in 1961: [15]

We can say we've made progress, the Voice of America says we've made progress, your professors tell you we've made progress, I tell you we've made progress . . . Yes, I can reel off statistics that would indicate that things are better than they were in 1890. The question is: Are they good enough for 1961? Are they good enough for the strength we need as a nation in 1961, and how do they compare to the progress made by other Americans in like time?

But there is no question at all that these changes have already made the world a new place for both white and Negro Americans in which both have to shed or shift their burdens and to see themselves and others in new ways. Negroes must acquire, as they move into this new world, nothing less than a new group identity with which to meet the new conditions of life.

This book attempts to report some of the beginnings of this change as I could glimpse them in interviews and conversations with individuals going through the experience. I have tried to discover and describe some of the elements of identity involved

---

14 *Ibid.*, p. 6.
15 In a lecture at Brandeis University, Oct. 16, 1961.

in this process, to see what some of these individuals saw as they looked back from their points of passage into the new world, and to share some of their sensations and uncertainties as they stepped out into it.

# 4. WIND AT THEIR BACKS

In this new world, Negroes accustomed always to feeling the big winds blowing against them now began to feel the new sensation of having the wind at their backs. Suddenly all the big facts of life and history—*they* out there—were working for them and not, as always before, against them. Great and important things happening to millions of people all over the world affected what was happening to them and what happened to them had become important to everyone. This was an enlargement that gave new shape to everything every man had in his mind about himself and about the world. Almost every individual I interviewed during this inquiry spoke of feeling this new sensation. It was experienced in different ways, located at different points in time, given different accents for the man in the street, for the middle class, for the intellectuals, but it was in essence shared by all.

Some spoke of their discovery that powerful forces had come to their aid and of the access of confidence this gave them. Thus, one of the younger leaders in the fight for equal rights:

All your life you were told that God was with us, but nobody else seemed to be. Well now I think Negroes have begun to get the idea that somebody is with us besides God. I began to get this feeling myself when I went into the Army, was sent from Texas to M.I.T. and began to discover that whites are *not* superior, that a Negro could be as good and even better. This feeling was broadened out after the war, the rumblings in India and Africa. I knew that two-thirds of the world was nonwhite, but it didn't come home to me until the Cold War came on and I realized that it would be a struggle for the loyalty of this two-thirds of the world and the winner would control the world. The United States couldn't be so dumb as to pass this leadership up just in order to keep the Negro down.

Or this, from a much older man, editor of a major Negro weekly:

I began to feel things when India won her freedom. I knew then it would reach me eventually. A new and powerful voice had become sovereign. Now I think the Negro man in the street has gotten to feel that this white man who is his brother had better straighten up and fly right or something is going to happen to him. You get a clear awareness of the fact that more and more colored people in Asia and Africa are coming into their own. It makes people want to lift up their chins, to want to go places, to feel they have a right to belong . . .

A writer spoke of the people in Montgomery:

Negroes have realized that the color thing is worldwide, that other people are faced with white supremacy, and if they can get rid of it, so can we. This was evident in Montgomery, where backward maids and cooks knew they were part of a world affair. They'd tell you they knew they were making history. They knew foreign reporters were there. Many had sons who were in the war. They'd link these things up. King would put this all in his sermons and speeches.

A noted professional:

I began to be sensitive to all this when with Hitler and World War II it became clear that race was emerging as an important factor in world affairs. Before that, Negroes had no real power on their side. They had goodwill, sentiment, morality, but no power. Since World War II, they have had real power on their side, legal power and a certain amount of political and economic power. But these would never have been enough without the weight of these large world changes working for us.

An aging churchman of the old school spoke of it all quite wonderingly:

I never expected to live to see the things I have seen happen. It has all gone far beyond my expectations. I always knew the Kingdom would come, I didn't know when, but I didn't expect this much so soon. Many people ask for a good more than I ask for. I haven't the daring of the young people to ask for complete freedom for everything. But I can testify myself to the change that comes over you when this dream of freedom comes true for our group out in some other part of the world; to see that people can get along better together than they do here in the United States. It makes you feel that it *is* possible.

A politican put it in his terms:

Between World War I and World War II, I never gave much thought to anything outside. Now the outside world is moving in. The darker people are coming up and moving. If this helps our fight, good!

A well-known public figure spoke of the effects:

There has been a loss of fear. How this came about I don't know but there is no question about it. The fear posture of the Negro has changed very markedly. Very difficult to say what brought this about. Indians say this is what Gandhi did for them, to make them lose their fear, to stop cringing. How does this happen to a man? One doesn't know, but I think this was the decisive factor in India, and here too the Negro has lost his fear. I don't think the Gandhi influence was direct in Montgomery where nobody even knew about Gandhi except Martin Luther King. The woman who didn't move on that Montgomery bus. She just didn't know why she didn't move. It had not been in her mind when she got on the bus. It was a reaction of the instant. Something had reached her. The big winds have been blowing, yes, but it is difficult to know what actually moves people . . .

A woman whose work brought her into frequent contact with Asians and Africans spoke of the effects in more personal terms.

I think all Negroes are affected in their feelings. Take me for example. In these meetings for the first time one has a feeling of acceptance and of being a human being on a par with one's fellow creatures. You can look him in the eye and know that he does not measure you with the black, yellow or brown yardstick, and when you look at him you can let that veil down too. With Americans an able Negro is something less than an able man or able woman, while in these encounters you become a man or woman. This gives the Negro the chance to compare the American white view of him and the view he gets of himself in another society where he doesn't have to be judged on the basis of his color.

A hardheaded younger intellectual put it bluntly:

The Negro intellectual gets a feeling of greater confidence. He sees the white American struggling unsuccessfully with new world problems. He is more confident that the superior-inferior classification is not holding up. He sees that it is not valid, whereas before he unconsciously accepted it. This includes me. My possibilities of career have been enhanced by the world situation in general, and the same goes for many other Negroes.

And this, from one of the best known of the younger writers:

There is a certain feeling of panic. I have had the impression that many white people I knew were insecure, baffled. They thought themselves so safe and now are not so any more. Ignorance, habit, sloth, fear, keep people from seeing each other's importance. This is changing now under the impact of insecurity. Out of the white man's fear largely, this is changing and Negroes are sensing that the worst is over and that time is on their side. This came to me, I think, around 1952 or 1953, at the time of the Korean War, or maybe more, really, from the time of Montgomery. I was in Paris during the Korean War. Whites I knew very well were showing this panic. Americans always thought themselves tough in mind and spirit. Now they discovered they weren't. To take you through reverses, you need a sense of who you are, and Americans lost this sense for the moment, with Negroes looking on, feeling a wry kind of disenchantment.

But most salient of all, appearing and reappearing in different forms in many of these responses, was the awareness that these new events were bringing to an end that crushing sense of *nobodiness* which has been the main burden of the Negro experience in American life. One of the major leaders in the civil rights struggle put it this way:

Remember, this all comes after all this time in which the Negro has been hearing the white man saying to him: "You come from nothing, you ain't nothing, you won't be nothing, and your children won't be nothing." I believe a good many American Negroes reach for the African resurgence only as an additional bolster to something they have been building up for themselves spiritually and mentally, a sense of rightness, a sense of their own value.

An older writer said:

What's happened to me is that it has given me a feeling of dignity. I mean this in a very specific and real way. A Negro of my generation never had any way of knowing that he was like anybody else, as good as anybody else. I remember my father saying to me before

I went to college: "Remember, you're as good as anybody else." He had to say that to me because there was nothing until then to give me this knowledge. The fact that what happens to the Negro in the United States is of consequence to what happens to American relations with the rest of the world has increased the sense of personal importance—I have felt this myself.

And most explicitly, a newspaper editor said:

Martin Luther King said in a speech at Cleveland some time ago that the Negro had come to a time when he could say to himself: I am somebody. Well now I would say that the Negro can say: I am *really* somebody.

In this new world, the Negro American has to see himself in entirely new ways in relation to past, present, and future. He is playing new roles, feeling new emotions, having new experiences unlike anything he has ever known before. He has to rearrange all that he has known and all that his history has imposed upon him. If he was *nobody* and is now becoming *somebody*, his need now is to discover *who he is*.

---

## PART TWO

# NEGROES
# AND
# THEMSELVES

# 1. *OUT FROM BEHIND THE VEIL*

Just as the failure to integrate Negroes has haunted the American democracy from its beginning, the question of their identity has haunted Negroes. Every man has to have some answer to the terrible questions: *Who am I? What am I?* For Negroes it was more terrible than for most because their history for more than three hundred years had largely deprived them of the means of making any satisfactory answer—indeed, of making any answer of their own at all. Instead, the white man's answer stood large before every Negro. The white man told the Negro he was an inferior being without history or place in the stream of human culture, that he was subject—past, present, and forever—to the total superiority of white men, the masters of the earth. Under conditions of slavery, enforced backwardness, oppression, and debasement, Negroes in varying ways accepted the white man's image of them and survived by building up their own inner defense against it and finding their own ways of expressing their energies and their hopes, their angers and their sorrows. Some found these outlets in dreams of heaven, some in their own unique ways of coping with life on earth, some at the cost of their fellows, but mostly at cost to themselves. Rejected by the white world, they rejected themselves and became victims of the self-hatred that the despised have so often acquired from their despisers. This has been the burden of many kinds of men in the comings and goings of history, but for few has it been more crushing. Negroes who came up generation after generation to defy and challenge this state of affairs had to struggle not only against the great white world, and not only against the fears and inertia of fellow Negroes, but also against the pounding assertion of the power of the white world's judgment. W. E. B. Du Bois put it with needle sharpness sixty years ago:

Behind the thought lurks the afterthought—suppose if all the world is right and we are less than men? Suppose this mad impulse [the demand for freedom and equality] is all wrong, some mock mirage from the untrue . . . a shriek in the night for the freedom of men who themselves are not yet sure of their right to demand it? [1]

Every man's identity is a unique product of his own endowments and the circumstances of his life. The circumstances shared by members of a particular group can shape some features of a common personality, a group identity—what Erik Erikson has called a *shared sameness*. It is made up out of the shared answers to the questions of personal identity, and these come out of the shared experiences of the group. For Negroes in America it is made up out of the stuff of their lives over three centuries, out of all the modes of adaptation, submission and resistance, out of their rage and despair, suffering and sorrow, their surrender and their striving. Hence all the familiar postures and outlooks, the aggressions and withdrawals of the ghetto, all the varieties of direct and indirect protest and defiance, the outlets for self-expression in the spirituals, jazz, the blues, song and poetry, the flights into piety, cultism, or pure fantasy, the resorts to violence or the lapses into apathy, and always also the protest and the rebellion. These and many other aspects of the Negro group identity are visible in the characters and great symbol figures familiar to all in the past, from Uncle Tom to Bigger Thomas, from Sambo to Simple, from Frederick Douglass through Booker T. Washington to Du Bois to Philip Randolph, from the unknown makers and singers of songs through W. C. Handy to Ella Fitzgerald and Marian Anderson, and the poets and writers from the pallid Phyllis Wheatley through Paul Laurence Dunbar and Countee Cullen to the passionate Richard Wright. For all of them the subjection and subordination of the Negro was the central fact of life, the big overpowering circumstance, and every individual identity was in some measure shaped by it.

So in a way, until day before yesterday, the Negro American had a kind of answer for whoever might ask him who he was—

[1] Du Bois, *The Souls of Black Folk*, p. 89.

he was a second-class citizen who could go here but not there, who could work at this but not at that, who could come and go within the gates of the ghetto but had to move with care outside of it. He was a man who had to contain the tensions of poverty and imposed inferiority, rejected by the white world in which he had somehow to make his life; a man who had to shape himself behind a veil of invisibility and exclusion. These were the familiar facts of life. This was the "expected" and "accepted" condition, and each man took his part of the common ways of coping with it.

But now great changes come, affecting every aspect of life for every Negro individual. Everything in the Negro's universe has to become something different. At the same time almost all of the old conditions continue to exist—the poverty, the ghetto, the discrimination, the exclusions. Negroes feel that big wind at their backs; it helps push them against the barriers that still hold them in. More and more they push out of their physical and mental ghettos. But now they move out onto ground that is still inhospitable or even hostile, strewn with obstacles, pocked with holes, and often even heavily mined against them. They have to keep up all their old caution, all their old guards. At the same time they also meet all the new conditions of life, of change and enormous difference, and they need a new scheme of life to cope with them. They have somehow to keep their bearings with the uneven pace of change, some of it coming fast, some of it slow, some coming here, none coming there; and the more things change, the more intolerable is the survival of what has not changed. The "faster" things move, the greater the frustration because they never do move fast enough. Some Negroes push out onto this new ground into the new conditions. Some hold back, fearful of losing, as James Baldwin has pitilessly reminded them, the crutch of their second-classness. For some younger people, on the other hand, the changes come too late and far too slowly; they are bitterly unwilling to accept their freedom, as the novelist Julian Mayfield has said, chip by chip. Behind all these, great masses remain, trapped in a poverty to which the new world, the new situation, the new sensations bring hardly any relief at all. The blowing winds therefore whip up their expectations without as yet making openings in the society that will let them through. This makes for a great and jagged melee of people and emotions and circumstances, a chaotic milling about as each person looks for some new way to fit together the pieces of life that used to fit before but fit no longer.

The tensions among Negroes become, then, less and less the tensions of submission and endurance and more and more the tensions of change and self-assertion. But both kinds of tension continue to coexist in almost every Negro individual. Perhaps "coexist" is not the word; they jostle each other in a constant and bruising inward turmoil as each person seeks to discover the new terms of life—the older person fighting both to hold onto and to throw off the older habits of mind and outlook; the younger person trying to find the new ground to stand on amid all the tangled fears and angers and despairs and exhilarations. Negroes today are still suffering most of the disabilities of second-classness, even as they are becoming aware that they need no longer submit to it, that times have changed, are changing, and will change a lot more. Neither old Southern college president, Mississippi farmer, nor boy on the streets of Harlem can remain as he was. All have to cut their ways through the fabric of outlook and personality inherited from the past in order to live in environments where they have to see others and to see themselves and to become aware of being seen by others in ways they never did before.

All the powerful assumptions and circumstances that until day before yesterday so largely shaped Negro personalities are now disappearing. The old group identity no longer fits the new social reality. The samenesses are ceasing to be the same. Like everyone else, Negroes are having to rearrange the truths and falsities of how they see others and how they see themselves. New images are flashing back at them off the surfaces of today's new experiences. Habits of lifetimes, of a whole group past, have to be broken. All of it, rudely or exhilaratingly, comes up for disposal, renovation, replacement. Twenty-five years ago the late great Kelly Miller of Howard sardonically summed up the group identity of Negroes in a single phrase: "A Negro is anybody who'd be Jim-Crowed in Virginia." Even in Virginia this definition no longer fits. The "Negro" is becoming someone else. The features of his new group identity will come out of the individual life experiences of millions of people who all around us now are feeling these new impacts and finding themselves in these new circumstances.

This is plainly a most complex affair with a host of mysteries locked up in it to which I certainly hold no key. I would not dare to enter the inner chambers where even novelists have trod so rarely, but I would look a bit into the anterooms where there is much in view even if it is not always clearly to be seen. For, like individual identity, group identity has its obvious and its subtle aspects, simple and intricate, visible and subterranean, and they would all, I am sure, yield differently to different kinds of exposure, the obvious becoming obscure and the simple complicated even as one tries to achieve a clearer view. I do not presume here to attempt any inclusive description of Negro group identity. My essay is more modest; it is to try to single out and examine only certain aspects of group identity which are seemingly the most obvious of all—*name, color, nationality, origins*—choosing these not to suggest that they tell the whole story but because I think they illustrate some of its most important parts.

# 2. *A NAME TO GO BY*

The entire history of Negroes in America has conspired to give them a group identity that was negative or blurred or both. When James Baldwin titles his book *Nobody Knows My Name,* he is referring to the fact that a Negro's individuality as a particular person is lost in the white world behind the identifying external mask he wears as a "Negro." This mask was fashioned out of all that went into the struggle for survival in a hostile white society. It was shaped mainly out of the myths and stereotypes created by whites for their self-appeasement and so largely accepted by blacks for their self-defense. Hence the Uncle Tom, the Sambo, the Stepin Fetchit, and all the other figures in this particular wax museum. But the problem of the Negro group identity is much more than the problem of this synthetic group personality. Nobody may know "who" the "Negro" is, but this is at least partly because the person who is Negro has also been kept by these circumstances from knowing who he is himself. Hardly anything illustrates this more dramatically than the fact that even as "Negro" he has had enormous difficulty in deciding what to call himself, what group name to go by.

When you begin to trace the matter back in time—and it goes back nearly 200 years—you find that the usages have varied and that preferences and arguments have swelled and swirled around a whole collection of labels: blacks, Africans, negroes (with the small "n"), Negroes (with the capitalization which became general usage only after a long struggle that ended only some 30 years ago and has still not ended in much of the South), Coloreds, Colored People, Colored Americans, People of Color, Ethiopians, Racemen, Negro-Saxons, African Americans, Africo-Americans, Afro-Americans, Aframericans, American Negroes, Negro Americans. Even a brief look into these differences is the beginning of discovery of some of the real inwardness of the Negro identity problem.

In the present generation the widest common practice settled on "Negro," an embattled word which has held its own against almost constant assault. Differences, however, persist in both opinions and usage. The term "colored" is still used almost as widely and not always interchangeably. The term "Negro" is still subject to challenge from various directions, and the argument about it, kept alive by its inner essence and rekindled by all our current events, still goes on.[1] Black nationalists keep insisting on "Afro-American" or just plain "African." [2] The push of this issue to the extremes of nonidentity is illustrated at one end of the spectrum by the common use of the term "group" or "group man" (in which context whites would be "the majority group" or simply "the other group"), and at the other by the Black Muslims, who reject "Negro" and insist on "black" or "black men" but carry the Negro individual's identity confusion to the ultimate dramatic extreme by requiring all their followers to abandon their family names (because they all come from white origins) and to substitute the most literal symbol of nonbeing —the Black Muslim calls himself by a first name followed simply by "X".[3] Cults with Islamic labels have long offered one way of escaping identification as "Negro." The predecessor of the present movement, founded in 1913, required its followers to "refuse longer to be called Negroes, black folk, colored people, or Ethiopians" but to be called "Asiatics" or "Moors" or "Moorish Americans." [4]

Like so many other critical aspects of the story of Negroes in America, this too is a subject still awaiting its author. Many Negro writers, scholars, and public figures have contributed

1 E.g., an exchange between Richard B. Moore, author of *The Name "Negro": Its Origin and Its Evil Use* (New York, 1960), and Editor James W. Ivy, who called the issue a "nonsense question" and was charged by Moore with refusing to face the arguments against "the vicious smear name 'Negro,'" *Crisis*, Dec. 1960, pp. 680–681; Mar. 1961, pp. 185–186.

2 E.g., William H. Cumberbatch, "'Negro' Or African, Which?" *African Opinion*, July–Aug. 1958, p. 8.

3 Lincoln, *Black Muslims in America*, pp. 109–111.

4 Frazier, *The Negro in the United States*, p. 358. Also Arthur H. Fauset, *Black Gods of the Metropolis* (Philadelphia, 1944).

their views to this controversy over a long period of time, but almost always necessarily in the form of an argument for this or that name. My own search produced no systematic study of the matter but considerable scattered material, some of it from the last century, some out of yesterday's newspaper or magazine. You can read passionate but closely argued debates of more than 50 years ago between such men as J. W. E. Bowen, Editor of *The Voice of the Negro*,[5] and T. Thomas Fortune, Editor of *The New York Age,* an argument which at the time led the New York *Tribune* (on June 10, 1906) to feature an entire page of solicited statements under the heading: WHAT IS THE PROPER NAME FOR THE BLACK MAN IN AMERICA? Or come down to the 1930's when the fight to win a capital N for Negro reached its climax (*The New York Times* magisterially and ceremonially granted proper-noun capitalization on March 15, 1930, with a heralding editorial announcement) and read the contributions of the salty-penned George Schuyler of the Pittsburgh *Courier,* the strong views of Professor Kelly Miller of Howard University,[6] and letters to assorted editors by assorted people with many different assorted opinions on the subject. There is an occasional attempt at a summary of the argument.[7] In the setting of his particular interest in the American language, H. L. Mencken examined the matter at considerable length in an article in 1944 which he called "Designations for Colored Folk," which was later incorporated into his work *The American Language*.[8] The subject is treated with uniquely rich detail by James W. Ivy in his article "The Semantics of Being Negro in the Americas," [9] but he deals chiefly with the race labels in the Portuguese and Spanish idioms of Latin America, referring sufficiently to race labels used by and about Negroes in the United States to show

[5] E.g., "Who Are We? Africans, Afro-Americans, Colored People, Negroes, or American Negroes?" *The Voice of the Negro,* Jan. 1906, pp. 31–36.

[6] E.g., Miller, "Negroes or Colored People," *Opportunity,* May 1937, pp. 142–146.

[7] W. N. Huggins and J. G. Jackson, *A Guide to Studies in African History,* New York, 1934, pp. 29–34.

[8] *American Speech,* Oct. 1944, pp. 161–174; *The American Language,* Suppl. One (New York, 1945), pp. 618–637.

[9] Written for the Second Congress of Negro Writers and Artists, Rome (Mar.–Apr., 1959), published in French under the title "Le Fait d'Etre Nègre dans les Amériques," *Présence Africaine,* (Fev.–Mai 1959), pp. 123–131.

how deep and far the similarities go. For a fuller study of this matter, someone is still going to have to go digging into mountains of such material with some sharp questions. All I have done is pick up specimens—some in libraries, others in the minds of people with whom I raised these matters. I can do no more than take a spectroscopic look at them to see if I can suggest at least the outlines of a structure and some of the inner composition of some of its parts.

The slave traders called their African cargo *negros* or simply *blacks,* these terms coming to be used synonymously with *slave.* Ivy locates an early example of this blending in a 1721 dictionary. A century later in 1819 a South Carolina court, indeed, held that the word "Negro" had the fixed meaning of a "slave." This has been the most commonly cited source for objection to the use of "Negro." It has been seen, as various writers have noted, as "a badge of shame" hopelessly freighted with its "slave origin and its consequent degradation." Closely associated with this idea and equally common as a reason for rejecting the word is the slippage of "Negro" into "nigger," the term that carries in it all the obloquy and contempt and rejection which whites have inflicted on blacks in all this time. This, many have suggested, may be "the clue to the whole business." [10]

[10] Ottley, *New World A-Coming,* p. 278. Ottley goes on to remark, as have many others, that "The term nigger is used by Negroes quite freely when out of the earshot of whites, sometimes having a good deal of affectionate meaning to them." This way of turning an insulting word into something casual, light, even affectionate or humorous, is a usage not uncommon in various quarters with such comparable words as *kike, wop, mick, spic.* This is a way of lightening the quality of the word, like Cyrano talking about his own nose, or saying-it-and-smiling, but it never really relieves it of its burden of contempt and self-contempt.

Even more hateful sounding, incidentally, is the word *Nigra,* which is the way "Negro" comes out when slurred, deliberately or otherwise, in Southern accents. Negroes in Atlanta told me with much cynical amusement about a white politician seeking Negro votes in a local election who was drilled sedulously to say *Nee-gro* when talking to Negro audiences and who reverted to his more normal *Nigra* when talking to whites. The word *Negress* is almost the most objectionable of all, being strongly held to be associated with both the auction block and with animals. It may be taken as a recent sign of the times that the Columbia *Record* of Columbia, South Carolina, accepted the protest of a group of local Negro women and announced it would cease using the term *Negress.* "We were not aware that the term was offensive," the editor wrote. Columbia's other paper, *The State,* ignored the protest. New York *Amsterdam News,* Apr. 21, 1962.

But it becomes clear even from a brief look that there are many other clues, much else to the business than this. Even limited scrutiny suggests that for Negroes the issue of the name to go by has been deeply entwined with all the deepest and unresolved issues of the flight from self imposed upon them by their whole history in this society: of color—that is, of relative lightness and relative darkness; of the ways in which they have related to their African origins; of all the ways in which they have striven to be both in and of the white society from which they were so consistently and so completely excluded.

The available record begins with the free Negroes who had come up out of the slave system by various means and had begun to group and to assert themselves at the time of the American Revolution and the establishment of the American Republic. The 1790 census noted 59,000 free Negroes in the population and although still called "Negroes" by whites, they had begun to distinguish themselves from the slaves by using the adjective "African." This was the name they attached to the new institutions they created for themselves at this time when they found themselves excluded from the established similar institutions of the whites. Thus the African Baptist Church (1779), the first African Lodge of Masons (1787), the Free African Society (1787), the African Methodist Episcopal Church (1796), and others. The first schools established for their children were called "Free African Schools" in New York and elsewhere.

By 1830, however, when free Negroes met together in their urgent common interest, the adjective "African" had been replaced by "Colored." When they met in Philadelphia that year, they organized the "Convention of Colored Citizens of America." They had generally begun by that time to refer to themselves as "colored people" or "people of color." Students of the period have apparently not dealt with this shift in name and I do not know what a new search through old papers would turn up on this score.[11] But I am willing to guess that at least two

11 In a note dated Feb. 14, 1962, responding to an inquiry from the author, Professor Howard H. Bell of Texas Southern University, a leading student of the Convention movement, said: "I have never seen the topic developed, nor did I find any great argument in the sources. 'African' seems to have been dropped before 1830."

sets of circumstances would be found to be part of the explanation.

The first is that in the intervening time a concerted movement had been started to get free Negroes to migrate back to Africa, whereas the overwhelming majority of free Negroes, especially in the Northern cities, wanted no part of any such migration. By the process of self-purchase, manumission, the efforts of various early abolition groups, and by natural increase, the number of free Negroes had risen by this time to 319,000, more or less evenly divided between Northern and Southern cities. Their freedom was tenuous and under constant threat. Their hardships attracted a certain kind of pious Northern white benevolence under which transportation back to Africa was seen as the best solution to the problem. On the other hand, the sheer existence of free Negroes was felt as a growing threat to slaveholding interests, and this attracted a certain nonpious Southern malevolence which seized readily upon the same idea. These interests were wedded in 1817 in the founding of the American Colonization Society, which received the ready support of certain state legislatures. Some Southern free Negroes accepted the Society's offer (in many instances manumission was made contingent upon willingness to sign up for the return to Africa), and from among these came the first boatloads of migrants who founded Liberia in 1821. By 1830 the number shipped by the society totaled only just over 1,400. As we shall have occasion to note in greater detail later,[12] there was an independent and recurring impulse among some despairing Northern free Negroes to look to Africa as a way out of hopelessness in America, but most Northern free Negroes vehemently opposed the Society's program and denounced it in strong terms, beginning in 1817 and every year thereafter in meetings in many cities. It seems reasonable to assume, therefore, that the label "African" was abandoned, at least by Northern free Negroes, because they were intent upon remaining Americans and rejected the schemes to send them, as "Africans," back to Africa.

But the choice of the term "people of color" or "colored

[12] "Back to Africa," Part III, ch. 2.

people" to replace "African" suggests the second set of circumstances clearly involved in this change. The term "African" had been used mainly by free Negroes in the North, most of whom had gained their freedom in the early years of the Republic. The clusters of free Negroes in the South, especially those in Charleston, South Carolina, and New Orleans, came out of a much older process. The first differentiation among the slaves was that made between the fieldhands and the house servants, and from among the latter came the issue of unions between white masters and slave women, often treated as a second family, given their freedom, means, and education. It was the descendants of such groups who developed their own special caste position (which included slaveholding of their own) and whose most visible mark of caste was their lighter color. This community in Charleston in 1790 formed not an *African* association, but the *Brown* Fellowship Society, "which admitted only brown men of good character who paid an admission fee of fifty dollars." [13] In New Orleans the even older and more aristocratic mixed descendants of the older French and Spanish settlers became a distinct group in the population and were called *gens de couleur*. It is presumably from this term, carrying with it all the connotations of higher caste associated with nonblackness and mixed ancestry, that the vague and essentially nondescriptive term *colored* or *people of color* was derived. With its adoption by the Northern free Negroes in place of "African" during the decade before 1830, it became the term of preferred and polite usage.

Although this term became one of general use and has persisted down through time until now, it has never stood alone or uncontradicted. At the very beginning, in the 1840's and 1850's, when some of the most militant and antimigrationist free leaders, despairing of ever gaining a decent status in America, became advocates of migration to Africa, there was some effort made to revive the use of the term "African." [14] Whites generally continued to use "Negro" although the abolitionist movement generally adopted "colored." Lincoln, Sandburg notes, was

13 Frazier, *op. cit.*, p. 77.
14 Howard H. Bell, "Negro Emigration Movement," loc. cit., pp. 132–142.

attacked by Southern sympathizers for shifting from "negroes," a term he still used in 1859, to "colored men" in 1860 and "free Americans of African descent" in 1862.[15] Frederick Douglass generally used "colored" in accordance with the preferred practice, but also used "Negro" and "black" as part of his effort to re-establish a sense of Negro identity. He used "Negro," he told a white audience in 1854, "precisely in the sense that you use 'Anglo-Saxon.' "[16] In referring to individual persons he continued as a rule to use "colored."

By whatever name he was called, the Negro in the closing decades of the nineteenth century found his status as a man and as a citizen driven lower and lower. It was at this time, in 1880, that T. Thomas Fortune came up with his effort to get Negroes and the society at large to accept the new term "Afro-American." Fortune wanted to get away from "Negro," according to Kelly Miller, because of "the historical degradation and humiliation attached to it," and, it is suggested, especially to get away from "nigger." Fortune wrote: "Until we get this race designation properly fixed in the language and literature of the country, we shall be kicked and cuffed and sneered at as a common noun, sufficiently and contemptuously characterized by the vulgar term. . . ." But Fortune wanted to do a lot more than merely do away with a vulgar term. He meant his term "Afro-American" to describe the different physical type that had been created in America by mixture with the white, as "a new race in this country approximating much nearer the American than the African type." "The term 'Negro,' " he wrote, "has been used to describe black people of Africa. It is not a term definitive of race affinities but of physical peculiarities of race of which color is the invariable index."[17] For Fortune too, this strongly suggests, a critical element in choosing the name to go by was the element of color and the distinctively "Negro" physical characteristics. The term "Afro-American," despite Fortune's doughty

[15] Carl Sandburg, *Abraham Lincoln: The War Years* (New York, 1939), v. II, p. 137, noted by H. L. Mencken, *The American Language*, Suppl. One, p. 621.
[16] Philip S. Foner ed., *The Life and Writings of Frederick Douglass* (New York, 1950), v. II, p. 304.
[17] *New York Age*, quoted by New York *Herald Tribune*, June 10, 1906.

championship and its adoption later as the name of the Baltimore *Afro-American,* never gained any wide measure of acceptance among Negroes and none at all in the general currency of the language.

But the argument, largely centering on the continued use of "Negro," went on and on, acquiring peculiar force around the years of the turn of the century. Booker T. Washington advocated the use of "Negro," and opponents of the word charged this against his general posture of submission. But along came W. E. B. Du Bois, no submitter, who not only espoused "Negro" but used "black" and stressed color almost obsessively in his own special struggle for the reassertion of Negro identity. It did not matter, he pointed out, whether they were called "African" or "Ethiopian" or "colored," but what mattered was who and what you were and where you stood in the society. This was the view expressed by many other leaders over the years, although the NAACP, founded in 1909 by Du Bois and others, followed the preferred usage among the middle- and upper-class Negroes and used "Colored." The Garvey movement a decade later did use "Negro" in its name (the United Negro Improvement Association) but much preferred "black" as a direct expression of its explicit and strong racial chauvinism.

Most of the present generation of Negro adults grew up simply accepting these confused and divided usages without questioning what they might mean. Among those I interviewed I noticed a fairly typical cleavage: members of what one might call the more traditional middle or upper class among Negroes almost invariably used "colored," and a few had strong views on the subject ("I never class myself as 'Negro,' " said an ex-college president. "I had to cease to be a 'Negro' in order to be a man"). The stronger "raceman" types had opposite views. ("My father always believed we should use 'Negro,' meaning black," said a noted labor leader. "As a term it has more strength than 'colored.' ") More generally the younger and more sophisticated either used "Negro" alone or used it interchangeably with "colored." When asked, most of them said they were aware of the disputes over the matter but did not think them important. Most commonly, they said they thought the objection to

"Negro" was its closeness to "nigger." Only a few thought there might be layers to the matter deeper than this, but this came out only when they were specifically asked. "I hadn't thought," said a noted educator, "that any matter of color was involved in this, but it is quite possible. Some four or five years ago there was a motel sign up somewhere near here [Atlanta] which said 'For Negroes.' A tax driver sneered as we went by it one day. 'He ought to know he won't get colored people's business with that sign.' And the fact is that the sign was changed sometime after that to 'For Colored.' "

Said another well-known scholar: "I am sure there is something about color in the use of 'Negro' and 'Colored,' though it is not always at the tip of people's consciousness."

In fact, just below the level of that more common consciousness, the issue of name confusion is intimately locked with all the central issues of Negro identity confusion: the flight from blackness; the flight from Negroness itself; the yearning to be white.

# 3. BLACK, STAND BACK

The flight from blackness and the yearning to be white have had a major part in shaping the Negro group identity down through the generations. It involved the more or less total acceptance of the white man's estimate of the black man, the more or less total rejection of self. This was a widely shared experience which took on many forms, but it would be hard to find a more explicit statement of it than the one made in a contribution to the argument over names in 1913 by William H. Ferris, author of a two-volume study called *The African Abroad*. Ferris had an entry of his own in the namestakes; he wanted the term *Negrosaxon*, because he believed that salvation for the black man lay in his complete adoption of white Anglo-Saxonism. He wrote:

> The Anglo-Saxon civilization is the highest and best yet evolved in the history of the human race. On the other hand, the word "Negro" originally referred to a native African black, who was a barbarian and a savage. . . . "Negro" calls up a black, kinky-haired and heavy-featured being. . . . [It] suggests physical and spiritual kinship to the ape, the monkey, the baboon, the chimpanzee, the orangutan and gorilla. . . . It is up to the Negrosaxon or Colored man to say which badge he shall wear, the badge of monkeyhood or of manhood, the badge of brutehood and bestiality or the badge of humanity. . . . What causes more of a shudder of repulsion to run through the frame than the phrase "a big burly Negro . . ."? The colored man who brands himself as a Negro thereby catalogues and labels himself as a being who is outside the pale of humanity.

Fortunately, Ferris goes on, most of the colored people in America were brought inside the pale of humanity by blood mixture. "While the colored people of America cannot boast of the manner in which they came by their white blood, they at least have this consolation—most of the Caucasian blood that

72

flows in Negrosaxon veins is the blood of Southern aristocrats."
Ferris believed that a full embrace of Anglo-Saxonism could
save even a black man. Citing some notable examples (such as
Alexander Crummell and Kelly Miller), he went on: "He cannot
bleach out his complexion or straighten his hair, or sharpen his
nose, or thin his lips. But in mind and character and disposition
he must become a black white man. After the Negrosaxon has
been made over into the likeness of the white man he can hope
to be made over into the image of God." [1]

This is, of course, a familiar phenomenon which has also been
called "identification with the aggressor." In wanting to become
like those who have dominated, despised, and rejected them,
Negroes have been behaving like members of many other dominated, despised, and rejected groups. All our various cultures
and subcultures are filled with examples. It became part of the
common experience of certain sections of the colonized peoples
during the Western imperial epoch; it was even shared for quite
awhile by certain kinds of Chinese. In the American culture it
has been plainly visible in the experience of successive immigrant groups as they went about relating themselves to the
dominant group in the society. Jews, who have been despised
and rejected for a longer time than any other people, have a
number of chapters of this kind in their long history. Bruno
Bettelheim's interpretations of what happened to some Jews in
the Nazi extermination camps suggests a recent and extreme
example.[2] More familiar and more common has been the behavior attached to the idea of "assimilation," the effort to shed
all vestiges of the Jewish identity by disappearing entirely into
the dominant group.[3] The equivalent among Negroes is, of
course, "passing" into the white population. But to "pass" is

[1] William H. Ferris, *The African Abroad* (New Haven, 1913), v. I, pp. 296–
311.

[2] Bruno Bettelheim, "Individual and Mass Behavior in Extreme Situations,"
*Journal of Abnormal and Social Psychology*, Oct. 1943.

[3] Kurt Lewin, *Resolving Social Conflicts* (New York, 1948), ch. 12, "Self-
Hatred Among Jews." For a picture of this experience among early nineteenth-
century German Jews, see Max Brod, *Heinrich Heine* (New York, 1957); for
vignettes of the same process going on among some of their descendants in twentieth-century America, Ludwig Lewisohn's novel, *The Island Within* (New York,
1928).

possible for only relatively few.[4] More generally people have to find other ways of assimilating the majority view of themselves and of expressing the self-rejection and self-hatred that follow from this. Among Negroes the forms and modes of this process are endlessly varied. One of the most pervasive of these has been the institution of color caste which raised "whiteness" to the highest value in all aspects of life. This meant everything pertaining to civilization, culture, religion and human worth. It became among Negroes an intricate system of social, group and personal relationships based directly on degrees of relative darkness and other degrees of physical Negroness, the shape and kinds of features, hair, lips, and nose which were "good" if they resembled the white's, "bad" if they did not. This was carried to the point of using artificial means—hair straighteners and skin whiteners—in the effort to close the gap between the two.

In coming to terms with himself, every Negro individual has had in one way or another to cope with the infinity of ways in which "white" is elevated above "black" in our culture. The association of white and black with light and dark and the translation of these quantities of light into polarities of "good" and "evil" and "beauty" and "ugliness" have taken place in the conventions and languages of many cultures, but in few has the conversion of physical facts into religious and esthetic values been worked harder than in our own.

## "Black" and "White"

The concepts and usages of black evil and white goodness, of beautiful fairness and ugly blackness, are deeply imbedded in the Bible, are folded into the language of Milton and Shakespeare, indeed are laced into almost every entwining strand of the art and literature in which our history is clothed. They can be traced down the columns of any dictionary from white hope to whitewash, from the black arts to the Black Mass, from blackbrowed and blackhearted to blacklist and blackmail. "I am black

4 Gunnar Myrdal, *An American Dilemma* (New York) 1944, pp. 683–8. Walter White, long-time secretary of the N.A.A.C.P., who himself had this choice, dealt with it in a novel, *Flight* (New York, 1926).

*but* comely," sang the Shulamite maiden to the daughters of Jerusalem, and on that *but* hangs a whole great skein of our culture.

The Bible's central theme of good and evil is constantly represented by the symbolism of "black" and "white" and "dark" and "light," beginning with God's creation of light to split the primeval darkness and continuing with the use of this imagery "from Genesis to the Apocalypse, and from the word of life to the shadow of death." [5] In the Scriptures the use of "black" as a negative word is consistent throughout, standing for sin, ignorance, wickedness, and evil. "My skin is black," cries Job in his great self-arraignment, using this figure to show how heavy was his burden of sin. Again in Job: "Let darkness and the shadow of death stain it; let a cloud dwell upon it; let the blackness of the day terrify it." Or in Jeremiah: "For this shall the earth mourn and the heavens above be black." And in the Epistle of Jude the famous phrase about "the wandering stars to whom is reserved the blackness of darkness forever." The word "white" is apparently used a good deal less in the Bible, and less consistently. Thus "the great white throne" of God in Revelation, the "white raiments" of the elders in Judges. But "white," though most often signifying beauty, purity, and elegance, is also more rarely used—as a literally descriptive word—in connection with leprosy, and has been associated in the language with pestilence and death. More consistent is the juxtaposition of "light" and "dark," the dark always being bad and light always good, from the original creation of light to divide it from the primeval dark and to show the way for men to see truth and good works and glory and the light of God himself: "In Thy light," sang the Psalmist, "shall we see light." There can be no question that when the Lord looked upon his work and found it good, it was the light that pleased him, not the dark. Where

[5] Harry Levin, *The Power of Blackness* (New York, 1958), p. 29. For many of these references, I am indebted to papers from my own M.I.T. graduate seminar, particularly by E. W. Gude, "Black and White" (1961), who examined the dictionaries and concordances of Shakespeare and the Bible, and also by Curtis H. Barker, "Black and White" (1960), who dealt with the ways in which words "fight back," i.e., how evaluative meanings outstrip and replace original or more objective meanings.

the references occur in the Bible to a literal blackness of skin, the association seems to retain its negative cast. "Look not upon me," adds the Shulamite maiden in the Song of Songs, "because I am black." A second such allusion is rather more equivocal. This is the reference in Numbers to the Lord's anger at Aaron and Miriam after they had spoken against Moses for marrying "an Ethiopian woman," the term "Ethiopian" signifying a person of black skin. The text suggests that the Lord was angry primarily because the offenders were jealous of Moses' special role as the Lord's man. If the issue here *was* color, than his anger was ironically vented: his punishing finger touched Miriam and she became *"leprous, white as snow."* I suspect, however, that Aaron was objecting to the Ethiopian woman not because she was black—the Israelites who came out of Egypt could hardly have been a lily-white race—but because she was gentile. In this case God either knew more about Moses' origins than Aaron did, or was simply less orthodox than his high priest—a not unfamiliar state of affairs.

The carry-over of the Bible's imagery into the common usage, visible in Chaucer and Milton, is richly illustrated in Shakespeare, whose own impact on the English language has hardly been less great than that of the Bible itself. "Black is the badge of hell / The hue of the dungeons and the suit of night," says the King in *Love's Labor's Lost,* in a passage of raillery in which the beauty of Rosaline (French and therefore presumably brunette) is called "black as ebony" and her admirer Biron chided for loving "an Ethiope." In quite another tone, in *Macbeth,* we come on: "The devil damn thee black—", again the symbolic joining of sin, the devil, and the blackness of skin which runs continuously from Job and the prophets through centuries of our literature. (Thus Fitzgerald in *Omar Khayyam:* "For all the sin wherewith the face of man is blackened. . . ."). In Shakespeare's first tragedy, *Titus Andronicus,* the villain is a black man. In *Othello* Shakespeare treats the theme with far greater subtlety. No doubt is left that Brabantio's rage is due in part to the thought that his daughter would run "to the sooty bosom of such a thing as thou," but the direct allusions to Othello's color are few. Perhaps the most ironic are those Shakespeare puts in the mouth of Othello himself, as where in the rage of his rising jealousy he says: "Her name, that was as fresh/ As Dian's visage is now begrimed and black/ As mine own," and where he cries out: "Arise, black vengeance!" He looks upon the sleeping Desdemona not wanting to shed her blood, "nor scar that whiter skin of hers than snow/ And smooth as monumental alabaster." When he has done the deed, the servant Emilia shrieks at him: "You, the blacker devil!"

One might travel many paths into some of the mysteries of this little-studied matter, whether in other cultures, including the African,[6] or in our own. These could run, in the latter case, from tracing the notions and characteristics attached to blondness or brunetteness (over the whole course of the Anglo-Saxon romantic tradition on down to the Hollywood illustrations, from Mary Pickford—partly contradicted, to be sure, by Garbo and Dietrich —and Theda Bara, and the convention requiring the cowboy hero always to wear a white hat and ride a white horse and the cowboy villain always a black hat and a black horse). One might pursue these themes into some of their deeper and more enigmatic courses, as Professor Harry Levin did in *The Power of Blackness*, in which he examines the imagery of black and blackness in Hawthorne, Poe, and Melville. But to lead us back to the aspects of the matter that touch us here most directly, let me only follow an allusion from his pages to William Blake's poem, "The Little Black Boy"—part of a collection published in 1789—in which the outlook imposed on the black child by the white society is quite neatly capsuled:

[6] During an American tour in 1959, Les Ballets Africaines, a dance troupe from newly independent and highly nationalistic Guinea, performed a dance described as traditional and even ritualistic, depicting the universal theme of the dual between good and evil. Both dancers involved were black men, the good spirit appearing dressed in a shining white tunic and headdress with white plume, and the evil demon, identically dressed, only in a dead black. Varying concepts and practices relating to the colors black and white have been attributed to different African tribes. These conventions are familiar and highly visible in other cultures and long predate contact with Western men, e.g., in the Chinese theatre the hero's conventional makeup is always white, the villain's always black, and the same goes for the depiction of good and bad in the art of Hindu-influenced Southern Asia, and for the coloring of the *wajang*, the puppets used in the most popular of all the traditional arts of Java.

My mother bore me in the southern wild,
And I am black, but O! my soul is white;
White as an angel is the English child,
But I am black, as if bereav'd of light.

My mother . . . began to say:
". . . And we are put on earth a little space
That we may learn to bear the beams of love;
And these black bodies and this sunburnt face
Is but a cloud, and like a shady grove.

"For when our souls have learn'd the heat to bear,
The cloud will vanish; we shall hear His voice,
Saying: 'Come out from the grove, My love and care,
And round my golden tent like lambs rejoice.' "

Thus did my mother say, and kissed me;
And thus I say to little English boy.
When I from black and he from white cloud free,
And round the tent of God like lambs we joy,

I'll shade him from the heat, till he can bear
To lean in joy upon our Father's knee;
And then I'll stand and stroke his silver hair,
And be like him, and he will then love me.

This raising of "white" and debasement of "black" has been marked deep on the minds of all through time and every "white" person has more or less unconsciously imbibed it as nourishment for his self-esteem. Like the English child in Blake's poem, he was already the color of the angels, while the black man could only yearn after whiteness, whether of character, soul or skin, and hope that by becoming "like" the white man—whether on earth or in heaven—he would come at last to be loved. This arrangement of things was communicated to all in our culture by all its modes and means, passed by osmosis through all the membranes of class, caste, and color of relationships, caressingly and painlessly injected into our children by their school texts and, even more, their storybooks.

Consider only one contemporary example, out of the Dr.

Dolittle stories, written by an Englishman, which have delighted
European and American children since 1920.[7] Dr. Dolittle, an
animal doctor who travels with an entourage of a dog, a duck,
a pig, an owl, a monkey, and a parrot, goes to Africa to cure
monkeys of a plague. Dolittle and his animal helpers become
the prisoners of a black king. In the king's garden the parrot
and the monkey meet the king's son, Prince Bumpo, who is pictured as an ugly, gnomelike black man with a huge nose that
covers most of his face. They hear him yearn aloud: "If only I
were a *white* prince!" The parrot promises that Dr. Dolittle will
change his color if he helps them escape. To Dr. Dolittle the unhappy prince tells his story:

"Years ago I went in search of The Sleeping Beauty, whom I had
read of in a book. And having traveled through the world many
days, I at last found her and kissed the lady very gently to wake her—
as the book said I should. 'Tis true indeed that she woke. But when
she saw my face she cried out, 'Oh, he's black!' And she ran away and
wouldn't marry me—but went to sleep again somewhere else. So I
came back, full of sadness, to my father's kingdom. Now I hear that
you are a wonderful magician and have many powerful potions. So
I come to you for help. If you will turn me white, so that I may go
back to The Sleeping Beauty, I will give you half of my kingdom
and anything besides you ask."

Bumpo refuses to settle just for blond hair and says: "I would
like my eyes blue, too, but I suppose that would be very hard
to do." The doctor concocts a paste which whitens Bumpo's face
and keeps it that way long enough for him and his friends to
escape, having first refused to give Bumpo a mirror because he
knew that the medicine would wear off and that Bumpo would
be "as black as ever in the morning." As they escape, the doctor
says, "Poor Bumpo." The parrot says: "Oh, of course he would
know we were just joking with him." The duck says: "Serve him
right if he does turn black again. I hope it is a dark black." Dr.
Dolittle decides that instead of apologizing he will send Bumpo
some candy when he gets back home.

   I do not know if Negro children have been readers of the

   [7] Hugh Lofting, *The Story of Dr. Dolittle* (New York, 1920).

Dolittle stories, but vast numbers of white children apparently
have—it came up in the first place when a discussion of these
matters in a seminar stirred the recollection of a graduate student of thirty, and an indirect question brought immediate recall of the story to my own daughter, then sixteen. It is not hard
to imagine the effect on white children who, as they chortle over
the good doctor's adventures with the animals, also take in this
vignette of the ugly black prince who wanted to be white in
order to be loved. It takes no great art either to imagine how
this tale might stab a black child or help give him all unknow-
ingly the same love for whiteness that it nourishes in the white
child.[8]

## Color Caste

The imprint on Negroes of this whole system of ordering
"black" and "white" has been seen and experienced by many
but studied by very few. Every "black" person obviously has

---

[8] An example of another kind, and earlier in time, is "The Story of Two
Little Lambs," in Maud Ballington Booth's *Sleepy-Time Stories* (New York) 1900.
A little white lamb strays from the flock and is lost and meets a little black lamb
in the forest. Says the little black lamb: "You are what they call a White Lamb,
and White Lambs have a good home and good things all the time, and they say
that they have a good Shepherd; but I am only a black one . . . some day when
we meet the good Shepherd (if we ever do chance to meet Him) He will take
us too, and bring us to the White Lambs' fold." To this the white lamb replies:
"I don't think He would like you very much for I have always been told that
He wants His Sheep and Lambs to have very white, white wool and you are all
black." The Shepherd Jesus comes to recover his stray white lamb and promises
that he can wash him clean and white again, and is about to leave when the
little black lamb speaks up and says he wishes he was one of Jesus' lambs too.
"But it's no use," he says, "for they say you only want White Sheep and Lambs
and cannot bear black wool, so I cannot be the sort of Lamb you want." To which
Jesus replies: "Did you not hear that I can wash away the stains and make my
little Lamb white again?" "But good Shepherd," interposes the little white lamb,
"that Lamb has always been black . . . It isn't your Lamb it's quite another
sort." Jesus is sad and angry. "Who said the Black Lambs were not mine? Who
said I do not want them?" So he takes up both little lambs, carries them to a
stream in which he washes them, "and when they came out they were both
white, as white as snow. They bleated for joy and jumped around the Shepherd,
and then they laid their little heads in His tender hand, and He stroked them
lovingly."

been called upon to reject or somehow deflect from himself the associations of evil and inferiority so powerfully attached to blackness. He has been called upon to do this, moreover, under conditions in which his ego was kept under constant assault from all the conditions of his life. That so many Negroes in every successive generation found the ego strength to meet and resist these identifications is in itself no small miracle. That a greater number accepted the white man's images as the truth about themselves is no wonder at all.

Out of this acceptance came the notions and practices of color caste among Negroes, the notions and virtue and nonvirtue attached to lightness and darkness, the placing of the highest value on nonblackness. This was, as we have already remarked, the basis for the separate identity of the *gens de couleur,* the underlying reason for the adoption of the term *colored,* and the starting point for the establishment of tight little groups of lighter-skinned Negro aristocrats. There is some suggestion that from the time of the forming of the "Brown Fellowship" in Charleston in 1790 until Reconstruction days, the practice of color caste remained locked in these small communities. This seems, at least, to be the meaning of the element of surprise in an exchange of letters between Martin R. Delany, who went to Charleston from New York in 1871, and Frederick Douglass. Delany, himself quite dark, wrote indignantly to Douglass of the attitudes and practices he found among the pre-Civil War free Negroes there, bringing from Douglass an astonished and angry response:

Can it be that the colored people of South Carolina are going to make such fools of themselves? . . . Are we to have, nay have we got a caste called the *Browns* in South Carolina? . . . I certainly unite with you in your hottest denunciations of that contemptible and senseless imitation of one of the meanest feelings that ever crept into the human heart.[9]

But color caste spread and grew, moved out into all classes

9 *Life and Writings of Frederick Douglass,* v. IV, p. 279.

among Negroes, and came to shape the attitudes and personalities of all who were touched by it.[10] "Among Negroes themselves," wrote James Weldon Johnson in 1912, "there is the peculiar inconsistency of a color question. Its existence is rarely admitted and hardly ever mentioned; it may not be too strong a statement to say that the greater portion of the race is unconscious of its influence; yet this influence, though silent, is constant." [11]

The first forthright scrutiny it ever received from scholars was in a series of investigations made in the late 1930's by a group of Negro and white social scientists and published in 1940 and 1941 for the American Youth Commission, especially E. Franklin Frazier, *Negro Youth at the Crossways* (Frazier probably dealt more frequently and more boldly with this matter in his works than anyone else); Charles Johnson, *Growing Up in the Black Belt;* W. Lloyd Warner, B. H. Junker and W. A. Adams, *Color and Human Nature;* and Allison Davis and John Dollard,

[10] The yearning after whiteness and color caste values governed not only Negroes in the United States but throughout the Americas. In the article already cited, James Ivy traces the matter not only through the terminologies used in Portuguese and Spanish but in the rich literature in both those languages. The late Franz Fanon, a Negro of Martinique and a psychoanalyst, wrote in *Peau Blanc, Masques Noirs* (Paris, 1952) with great force and passion of the ways in which these same pressures shaped the black men who came under the domination of France.

In shapes that await someone's closer look, the matter also appears in African settings. E.g., in *Drawn in Color: African Contrasts* (New York, 1962, pp. 85–86), Noni Jabavu, daughter of a distinguished South African educator, quotes a cousin of hers: "Funny thing about those up-North people. All the ones who came were so *black* . . . We were a little taken aback, then jumped to the defense of the East Africans . . . 'Don't talk rubbish! Haven't we got our dark-complexioned ones?' The cousin clung to his point . . . 'Why is it the ones who come south all happen to be this black-as-sin type?' We at once stopped laughing and winced at the idiom. We were shocked to have to admit that we had all observed it . . . He was speaking of an ugly thing, being blunt and unashamed about the colour prejudice that we all knew and felt . . . In months to come I was to be astounded to find this same preference for copper-coloured complexions lurking even among the Ugandans themselves whose own deep colouring is artistically complete and reminds you of the look of rich, dark fruit when the bloom is on it. These secret dissatisfactions made me wonder if there weren't more intricacies than meet the eye in the complex attitudes about colour which arouse emotions the world over."

[11] *The Autobiography of an Ex-Colored Man* (New York, 1928), p. 154 (orig. pub. 1912).

*Children of Bondage.*[12] They showed that at all levels in the Negro population in both North and South shades of relative darkness and lightness had become tightly related to social, moral, and esthetic judgments, and affected relationships of all kinds, from playmates among children to marriage mates among adults. Until these studies appeared, showing the "unimaginable bitterness and antipathies [that] rage within the veil of color," [13] very little had ever been said in print about this pervasive fact of Negro life.

Apparently its first appearance as the central theme of a novel was in Wallace Thurman's *The Blacker the Berry* (New York, 1929) which brought out into the open, according to Langston Hughes, "a subject little dwelt upon in Negro fiction." The title comes from a folk saying often defensively on the lips of the darker skinned, especially the women: "The blacker the berry, the sweeter the juice." Thurman's heroine Emma Lou is a dark girl whom he takes through every kind of Negro milieu, mercilessly depicting the hurts and the cruelties inflicted upon her. These begin when she is still in her cradle with the scorn and derision of relatives ("Try some lye," they would joke viciously to her mother, "it may eat it [the blackness] out. She can't look any worse!"). It goes on with the hatred of her mother, who sees her daughter's darkness as her penalty for marrying a dark man of whom she was ashamed. Emma Lou goes to school in Los Angeles where she hopes to find a kindlier cosmopolitanism, but she is snubbed by lighter Negroes there too. She goes to Harlem where she finds all the better jobs—even at the menial levels of restaurant work—restricted to lighter-skinned girls, and where she must even listen to the raucous taunts of

[12] See also Myrdal, *American Dilemma*, notes 12–39, pp. 1382–1386. For a useful search through the journals of psychology and psychiatry, I am in debt to a 1959 Harvard undergraduate paper: Arnold R. Isaacs, "Self-Rejection and Color Caste in the Negro Community." This literature is extremely small, yielding up very few items dealing specifically with color caste as such. Two articles in the *Psychoanalytic Review*, over a wide time interval, turned out to be more in the nature of personal testimony than studies, though not less interesting on this account: Charles H. Gibson, "Concerning Color," (Oct. 1931), pp. 413–425; and Gilbert Balfour Bovell, "Psychological Considerations of Color Conflicts Among Negroes" (Oct. 1943), pp. 447–459.

[13] *Journal of Negro History* (Jan. 1942), p. 103.

hoodlums she passes on the streets, their voices carrying after her with: "Man, you know I don't haul no coal," or singing a common ditty:

> A yellow girl rides in a limousine,
> A brownskin rides a Ford,
> A black girl rides an old jackass,
> But she gets there, yes, my lord.

There are many variations on this theme, the following being one of the most common:

> White, you're right,
> Light, you can fight,
> Brown, stand around,
> Black, stand back!

Emma Lou makes a friend of a West Indian girl who is also suffering the slings and arrows of rejection as a "monkey chaser," but even here the circle is rounded for her by a West Indian landlady who turns her away because, Thurman explains, "persons of color don't associate with blacks in the Caribbean Islands she had come from." He takes us with his heroine through the common practice of skin bleaching, the use of all sorts of preparations and powders on which great fortunes were made in the ready market among dark-skinned women. She even tries arsenic wafers, which she had heard increased skin pallor, but only gets sick, and all the ointments and solutions only serve to give her rashes, burns and irritations. At work and at church, she goes on seeking acceptance without finding it, and when a "yaller nigger" shows interest, she is flattered "that a man as light as he should find himself attracted to her," but then she finds she despises him for this very reason. She is drawn back to the man who had most brutally misused her, but even he, at the bottom of the pit of misfortune from which she tries vainly to lift him, feels free to step on her at will; this finally forces her to look squarely at herself and her life. Thurman, a gifted writer who died very young, brings his dark heroine at the end to a positive affirmation of strength: "What she needed to do now was to accept her black skin as being real and unchangeable, to realize that certain things were, had been and would be, and with this in mind to begin life anew, always fighting, not so much for acceptance by other people, but for acceptance of herself and by herself." She can do this, but only at the price of achieving a terrible hardness of spirit.

Not many other writers even yet have chosen to deal explicitly and at length with the theme of lightness and darkness in Negro life. It is deeply enfolded—indeed, often hidden—in the writing of Langston Hughes. Saunders Redding comes back to it again and again in his work, but almost always glancingly or in brief episodes through which he still manages to show how enormously important it is to him. In a small part of the first chapter of his *No Day of Triumph*,[14] for example, he writes of his two grandmothers between whom there lay a deep abyss: "One was yellow, the other was black." He tells how as a small boy who already knew there was "a stigma attached to blackness," he realized that for his Grandma Conway blackness was not merely a *blemish* but a *taint*. Another is his poignant account of a girl, a distant relative, who never overcame the handicap of her darker color and ended up by dissolving as a human being. In *The Third Generation* (1954) Chester Hines writes about a woman who is the product, three generations removed, of a union between a plantation lord and a slave. She is white in appearance and is wedded to this whiteness with an intensity that is a sickness. This is the way in which the sins of her forebears are visited upon her, for her obsession drags her, her husband, and her children, into various kinds of self-destruction.

In *Proud Shoes*[15] Pauli Murray gives us a portrait of her grandmother, who was actually just such a woman, herself the daughter of a plantation owner and a slave who was mostly Cherokee Indian. She built her entire identity around these facts of her origin and her first loyalty was not only to her "whiteness" but to her "Southern aristocratic whiteness." Thus when a neighbor thinks to insult her by calling her "a half-white bastard," she retorts:

[14] (New York, 1950) p. 88.
[15] (New York, 1956) p. 88.

Hmph! You think I'm insulted? I'll tell anybody I'm a white man's child. A fine white man at that. A Southern aristocrat. If you want to know what I am, I'm an octoroon, that's what I am—seven-eighths white. The other eighth is Cherokee Indian. I don't have one drop of colored blood in me and I don't have to mix in with good-for-nothing niggers if I don't want to.

"Anyone who has been part of a family of mixed bloods in the United States or the West Indies," writes Miss Murray, "has lived intimately with the unremitting search for whiteness. To deny that it is part of one's heritage would be like saying one had no parents." The form it took was the unending obsession with color:

The world revolved on color and variations in color. It pervaded the air I breathed. I learned it in hundreds of ways. I picked it up from grown folks around me. I heard it in the house, on the playground, in the streets everywhere. The tide of color beat upon me ceaselessly, relentlessly.

Always the same tune, played like a broken record, robbing one of personal identity . . . It was color, color, color all the time, color, features, and hair . . . Two shades lighter! Two shades darker! Dead white! Coal black! High yaller! Mariny! Good hair! Bad hair! Stringy hair! Nappy hair! Thin lips! Thick lips! Red lips! Liver lips! Blue veined! Blue gummed! Straight nosed! Flat nosed!

Brush your hair, child, don't let it get kinky. Coldcream your face, child, don't let it get sunburned! Don't suck your lips, child, you'll make them too niggerish! Black is evil, don't mix with mean niggers! Black is honest, you half-white bastard. I always said a little black and a little white sure do make a pretty sight! He's black as sin and evil in the bargain. The blacker the berry the sweeter the juice! [16]

The unremitting search for "whiteness" naturally produced its counterpart in a defense by aggressive reassertion of blackness. Among the masses of black or darker people, who in the past were predominantly of the lower economic groups, elementary self-defense took the form of a strong counterprejudice against the lighter skinned. The popular idiom was (and still is) full of lively expression of feelings about the "yellow niggers," many of them counterthrusting hard and deep at the assumed

16 *Ibid.*, p. 270.

illegitimacy of the "yellow bastards," whether in the present or past generations.[17] Thus "yellow" became, like "black," a fighting word in many situations, touching areas of great sensitivity and ambiguity even when used more or less lightly in the common parlance.

For a long time the defense of blackness was identified with race chauvinism and held out at the edges of Negro life. It was wrapped up with black nationalism, and this was the stuff of extremism, as in the case of Marcus Garvey, whose appeal in the 1920's was made, as we shall see, to the dark and the poor against the better off and lighter skinned. It was, in fact, Garvey's brutal exposure of this deep cleavage which made many thoughtful Negroes realize how costly color caste had become. The beginning of the end of its most egregious forms dates from that time. Negro writers, poets, and scholars had again and again over the many years tried to resist the erosions of color caste by insisting, among other things, on the virtues of blackness. W. E. B. Du Bois, himself one of the lighter Negro leaders and one of Garvey's prime foes and targets, had ceaselessly carried on a campaign on this score in all his writings, referring caressingly always to "warm ebony" and "satin black" and "golden brown."

Given the persistent weight of the white world on all the circumstances of Negro life, color caste was not easily countered. The studies of Frazier, Johnson, Warner, and others show how deeply both the offensive and defensive forms of this caste system had rooted themselves in the population up through the 1930's, and although there is little clinical material, what little there is testifies to the critical importance of color caste issues in the lives of individuals who did finally break down under the accumulated pressures of this kind of life experience.[18]

But even a generation and longer ago, the sharp edge of changing circumstance was already undercutting color caste among Negroes. There was, as I have suggested, the sobering experi-

[17] Cf. E. Franklin Frazier, *Negro Youth at the Crossways* (Washington, D.C., 1940), pp. 51–53, Charles S. Johnson, *Growing Up in the Black Belt* (Washington, D.C., 1941), p. 262.

[18] E.g., see the case material in Abram Kardiner and Lionel Ovesey, *The Mark of Oppression* (New York, 1951).

ence of Marcus Garvey's violent color chauvinism. There were also changes beginning in the Negro community which, while they came out of the common yearning to be "white"—i.e., better off—in culture and mode of life, did begin to counteract the practice of assigning automatic value to degrees of actual physical whiteness. The push of rejection which had shunted so many into numbness and apathy prodded others into a fierce drive for achievement. Darker-skinned men came up from the lower economic rungs and won new status for themselves through education and financial success. This was not just a matter of a few exceptional achievers but of a sizable class of men of the generation that grew up after the First World War, followed by a still larger group of those who came up out of the depression and into the war years as they matured. As E. Franklin Frazier pointed out, this new class of men largely shouldered aside the older mulatto middle class. Instead of family and color, they established position and money as the chief criteria of status in the Negro community. At the same time, however, in pursuit of the prevailing color caste values by which they were still governed, such men almost invariably married lighter-skinned women. The showing of these men and the frequency of these marriages eventually had a certain taming effect on the overall expression of color caste prejudice and, more important, also began to shade down a substantial segment of the population into increasingly common shades of brown. It was already becoming bad form in many quarters even 30 years ago to express color caste prejudices openly even though they were still widely held and practiced. Writing of the Negro upper crust in the 1950's, Professor Frazier said it still had an "unavowed colored snobbishness which has ceased to have much importance." [19]

In this, as in all else affecting Negro life, the pace of change quickened as we moved into the 1960's. Many of the old patterns of behavior still exist and still govern many people, but they are all but lost in the great swirl of new relationships and new attitudes. The effect is that of a kaleidoscope in which all

[19] E. Franklin Frazier, *Black Bourgeoisie* (Glencoe, Ill., 1957), pp. 198–199.

the old images and postures are mingled with new pictures and new attitudes, and the view you get depends on where and when you look and with whom you talk at any given moment. This jumbled scene, like a vast mural with a host of sharp details, emerges so clearly and so vividly from the interviews and conversations on which this study is mainly based that I turn to them now for vignettes of this process in motion. But even as I draw them from my notes, I must remind the reader that they date mostly from between 1958 and 1960, and that whatever was described as rapidly changing then has changed even more since. First, then, for varying views of the amount and pace of change and of the shape of the transition:

Negroes are less sensitive about color now, less self-conscious about it when they are among whites. You rarely find a Negro who does not now more easily discuss the matter. Prejudice is vanishing. You will still find it in the old strongholds of the past, in Charleston and New Orleans, a lot less still in Washington. I think this change has simply come out of the crucible of the struggle for equality in which people have learned certain elementary lessons. This is the main explanation.

This is gradually melting away. You just don't hear anything any more about black, yellow, mulattoes, half whites, octoroons, the kind of terms that were fashionable 40 or 50 years ago.

I hear far less about the blue-veined society among Negroes now than I used to. I don't hear references to color, except in jest. In the past to call a man a "black S.O.B.," was the worst possible epithet, and not because of the S.O.B. part alone, but "black" itself was derogatory. I think there may be a difference now, an absence of emphasis of skin color rather than any new positive affirmation of the virtues of blackness.

There is a lessening of color prejudice within the group. They are not as bad as they were. It's a touchy point. Negroes have not been frank on this. "Mixed blood," or "mulatto," one still doesn't know what word to use. In my upbringing, the matter of color was not to be mentioned. We could never say a man was "black" and never use the adjective "yellow," because of its connotation. "Black" was a fighting word and anyone of mixed origin would flinch at the use of the word "yellow." Langston Hughes thought his family here, the

Langstons, rejected his mother because of her color and he was always sharp on Washington's middle class because of its color snobbishness. This is changed now generally. It is still true that men select the lighter wife; the darker woman has a hard time, but not as hard as it used to be.

This has changed enormously. Except that I have to say that only yesterday I visited a church in Macon, Georgia, and here were some 50 kids, all little light-colored mulatto kids. At least fifteen of them looked white, all the others were shaded up a sort of brown, but with straight hair. Only a few darker people were there. The First Congregational Church here in Atlanta used to be like that. The younger generation here is much darker. For the most part it is dark brown and black now. There are no gradations of this left in Atlanta society; a man is all right, whatever his color, if he has good prospects, and I think there is no disadvantage for the dark girl if she has good family. I don't get around in society much, but look at the campus queens and the drum majorettes! They have changed enormously. There are more mixed marriages. This sort of thing has been going out . . .

We are getting away from these color attitudes, though too slowly. This is the damndest thing that ever happened to the Negro race and it's fortunate we are getting away from it. It is not popular anywhere now to admit such feelings. Now, as in the white world, it is more subtle. I was at an affair the other night, a coming-out party, and there were not more than five dark people there. And we started to talk about it, it was so noticeable. The party was at the Belmont Plaza; the mother very light, the father very black, the girl brown. The mother is Southern born and holding on to all her old connections and attitudes. It was really the mother's party, not the girl's at all.

I don't really know if color ideas are changing. I hear it spoken of less frequently than even ten years ago, unless I am selectively not hearing it any more. It is not uncommon now to get cases [in a clinic] based on color rejection. Any Negro family that is honest will admit that color is important in the self-image of themselves and their children. This is still prevalent although there is some evidence of change. When I was in college it was an inviolable rule that a successful man had to marry a fair woman. I don't think this trend is as marked now as it was then, 20 years ago.

The change has been from shame to pride. For a long time in my life I would never admit I had a wish I wasn't colored. It was my private wish. I would feel guilty about it. As late as my college days, I would think: Oh boy, if I weren't colored . . . I used to think that blackness, usually identified with Africa, was ugly and that Caucasian features were beautiful. I don't think that any more. I find myself wishing sometimes that I was darker. I feel myself looking at some darker people now and having a feeling of admiration, even envy, where not so long ago I would have thought they were ugly. Now in marriage the question of color would not be a problem the way it was in my younger days.

Standards of beauty lie close to the core of the whole business of color caste. Negroes generally adopted the models of "white" or "Caucasian" good looks that filled the moving-picture screens, billboards, newspapers, and magazines, and the greatest favor and preferment went to those Negro men and women who most closely approximated these standards. Aggressive dark men could, as we have seen, lift themselves above color caste discrimination by their success, but a prime reward of their success was the chance it gave them to reject dark-skinned women and to take lighter-skinned and less Negro-looking women to be their wives. This left the dark Negro woman the least desired and the least admired. She became the carrier of the heaviest part of the burden of the color caste system, and that is why her status now is the real key to the extent of its passing. The evidence seems to be that her position has changed much, but still less and much more slowly than that of all the other actors in this drama.

In the 1930's the very black and very Negro Mrs. Mary Mc-Leod Bethune presented a new model not of beauty but of high achievement that made a considerable dent in color caste attitudes. Mrs. Bethune, daughter of ex-slaves, noted educator, frequent visitor to the Roosevelt White House, was the founder and president of the National Council of Negro Women, a holder of important government posts, and a spokesman to whom everyone listened. One of our panelists said of her:

Mary McLeod Bethune became the greatest Negro woman in the country and was worshiped by all and came to represent the hopes of the race. Nobody could think ill of black women after her.

Mrs. Bethune did not, of course, quite manage to cast her brighter light over *all* black women, but she did play an important role in beginning to change the perceptions of others, as in this self-examination:

When you are ashamed of something, you turn away and don't look at it or you never look deeply. When you are no longer ashamed, you look and you begin to appreciate it. When I first saw Mrs. Bethune, I thought, My God what an ugly woman! But later I could only think of what a grand lady she was. Then sometime about 1952 or so, the first time I was shockingly aware that I was thinking that a black girl I saw with kinky hair was beautiful, a girl I saw at the University of California with her hair pulled back. I saw that she was beautiful, a black girl with Negro features. In my family there was every color, from white as snow to black as coal. When I was a young fellow, I remember four or five Negro dance teachers, always pretty in the American Caucasian sense, like Lena Horne. Now I see an almost deliberate kind of native naturalness. I think of Pearl Primus, the dancer. The dark woman's disadvantage is rapidly disappearing. The number of men who would marry women darker than themselves is far greater than in my generation.

There is probably no such thing at this moment as an inclusively accurate description of this changing pattern of experience. Each individual has his own version, his own accent, agreeing with all others only that things are not as they were. Some examples:

In 1955, I heard an ad over the radio for a cosmetic: "Are you too dark to be loved?" I got sore and called the station, and the girl there told me the same ad was running in my own paper, the *Afro-American*. And it was. I told the publisher I thought this sort of thing was perpetuating among Negroes the idea that a light Negro was better than a dark one. He agreed and said the language of the ad had to be changed. Here in Harlem now a dark girl would have very little to remind her of it. It is too polyglot. Now black girls figure in our cheesecake pictures as well as white or light girls. Formerly if I sent a photographer out and said, "Get us some cheesecake," he would just automatically get as close an approximation to the Nordic as you could get. But I called our photographer in and said "Let's not have any of this leapfrogging over the dark person."

Now you take the Press Photographers' ball, the Elks' beauty contest—you know, where the judge holds his hand over the girl's head and goes by the applause—and I've seen crowds give the applause to the dark girl even though the fair girl was better looking.[20]

In the old days the Negro beauty queen was indistinguishable from white. She was practically white. In the last 15 or 20 years the color ideal has been browning down and from "good hair," that is straight hair, we have now come to where Negro type of hair can be fitted into popular coiffures. The beauty queen at Howard could not be darker than brown, in some Southern schools she could be darker brown, but some other schools are worse on this than Howard.

Negroes laugh about whites and sun tan and getting their hair curled. There *is* a new appreciation of blackness; a black girl is more acceptable now than before, but she still needs white features, still has to be chiefly in the *Saturday Evening Post* style, that is closer to the white standard of beauty. But there is a certain relaxation on the item of color. A brown man will marry a black woman now, where he wouldn't have 15 or 20 years ago.

When I was growing up, the fair-skinned girl was the more desired. Now this is not true. Brown is the color now—"I found a fine brown," a man will say. People can now find a black girl beautiful, whereas 40 years ago nobody would have. At the Comus Club dance in Brooklyn I've seen the color darkening for a long time. Thirty years ago little dark girls wouldn't come because they didn't have a good time. Now they show their dark shoulders and they're enchanting. Hair straightening is still in among women but going among men. When I was in college men used to use some gooey stuff to straighten their hair, called Congolene. Getting your hair "conked," barbers would rub it in. You see very little of this now.

The great hair question is on its way out. Some girls I know, not many, and some men, just don't bother any more about hair. They don't spend hours and weeks on it. It's getting to be the mark of a

---

[20] The switch in behavior sometimes produces ironic results. In New York, where hitherto lily-white enterprises have begun to open places for Negroes, they are often likely to want their new virtue to be as visible as possible. The patterns of change are infinite in their variety, but some kind of turning point was reached in this matter when a Negro model who had failed to get on a certain TV show complained to the New York State Commission on Human Rights that she had been "turned down on the basis that she 'was not colored enough.'" New York *Amsterdam News*, April 28, 1962.

square to pay attention to hair from this point of view. This is developing this way, I notice, in musical circles and backstage in the show and art world, mostly among young people. In Harlem there's a sharp line between those who do and those who don't fiddle with their hair. For men this is "conking," for women "processing." If you conk or process your hair, you've got to keep it dry, keep out of the rain, etc. Many people just can't be bothered any more. The changes in this are mostly hidden, but they are perceptible. Ideas of beauty are changing more slowly. Look at Poitier, very black, very Negro, very beautiful. But Harry Belafonte is still the hero; girls are not putting Poitier up on their walls. The girls' idea of beauty is still Lena Horne and Dorothy Dandridge, though we do have Pearl Bailey to give hope to little black girls who would try to bleach their skin. There is much less bleaching now.

Skin whiteners have lost a good deal of their appeal. Hair preparations now tend to stress neatness and fashion rather than straightness. In the 1920's one heard only straight, straight, straight. Now more people have the feeling of doing with what they have. The desire to appear like the majority is as old as the society, but you don't need straight hair to achieve things. I heard a woman say just the other day that in times gone by she could remember that darker girls hardly ever went anywhere, while light girls would venture forth and "pass" into movies, restaurants, and so on, and come back and boast about it. But now everybody can go to these places. Time has caught up with these special advantages for lightness. Here in New York they have melted away.

Later in these pages we shall be taking a longer and closer look at the intimate entwining of all these shapes of the Negro group identity with the issue of relationship to Africa, both in the past when it was so deeply submerged and now when it has so dramatically emerged. Here let me simply suggest how these interactions were seen by these individuals in relation to color caste, beginning with the account of a young woman who was at the time we talked just twenty-one and still an undergraduate at Howard University in Washington:

When I was a child in elementary school I was called "a black African" because of my color, more or less an insult. . . . When I came here [to Howard] I was very color conscious. All the queens of the courts when I first came here were light skinned. Now we're getting away from it. Several girls my color have been elected queens of a court. At times I feel pretty bad. Recently had several isolated instances where darker girls were treated by lighter girls as though they were less of human beings, though it is never put on that basis openly. This came up in the Greek letter sororities. A dark girl has to have something special in her favor to get in, whereas a light-skinned girl just has to be light skinned. I think we're moving away from this a good deal now. It is openly discussed, there is a greater realization of it. It is quite possible that there is a connection between this and Africa. American students used to joke about the way the Africans looked, their hair, very dark, very Negro. Now dark-skinned Negroes are just beginning to find a place in this community and so are the Africans, who are more respected now because of independence but are not really integrated as they should be. People are getting more educated, possibly realizing their common ancestral background. Some American students are getting more nationalistic about Africa and the relations between African and American students is criticized a good deal in the university paper.

And some others:

I don't think Africa has anything to do with the changes that have been coming for more than a decade and even since before World War II. But I do think the emergence of Africa will accelerate the vanishing of these distinctions among Negroes. Nkrumah stands for something new in this respect too. Seeing black men in the regal majesty of dignity and power will probably wipe out whatever is left of prejudice against blackness.

I think Africans are making black more acceptable. Africans with status are bound to make this difference. As African-American relations emerge, attitudes about color in America will change, both for whites and Negroes.

Africa is now emerging affirmatively and blackness is benefiting from it.

Color is not such a big thing for Negroes any more. As for women, the most beautiful girl I have ever seen in my whole life was a jet-black girl with narrow features, slanting eyes, thick dark hair, exquisite figure—a Ga woman I saw in Accra, a schoolteacher.

The African type is now no longer grotesque or so different. Nkrumah is seen as a handsome man, dignified, with a strong face.

Only 20 years ago he wouldn't have been seen this way. The African girl here makes no effort to straighten her hair, while American girls' ideal is still the white model and they are getting closer to it with their waves and curls. Men on the other hand don't touch their hair so much now; they keep it close cropped. Only Africans let it grow long, partly out of the new pride they have in themselves.[21]

I heard an almost white Negro woman at a Nkrumah reception say: "I'm so proud of being black!"

[21] In her *Amsterdam News* column (May 5, 1962) Poppy Cannon White wrote, under the title "Hair and History": "Manufacturers and marketers of hair-straightening preparations and even some of the beauty parlors are said to be worried about the African trends. Just the other evening on a television recital, Metropolitan Opera tenor George Shirley appeared . . . wearing white tie and tails, with his hair quite long and natural, in a manner which has already become identified with a number of leading diplomats from Africa . . . Even more startling is a similar trend among the ladies, South African Miriam Makeba is said to have started the fashion . . . Already there are rumors that certain style-setters are dreaming up new types of permanent waves calculated to transform straight or semi-straight hair into tight, springy twists . . ."

But the new style obviously still had a long way to go to more common acceptance. On the following pages of the same issue of the *Amsterdam News* were ads for "hair-weaving": HUMAN HAIR, COLOR BLENDED TO MATCH PERFECTLY, WOVEN TO YOUR OWN HAIR, CANNOT COME OFF, DEFIES DETECTION; or again: CHANGE YOUR HAIR-DO AS EASILY AS YOU CHANGE YOUR DRESS . . . CHIGNONS, BRAIDS, FINE CURLS, CLUSTERS . . . The new fashion in wigs in the society at large was going big in the Negro market as well. In *Ebony* the same week (May, 1962) there were twenty ads for hair preparations: REPEATED USING RESULTS IN IMPROVED SOFT-SILKENED HAIR; and eight for skin preparations: MAKES YOUR SKIN LIGHTER, BRIGHTER. LIGHTER, LOVELIER SKIN BEAUTY FOR YOU!

# 4. *SOULS SO DEAD*

In nationality, as in name and color, the Negro identity has remained blurred, obscured behind the veil of alienation, ambivalence, confusion, and duality. Always present in the complex of Negro life, the issue of nationality has been stirred in fresh ways in recent years by the African emergence. In this connection, a noted scholar told me of a journey he made to the Gold Coast—it was in 1955 before it became Ghana—and of a conversation he had there with the chief of police of Accra, an African:

He asked me what *nation* I came from. I was confused by this until I realized that he meant what *tribe* I derived from, and I explained that no American Negro was in a position to identify his tribal origin, that *my* nation was America. He said: "You see, this is one of the errors in trying to equate Africans and American Negroes. Why *every* African knows *his* nation!"

The irony in this exchange had more than one fold to it: the African was just being caught up in events that required him to enlarge his concept of his *nation* from his tribe to the larger idea of *Ghana*, an enlargement obviously not easy for him to make. On the other hand, the Negro from America could reply that he was American, that he knew *his* nation, while being fully aware that the real question was whether his nation knew *him*.

Of this condition Du Bois, again, 60 years ago wrote these vivid and often-quoted words:

... The Negro is a sort of seventh son, born with a veil, and gifted with second sight in this American world—a world which yields him no true self-consciousness, but only lets him see himself through the revelation of the other world. It is a peculiar sensation, this double-consciousness, this sense of always looking at one's self through the eyes of others, of measuring oneself by the tape of a world that looks

97

on in amused contempt and pity. One ever feels his two-ness—an American, a Negro; two souls, two thoughts, two unreconciled strivings; two warring ideals in one dark body whose dogged strength alone keeps it from being torn asunder.[1]

The goal of the Negro's struggle for identity in America has been to resolve this twoness, to shake the blur into some single or coherent image that he could have and hold of himself as a person and as an *American*. This has not been peculiarly the Negro's problem, as James Baldwin reminds us, quoting Henry James: "It is a complex fate to be an American." The label "American," Baldwin goes on, has remained "a new, almost completely undefined and extremely controversial proper noun." [2] Only for the Negro it has been more complex, more undefined, and more controversial than for anyone else. He has been in America longer than most of those who now so much more easily are "American." He was cut off more completely from his roots than any others who came here and shaped his culture and personality out of the materials of his life in America. Finally, his life was dominated by his exclusion from the surrounding society, the denial of his essential manhood and even of the most elementary of birthrights—his nationality. A war was fought in part over his status and the rights of American nationality were explicitly and constitutionally guaranteed to him. But even after this, for nearly a hundred years he continued to stand outside the pale while wave after wave of later-comers rolled past him and over him and within a generation or two more or less painlessly assumed their new national identities as Americans.

Nationality is a word of many definitions and a status with many different meanings. But in the age of the modern nation state it is perhaps the most elementary form of any group identity, throwing its common mantle over rich and poor, good and bad, tall and short, top and bottom—over all who live on the ground it covers. Having a nationality makes one's nation an enlargement of "home" as defined by Robert Frost—the place where, when you have to go there, they have to take you in. To

---

[1] *Souls of Black Folk,* p. 3.
[2] *Nobody Knows My Name* (New York, 1961), p. 3.

be deprived of nationality is to be thrown out in the desert of homelessness. To be without it—a fate experienced by millions in this Era of the Refugee, the Stateless, and the Displaced Person—is to learn, as Hannah Arendt has pointed out, that "the abstract nakedness of being human" is not enough to entitle one to "human rights," that in fact in our age nationality has become the "only remaining and recognized tie with humanity." [3]

Negroes in America learned this long ago in their own unique version of this tragic experience. They were placed yet forever displaced, rooted yet held rootless, included yet relentlessly excluded; their twoness, *American* and *Negro,* made them both national and alien at the same time.[4] In America, through their history Negroes have struggled to shake off this duality. This struggle has known more of defeat than of victory, and the frustration has led some Negroes simply to stop trying vainly to become *American* and to try to become something else that would be *Negro.* Out of this came the flickering dream of Negro nationalism that has been part of this story almost from its beginning.

More has been written about Negro nationalism than about most of these other interlocking aspects of Negro experience. Never yet fully or closely studied, still it has often been sorted out, described, and interpreted in various ways.[5] In its most literal and explicit form, Negro nationalism proposed that Negroes who were denied their nationality as Americans should

[3] *The Origins of Totalitarianism* (New York, 1958), p. 300.

[4] "We're aliens in an alien land," said the father of J. Saunders Redding to his son as he sent him off to college. "And yet," Redding continues, "he had fought the Garveyites' dream of going 'Back to Africa'; had applauded the deportation of Emma Goldman; on every day of national memorial had hung out the flag, and when the breezes of May, the suns of July, and the snows of February rent and seared it, had bought another." *On Being Negro in America* (New York, 1951), p. 44. "In poem after poem," writes Arthur Davis, "Cullen states or implies that the Negro in America is a perpetual alien, an exile from a beautiful sun-drenched Africa, his lost homeland." "The Alien-and-Exile Theme in Countee Cullen's Racial Poems," *Phylon,* 4th quarter, 1953, p. 390.

[5] E.g., August Meier, "The Emergence of Negro Nationalism," *Midwest Journal,* nos. 1 and 2, 1951–1952; Herbert Aptheker, "Consciousness of Negro Nationality: An Historical Survey," *Political Affairs,* June 1949; Wilson Record, "The Negro Intellectual and Negro Nationalism," *Social Forces,* Oct. 1954–May 1955; E. U. Essien-Udom, *Black Nationalism* (Chicago, 1962).

seek a nationality of their own. It proposed that they leave the United States and find another land somewhere else which they could call their own, their native land where they could at last, by regaining respect for themselves, win the respect of others. In 1849—at a time when many militant free Negro leaders lost hope in the antislavery fight and became advocates of migration to Africa—J. Mercer Langston, an ancestor of Langston Hughes, said bitterly: "We must have a nationality before we can become anybody." This theme has reappeared in every generation in the words of despairing men who proposed that Negroes leave America and seek their manhood elsewhere.

Schemes for migration dot this history, both before the Civil War and since, with plans coming up to go to Canada or Mexico, to Haiti or South America, but most commonly to Africa. There have also been proposals at various times for creating a separate state for Negroes right here, as in the movement for a "forty-ninth state" and in the program of the Communist Party, which vainly tried to win Negro support in the 1930's by proclaiming them a "nation" and calling for "self-determination in the Black Belt." [6] More currently, it is the central political plank in the program of the so-called Black Muslims, at present the largest of the "nationalist" movements among Negroes, who demand that several states be detached from the United States to provide land for a new and separate black nation.[7]

But even Negroes striving to become accepted as Americans still had the need to recognize an ethnic identity which they accepted for themselves. This raises problems of Negro identity which go far beyond the simple matter of nationality and call for answers more complicated than civil rights or migration. This has to do with the feeling of being alienated not merely from a country but from the whole human race. It stems from the crushing judgment of the dominant white world that Africa, whence all the black men came, was "a continent without history," and that its people had added nothing to the record of

[6] See Wilson Record, *The Negro and the Communist Party* (Chapel Hill, N.C., 1951), pp. 55ff. and *passim.*

[7] See Lincoln, *Black Muslims in America,* pp. 94–97; and Essien-Udom, *op. cit.,* pp. 262–264.

human accomplishment. Under the immense weight of this judgment, Negroes turned away from their blackness, and this meant turning away also from Africa. Some Negroes, however, resisting this exclusion and rejecting flight, undertook to re-establish a self-respecting ethnic identity by rediscovering the place of their black forebears in the stream of human history. This meant rediscovering Africa, and it usually also meant coming to see black men everywhere as a *nation*, all having a common identity and a common allegiance stemming from their common African origin. They shared this common identity whether they were still in Africa or scattered elsewhere in the world and blended with many other strains of men and streams of culture. The nature of this "nationhood" of Negroes, like that of Jews in the Diaspora, remains moot, with the issue shifting in more recent years to the racial grounds of *negritude*. This is the idea that black men are of a common nation not merely because they all had ancestors in Africa but because a mystique arising out of their common blackness itself somehow binds them together. The idea of Jewish nationhood (which also had its mystiques) remained abstract until the re-establishment of the State of Israel forced Jews to try again to resolve their two-ness. In much the same way, the idea of Negro nationhood re-mained in obscurity while Africa remained submerged, and comes into view again now that Africa has emerged and reshaped itself into dozens of new states. This compels Negroes every-where to re-examine and redefine their sense of their relation-ship to the continent of their origins. Let us try, then, to see how all these matters come together at the place that Africa has occu-pied—and is now coming to occupy—in the universe of the Negro American.

PART THREE

———————————— ❁ ————————————

# NEGROES
# AND
# AFRICA

# 1. *THE HAZY PRESENCE*

Down through the generations Africa has persisted as a hazy presence in the universe of Negro Americans, an image now receding, now advancing, taking on different shapes, occupying different places in Negro mental landscapes. Now it is the ancestral land, dimly known, forgotten, denied, or thrust away both as a place and as a memory, dark, torrid, dangerous, a deeply unwanted piece of oneself. Or now it is, as the white man had said and his Providence had ordained, a savage, heathen land awaiting a tardy redemption on which even Negro slavery in America could be seen as a deposit. Or again, it is the shadowy wisp of a far past, nostalgically or romantically remembered, or woven unrecognized into bits and corners of a great folklore. Or a promised land, a refuge from present evil, the land of manhood and nationhood restored, the womb of a past in which no white man lived, and can now be yearned after and regained. Africa has been all this and much else to Negroes of every kind. In one way or another, at one time or another, these notions or emotions have linked the Negro American to Africa and have been part of his history and his continuing struggle to locate himself in the world.

Almost all the particulars of this matter still await chroniclers who, if they will only look, will find great troves waiting for them in materias barely touched before. It is not a mere matter of chance or unstudied neglect that this is so. More than one kind of barrier has stood in the way of this exploration. Nearly 65 years ago the Honorable J. C. Smyth, a Richmond editor and former Minister to Liberia, opened an address to a missionary conference on Africa with these words:

[Negroes] are averse to the discussion of Africa, when their relationship with that ancient and mysterious land is made the subject of discourse or reflection. The remoteness of Africa from America may be a reason for such feeling; the current opinion in the minds of the Caucasians, whence the American Negroes' opinions are derived, that the African is by nature an inferior man, may be a reason. The illiteracy, poverty, and degradation of the Negro, pure and simple, as known in Christian lands, may be a reason in connection with the partially true and partially false impression that the Negroes, or Africans, are pagan and heathen as a whole, and as a sequence hopelessly degraded beings. These may be some of the reasons that make the subject of Africa discordant and unmusical to our ears. It is amid such embarrassments that the lecturer, the orator, the missionary must present Africa to the Negro in Christian America.[1]

More than a generation later, in 1937, Carter G. Woodson, founder of the Association for the Study of Negro Life and History, wrote:

Negroes themselves accept as a compliment the theory of a complete [cultural] break with Africa, for above all things they do not care to be known as resembling in any way these "terrible Africans." [2]

And in his autobiographical volume, *Dusk of Dawn,* Du Bois wrote of Negroes "who had inherited the fierce repugnance toward anything African, which was the natural result of the older colonization schemes. . . . They felt themselves Americans, not Africans. They resented and feared any coupling with Africa." [3]

It seems fair to say that all these words might have still been accurately applied to almost any group of Negro Americans until barely the day before yesterday and still apply to a great many Negroes even today, for the notion of kinship to Africa has carried with it through all these years these same "discordant and unmusical" echoes, has filled people with these same "embarrassments" or that same "fierce repugnance."

This attitude, common among Negroes through most of the nineteenth century and in all the following decades until now,

1 "The African in Africa and the African in America," *Addresses and Proceedings of the Congress on Africa, Dec. 13-15, 1895* (Gammon Theological Seminary, Atlanta, Georgia, 1896).
2 *Journal of Negro History,* 22, 1937, p. 367.
3 *Dusk of Dawn* (New York, 1940), p. 275.

has been challenged and contradicted from time to time by various movements and ideologies, by exhorters to race pride, by the labors of individual scholars and writers, great and obscure. But it has never been brought to a point of major revision until now. This has come about because only now has Africa itself begun to take on a new character, to stand in a new light, to assume a new place among the continents, and to play a new role in current history. In doing so, Africa challenges the judgments of the hitherto dominant white world. And now, too, that white world has shrunk and its power to impose its judgments has begun to ooze away, including the whole bag of its imposed attitudes and relationships, its ethnocentric histories, its self-serving doctrines and justifications. This is what is "new" in the world. It is happening so swiftly that a grown man cannot easily keep pace with the changes it demands of him: of the white man, to learn how to cope with the loss of the political, social, economic, and psychological privileges which for so long came as part of his birthright; of the black man, to displace and replace those deeply imbedded parts of his character and personality created by him or for him by all the conditions of his existence up until now.

Alike in relation to Africa and to his own society, the Negro American now moves in and between parts of two worlds—the world of new breakthroughs and conquests of freedom, and the world which still tries to hold him in the vise of the past. About Africa his mind takes in the great changes, the new figures, new images, new emotions, the new and exhilarating appeals to prideful and beneficial association, while still holding somewhere deep within, all that was put there about Africa and his kinship to it in years long gone by. This makes a great and painful tangle which will not be quickly or easily undone.

There is, to begin with, the literal matter of survivals, the specific links of ancestry and culture that connect the Negro American with his African forebears and their contemporary descendants. The circumstances of the Negro's history in America have made neither of these links easy to trace or to describe with any great exactitude. Both have been subject to some scholarly inquiry and a great deal of controversy. Happily it is not needful for our present purposes that we should know to the last drop or digit the measured extent of African ancestry among Negroes, or decide whether or not there are any remnants of ancient African culture to be discovered in some Negro folkways or aspects of "Negro" personality. The nature of the Negro American's African identity does not and will not depend on these precisions.

The facts about ancestry are somewhat more tractable than the issue of culture, if only because the largest of these facts is plainly visible, namely that the Negro did come in his first great numbers from Africa and has since, like almost all others who populated this land, become a blend of all the strains of men around him. Statistics to show the exact extent of this blending are harder to come by. The United States Census used to make a crude distinction between "mulatto" (presumed to be of mixed origin) and "black" (presumably "pure"), but this count was so clearly defective that the Census Bureau dropped it in 1900 as "misleading." It was tried again in 1910 and for the last time in 1920, but with unimproved accuracy, showing in the latter year 15.9 percent "mulatto" and 84.1 percent "black." More serious attempts at measurement, pioneered by the anthropologist Melville J. Herskovits, subsequently reversed these proportions, leading to a guess that at least three-quarters of all Negroes in the United States were of mixed descent. Other studies suggest that the surviving percentage of any sort of "pure" African ancestry, whatever that might be, would be smaller still.[4]

These statistics still await refinement, but it is clear that however the percentages fall, a great many Negro Americans are now a good deal less *African* than they are a great many other things, and that if they have ancestors in Guinea or Ghana, they also have ancestors in every corner of Europe from which men came to America, as well as among the American Indians whom they all found here when they came. If many Negroes came to attach more value to one set of forebears than to another, they

---

[4] See Louis Wirth and Herbert Goldhamer, "The Hybrid and the Problem of Miscegenation," Otto Klineberg ed., *Characteristics of the American Negro* (New York, 1944), pp. 268–272; Myrdal, *An American Dilemma*, pp. 120, 133.

were simply reflecting the pressures of the environment, trying
to improve their status in a world which elevated the white and
degraded the nonwhite—the Negro most of all—by every device
that white power and talent could devise. This led many Negroes to prize their white ancestry while never permitting them
to divest themselves of their African blackness even if, as they
used to say, it amounted to no more than "one drop" of their
blood. This is what gives the fact of African ancestry such a peculiarly meaningful place in the makeup of any Negro no matter how biologically far he may be from his African origins. It
becomes not a matter of reason or statistics, but of mythologies
imposed by men with power on men without power. And this
leads to a next question: If not so much by the genes, then how
much by their culture are Negro Americans still African?

The question of African survivals in Negro-American culture
has been argued for more than two decades. Herskovits claimed
to have found African origins for certain modes in dancing,
music, art, some religious practices (e.g., baptism) and certain
familial and sexual practices attributed to Negroes. In retort,
Frazier and others have held that only the most insignificant
vestiges of the ancestral culture survived the passage from Africa into American slavery (fewer vestiges, all agree, in the
United States than in parts of Latin America) and that in all
its essential shapes and details the culture of the Negro American has been formed by his experience in the American environment and his participation in the making of the American
culture itself.[5]

Very few Negroes were ready to enthuse over Herskovits' insistence on closing the cultural gap between them and their
African background. Since he wrote avowedly "to give the Negro an appreciation of his past," his work was generally well
received by those devoted to the same purpose, including Carter

[5] Cf. Melville J. Herskovits, *The Myth of the Negro Past* (New York, 1941);
Frazier, *The Negro Family* (New York, 1939) and *The Negro in the United
States*. See Myrdal, *op. cit.*, note 32, p. 1394, and especially note 2, p. 1425, for
references to other Frazier-Herskovits exchanges. Cf. also Lorenzo D. Turner,
"African Survivals in the New World with Special Emphasis on the Arts," *Africa
Seen By American Negroes*, John A. Davis, ed., (Paris, 1958).

G. Woodson, founder of the *Journal of Negro History*. But even Woodson at one point mildly advised the ardent anthropologist to restrain his impulse to make much out of little lest he become a "laughingstock." [6] On the other hand, Woodson did not hesitate to challenge Frazier's contrary views by accusing Frazier of being ashamed of his African heritage.[7] In *An American Dilemma* [8] Gunnar Myrdal and his associates avoided coming to any conclusions about this issue, suggesting instead that the bits and pieces of truth on all sides were probably being obscured by the argument.

In the preface to a 1958 reissue of *The Myth of the Negro Past*, Herskovits acknowledges that nothing has been added to the substance of the argument, that there has been no new research in the "Afroamericanist field" in the United States. He welcomes a greater receptivity among Negroes for his general thesis of the greater worthiness of the Negro's African past, an attitude he attributes to world changes and the new African emergence. He continues to suggest that rejection of the claim that there are important African survivals in Negro-American culture is equivalent to rejection of any identification of Negro Americans with their African past. It would seem to be helpful, however, now that the whole question is being reopened for so many people, not to allow these issues to become more than necessarily confused.

The merit of ancient African cultures as a heritage for Ne-

[6] "[Dr. Herskovits] deserves much credit for his painstaking research in this field, but he should restrain himself from positing too much on the few facts which he has discovered. Else he may become a laughingstock, as did W. D. Weatherford in his study of Africa. The latter reached the conclusion that the 'razor-toting habit' of the American Negro is the survival of the African custom of the natives who have to carry with them all the time a large knife to cut their way through the thick grass and undergrowth in the wilds of that continent." The *Journal* went on to note that a writer in a Southern journal had already attributed to Prof. Herskovits the finding that the "bad nigger" had "originated in Africa" and had provided the model for "white desperados." *Journal of Negro History*, 24:2, 1939, p. 235.

[7] "Woodson said I took the position I did because I was ashamed of my African heritage. But I said I'd be proud of this heritage anytime I could find it. I was not ashamed of my African background." Frazier, in conversation with author, Aug. 1, 1958.

[8] P. 930.

groes to be proud of, or at least not ashamed of, is one thing.
The issue of how much identifiable Africanism still remains in
this or that facet of the customs, behavior and personalities of
Negro Americans is another thing. A Negro's view of his relationship to Africa covers much more than the possibility that
the way he dances, sings, or responds in church had roots in
some dim tribal past. There are vast numbers of Negroes who
do not dance or sing that way—or any way at all!—who do not
respond that way in church, who have had families consisting
of both fathers and mothers; and all these Negroes too must face
up in some new way to the fact of their ultimate African kinship.
The question of how *African* any Negro Americans may still be
is but the smallest part, really, of the large and truly crucial issues raised by the great re-examination, now just beginning, of
what Negro Americans are to Africa and what Africa is to them.

The literature on this dispute over African cultural survivals
is quickly exhausted. When we look beyond it for more light on
all the many other aspects of the problem of the Negro's African
kinship, we find peculiarly little. Africa again becomes a hazy
presence.

Negro scholars and writers of the last two or three generations have had the enormous task of lifting the Negro's place in
American life out of the mire of ignorance, prejudice, and
obloquy in which so much writing and scholarship—by whites—
had confined it in the past. With but rare exceptions they have
been concerned with the Negro (and, indeed, each one with
himself) not as African or ex-African, but as American. Almost
all historians, novelists, essayists, pamphleteers, have started
from this same threshold. Hence in the great bulk of writing by
Negroes about Negroes, the theme of Africa figures briefly, if at
all, as the point of departure into slavery, the introduction to
a tragic history, or as the merest allusion to origins, all quickly
submerged under the greater and far more pressing immediacies
of the Negro in his American environment.

The literature by Negroes about Africa is not large, yet
neither is it insignificant. A check list of such works compiled
by Mrs. Dorothy Porter of Howard University in 1958 listed

325 titles by 149 authors. One large group of these deals with Liberia in its various aspects. Another consists of accounts by missionaries and other travelers, almost all dating from the nineteenth century. Another group of titles marks the development of that school of writing marked earlier by writers like George Washington Williams, and later W. E. B. Du Bois, Monroe Work, and Carter Woodson, chiefly intent upon re-establishing a heritage, both in America and Africa, for Negroes to take pride in. They wanted to overcome the shame and inferiority carried out of slavery, and to show that before his enslavement in America the Negro had an African heritage worth remembering and cherishing. A third major group of titles in Mrs. Porter's list deals with Africa in world politics, the object of colonial wars, exploitation, Western white rapacity. Here again, Du Bois is heavily represented, and after him other students of world affairs such as Rayford W. Logan and Ralph Bunche. The list shows a scattering of titles of older works on the anthropology, the flora and fauna and art of Africa, swelled in more recent years by the output of the first of the younger Negro scholars who have joined in the general rush of rediscovery, producing new studies in the sociology, politics, and economics of changing Africa in the manner of their various scholarly disciplines.

But very little of the literature listed by Mrs. Porter bears directly on the mutual relations of Negro Americans and Africans except as these appear incidently in the writing of missionaries and travelers or in the works of those with hortatory or propagandistic purposes. There are barely 20 titles in the list which touch these themes more or less directly, and most of these date to the last century, e.g., the essays of Reverend Alexander Crummell and Bishop Henry McNeal Turner. Louis R. Mehlinger's study of the attitudes of free Negroes toward African colonization schemes in the last century, published in the first volume of the *Journal of Negro History* in 1916, opened a subject that was finally explored at greater length in a doctoral thesis completed in 1953 and still unpublished.[9] Personal accounts of re-

[9] "The Attitude of the Free Negro Toward African Colonization," *Journal of Negro History*, July, 1916, pp. 276–300; Howard H. Bell, "A Survey of the Negro Convention Movement, 1830–1861," unpub. thesis, Northwestern University, 1953.

cent journeys of rediscovery, like Richard Wright's *Black Power*, are still very few in number and deal in any case with the freshest experience. On the past, a great deal of work of inquiry and scholarship has to be done if this aspect of the Negro's story is ever to be brought into focus with all its complicated diversity and detailed substance.[10] Still, to understand what I found to be the patterns of thinking about Africa in the minds of the Negroes I have interviewed, it was needful to go back and learn something of how these patterns were shaped from the past. In the outline that follows I try to identify some of the main elements of this history so far as some brief gleanings could bring them into view.

[10] The subject is barely opened in *Africa Seen by American Negroes*, John A. Davis, ed., a special issue of *Présence Africaine* published by the American Society of African Culture in 1958. Another recent approach was made by Earl E. Thorpe, "Africa in the Thought of Negro Americans," *Negro History Bulletin*, Oct. 1959. For an indication of what such inquiry can bring forth see George Shepperson, "Notes on Negro American Influences on the Emergence of African Nationalism," *Journal of African History*, I:2, 1960, pp. 299–312.

# 2. "BACK TO AFRICA"

The possibility that vagrant bits of ancient African cultures may have survived among some American Negroes is of far less moment in this history than the fact that again and again Africa has been seen as the place to which Negroes might go or be sent back and thus solve the problems created by their enslavement and their existence in an unhospitable white world. This notion of a return to Africa has sprung up repeatedly during the last 200 years or so, appearing in different places and for different reasons among both Negroes and whites.

As advocated by whites, a first mention is made of a New Jersey man who urged repatriation of Negroes in 1714, and the theme keeps reappearing at intervals all the way down to 1939, when Senator Theodore Bilbo of Mississippi asked Congress to pass his bill providing for deportation of Negroes to Africa. In almost every case this has been an effort to solve a problem by making it go away. As urged by Thomas Jefferson upon the Virginia Legislature in 1777 and elsewhere by like-minded individuals, it was seen as a form of emancipation and a redress for evil done. As it developed with the formation of the American Colonization Society in 1817, it appeared more clearly as an effort to satisfy both the troubled consciences of New Englanders and the hardheaded wish of Southern slaveholders to get rid of the minority of free Negroes in their midst because it was feared they might disaffect the enslaved mass. Saunders Redding quotes a dispassionate summary, written by the abolitionist Judge William Jay in 1834, of the different motives out of which different groups were supporting the Society:

"First such as desire sincerely to afford the free blacks an asylum from the oppression they suffer here, and by this means to extend the blessings of Christianity and civilization to Africa, and who at the same time flatter themselves that colonization will have a salutary

114

influence in accelerating the abolition of slavery. Secondly, such as expect to enhance the value and security of slave property, by removing the free blacks; and, thirdly, such as seek relief from a bad population without the trouble or expense of improving it." [1]

Under these mixed auspices the colonization movement had a fitful history that lasted through most of the nineteenth century. In 1821 the Society sponsored the boatload of migrants who founded Liberia. But by the eve of the Civil War, barely 8,000 free Negroes (out of a national total of about half a million) had joined the migration. Still smaller numbers were recruited thereafter. The overwhelming majority of free Negroes reacted to these colonization schemes with mistrust, rejection, and resistance. They expressed themselves year after year in convention after convention in many cities and states, denouncing the Colonization Society as "officious and uncalled for" and rejecting "banishment from our friends and home." Or again: "Why should we leave this land, so dearly bought by the blood, groans, and tears of our fathers?" If any were moved, as some were, to favor any kind of migration, it was not to "a howling wilderness across the seas," as one Boston meeting put it in 1831, but rather to some part of the newly opening American continent, or else to the Caribbean, or to Central or South America where, some believed, a chance for free growth was still to be had. [2] This was when Northern free Negroes in their anxiety not to be coupled with Africa, especially as prospective migrants, began to abandon the word "African" as the descriptive adjective for many Negro organizations, and the term "colored" began to appear more widely in its place.

Still the idea of a return to Africa has had a vivid life of its own among Negroes through much of this time. One may guess that the first generations of slaves only slowly yielded the dream of returning home. [3] But we know that from the first days of the

---

[1] Redding, *They Came in Chains* (New York, 1950), p. 76.

[2] Mehlinger, "The Attitude of the Free Negro Toward African Colonization," *loc. cit.*

[3] It has been argued that the "home" so often mentioned in slave songs and spirituals was not heaven but Africa. Cf. Thorpe, *op. cit.;* Miles Mark Fisher, *Negro Slave Songs in the United States* (Ithaca, N.Y. 1953).

new American republic there were free Negroes who gave thought to a new life in Africa as an alternative to the struggle to become as free as other men in newly free America. In the new nation of the equally created, the "free" Negro could hope for little more than a pariahlike existence. Rejected by the dominant white society as citizens with equal rights, the excluded Negroes defensively separated themselves. They built their own little closed societies and established their own churches to worship the God of the believers in the brotherhood of man. This process of rejection and separation had its own logic. It led some whites of uneasy conscience or special interests to become advocates of repatriating Negroes to Africa. It led some Negroes to consider the ultimate option of going rather than staying—of going back to Africa.

## The Option of Despair

Indeed, the idea of going back to Africa was the ultimate option of the man who ceased to hope that as a Negro he might still be able to live decently as a free man in the land of the free. There were always other options: endurance, accommodation, Uncle Tomism, Samboism, sloth, fantasy, religion, violence. A Negro could stand on the white man's ground and fight for his equal rights as man and citizen. Or else he could escape to some kind of freedom lying beyond the white man's power to deny it, whether into some secret self, into the ghetto, or, as a wistful dream, away somewhere all the way across the sea back to Africa. These choices have shaped some of the major themes in Negro life in America, a kind of dialogue often interrupted but never ended, figuring in all the annals from then until now. On the one hand, the death of Crispus Attucks as the first man to fall in the fight for American freedom in the Boston Massacre in 1770 can be seen perhaps as a first symbol of the Negro hope to share in that freedom. On the other hand, there was the action of the free Negroes in Newport, Rhode Island, who in 1787, just as the republic was being born, formed the "Free African Society" to advocate repatriation to Africa. These contending impulses have moved men in generation after generation and the passage from the one to the other has sometimes occurred within the single spans of some very remarkable individuals indeed.

Consider the story of Paul Cuffee, free Negro, Quaker, and a bold enterpriser who sought to "integrate" in his own day by proving his worth, building, sailing and trading in his own ships out of Boston, stoutly refusing to pay taxes until his right to vote was acknowledged by the Commonwealth of Massachusetts. But Paul Cuffee apparently decided that the hope of true freedom and equality lay in a return to Africa. In 1811 he made a reconnoitering voyage to Sierra Leone and in 1815 at his own expense took a shipload of 38 free Negro migrants to settle there.

This affirmation first of hope and then of despair, the pattern of fighting hard to be free and then coming to believe that the only road to freedom was the road to escape, appears in the lives of others whom we can glimpse through the years. John B. Russwurm, coeditor of the first Negro American paper, *Freedom's Journal*, was first a strong opponent of colonization, but then became, in 1829, an ardent migrationist and eventually migrated to Liberia himself. Another striking figure of the same period was Martin Robinson Delany of New York, a Harvard-educated physician, author of novels and essays, who denounced the American Colonization Society as "anti-Christian in its character and misanthropic in its pretended sympathies," and who in a memorable passage also said:

Our common country is the United States. Here were we born, here raised and educated; here are the scenes of childhood . . . the loved enjoyments of our domestic and fireside relations, and the sacred graves of our departed fathers and mothers, and from here will we not be driven by any policy that may be schemed against us. . . . We are Americans, having a birthright citizenship—natural claims upon this country—claims common to all our fellow citizens which may, by virtue of unjust laws, be obstructed, but never can be annulled.[4]

But by 1852 Delany had become a migrationist, seeking escape

[4] Meier, "The Emergence of Negro Nationalism," p. 101.

first elsewhere in the Americas and then in Africa. He answered the reproaches of William Lloyd Garrison with these words:

I am not in favor of caste, nor a separation of the brotherhood of mankind, and would as willingly live among white men as black, if I had an equal possession and enjoyment of privileges. . . . If there were any probability of this, I should be willing to remain in the country, fighting and struggling on . . . But I must admit, that I have no hopes in this country—no confidence in the American people—with a few excellent exceptions—therefore I have written as I have done. Heathenism and Liberty, before Christianity and Slavery! [5]

He had come to the conclusion: "We must make an issue, create an event, and establish a national position for ourselves." He devoted himself thereafter to a number of unsuccessful migration schemes until the coming of the Civil War revived his hopes, and he went forth to fight for his cause in the uniform of a major in the Union Army. [6]

Across all of his years the great figure of Frederick Douglass stood firmly against the impulse to flee. In 1853 he said:

We are here and here we are likely to remain. Individuals migrate, nations never. We have grown up with this republic and I see nothing in her character or find nothing in the character of the American people as yet which compels the belief that we must leave the United States. [7]

Douglass returned often to the charge against the colonization schemes, and he was especially scornful of the argument that by going back to Africa and encouraging development there American Negroes would thereby help break down slavery in America. This idea, he wrote, "proposes to plant its guns too far from the battlements of slavery for us," and has to be based "upon the lying assumption that white and black people can never live in the same land on terms of equality. Detesting this heresy as we do . . . we shun the paths that lead to it, no matter what taking

5 Quoted by Meier from Carter G. Woodson, ed., *The Mind of the Negro as Reflected in Letters Written During the Crisis, 1800–1860* (Washington, D.C., 1926), p. 293.

6 Howard H. Bell, "The Negro Emigration Movement," *loc. cit.*, pp. 132–142.

7 Mehlinger, *loc. cit.*, p. 295.

names they bear, or how excellent the men who bid us walk in them." [8]

In 1872, Douglass again:

Our broad and fertile prairies are to be tilled, our rich mines are to be opened and developed, work for millions on millions is abundant in this country, there is nothing in reason why anyone should leave this land of progress and enlightenment and seek a home amid the death-dealing malaria of a barbarous continent . . . All over the North and South are emissaries of the Colonization Society, in the one section begging money to carry out their diabolical scheme of enticing from this land of progress to a land of barbarism a useful and needed population of workers; in the other section giving encouragement to negro-hate by impressing the people with an idea that the black man has no right here as a freeman. [9]

But other men, also strong (though not quite so strong), lost hope in Douglass' dream of the black man as a free man, and they had much reason to despair. As we have already noted, the years after Reconstruction, the peak years of Western white supremacy all over the world, were, in Rayford Logan's phrase, the years of the nadir for the Negro in the United States. All his rights as a human being and citizen—so deeply imbedded in the cause over which the nation had just nearly torn itself apart— were now smothered by vindictive, weary, complaisant, or indifferent white men South and North. Some whites, whether benevolently or malevolently, snatched again at a chance to make the whole problem go away, or at least farther away. State and Federal legislative hoppers were filled with schemes for the migration, emigration, or expulsion of Negroes to more distant American territories, to the Caribbean, and sometimes all the way to Africa. At the same time, in some Negroes too the desire rose to get quit of it all and to seek chances of a decent life somewhere else on fairer terms. There was the "Great Exodus" of 1879, led by Moses "Pap" Singleton, from the South to Kansas, Iowa and Nebraska; the effort led by Edwin P. McCabe, to create a Negro settlement in Oklahoma territory; and the depar-

8 *Life and Writings*, v. 2, pp. 443–4.
9 *Ibid.*, pp. 301–2.

ture of several vessels chartered by bands of Negro migrants which sailed for Liberia between 1877 and 1895.[10]

Perhaps the best-known Negro migrationist of this period was Bishop Henry McNeal Turner of Georgia, a longtime and doughty fighter, chaplain in the Union Army, member of the Georgia Legislature during Reconstruction, and church leader. After the Supreme Court in 1883 killed the Civil Rights Act of 1875 and the states plunged ahead to deprive the Negro of everything but his bare existence, Bishop Turner summed up the end of his own long dialogue between hope and despair in these harsh words:

There is no manhood future in the United States for the Negro. He may eke out an existence for generations to come, but he can never be a man, full, symmetrical and undwarfed. . . . The colored man who will stand up and in one breath say that the Negroid race does not want social equality and in the next predict a great future in the face of all the proscriptions of which the colored man is the victim, is either an ignoramus or is an advocate of the perpetual servility and degradation of his race. The whites will not grant social equality to the Negroid race, nor am I certain that God wants them to do it. And as such, I believe that two or three millions of us should return to the land of our ancestors, and establish our own nation, civilization, laws, customs, style of manufacture, and . . . build up social conditions peculiarly our own, and cease to be grumblers, chronic complainers and a menace to the white man's country, or the country he claims and is bound to dominate.[11]

## The Inscrutabilities of Providence

Bishop Turner, like Martin Delany, had been driven to conclude that there was no future in manhood for Negroes in Amer-

[10] Logan, *The Negro in American Life and Thought, The Nadir,* esp. pp. 126–139, 187–190.

[11] "The American Negro and the Fatherland," *Addresses and Proceedings of the Congress on Africa,* pp. 195–198. In 1893, Bishop Turner said: "The Negro . . . is an outlawed inhabitant of the country, for a people divested of their civil rights can hope for nothing but degradation and contempt." Quoted in C. A. Bacote, "Negro Proscriptions, Protests, and Proposed Solutions in Georgia," unpub. ms. See also Bacote, "Some Aspects of Negro Life in Georgia, 1880–1908," *Journal of Negro History,* July 1958.

ica, and that they had to seek their freedom in Africa. But whereas Delany had boldly chosen "heathenism and liberty before Christianity and slavery," Bishop Turner joined those who argued that the return to Africa would serve a great spiritual purpose. "God brought the Negro to America," summarized his biographer, "and Christianized him so that he might go back to Africa and redeem that land." [12] This was the idea that the Negro's whole history, the wrenching away from the homeland and the long term of bondage had all been part of a divinely mysterious scheme to open the way for Christ in Africa, to deflect the threatening sword of Islam, and to show the pagan brothers the path to grace. This idea had obvious advantages for those white Christians who hoped to solve their own unhappy dilemma by shipping Negroes back to Africa, and it had long been used in the propaganda for the various colonization schemes. It was also an idea that moved Negroes who wanted to migrate, who could see in America only an Egypt, and in Africa a Promised Land. This great spiritual sanction made migration seem not a flight but a mission. They would go not merely to seek a portion of the kingdom on earth in Africa for themselves, but a portion in the kingdom of Heaven for the Africans. These mixed spiritual and temporal emotions and motives appear often in the arguments of the times. At a convention of free Negroes in Baltimore in 1852, for example, while a "mob" of opponents milled around outside and hecklers interrupted him inside, a migrationist named James A. Handy declared that "Providence was moving in its mysterious and inscrutable way" to redeem Africa by opening the way for "a part of her crushed children" to be "delivered from immolation, then born, elevated and blessed under redeeming auspices," only now to hear the thundering voice of Heaven say: "Arise and depart, for this is not your rest." And the new destination was Africa because:

. . . emigration is the only medium by which the long closed doors of that continent are to be opened; by her own children's returning, bearing social and moral elements of civil and religious power by

[12] M. M. Ponton, *Life and Times of Henry M. Turner* (Atlanta, Ga., 1917), p. 77.

which that continent is to be resuscitated, renovated, and redeemed.[13]

Thus Africa's lost children were to bring home with them not only God's word but "civil power." Their purpose was plainly set forth in the call to this same convention which declared that free men of color had:

become more sensible of their own anomalous and degraded condition, and the result is a yearning to be free like those around them, to have a land all their own, to have rights unquestioned by any superior color, to go wherever such privileges may be obtained . . . a land where, from simple citizenship to the highest post in the government, all is free and open to them, and where character, enterprise, education, and honorable ambition, have all their appropriate rewards in the order of the state.[14]

But by Bishop Turner's time, toward the end of the century, the white men of several European nations had busied themselves with establishing their own "civil power" in various parts of Africa. Even as a wishful dream, the thought of black men building their own nations, becoming their own presidents, governing themselves in Africa, now faded away. At a conference in Berlin in 1884 the powers scrambling for pelf and position in Africa agreed on the terms and boundaries of a partition. Virtually all of the prospective homeland for black men and mission fields for black Christians were now pre-empted by white men, along with the rest of the available earth. Only the feeble little state of Liberia managed to survive (although it lost territory to the French and British), and Ethiopia, which threw back Italian invaders in the great battle of Adowa in 1896. Around all the rest of Africa a scaffolding of white power had been built by the century's end, strong enough to restrict the black man's freedom inside or to deny it to any black man who might come seeking freedom from without. This is what Booker T. Washington saw in 1899 when he gave answer to Bishop Turner and other advocates of migration to Africa:

[13] Quoted in "A Typical Colonization Convention, Documents," *Journal of Negro History,* July 1916, p. 332.
[14] *Ibid.,* p. 319.

I see no way out of the Negro's present condition in the South by returning to Africa. Aside from other insurmountable obstacles, there is no place in Africa for him to go where his condition would be improved. All Europe—especially England, France and Germany —has been running a mad race for the last twenty years to see which could gobble up the greater part of Africa; and there is practically nothing left. . . . A return to Africa for the Negro is out of the question, even provided that a majority of the Negroes wished to go back, which they do not.[15]

Now, even when he merely dreamed of a beckoning ancestral homeland, the Negro had to settle for less, whether he wished to regain Africa for his own kingdom or for God's. In the face of the universality of the white man's power, even the most wishful fantasies had to be shrunk and reshaped. There was no escape to Africa now. The road to emancipation, said Booker T. Washington, lay through submission and toil, moving slowly but surely up the rungs of economic advancement toward some better day. The white man's take-over in Africa also pressed the missionary impulse into more accommodating shapes. Faithful flocks in Negro churches continued to give their meager support to a dribbling handful of Negro missionaries in Africa. But there was a certain fading of the image of the black Christian, purged and saved through the ordeal of slavery, returning to redeem his African brethren for the Lord. For it now appeared that Africa was not going to be saved after all by its returning black children. By decree of that more-than-ever inscrutable Providence, it appeared that this was going to be accomplished by Africa's new white masters and *their* bearers of the Gospel. Whether out of self-conscious expediency or unconscious needs to find benevolence in unchallengeable authority, it became necessary to look upon the European conquest of Africa and find it good, or to be careful to look only where good could be found in it. This became the common posture of the time. For example, in a greeting sent to a missionary conference in 1895, the great Negro educator and statesman Edward Blyden wrote from his post as Liberian Ambassador in London:

[15] *The Future of the American Negro* (Boston, 1899), pp. 159–160, 164.

Such is the enthusiasm here for opening Africa, that when it was learned, only a few days ago, that the so-called King of Ashantee was placing obstacles in the way of England's efforts to bring that country within the pale of civilization, a magnificent expedition was organized at once . . . not so much to fight as to convince the refractory chief of Coomassie, and all others like him, how utterly useless it is . . . to oppose . . . the magnificent work of Africa's regeneration.[16]

## The Missionary Impact

Despite all obstacles, Negro missionaries have for many decades taken part in the "work of Africa's regeneration." The history of these missionary efforts in Liberia and elsewhere in Africa is little known. It still lies largely scattered in a literature of individual, church, or denominational accounts; another subject awaiting its author. From the scant literature available,[17] it appears that Negroes went to Africa as missionaries only in small numbers—no precise figures are available—and all but a few of these were sent and thinly supported in the field by Negro churches at home. With but rare exceptions, the large white Christian denominations seldom wished to send Negro workers into the African vineyards. Even when they did wish it, they seldom did so, and when they did, they did it sparingly and not for long. This too came out of the complex of fears and ambivalences suffered by so many white Christians where Negroes were concerned.

It was also due in part to the fact that the white rulers in most of Africa did not want Negroes coming in from America as missionaries. It was feared they would upset Africans' ideas of how a black man was supposed to look, act, and sound. It was thought, as one Negro churchman suggested, that "the American Negro might help the African to awaken." Colonial authori-

16 *Addresses and Proceedings of the Congress on Africa,* p. 16.
17 Cf. Wilber Christian Harr, "The Negro as an American Protestant Missionary in Africa," unpub. Ph.D. Thesis, University of Chicago Divinity School, 1945; Bodine T. Russell, "What are the Policies, Practices, and Attitudes of the Foreign Mission Boards in North America with reference to the Sending of American Negroes as Foreign Missionaries?" Unpub. M.A. thesis, Presbyterian College of Christian Education, 1945.

ties often did not welcome missionaries of any color, implicitly recognizing the subversive character—or at least the embarrassing potentialities—of the Christian Gospel. But while it might ordinarily be deemed safe enough and even useful in the hands of its white guardians and interpreters, bearers of it in black hands could be quite another matter. The record indicates that most of the white colonial authorities in Africa ruled that if any black souls were going to be allowed to be saved at all, it was going to have to be done by white soul savers. The white government of South Africa was especially fearful on this score and placed major obstacles in the path of the African Methodist Episcopal churchmen—including the redoubtable Bishop Henry Turner—who came to that country from the United States to persuade some South Africans to form a church of their own under A.M.E. auspices. A report in 1899 said that the American Negro Methodists were "suspected of fomenting a rebellious spirit among the natives of South Africa against the British government." [18] Such fears were not often well founded in any immediate sense except as they rose from the deep and chronic insecurity of the white men in Africa resulting from the relationship they had established with the blacks. Every once in awhile this inner logic proved itself with results disquieting to white men. An example was the case of John Chilembwe, a young man of Nyasaland, who was brought to the United States by a white missionary, the Englishman Joseph Booth. Chilembwe received some education in this country, returned home, and in 1915 led an abortive uprising against white rule in his homeland.[19]

The history of the American Negro missionary effort in Africa lies beyond the reach of these pages; let it be hoped that its own special mix of devotion, pathos, and irony will not be lost in the chronicling of the larger missionary enterprise of which it was a unique part. What I am concerned with here is the im-

[18] *The Independent,* New York, Nov. 30, 1899.
[19] George Shepperson and Thomas Price, *Independent Africa—John Chilembwe and the Origins, Setting, and Significance of the Nyasaland Native Rising of 1915* (Edinburgh, 1958). A shorter account by Shepperson is "Education Sponsors Freedom—The Story of John Chilembwe," *Negro History Bulletin,* Jan. 1952.

pact of Negro missionaries not on Africans in Africa but on their fellow Americans here at home, especially on members of our interview panel who spoke often of the church as the source of some of their earliest notions about Africa.

Despite all the adversity, the rejection by white churches at home and by white authorities in Africa, the passivity of Africans in Africa and the large apathy of Negroes at home, the Negro missionary effort persisted. It established and maintained a certain continuous contact between Africa and American Negroes through mission and school enterprises, mainly in Liberia but also in a small scatter elsewhere in Africa. Africans and Americans traveled back and forth, and a small number of African students began coming to American Negro schools and colleges. A constant appeal was kept up in Negro churches to support these various undertakings, and this was a key point of contact between Africa and the large mass of faithful churchgoers. Rayford Logan has suggested that "American Negroes who grew up in the early part of this century probably first heard about Africa when a minister, priest, or missionary appealed for funds to support missions there." [20] Whether or not it came first, the impression in church certainly came early, giving Negro children for the first time some details about the vaguely known ancestral homeland, or strongly reinforcing in the authoritative and much friendlier atmosphere of the church what they had already heard about in school.

Up to a certain point, churchgoing Negroes simply reproduced the experience of their white churchgoing counterparts in doing their duty toward the heathen abroad. It was part of the ritual of piety to add coins to the collection to support the good work in distant parts, to help save some of those benighted unfortunates who bowed down to wood and stone in so many parts of the earth where every prospect pleased and only man was vile. Until most recently this was the setting in which great masses of Americans received crucial bits of their education about the remoter parts of the world and took in the large generalized images of outlandishness attached to the people who

[20] "The American Negro's View of Africa," *Africa Seen by American Negroes*, p. 218.

inhabited them. This writer has recorded some of the effects of these Sunday morning encounters as they pertained to the Chinese and Indians,[21] and found himself once again sharing familiar experiences when in these talks with Negroes the missionary images of Africa began to emerge.

But here we come upon a critical difference. From these images of the absurd or sinful deficiencies and backwardnesses of heathen people far away, white American Christians could and did derive a pleasant sense of their own indubitable superiority. The Negro Christian hearing about Africans was having a much more complicated and much less satisfactory experience. These grotesque and ignorant savages were his own kin. If he reached out to them with Christian succor, it was partly to rescue himself from the stigma of his continued relationship to them. If he felt superior, it was at the cost of accepting the white man's view of his own origins; of feeling grateful for having been rescued and carried so far from his own past. To act with Christian charity toward his African cousins was a way of refuting the white man's constant inference that the black African's savagery was but a mirror of the Negro's own. Thus in a unique and painful way the Negro's encounter in church with the African heathen was often—far below the levels of conscious awareness—a meeting with himself.

Only rarely did these images of Africa acquired in church come down through the years even in faintly positive tones. One example:

Our church was the A.M.E. Church in St. Paul and we always had a bishop in Africa, and here I had very early contact with it. I got the typical missionary viewpoint, of people badly needing help, with some warmer overtones because of the special interest and identification of our church. It was different, say, from the Lutherans or Episcopalians doing the same thing. Our mission and our bishop gave us a little closer identification with those people over there, though nothing was very clearly described that I remember.

Sometimes the tone was nearly neutral:

[21] *Scratches On Our Minds.*

From missionaries I knew about Africa, the slave trade, about Liberia . . .

Everybody wanted to convert the African. Heard about missionaries taking God to Africa, saving them from idolatry . . .

First heard of Africa in church, where the missionary plate was passed around every Sunday for the Lott Carey Convention doing missionary work in order to take the word of God to the benighted heathen of Africa . . .

I must have been at least ten or eleven, I remember my father commenting on some Negro missionary as a fine Christian man making the great sacrifice of going to Africa.

But when we come to the somewhat more detailed recollections of what had been heard in church, we begin to come upon items like these:

In the church I went to in Americus, Georgia, when I was a little boy . . . I was given the missionary's concept, and the picture we got of African people was of ugly, unkempt, naked savages who had to be civilized. We had to take them Christianity and the Bible . . .

Returning missionaries painted a very disturbing picture . . . cannibalism, polygamy, illiteracy, primitive way of life, and worst of all, not Christians.

I used to go to missionary meetings and always heard such horrible things about Africa . . . I imagined it as a horrible place to live . . .

As a young boy [what I got was] all negative, cannibalism, Sunday-school literature, naked women, heathen, tribal masks, shame, savages.

Our own Negro churches confirmed and exaggerated all of this . . .

Missionaries spoke of the Dark Continent, the noble missionaries, the poor Africans eager to get the word of God. I am afraid they supported in the main the initial images from the geographies of wild, savage peoples . . .

Finally, this summary comment, from a member of the panel who is himself an official of high rank in a major Negro church:

What about the missionary picture of Africans? Well, we couldn't raise money if we said the Africans were rich and beautiful. But few have known how to present it. I remember hearing Bishop John Bryant Small, a West Indian who had been a soldier in the British Army and then became a missionary in Africa. His story of Africa was my first great impression of Africans, a dignified story, mixed, good and bad, but a story of greatness. But only a few could deal with it this way. Most of the missionaries brought back sensational and ridiculous stories in order to capture and hold their audiences. It is from this that the average Negro has gotten the idea that the African is inferior to American Negroes. If anything, I would say that white missionaries have pictured the African in brighter colors than the Negro missionary has. He has been more understanding. The Negro was looking on the surface, looking for American culture and way of life, and would come back and stretch the differences. He would try to tell the funny and odd things to keep the audience laughing. He would talk about nudeness. To hear these Negroes talk you would think the whole thing in Africa is nudeness. It made a very false impression.

## The Liberian Embarrassment

Most of the Negro missionary and educational effort was concentrated in Liberia; most Negro contact with Africa has been with Liberia. Founded in 1821 by one of the few groups of Negro migrants which ever actually crossed the sea from America to Africa, it soon became and has remained a source of controversy and heartache among many Negroes. Back from Liberia on a visit to this country in 1891, the noted Episcopal minister and missionary, Alexander Crummell, was kept busy saying things like this:

It is very common nowadays to hear this little Republic referred to as evidencing the incapacity of the Negro for free government, and nothing is more constant, nothing more frequent than the declaration that "Liberia is a failure!" ... Nothing can be more ignorant, nothing more stupid than these utterances.[22]

[22] *Africa and America, Addresses and Discourses* (Springfield, Mass., 1891), p. v.

But such utterances continued to be heard on through the years because Liberia apparently never—until quite recently—provided much basis for other opinions except among its leaders' most devoted friends. Some of these friends worked hard to promote progress in Liberia over the years past, and there are many who stoutly defend the record against the universal belittlement. But to judge from those I interviewed, the more common feelings about Liberia are defensive embarrassment or—what amounts to the same thing—a defensive indifference. The reason for this goes back to the charge echoed by Reverend Crummell 70 years ago, that the poor Liberian performance proved something about the capacity of Negroes in general. Both those who have tried to help Liberia and those who washed their hands of it were moved primarily by this conviction. The unhappiness with Liberia had to do in part with the lack of development in the country over most of its history. But it bore even more heavily on the nature of the regime created by the migrants from America, called Americo-Liberians and now estimated to number some 15,000, and imposed on the indigenous tribes of the country, now guessed to number about 1,000,000. The embarrassment reached a certain climax in 1930 when a League of Nations commission of inquiry reported the continued existence of slavery in Liberia. Forced laborers rounded up in the Liberian hinterland were delivered to French and Spanish users outside of the country in conditions that differed little from actual slavery. The president of Liberia and some of his highest officials were shown to have profited from this slave trade and were forced to resign.[23]

Although the picture of Liberia is shifting too as it seeks to find its place in the new circumstances of emergent Africa, I found that by far the great majority of individuals I interviewed in 1958–59 preferred to ignore the subject of Liberia altogether and to concentrate their recent interest in Africa on the new state of Ghana and its upcoming neighbor states in middle Africa. There were some defensive remarks about Liberia and a

23 Cf. George Schuyler, *Slaves Today: A Story of Liberia* (New York, 1931); W. E. B. Du Bois, "Liberia, the League, and the United States," *Foreign Affairs*, July 1933.

few individuals remarked their unhappiness over the recently published account of Liberia included by John Gunther in his *Inside Africa,* published in 1955, which seemed to them unduly negative. On the other hand no one was willing to go as far as Du Bois who in 1940 unblinkingly referred to Liberia as "a continuing symbol of Negro revolt against slavery and oppression." [24] References to Liberia in the interviews ran more commonly like this:

People don't think about Liberia. I don't think they are hostile, just indifferent or ignorant or both, and this is just as well . . .

American Negroes hope Ghana doesn't become another Liberia . . . The interest of American intellectuals in Africa was tortured for a long time by the failure of expectations, the treatment of the natives, and the corruption in Liberia . . .

I didn't like the Liberians. They have all the negative standards of Negro Americans and none of the positive features . . .

Liberia has always remained a nonentity in the Negro's mind. I never knew about it, never heard about it, never did a damned thing about it!

I rarely think of Liberia because I don't want to. I think of Liberia as a mistake, a political mistake . . . Liberia is like Mississippi. I try to block out Liberia when I think of Africa. I think of South Africa for this reason, a place of torment, but not stagnated like Liberia.

You know Americo-Liberians were hostile to American Negro immigration. It is well known that the ruling class in Liberia was hostile to American Negroes so that Negroes couldn't go into business there. The Liberians were held down for a long time, and Americo-Liberians simply imitated the white colonialists.

The least to be said from our evidence is that whatever Liberia was, it was no African beacon of hope for American Negroes, no source of uplift for the American Negro spirit. It had the ardent and faithful devotion of a handful of friends among American Negroes, but they did not change the situation either in Liberia or among their fellow Americans. Liberia has never

[24] *Dusk of Dawn,* p. 239.

looked like a promised land, least of all to Negroes at the turn of this century. If there was an ultimate option in Africa, it was at that time more than ever a wishful dream. At his nadir in America in 1900, the Negro had nowhere else to go but up; and that is the direction in which he now slowly began to move.

The new voice in the dialogue appeared in the sharp, insistent, spurring accents of a young scholar named William E. Burghardt Du Bois, who had come to Atlanta University from Massachusetts via Fisk, Harvard, and Berlin. In 1903, Du Bois openly challenged the submissive posture and gradualist philosophy of Booker T. Washington. He called upon Negroes "to strive for the rights which the world accords to men," *viz.*, "the right to vote, civic equality, and the education of youth according to its ability." In 1905, Du Bois and a group of his friends met at Niagara, New York, and issued a manifesto of demands for full citizenship:

We will not be satisfied to take one jot or tittle less than our full manhood rights. We claim for ourselves every single right that belongs to a freeborn American, political, civil, social; and until we get these rights we will never cease to protest and assail the ears of America.

In 1910 the Niagara group was succeeded by the National Association for the Advancement of Colored People, launched by a group of prominent white and Negro leaders, with Du Bois as its director of research and editor of its organ, *Crisis*. These events marked where the tide changed and a great pressing forward began. The NAACP launched the long struggle for rights through the courts, in the public prints and forums of the nation. Then came the First World War, bringing on its great upheavals and uprootings, its migrations, its mobilizations, and for Negroes its great new hopes of emancipation. Briefly roused, these hopes shriveled at the war's end as the walls of the white American world once more closed in around them. The historic dialogue resumed. The new taker of the ultimate option appeared directly on cue, a caller to the wishful dream, a black West Indian prophet named Marcus Garvey who summoned the weary Negroes of America to stop following after their false white gods and false white hopes and to follow after him, back to black Africa.

## Marcus Garvey

Marcus Garvey, the "Provisional President of Africa," never set foot on African soil and never sent a single Negro migrant back to settle there, but his name stands for the greatest "Back-to-Africa" movement in Negro history. His figure hovers somewhere in the memory of every member of our panel, and echoes of many things he said can be clearly heard now in the words of many who were embarrassed by him while he lived.

Garvey was a Jamaican who came to the United States in 1916. Over his Universal Negro Improvement Association he raised the banner of black-race purity, and he summoned the Negro masses to join him in returning to the African homeland, which he promised to win back for them from its white masters. By 1920 he claimed four million dues-paying members; by 1923, six million. Even his most ardent belittlers admitted he had hundreds of thousands of followers. He sank most of the money they gave him in his Black Star Steamship Line, which was going to provide the means for returning to the promised land but managed only to founder after a series of costly misadventures. He was convicted of using the mails to defraud in 1923, went to Atlanta Penitentiary in 1925, was pardoned and deported by President Coolidge in 1927, and died obscurely in London in 1940 at the age of fifty-three.

In the brief high years of his career Garvey became an international figure, center of turmoil and controversy, constantly attacked and attacking. European colonial authorities in Africa kept an eye cocked on him from afar and kept his paper, *Negro World*, from entering their precincts. In the United States all the best-known leaders among Negroes and most of the educated, aspiring American Negro middle class reacted strongly against him as a West Indian interloper, a bizarre mountebank, an irresponsible demagogue, a cheat and fraud, a wild dreamer, and, most of all, as a black racist who with brutal tongue and phrase rejected men of mixed descent far more violently than he rejected the whites themselves. But he was also the man who created the most spectacular mass movement seen among Negroes before or since. With his appeal to race pride, he reached into the lowest levels of the Negro masses and won a following that no Negro leader or group, not even the churches, had ever touched before. Instead of pie in the sky, Garvey promised Africa. For a brief flash of time Garvey made it seem that Africa did lie, reachable, at the end of the streets through which his followers marched; the homeland where a new life for the race could begin, where he saw "a new world of black men, not peons, serfs, dogs, and slaves, but a nation of sturdy men making their impress upon civilization and causing a new light to dawn upon the human race."

In his heyday Garvey wrote much and spoke much and was much written about. After his eclipse, his name and history were kept alive by small surviving bands of the faithful. His swift passage across the scene was only briefly noted in the appropriate places in occasional books. Garvey went largely unstudied and unchronicled for nearly a generation after his movement collapsed. Some re-examination of his movement has begun to appear in journal articles and theses in the last ten years or so. The first and so far still the only serious book-length study of him appeared in 1955. It is with material drawn from these sources [25] that we will attempt here to locate Garvey's place in this short history of Negro links to Africa.

In his appeal to Negroes to follow him back to Africa, Marcus Garvey gave his own shape and his own accent to every major theme that had already appeared on this subject in the past, and

25 Edmund David Cronon, *Black Moses, The Story of Marcus Garvey and the Universal Negro Improvement Association* (Madison, Wis., 1955); Robert Hughes Brisbane, Jr., "The Rise of Protest Movements Among Negroes since 1900," unpub. thesis, Harvard University, 1940, and "His Excellency the Provisional President of Africa," *Phylon*, 3rd quarter 1949; Record, "The Negro Intellectual and Negro Nationalism," *op. cit.* These studies provide ample bibliographical notes and footnotes which will lead any interested student back to the living details of the Garvey story. The quotations from Garvey that follow in these pages are, unless otherwise indicated, drawn from these sources.

he added some themes that had never so explicitly been there before. Like all his predecessors in the Moses role, Garvey came offering an escape from despair, and the despair among Negroes in the aftermath of the First World War was as deep as, and perhaps less bearable than, any they had known before. The great sweeping events of the war had enormously dramatized both the rise of new hopes and their collapse. All the magnitudes were large—the movement of people from South to North, from lonely fields and furrows to crowded streets and factories, from smaller communities of known victimizers to the encounter in the great cities with large faceless masses of hostile whites. There was the experience in the armed forces, and for some the journey across the sea, the exposure to a great mass of new impulses and new ideas. The ideas were large too: the war was for freedom, to make the world safe for democracy. Like subject peoples all around the globe, Negroes in America thought this included them. All these hopes and expectations were struck down; the Ku Klux Klan, lynch mobs and rioters rode right over them while the rest of the society simply looked on. Most of the millions of Negroes in the country hugged what cover they could from this storm, as they always had in the past; most of them never even heard of Garvey. But there were other millions in large cities now who did hear of him; great numbers who heard him, and large numbers who stepped out after him when he called.

Like others before him who had seized this ultimate option, Garvey urged his people to leave the white man's land to the white man and to seek a place of their own where the black man could be his own man:

> If you cannot live alongside the white man in peace, if you cannot get the same chance and opportunity alongside the white man, even though you are his fellow citizen . . . then find a country of your own and rise to the highest position within that country . . . [We need] a government, a nation of our own, strong enough to lend protection to the members of our race scattered all over the world, and to compel the respect of the nations and races of the earth.

And the black man's nation, of course, was to be found in

Africa, a homeland waiting to be reclaimed from the white men who held it. Garvey summoned up his Negro hosts—he counted them up to an imaginary 400,000,000—to fight for their own home soil:

> If Europe is for the Europeans, then Africa shall be for the black peoples of the world. We say it, we mean it . . . The other races have countries of their own and it is time for the 400,000,000 Negroes to claim Africa for themselves . . . The Negroes of the world say, "We are striking homewards toward Africa to make her the big black republic." And in making Africa a big black republic, what is the barrier? The barrier is the white man, and we say to the white man who now dominates Africa that . . . we mean to retake every square inch of the 12,000,000 square miles of African territory belonging to us by right Divine . . .

Garvey dressed himself and his followers in titles and fancy uniforms, organized them into Royal African Legions and Black Cross Nurses, and marched them through Harlem. The bizarre show made the white world laugh and sensible Negroes wince, but some of his words stabbed deep into those who could hear him:

> The white man need expect no more Negro blood shed on his behalf. The first dying that is to be done by the black man in the future will be to make himself free [and when this is accomplished] if we have any charity to bestow, we may die for the white man. But as for me, I think I have stopped dying for him.

Garvey called not only for blood, but for *pure* blood. Garvey spoke the language of an all-out black racism. When he called upon his people to reforge their kinship and connection to Africa, Garvey called on *black* men for this, men without white taint. The racist note had been heard in this dialogue from the very beginning, but Garvey made it his central crashing theme. On this score he was bolder and more violent than the strongest-tongued "raceman" who had ever at any time pressed Negroes to meet the racist white man on his own terms. He called for a pure black race to stand by itself apart from a pure white race, and he reserved his most poisonous scorn for Negroes of mixed ancestry, who in his time made up virtually the whole top social and economic layer of the Negro population. Against them, Garvey unhesitatingly aligned himself with the white racists:

The black and white races are now facing the crucial time of their existence. The whites are rightfully and properly crying out for a pure white race and the proud and self-respecting blacks are crying out for a morally pure and healthy Negro race. Between both we have a new school of thought, advanced by the "near white" or "colored man," W. E. B. Du Bois and his National Association for the Advancement of Colored People, who advocate racial amalgamation or general miscegenation with the hope of creating a new type of colored race by wiping out both black and white.

Garvey's black racism was a deep and vital part of his appeal, perhaps the deepest and most vital of all. It was addressed in the first place to the larger numbers of his fellow West Indians in New York, immigrants who had come out of the profoundly color caste-ridden system in the Caribbean and who formed a considerable part of his core following. But after them, Garvey's ultraracism also directly touched deep chords of response among the lower-class Negroes crowding the war-swollen ghettos of New York and a few other big cities. These people tended to be more commonly black, or at least blacker, than members of the predominantly "mulatto" or lighter-colored middle class. Garvey summoned up in them all the deeply stored resentment, even hatred, created by the American Negro's own deeply imbedded color caste system.

In lighter Negroes Garvey aroused fear and repugnance. They were stung to outrage—often complex and ambiguous—by his attempt to read them out of the race as impure "near whites." All the best-known and most articulate Negroes of the time fell into this category; they stood up against Garvey, fighting the Negro cause as they saw it but fighting also, desperately, for themselves. Under all the blows of the time, these men were suffering their own doubts, ambivalence, and alienation. But Garvey forced them to cling all the harder, despite all the adversity, to the hope for a future based on equal rights in American society. Even where they carried within them their own racial feeling (and who can say that men like Du Bois, A. Philip

Randolph, and James Weldon Johnson did not?) Garvey denied it to them because they were not black or not black enough. Even if any one of them had felt the impulse to see if there was indeed any reality in the prospect of an escape to Africa, Garvey cut them off from it; they were not *black* enough. Garvey tied the race and Africa to *blackness,* and in ways deeper than most Negro leaders either knew or would acknowledge, this made him their mortal foe.

These leaders saw Garvey's movement primarily as a mad, capering chimera in which people could only be cruelly deceived and defrauded and the larger Negro cause damaged. Where Garvey also made the matter an issue of race and color in its bluntest and most personal form, he only sharpened and embittered the controversy, and in the fray he forced some notable men to dispute with him on his own terms. Randolph called Garvey a "supreme Negro Jamaican jackass" who had come out of "the mudsill of Jamaican society." In a phrase that Garvey gleefully hugged to himself and repeated to cheering admirers again and again, Du Bois called Garvey that "little fat black man, ugly, but with intelligent eyes and a big head." Garvey retorted that Du Bois was "a mulatto whose white blood despised the black within him." Du Bois, who had his own racial ideas and his own vision of a new Pan-Africa (his first Pan-African Congress had taken place in Europe in 1919), saw the Garvey threat in these terms:

Here is Garvey yelling to life from the black side a race consciousness which leaps to meet Madison Grant, Lothrop Stoddard and other worshippers of the great white race. . . . If with a greater and more gifted and efficient Garvey, it sometimes blazes into real flame, it means world war and eternal hate and blood.

Partly under the pressure of his opponents—who successfully put the law on him—but mostly by his own actions, Garvey brought his own movement crashing down. He punctured much of his appeal and showed his essential lack of contact with American Negroes by carrying his racism to the point of making public common cause with the Ku Klux Klan. He approved its white racism; it supported his plan to take the blacks back to Africa.

But even among his West Indian followers, to whom the Klan was perhaps a less meaningful symbol, the high emotion generated by his demagogy and showmanship began to need more substantial nourishment. There was some excitement in the sailings of two vessels which got to the Caribbean but never to Africa. But the Black Star Line soon went down in a storm of wild mismanagement. Garvey's high-handedness and lack of touch with reality finally overtook him. He went to prison, and his organization fell apart into fragments. The larger masses which had sought relief or escape through Garvey were forced to seek it elsewhere.

Marcus Garvey was well remembered by all but a few of the youngest members of our panel, and even they had heard or read of him. Some of the older and best-known members of the group, like Du Bois and Randolph, were among the most prominent of Garvey's opponents. Others, like Frazier, had observed him closely at firsthand or had heard him speak, watched his parades, or followed from a distance the controversy about him in the press. Then there were those who had been children in Garvey's time and remembered how their families had reacted. All but a few of these individuals came out of backgrounds that were either already middle class or aspiring to that status or were of clearly mixed descent, and their responses to Garvey were patterned accordingly.

For some the recollection is dominated by the strong feeling about West Indians that ran among American Negroes in those days:

As a kid I heard about Marcus Garvey. We used to sing a song ridiculing him. It went like this:

> Marcus Garvey is a big black monkey man,
> Marcus Garvey will catch you if he can.
> All you black folks get in line,
> Buy your tickets on the Black Star Line.

Other examples reflect the difference of class and education between those who followed Garvey and those who did not:

I heard Garvey speak on a few occasions in Cleveland, once at Howard. I was never attracted. There was a certain intellectual snobbery about this. Garvey did not have a literate following and he was given to gaudiness, parades, and fantasy and grand eloquence. I looked down my nose at this sort of thing.

I remember hearing my father talk about Garvey. He never liked him; thought he was a crook. He laughed about the Back-to-Africa movement . . .

Among people of education, the idea of going back to Africa has always been absurd . . .

Garvey was able to attract all Negroes who wore red underwear, I mean the lower class. I was too young or too ignorant to know too much about it . . .

Garvey attracted frantic, insane people. My brother and I once had to run for our lives when we scoffed at some of them . . .

The Garvey movement occurred while I was in college. . . . It was the uneducated who fell in line . . . a herd led by a skillful manipulator. . . . This was not for our kind of people, physicians, schoolteachers, civil servants . . .

His appeal was mostly to the lower masses. . . . He was the man who led big parades of ignorant people down the street selling pie in the sky.

Garvey came during my school days. He was much discussed and ridiculed in my family. He was playing into the hands of the Bilbos; he was unrealistic. He assumed we were not first and last of all Americans. My folks went too far back in Washington and Virginia to be interested in the Garvey movement . . .

For many the stronger focus was on the notion of going back to Africa:

I shared my father's views. This was *my* country, and I would rather fight for what I had here than go back to Africa . . .

I know of no well-educated Negro who believed Marcus Garvey was on the right track. Thirty years ago the average Negro with education or any advantages had very little interest in Africa; resented the implication that he should be. The popular phrase was:

"I haven't lost anything in Africa and I'm not going there to find it." . . . Most trained Negroes rejected Garveyism as a burlesque act . . .

I rejected the idea of any Negro identification with Africa on a large scale. Any man who talked of Africa as a home for Negroes was simply foolish. It was pure hokum. Most Negro intellectuals looked at it this way. I saw a Garvey parade in Chicago. He wore a yellow cap and rode a horse. I thought he was a mountebank.

Mentioned somewhat less often but running through all these reactions, clearly visible even when it was being unnoticed or unstressed, ran the black thread of color:

It was a black chauvinistic movement . . .

The theory was to unite the Negroes to go black and do black . . .

Garvey was a transplanted black man who wanted to do everything black and establish a black country in Africa. . . . But *this* was *my* country, where *my* people were born . . .

Garvey was able to tear the Negroes apart in this country. He set Negro against Negro, the light against the dark. If he had been efficient and honest, there is no telling where the thing would have gone . . .

There was very little crossing of line then on the color question: black against light, West Indian against American, Garvey against Du Bois . . .

The Garvey story was clearly more than just a bizarre episode, and Garvey himself something more than a race-mad clown. He linked himself to ideas and emotions that have had a continuing relevance: Africa, the Negro's relationship to it, and the Negro's view of himself.

For one thing, Garvey made himself the first prophet of a free Africa. "I know no national boundary where the Negro is concerned," he proclaimed. "The whole world is my province until Africa is free." Whether addressing his West Indian followers or Americans, or in the last years in London, where young African expatriates were within hearing, Garvey never abandoned the messianic note: "No one knows when the hour of Africa's redemption cometh," he proclaimed. "It is in the wind. It is coming. One day, like a storm, it will be here." To some Africans his words came as a summons. One of his readers, for example, was a young African named Kwame Nkrumah studying in the United States in the late 1930's who later wrote: "Of all the literature I studied, the book that did more than any other to fire my enthusiasm was *The Philosophy and Opinions of Marcus Garvey.*" [26]

Barely twenty years later Nkrumah became head of the first of the new African republics. In December 1958 he opened the first All-African People's Congress at Accra with a tribute to Garvey, and when his new black state established its own fleet of merchant ships, he called it the Black Star Line.

What Garvey made Africa mean to the Negroes in America who briefly listened to him is still another matter. He summoned black men to rise with him and go back to Africa. He cast his words upon the winds, and the response came pouring in upon him in great human tides and floods of money. Yet no migration ever took place, nor did Garvey ever apparently make any serious moves toward launching one. He did send a probing mission to Liberia. (One individual I interviewed remembered that his brother had been a member of that mission. "He nearly stole Liberia for $50,000," he said.) But the would-be vanguard of the Garveyite mass was repulsed. The Liberians wanted no part of an invasion of freedom-seeking kinsmen from America led by a half-mad Jamaican prophet. No plans for anyone's actual return to Africa ever moved beyond this point; in Garvey's program the central theme, Back-to-Africa, remained pure fantasy. It was "not that he was a conscious liar," observed Du Bois in 1923, "but dream, fact, fancy, wish were all so blurred in his thinking that neither he himself nor his hearers could clearly extricate them." It was this fantastic quality, among other things, that led Ralph Bunche, in a study he made in 1940 for Gunnar Myrdal, to the view that Garveyism had been pure escapism, a large movement because there was a large desire for

26 Kwame Nkrumah, *Ghana* (New York, 1957), p. 45.

escape, but not to be taken seriously as a sign of the readiness of Negroes to go back to Africa.[27]

Garvey presumably meant himself to be taken quite literally when he spoke of the return to Africa, but apparently few of his followers did so. Even of Garvey's West Indian immigrant following, Claude McKay wrote:

They gave Garvey all the money he needed to institute his programme. But only an infinitesimal few of these people really desired to go—*back to Africa*. And obviously Marcus Garvey himself had no intention of going back to live in some corner of the vast land of his ancestors. But Back-to-Africa on a Black Star Line was magical propaganda.[28]

Perhaps what most of his listeners heard was a man calling them back to themselves, to stop forever seeing themselves in the white man's eye. As E. Franklin Frazier, then a young but already sharp-eyed observer of Negro life, remarked at the time: Garvey made people "feel like somebody among white people who have said they were nobody."

One of Garvey's attorneys at his trial tried to express a similar idea to the jury:

If every Negro could have put every dime, every penny into the sea, and if he might get in exchange the knowledge that he was somebody, that he meant something in the world, he would gladly do it. . . . The Black Star Line was a loss in money, but it was a gain in soul.[29]

Among all those I interviewed there were barely half a dozen who had either positive recollections about the Garvey movement or positive afterthoughts about it. These were in every case attached not to the Back-to-Africa theme or the color issue (these were minimized, indistinctly remembered or just "forgotten")

[27] Garvey's widow, Amy Jacques Garvey, offered this interpretation in 1960: "As a matter of fact, the term Back-to-Africa was used and promoted by newspapers, Negro newspapers mostly, to ridicule Garvey. There was no Back-to-Africa movement except in a spiritual sense." "The Ghost of Marcus Garvey," *Ebony*, Mar. 1960.

[28] Claude McKay, *Harlem: Negro Metropolis* (New York, 1940), p. 150.

[29] Quoted in Ottley, *New World A-Coming*, p. 79.

but rather this element of pride in self. Here are three examples, all from individuals of West Indian background who were children in Garvey's time:

My mother was a member of the UNIA. As a child I went to meetings with her. . . . I have no recollection of the color issue in connection with the Garvey time. . . . I don't think my mother ever seriously thought of going to Africa. She had no deep or burning desire to do anything like that. I think she joined the Garvey movement to get identity. She was an alien accepted by nobody, neither the Negroes nor the whites . . .

I was just a youngster and I was excited by the parades and the ritual. I only got a little of the content. It was glorious and uplifting for the Negro. I never even thought about the idea of going back to Africa. My people were already immigrants and certainly weren't thinking of making another move . . .

My mother was an intense Garveyite. She bought stock in it. I was very young and to me it meant excitement, fervor. I went to meetings with my mother to Liberty Hall. . . . She lost money in its ventures and was disillusioned, but not in the principles involved. She kept a certain pride in it, and still does. The Back-to-Africa part was not important. Pride was. Negroes should have something of their own. And the blackness, this was not taken literally, as far as I can recall. My mother isn't black. I don't recollect this part of it. All my memory of the Garvey movement is positive. My mother's explanations, seeing the parades, my mother's reproduction of the black Christ and the brown dolls.

But there is no way, even by the most selective kind of remembering, to get away from the central theme in Garvey's appeal: in calling them back to Africa, back to themselves, he was calling them back to their *blackness*. " 'Negro, Black, and Africa,' the magic words repeated again and again," wrote McKay, "made Negroes delirious with ecstasy." [30] Garvey did not mean this only symbolically, although many no doubt took it that way and some of his lieutenants were far from black themselves. Garvey was not merely summoning Negroes from the false lure of white values, white ways, white cruelties. He meant it literally; he

30 McKay, *op. cit.*, p. 151.

dreamed of a pure black race regaining a proud posture in the world, and he had as much contempt for "race mixers" as the most fanatic white racist, and even more contempt for those whose race had already been mixed beyond repair.

Garvey's brutal assault on the issue of color among Negroes forced it out onto the surface of things where it had rarely been seen before. He dramatized it, deliberately setting dark Negro against light Negro. By bringing them out into the open in their most blatant and dangerous form, Garvey forced a certain change in the currency of these prejudices though not in ways that he intended. The inner shame over blackness was by no means exorcised but after Garvey it was never again quite the same as it had been. It can be said that the beginning of the crumbling of the old color caste really began from this time in the 1920's, because Garvey made so many more people so much more sharply aware of the cleavage and of its cost. Color caste attitudes after that were much less flagrantly held or expressed. Leaders of Negro protest movements in the years after Garvey were made especially conscious of this problem and tried more strenuously than ever before to close the gap between themselves and the masses of darker people below, and thereby to broaden the base of struggle for civil rights.

On the other hand, Garvey drove Africa still further away beyond the American Negro's horizon. He did this partly by making Africa seem such an ephemeral dream that the same emotions that had led many people to him guided them afterward to Father Divine, a newly risen religious cultist who said he was God and whose Kingdom was made to look much closer than Garvey's Africa. Garvey also accomplished this by linking the African dream so explicitly to blackness. If the call back to Africa did mean a call back to blackness, there were simply too many Negroes of irretrievably mixed descent who not only could not respond to the call but desperately did not want to do so. If any link was ever to be re-established between them and Africa, it would have to be on some other plane not yet in sight. Meanwhile those Negroes who dreamed the black-African dream continued to do so only at the fringes of real life, whether it was shaped by Garvey's wild fantasies, by the cult of glorified black primitivism that also flourished in the Harlem Bohemia of the time, or by Du Bois' wider vision of Pan-Africanism.

## Stanley, the Congo, and Royal Relatives

I mention at this point the literary African vogue of the 1920's and Du Bois' Pan-African movement only to establish them here as markers to indicate two more points of contact between American Negroes and Africa. Let them be well marked, for we shall be coming back later for a longer look. As we go by, however, it should be noted that these were both matters that reached significant Negro reading publics. Du Bois wrote extensively of Pan-Africanism in *Crisis,* in those years the periodical most widely read by Negroes. It was mentioned more often in our interviews than any other single publication. The romantic African cult had a smaller audience, but some of the more important poets who reflected some of its themes were very widely read. Langston Hughes was one of these, and Countee Cullen's poem "Heritage" was mentioned repeatedly in this connection.

Besides these, a variety of other associations of various kinds also turned up fleetingly in the interviews, crossing most of the same years we have been considering. I will confine myself here simply to reporting them as they appeared. The most important of these were also literary, for it would seem that wherever there was exposure to books or reading in Negro homes, an important part of it had to do with Africa. Some of this came from missionary publications. Frequent reference is made to Du Bois' *Souls of Black Folk* and to the books of Carter G. Woodson. But some of these reading memories went even further back to show that in some Negro homes there was great interest in the Stanley-Livingstone story:

As a child I read the Stanley story. I had a red book about the strange and exotic things in Africa, pygmies. My father had lots of missionary books about Africa. The *In Darkest Africa* sort of thing . . .

When I was a little boy and could first read, I had books on Stanley, Livingstone and things like that . . .

I knew about Livingstone; we had Stanley's book illustrated, a fat brown book . . .

I remember my father reading to us, when I was seven or eight, from a book called *With Stanley in Africa.* He used to read it to us and talk about Africa, about slavery, what they had done to Africa, and tell us that Negroes had been kings when white men were savages . . .

I read Stanley's *In Darkest Africa* when I was about twelve or thirteen. I read everything he wrote . . .

One younger man brought up out of his boyhood years a vignette of Arthur Schomburg, the collector and then the curator of the country's most notable collection of Africana, housed in the public library on West 135th Street in New York:

When I was twelve or thirteen I used to go to the library to get books, and there I met Mr. Schomburg. He used to talk to me a lot. He respected me, never treated me as a child, and this kept me coming. They had African sculptures on the second floor and I got curious about them. I began to read a lot about Africa. Its history was a real eye opener to me . . .

Some members of our panel recalled an early awareness of certain events in Africa communicated by the press, from the pulpit, or by talk in the family circle at home:

Of course we all knew about Menelik's defeat of the Italian Army at Adowa in 1896, and about the wars of the Zulus in South Africa. I used to hunt out information about these things in the library at Syracuse . . .

More frequently mentioned were King Leopold's atrocities in the Congo:

We heard of the Belgian Congo, the crimes of Leopold. I remember my mother talking about how they chopped people's ears off. She read about it, either in Trotter's *Guardian,* or in *Crisis* . . .

Of course I had heard of the Belgians in the Congo way back . . .

I heard old Rev. Sheppard talk about the Congo, Leopold cutting people's hands off . . .

The conduct of the Belgian King Leopold, the mutilation of people in the Congo. We had a Negro missionary named Sheppard who came to Morehouse, or to the church in my home town, I forget which, and described all this. It made an indelible impression on me . . .

I think clearly of the feeling of divine retribution during World War One. I mean that what the Germans were doing to Belgium was inflicted on them for what they had done to the people of the Congo, the Congo atrocities. This was preached in the churches. I heard it constantly.

And in some Negro families this word was passed on down from generation to generation, for one of the youngest of our panelists, who was only a small child in the 1930's, remarked:

I didn't know a thing about Hitler, but I had heard about Leopold in the Congo! [31]

Some associations with Africa were of a more directly personal kind, encounters with African students at school occurring at places like Tuskegee, Howard, Morehouse, Fisk or Lincoln. In one case it was the experience of having the great James A. K. Aggrey, the West African leader and educator, as a teacher at Livingstone College in North Carolina. In a few much more unusual instances it was a matter of actually having African relatives of fairly recent date. This came about, it appeared, through marriages made in this country by some of the rare African travelers of a generation or two ago. In one or two of these cases the relationship was a very explicit one. Sometimes it was rather more obscure, and almost always it involved some reference to royal backgrounds, especially in brown Madagascar:

There is a legend in my family that one of our ancestors on my mother's side three or four generations ago was supposed to have been a princess of Madagascar . . .

I met my first African prince about 1928 or so, a songwriter

31 For references to Negro-American interest in Leopold's Congo, see Shepperson, "Notes on American Negro Influences on the Emergence of Africa Nationalism," *loc. cit.*, p. 305, notes 41–45.

named Andy Razal. His mother was a Negro girl from Kansas City who went to Madagascar and married the son of a royal prince just before the French did away with royalty there . . .

You would hear many stories of people claiming to have an African prince in their family history . . .

The matter of blackness of color, which scarcely ever fails to come up in any part of this discussion, also appears here:

If you look up the first press release on the election of Robert Moton as President of Tuskegee [in 1915] you will find that Moton, big and black, described himself as "a descendant of an African prince." He obviously thought of this as giving him prestige. Mrs. [Mary McCleod] Bethune was also identified this way in early books. I would guess that purity of stock reflected in color, and the blacker the family background, the greater the tendency to identify with Africa; the lighter the background, the greater the tendency to identify with the lighter ancestors. People who were black capitalized on Africa.

From these more remote, fragmentary, or occasional associations, we come now to the next time after Garvey that any considerable number of Negroes became involved with Africa; this was their reaction to Italy's attack on Ethiopia in 1935.

## The Ethiopian War

The very name "Ethiopia" had more than one dimension in the thinking of Negroes. It had long been—as in the Bible and in Shakespeare—the broad and nearly generic term for the whole universe of dark-skinned people in olden times. The day when "Ethiopia's hand shall stretch forth unto God" would be the day of liberation for all dark-skinned people everywhere who had been submerged under white mastery for so long. "Ethiopian" was an adjective associated with part of the ancient and prideful history of black men and their role in the early civilizations of man. Whether as "Ethiopian" or in its other common form, "Abyssinian," this descriptive adjective was used in many names and associations; it is the name borne by the largest Negro church in New York City. It was also a name favored by some extreme racialists—in 1932 there was an "Ethiopian Peace Movement" in Chicago still carrying the banner of "Back to Africa" from the days before Garvey fell. When the Italian assault came the fading Garvey, speaking from his London exile, again summoned his black hosts, this time to come to Ethiopia's aid. But Negroes needed no spur from Garvey to be stirred by Ethiopia's plight. The Italian attack revived all the pride that Negroes of an earlier generation had shared from afar when the Ethiopians threw back the first Italian invaders in the famous battle of Adowa in 1896. That victory still stood as the single successful repulse of white men by black in Africa, and Haile Selassie could appear now as the symbolic defender not only of his country but of Negro self-respect everywhere. John Hope Franklin summarized this view: "Ethiopia was a Negro nation, and its destruction would symbolize the final victory of the white man over the Negro." [32] Besides racial spurs, Du Bois' Pan-Africanism had helped create a small, narrowly held, but sophisticated interest among Negroes in the whole issue of imperialism, colonies, international politics, and the prospects of African freedom from European domination. Also by the mid-1930's, the Communist Party was at the peak of its effort to win Negro adherents, and it mounted a major campaign to mobilize Negroes around the issue of the Ethiopian war.

Together or separately, all these sources of feeling about Ethiopia helped produce a considerable response among Negroes. It was no massive movement like Garvey's; the Ethiopian issue came even less close than Garvey did to the great bulk of the Negro population. But neither was it a small affair. In many cities mass meetings were held, funds raised, popular feeling greatly aroused. It was an excitement that appears still quite fresh in the memories of most of the members of our panel, coming up with particular sharpness among those who were young at the time:

I was up to my gills in the Ethiopian war. I followed every tiny step of it. "Ethiopia shall stretch forth her hands . . ." You knew

32 *From Slavery to Freedom* (New York, 1947), p. 558.

what the Bible had predicted. And you knew about Adowa in 1896 and here were the Italians back again. It was a great spectacle . . .

The *Courier* sent J. A. Rogers to Ethiopia and gained 23,000 circulation with an interview with Haile Selassie . . .

The Ethiopian war made me bitter; it frightened me. We had Italian neighbors and I fought that war every day. My mother was very excited about it. I just knew the Ethiopians were black and therefore we were for them . . .

Even as kids we identified with the Ethiopians. Never had the same feeling about Czechs or Jews. There were protest meetings about Ethiopia, largely Negro meetings. I grew up amid a certain social awareness, but the only foreign thing in it was Ethiopia . . .

I remember the newsreels, fighters with spears, and our people in a passion over it, my mother attacking the Pope about Ethiopia, blessing those monsters. When the Pope died that was the thought that came into my mind.

One major effect of the Ethiopian war was to give large numbers of Negroes for the first time a sense of involvement in world events. Japan's invasion of Manchuria in 1931 and Hitler's rise to power and his march into the Rhineland in 1935 had produced negligible or ambivalent reactions among Negroes. The Spanish civil war, starting the next year while the Ethiopian war was still going on, touched only the well-informed intellectuals or the Communist-influenced radicals. But Ethiopia gave Negroes their own handle to world affairs, and it opened the door on the world to many who had hitherto hardly known it was there. One of our panelists put it this way:

There were glimmerings of these things before . . . but it was around the Ethiopian affair for the first time that there was a crystallizing of attitudes among American Negroes toward colored peoples outside the U.S. . . .

John Hope Franklin has put the matter even more strongly. With Italy's attack on Ethiopia, he has written, "almost overnight, even the most provincial among American Negroes became international minded." [33]

[33] *Ibid.*, p. 558.

But two elements in the situation thinned out these emotions and dampened many of these responses.

First, the involvement of the Communists brought on a great muddying of the whole affair. Their call to action had not only been to get help to Ethiopia but also to stop help from going to Italy. The pressure on the United States Government was to get it to halt shipments of wheat and other vital supplies to Italy. The issue before the League of Nations was the issue of sanctions, especially on the shipment of oil to the Italian war machine. But then it developed that even while Maxim Litvinov, the Soviet Foreign Minister, had been making his eloquent appeals for Ethiopia at Geneva, the Soviet Union had gone on supplying Italy with oil and wheat, and moreover, at premium prices. A din of controversy arose over this exposure of Russian Communist cynicism. Many Negroes who had been drawn into the issue in the first place by Communist appeals began drifting away from it with a certain cynical despair of their own: white Italian Fascists and white Russian and American Communists were all equally poison for the black Ethiopians.[34]

The second element that cut away at this movement of sympathy for Ethiopia was the black Ethiopian himself, and he cut much deeper and hurt much more. For while Negroes in America were enthusiastically identifying with Ethiopians, Ethiopians were rejecting any identification with Negroes. They described themselves as sons of Ham and not "Negro" at all. American Negroes might see Ethiopia as a "Negro nation" but Ethiopians did not, and what is more, considered the suggestion insulting. A few Negroes in America knew of this attitude, but most did not. Only in 1936, when Haile Selassie's nephew came to the United States and refused to appear at a great rally organized for him in Harlem, did the Ethopian view of Negroes begin to be more commonly known. There was nothing much new in discovering white duplicity at the black man's expense; it was much harder to suffer the indignity of being rejected by the embattled black Ethiopian even as one was cheering him on. In

---

[34] For a detailed account see Wilson Record, *The Negro and the Communist Party*, pp. 137–141. Cf. McKay, *Harlem: Negro Metropolis*, p. 226.

this country the blow was passed over in angry embarrassment.[35] When Haile Selassie fled to London, Garvey tried to contact him but was snubbed, and it was reported that "the emperor did not desire any contact with 'Negroes.' " At this, Garvey, who had in his own great days called himself the "Lion of Numidia," trained some of his heaviest vocabulary on the Lion of Judah:

Haile Selassie is the ruler of a country where black men are chained and flogged. . . . He proved the incompetence of the Negro for political authority . . . The emperor's usefulness is at an end. He will go down in history as a great coward who ran away from his country . . . The Negro Abyssinian must not be ashamed to be a member of the Negro race. If he does, he will be left alone by all the Negroes of the world . . .[36]

In later years Ethiopian behavior improved. One of our Washington panelists recalled the occasion when an Ethiopian delegate came to a wartime conference in Washington in 1943 and was not given room in any downtown hotel. "We had to put him up at Howard," he recalled sardonically. "He told me with tears in his eyes that he would never come back to Washington until he could be treated decently." In 1954 when Haile Selassie visited this country, James Hicks recalls that he was sent to get an interview with explicit instructions to get a statement from the Emperor on his views about American Negroes, and that this time the Emperor was prepared with a statement proclaiming the "kindred feeling" of his people for Negroes. But something less than kindred feeling was generated by a young Ethiopian guest on a television panel program in 1958 who made a very special point of insisting that Ethiopians were not "Negroes" and had nothing in common with them at all. Nowadays much less seems to be made of this matter, but Ethiopia does not figure prominently in the new shape of Negro interest in Africa.

[35] "Aframericans are not generally aware that many other Africans besides Ethiopians object to being called Negroes, because they regard it as a name fit for black slaves. The Ethiopians will not even allow themselves to be designated as Abyssinians, because it is Arabic for slave. Yet because of this propaganda against the Ethiopians, many Aframericans refused to identify themselves with the Help Ethiopia movement." McKay, *op. cit.*, pp. 175-6.

[36] *Ibid.*, p. 176; Cronon, *Black Moses*, p. 162.

"Somehow," said one individual, "when I think of Africa I never do think of Ethiopia. But I must say," he went on, "that I really don't mind now those Ethiopian objections to being called Negro. I really have no strong feelings about it."

# 3. *THE HEART OF THE MATTER*

Our review of all this history has shown—at the very least—that there has actually been a great deal about Africa, hazy or not, in the universe of Negro Americans down through all the generations. We have seen that while some individuals now and again reached out for their African identity and some even tried to make it the central stuff of life, by far the greater number of Negroes preferred to keep it at a remote distance or to let it pass from sight altogether. We have seen that some Negroes have from time to time wanted to go back to Africa, but that this was almost always a dream of desperation; that by far the greater number, no matter how desperate, refused to dream this dream and doggedly went on trying to win through to a free life here in the American society where they felt rooted enough. A complex cluster of things about each person went into the making of this choice. It was made out of parts of his own unique character and parts of the whole of the history of the Negro in America. But somewhere in it always, whether he embraced it or fought it, was that "aversion" to Africa of which J. C. Smyth spoke so bluntly 65 years ago, and which keeps appearing in all parts of the record, both before that time and since. It is time now to try to explore the nature of that "aversion" itself, and for this we must go back again to the childhood recollections of those who joined with me in this inquiry and see what we can learn about it from them.

There is a considerable literature on how Negro children find out that they are Negroes and what this comes to mean to them. When we look into this literature, we come upon a striking fact: the African background seems to lie so deeply buried under so many other layers of the harsh experience of self-discovery in Negro childhood that it hardly ever appears in these accounts at all. If it does, it comes in glancingly only now and then and is hardly seen. We have by now a small but by no means negligible accumulation of psychiatric, psychological, or sociological case-study material dealing with Negroes. A combing of a substantial sample of this literature suggest that here, where the stress is so often on childhood and youth, the subject of the African back-ground comes up rarely or not at all. The active or passive "for-getting" about Africa seems to have extended virtually to all the question askers and all the question answerers in what are often otherwise quite searching inquiries.

In 1940–41 appeared the remarkable series of studies made for the American Youth Commission by a group of social scien-tists headed by Franklin Frazier, Charles Johnson, Allison Davis, John Dollard, W. Lloyd Warner, and others.[1] These works ex-amined the shaping of the Negro personality under the pressures of segregation and discrimination in American life. Teams of interviewers, using a great variety of methods, interviewed, tested, or otherwise examined hundreds of Negro adults, youths, boys, and girls on some of the most intimate matters of their lives. The results were spread on a vast and full canvas—pictures drawn with everything from the thin stylus of psychoanalysis to the broad flat brush of sociology. There was more about Negro color attitudes in these studies than had ever been seen in print before. Yet the word "Africa" does not appear sufficiently to be included in the indexes to any of these volumes and is but fleet-ingly mentioned in the great mass of interviews and other mate-rial. In the lengthy batteries of tests and instruments used for one of these studies, the nearest thing to an African allusion ap-pears in a single item in a long schedule of statements on a true-false test, *viz:* "Negroes would still be heathen savages if it were not for the work of white people in educating them and bring-ing them Christianity." [2] In *Negro Youth At the Crossways,* Franklin Frazier alludes in an appendix to the issue of African survivals.[3] In the remaining volumes it apparently does not get mentioned, either in the body of the material or in the sum-maries and analyses made by the senior inquirers.

---

[1] See pp. 82–83 and Bibliography.
[2] Johnson, *Growing Up in the Black Belt,* p. 352.
[3] P. 277.

In a collection of papers done for the Myrdal study and published under the title *Characteristics of the American Negro*,[4] the index shows six entries pertaining to Africa, five of which deal with some comparative testing done in Africa, and the last of which discusses the place of origin of the slaves carried off to America. In the Myrdal volume itself[5] the index to its 1,500 pages contains 11 references to Africa, and these deal with: the places of origin of slaves, the indicated degrees of African ancestry among Negroes, the efforts to raise the level of appreciation of the African heritage, the disputed issue of African cultural survivals, the "Back-to-Africa" appeal of the Garvey movement and a mention of the possibility of its revival.

In *Mark of Oppression* the authors say at the outset:[6] "For our purposes the African background of the Negro is important only with regard to the extent that his aboriginal culture survived in his new habitat [*sic*]," and they settle the matter for themselves by accepting Frazier against Herskovits and by beginning their discussion of "Negro psychology" with "slave psychology." The bulk of the book is given over, however, to the details of 25 case histories of persons who were driven—mainly by their color caste problems—to seek psychiatric help. In all these case histories the nearest thing to an allusion to Africa is one subject's strong rejection of the term "Negro" and her preference for "Afro-American."

In an intensive examination of the group identifications of 25 Negro girls in New York, Margaret Brenman[7] refers once to the "pure 'African' type," meaning a person of Negroid appearance, as suffering a disadvantage in social life. One of her subjects refers indirectly to Africa in telling of her father's interest in the Garvey movement. Another, who had made "tireless efforts . . . to build up a 'racial' past," is quoted as saying:

Anything African is supposed to be something to be ashamed of.

[4] Edited by Otto Klineberg, 1944.
[5] *An American Dilemma.*
[6] Kardiner and Ovesey, p. 38.
[7] Margaret Brenman, "The Relationship Between Minority-Group Membership and Group Identification in a Group of Urban Middle Class Girls," *Journal of Social Psychology*, SPSSI Bulletin, 1940, 11, pp. 171–197.

I've often wanted to know what tribe we came from originally; Mother told me it was the Zulu tribe, so I went to the Museum of Natural History and looked up the pictures of the Zulu tribe. It made me feel good.

These allusions brush close, as we shall see, to matters of the most central importance. But the single most precise reference of this kind turned up in a study reported by Edward K. Weaver,[8] who asked 30 children at an elementary school in the South: "When did you first discover that you were a Negro?" In one and only one of the answers does the African association appear:

They were told I was a cannibal and evil. I can remember when I was real small how children would be drawn away from me by their mothers and told that I was a black African cannibal and that black is evil.

Weaver does not identify the "they" in this passage, but it seems almost certainly to refer to other Negro children. This child here reports a crucial experience that is centrally significant, namely, the association by Negroes at a critically early age of the notions of *African, black, evil,* with *cannibalism* thrown in for good measure as the ultimate form of uncivilizedness.

There may be a few more such vagrant flashes to be found in this literature by more exhaustive and more diligent search, but I believe they would still be few and still vagrant and would not be likely to make the references to Africa in this connection seem any less sparse.[9] Whatever its degree, however, this sparseness is clearly not accidental. Why, we have to ask, do references to Africa appear so rarely or not at all, in these studies of how Negroes view themselves?

[8] Edward K. Weaver, "Racial Sensitivity Among Negro Children," *Phylon,* 1st quarter 1956, pp. 52–60.

[9] No such allusions appear at all, e.g., in such articles as that by K. B. and M. K. Clark, "The Development of Self and the Emergence of Racial Identification in Negro Preschool Children," *Journal of Social Psychology,* 10, 1939, pp. 591–599, and "Skin Color as a Factor in Racial Identification," *loc. cit.,* 1940, 11, pp. 159–169; Charles I. Glicksberg, "Psychoanalysis and the Negro Problem," *Phylon,* 1st quarter, pp. 41–51; Henry J. Myers and Leon Yochelson, "Color Denial in the Negro," *Psychiatry,* Feb. 1948, pp. 39–46; etc.

It is true that in these pioneering inquiries all those involved stood in the nearer foreground of Negro American life,
and heaven knows there was enough to preoccupy them there in
vast areas which had at that time only barely begun to come
under scholarly scrutiny. At the same time, it is also clear that
for most of the people who figure in these studies, whether as
inquirers or subjects, the African association was in fact so dim
and slight as to be pretty nearly nonexistent. The subject simply
never came up. But again, we come now to ask, *why was this
so?*

There are certainly several different answers to this question,
none of them "wrong," and none telling quite the whole story.
But I suggest—speaking, of course, particularly of the Negroes
involved—that the African association was dim for most of these
individuals because it had been driven down so far and so deep
that the askers simply "forgot" to ask about it and the answerers
simply "failed" to mention it. As a result, in the seeking out of
the elements involved in the early shaping of self-knowledge in
the Negro child, the connection to Africa was quite "over-
looked."

I came to this opinion because in my own interviews I found
that in nearly every instance the early discovery of the African
background was in fact a prime element in the shaping of each
individual's knowledge of himself and his world and his attitudes toward both. In these interviews the subject of the African
background did come up, partly because the subject was much
closer to the surface of most people's minds by 1958–59 than it
had been even two or three years before—much less twenty or
forty—but it came up mainly because I raised it. I did not do this
with any sharp prod. I simply asked individuals to tell me what
they could of their earliest recollections connected in any way
with Africa or Africans. The answers varied much in tone, full-
ness, and candor, plucking sometimes at a point of departure
in the years of youth or even later, often circling far around in
time, but almost always coming back eventually to the childhood
years, the early grade-school ages of six to nine or so, or even
earlier.

The earliest recall is of the "osmosis" variety; the breathing in of knowledge from the environment:

I guess I've heard of Africa all my life . . .

I was never unaware of Africa . . .

Probably before I learned to read.

I have always known about Africa, I can't name the beginning . . .

I've been aware of Africa since I've been aware of anything; that we had descended from Africans . . .

This first awareness was of only the barest and most elementary facts: there was a place called Africa, the place we all came from long ago, the place from which the slaves had come. Yet even this first knowledge, coming to the child in his pre-school home setting, could come bearing qualities of feeling which the child insensibly took in. Sometimes there are glimpses of parents trying to insulate their children for as long as possible from the hurtful harshnesses of the outside. This protection is against a lot more than "Africa" but it usually includes it, and it adds "Africa" to the process of later discovery, which is almost all painful. In homes where strong "raceman" attitudes governed, it is strongly indicated that the information often came prearmored against future attack: Africa was the ancestral land, a great and special place from which great and special people came, and the white man lied about it just as he lied about everything else. Where the influence of church connections to Africa was strong, this early image was more likely to be cast in a kind of benevolence that was intended to be reassuring, but nevertheless still was of a dark and dangerous place—happily, quite far away—inhabited by a mass of heathen, uncivilized, black (but also very distant) kin toward whom one had the duty to be helpful. Sometimes, finally, the beginnings of the "aversion" to Africa appear in the simple and unavoidable association of "Africa" with "slavery," because for many people the slave past was the source of all shame and weakness and it was best to blot it out of mind and memory, and Africa along with it.

It is obvious that whatever the varieties of experience, even

this earliest awareness of the African background quickly became something much less elementary. It was linked with other
vital matters, with attitudes, feelings, values, patterns of behavior coming from one or both parents, coming out of the
family's particular place in the Negro scheme of things, or, soon,
coming upon the child from the outside. It took on a continuous
and continuing character, playing its peculiar part in each person's self-discovery and becoming imbedded in the common
usages and habits of mind and speech in everyday life. And here,
to begin to illustrate the nature of these complications, I ask the
reader to reach back among the many individuals glimpsed in
the pages of those previously quoted studies and take the hand
of that one lonely child and hear again his cry of pain and anger
at being taken for *cannibal, evil, black, African*—for he is the
one who tells us that what we have been learning is not "new,"
only unnoticed or ignored, unmentioned or, until now, unmen-
tionable, and this because it is so close to the real heart of the
matter.

Insofar as I dare generalize from my certainties about the particular individuals I have interviewed, I suggest that the heart
of the matter is this: that the systematic debasement and self-
debasement of the Negro in this white world has begun with or
been underpinned by the image the Negro child has gotten of
the naked, savage, uncivilized African. I think I can pinpoint
this even more specifically and say that for the Negro school
child it was the picture of his contemporaneous ancestor that
stared out at him from the pages of one of the first books he
ever held in his hands. Wonderingly he turned the pages of the
geography text from which he was to learn the nature and shape
of the world and there (*"down on the right-hand side of the
page!"* remembered one person) was the portrait of his origins,
the picture of himself, the reason (as the text often inferred or
flatly said) for his lowly backwardness and his dim prospects.
The memory of those pictures is etched so sharply on so many
of these minds that they would come off in swift prints, every
detail vivid, every emotion alive, even after 40, 50, even 60 years;
a moment of discovery never really lost again, though often long
hidden in deep, deep places and brought up only now to view,

perhaps because only now this particular button of the memory had been pushed, or perhaps because it is easier to face this memory now that the defense against it can be so much stronger. Some examples:

I opened a geography and saw Africa represented by a naked African with a headdress, some feathers around his middle and a spear . . .

In the books there were pictures of black-complected people with ugly-looking hair . . .

In Frye's geography . . . horrid pictures of cannibals and savages . . .

. . . a typical representative [of each of the five races] and the African was shown with an elongated head and prognathous jaw, and it said the black race alone had made no contribution to civilization.

We were shown people, wild, pagan, hopelessly inferior, heathen-looking animalist types. Even the Indian was painted with greater dignity than the Africans in these books. It must have been in the primary grade at six or seven that I saw these pictures.

In Carpenter's geography. It had the continents and the five races. . . . They selected the best Nordic type for the white race and the ugliest to represent the Negro, the picture of an African tribesman with a bone through his nose, earrings, and a fuzzy mop of hair.

One man said it all, swiftly and succinctly in these sharp, angry sentences:

In the fourth grade, those pictures of the races of man . . . with a handsome guy to represent the whites, an Indian with a feathered hat, a Chinese and an East Indian, and then a black, kinky-haired specimen—that was *me*, a savage, a cannibal, he was just the tail end of the human race, he was at the bottom. . . . That picture in the book was the picture of where and what I came from. I carried that idea along with me for years.

I believe that here, by the side of these children, remembered in their classrooms, heads bent over these books so long ago, we are brought close to the most critical elements in Negro responses to the African background. Let us peer over their shoulders, then, and try as best we can to look at those textbook pages with their eyes. What were they seeing?

If they were looking at some of the same textbooks now before me [10] they were probably seeing a set of five pictures grouped on a page to represent the "five races of man," or else samples of the five spread out over several pages. Usually the largest, always in the center or the most prominently placed, was the representative of the "white" race. For this role, the publishers usually cast a dignified-looking gentleman dressed in the Sunday best of the time, with stiff mustaches, stiff collar and smooth lapels, high of brow, clear of eye, with a calm, assured, vigorous look about him. In one of these arrangements he is an Emersonian figure of a man, shown seated in his library, shelves of books behind him, tomes on the table and floor, a globe and telescope close to hand, and a small child at his side, obviously imbibing his kindly and patient wisdom. In another text, where the preferred stress was apparently on beauty rather than brains, the representative of the "white" race was the head of a Greek statue, its classic features in frozen profile. Its caption, added with objective grace: THE WHITE RACE—AN IDEAL HEAD.

The representatives of the other races adjoin or surround the "white" prototype. The "brown" man or "Malay" is here a sharp-faced, glint-eyed individual with a white turban wrapped around his head; or there he is dressed in a graceful robe and carries a shiny kris, or wavy sword, in his hand. The "red" man or "Indian" is a virile, stern-faced man with a feather in his hair, or in another instance, in the full dress of a chief standing against a background of tepees. The "yellow" or "Mongolian" specimen appears in a variety of guises, here a well-dressed Chi-

---

[10] Cornell's *Grammar School Geography* (New York and Cincinnati, 1860); Warren's *Common School Geography* (Philadelphia, 1870); A. C. L. Arnold, *This Living World* (Boston, 1875); Frye's *Complete Geography* (Boston, 1897); Frye's *First Course in Geography* (Boston, 1906, 1917, 1920); Ralph S. Tarr, *New Physical Geography* (New York, 1912); V. M. Hillyer, *A Child's Geography of the World* (New York, 1929); Van Loon's *Geography* (New York, 1932). I am indebted to Mrs. Laura Farnsworth for locating these and other texts in the New England Deposit Library, and to E. S. Whitney Thompson for his M.I.T. seminar paper, "Elements in the Image of Africa and Africans as Presented in Geography Books," Jan. 1960.

nese merchant type with drooping mustaches and a round black hat, or there an artist's conception of what appears to be a lordly Japanese aristocrat surrounded by kneeling servants.

In all these cases the "black" or "African" or "Ethiopian" man invariably appears, by great contrast to all the others, at his most primitive. Thus alongside the Emersonian white man in his study, the Japanese aristocrat, the Malay nobleman, and the Indian chief—all obviously selected to depict the highest social rank in each case—a comparable figure might have been an African chief in *his* best clothes. Instead, in this particular instance, the "African" appears as a prehistoric figure of a man, naked, stepping out of primeval ooze, carrying an antedeluvian club and shield. In another example of this style of contrast, one text classifies the states of man as "savage" (who are "all black or red"), "barbarous" ("chiefly brown"), "half civilized" ("almost wholly yellow"), and "civilized" ("almost all belong to the white race"). In the accompanying set of illustrations the "savage" state is depicted by two black men fighting, one with a club, the other with a spear. At the "civilized" end of the scale we discover that Emersonian man again, complete with books, globe, telescope, maps, and small boy reading.

It is this enormous contrast, presenting the black man at his least elect and the white man at his most distinguished, that leaps first of all to the eye from all these pages. It appears no less even in those portrayals where the intent is strictly to show different physical types and where this is done with some degree of straightforwardness. In one of our examples the African appears in profile, with heavy prognathous jaw, thick lips, flat nose, a striking, even handsome face, lent a certain air of barbaric rakishness by a necklace gleaming on his bare black neck, and a heavy ornmental ring of gold dangling from his visible ear. The white man in this set is, again, an impeccably dressed bourgeois gentleman, style of about 1912. This kind of deck stacking with pictures has gone on continuously from way back then until now.[11]

[11] I am indebted to my son for calling my attention to the 1947 edition of *Compton's Pictured Encyclopedia*—a major item in his own early boyhood library—in which we again find (Vol. 12, p. 11) an arrangement of pictures of

Even before we outgrew the crude anthropology of the "five races" it was obviously possible to select from a wide variety of types with which to fill the indicated boxes. It is hardly necessary to dwell upon the inward persuasions that led to the choices that were generally made. If you can imagine inverting the biases consciously or unconsciously at work in this process, you might then see the "white race" represented not by a Greek god or Benjamin Franklin or the model of a Harvard professor but, say, by a picture of one of the Jukes, a mugshot of Al Capone, or, to make the selection on more purely esthetic grounds, someone with the looks of Charles Laughton, W. C. Fields, or Maxie Rosenbloom. The "black" man in such a case could appear not as a primeval savage or a stupid and ugly villager but, say, as a haughty Zulu chief, or even with the leonine head and strong face of Frederick Douglass, or, if we come down to more familiar times and faces, someone with the look of Jackie Robinson or Sidney Poitier, Sekou Touré or Jomo Kenyatta.

Other varieties of such self-defensive inversions were in fact beginning to appear late in the last century in the so-called "race" literature produced by some Negroes, countering the universal debasement with a doggedly insistent self-glorification. This defense had its value, and among some of our panelists remembering here their childhood experiences there were a few who were able to fall back on these counterclaims as bulwarks against the universal assault. But far more commonly the Negro child had little or nothing with which to withstand it. The evidence of the black man's inferiority was borne in upon him with all the weight and authority of the all-knowing, all-powerful, all-surrounding white world—all the irresistible force of white learning set down in books.

The portrayals that came upon the Negro child in the school placed the "black" man (who was supposed to represent him) or the "African" or "Ethiopian" (his ancestors or kin) at the bot-

---

"the five races of mankind." Here the "African Negro" appears as a vacant-faced African villager. The brown man is a "Malay chief," a handsome fellow with a great mustache. The American Indian is a chief in full headgear. The yellow man is a richly attired Chinese. The white man is represented by a picture of Benjamin Franklin.

tom of every scale used to give value to men. They made him the least of all men in his attributes and his achievements, with the least of history, the least of culture, the least of brains, the least of beauty, the least of everything. If he did not take this in from the pictures, it was spelled out in the text, which told him that Negroes were members of the "lowest and most degraded class" of mankind, that the "white race is superior to all others in intelligence, energy, and courage," "that the Ethiopian is unintellectual and unprogressive" as compared to the "active and enterprising, highly developed" white man. (By this particular account, incidentally, the "Mongolian" race is "sullen and sluggish" while the American Indian is "stern, moody, not emotional.") Here is a passage from a text called *The Earth and Its Inhabitants,* published in New York in 1886:

According to physiologists, the blood of the Negro is thicker and less red than that of the whites. It coagulates more rapidly and flows more sluggishly. The Negro, like the yellow Asiatic Mongol, is of a less sensitive temperament than the European. He suffers less under surgical operations, and runs less danger from their consequences. His nervous life is less intense, his pulsation less active, than that of Europeans. . . . Unfortunately for themselves, the Negroes are the most docile and devoted of servants. Anthropologists have remarked on their essentially feminine type as compared with that of the whites. They are generally noted for their soft voice, scant beard, delicate articulation, pink nails, velvety skin, and rounded muscles. . . . They are timid and inquisitive, jealous and coquettish, great gossips and scandal-mongers, quick to love. . . . Like so many women, they also delight in abject submission, even sacrificing themselves for those who despise and oppress them. Hence from the remotest times, the blacks were most highly esteemed as slaves.

The Negro child must have read passages like this with a sinking feeling; the knowledge he acquired from it dropped somewhere into the deepest bottom of his being. He already knew or was in the process of painfully or subtly discovering that he and his family and all Negroes lived at a level well below the whites, that they had been the white man's slaves, and were now the lowliest of folk in every department of American life. He was also learning that Africans were black people in Africa also living under the power and rule of the white man, still living in primitive ways, uncivilized by all the Western, modern, Christian, *white* norms which his family and all his people basically accepted as desirable and superior.

What the textbooks did now was to "confirm" and "explain" both these facts by citing the authority of both nature and history. This inferiority, they "showed," came out of the black man's inherent racial character, and this was "shown" not only by his status here and now but also by the whole history of his kind; not merely their history of shameful enslavement in America but even their remoter history on a dim and dark continent in a dim past which had left neither literature nor monuments, coming on down to the present in which they were conquered people and burden bearers for the superior white man.[12] In this way even the simple truth that a great many Africans were living in Africa in primitive ways became a hateful truth, and pictures of them, even the simplest and most straightforward pictures, became hateful pictures. To the extent that the Negro child identified himself with these Africans in the pictures, he accepted proof of his own lower worth and justification for his own lower status. This was reason enough for him to dissociate himself from them in any way he could, to look away in painful rejection, to say, or hear his parents say,[13] that he had nothing to do with those Africans, that he was civilized, Christian, did not live in any jungle, did not go about naked, and neither did his folks or anyone he knew.

[12] In his novel *Stranger And Alone* (New York, 1950) pp. 42–48, Saunders Redding has sketched not a child but a college student being introduced to the subject of black inferiority by a white professor, sitting "through lecture after lecture feeling his selfhood to be no proof against those drumming words, feeling that he was hearing the indisputable artillery of scientific truth." He found this "truth" in his books, "supported by footnotes and cross references" and all he knew, all he had seen, felt, heard, read, supported them. "He stared at himself in the mirror and desperately wished he were white."

[13] There is a glimpse of this, from over a high, high wall, in Booth Tarkington's *Penrod and Sam*, in an incident in which Penrod and Sam, playing at being in the jungle, get two Negro boys to strip down to play the roles of black beaters for the hunt. The mother of the Negro boys appears with a lath in her hand and whacks both her boys. "My goo'ness, if yo' pappy don' lam you tonight!" she is made to say. "Ain' you got no mo' sense 'an to let white boys 'suade you to play you Affikin heathums?"

The response spirals down, a landing below mere backwardness and primitiveness to the darker level of savagery. Not merely in these textbooks but in a thousand subtle ways all the white man's ways toward the Negro suggested his inner view of the black man as an animal, simple and childlike when well tamed, but down deep somewhere not merely primitive but primeval, full of nameless mystery and violence that might burst forth at any time. All the wild and savage instincts of unregenerated man were seen as infinitely closer to the surface of a black skin than to a white, and this was intimately linked to the sexual urges and fears that have played their own deeply complicated role in the relationship between Negroes and whites in American society.[14] These pictures of his black-skinned contemporaries, living now in Africa, their bodies naked and daubed, wearing the feathers and skins of the birds and beasts with whom they shared the jungle, and sometimes described as cannibals, all of this spoke for a great and fearful animalism that the Negro in America was made to feel was the source of his own untouchability. This too, in whatever wordless thoughts, the Negro child felt as he contemplated these images of himself, and this is what he shrank from in them.

By a thousand invisible channels, through all the great fine mesh of capillaries in the white man's vast and all-enveloping system, this was the only "truth" the Negro child got: that his people, insofar as they were African, were ignorant, primitive savages who had added nothing to the stream of human culture and existed today only at its outer edges, that this was why *he* was hopelessly behind, backward, inferior himself, and had to be grateful for the benevolence and grace that had saved him, even though it was via slavery, from the worse fate of his forebears. All the ambivalent angers and confusions over this experience are poignantly recalled from his boyhood by a man who rose to be a noted leader in his field:

14 Writing of propaganda against the Negro, Carl Rowan gave this example from the 1905 novel of Rev. Thomas Dixon, *The Clansman:* "One drop of Negro blood makes a Negro. It kinks the hair, flattens the nose, thickens the lip, puts out the light of intellect, and lights the fires of brutal passions," *New York Times,* National Urban League Supplement, Jan. 17, 1960.

The textbook pictures made you ashamed, and white kids would point to them and (in effect) say: these are *your* forefathers. Ain't you ashamed of your ancestors, and ain't you glad we rescued you? I got a lot of this. We *were* ashamed. *I would fight over this even though I agreed with it.* It was all I knew and I had no skill to measure it by.

He tried to beat back with his fists what he believed to be the damaging truth about himself, fighting back blindly in angry protest and rejection of the fate this "truth" imposed on him.

This "truth" pursued him not only in the alien classroom or the hostile streets, but also as we have already seen, into his own church where accounts by or about missionaries, even when more benevolently cast, had very much the same overall effect. But these images of Africa and Africans were magnified most of all through what had become, in these same growing-up years of most of the members of our panel, the most powerful of all the mass media: the moving picture. The neighborhood movie house, its pictures about Africa, and the feelings aroused by them appear again and again in these recollections:

This was Philadelphia with all the Negroes sitting upstairs and all the whites downstairs. When a picture about Africa and Africans would come on the screen there would a great howl from upstairs, like a kind of laugh. It was something funny, and I always wondered why. I didn't know why. I had the feeling they were laughing at themselves and didn't realize it . . .

I remember a movie of British troops landing and dispersing a mob of howling Africans and saving whites, and the Negro kids in the Howard theater howling with glee and applause for the English . . .

The movies, always some tribal group and some missionary in a pot, or Africans thinking that every white blonde that came along was a goddess. I was glad I wasn't African. It made me think I wasn't so bad off . . .

Always a bunch of tribesmen with rings in their noses, all Africans were supposed to be savages. . . . I don't think I felt myself akin to those savages. Africans were so very different from the kind of people I knew. At that time "African" was synonymous with cannibal . . .

I hardly ever went, but every once in awhile I did see savages. There was something painful, sort of embarrassing about it. I suppose it was because that savage was black like me and was making a fool of himself in front of the whole white world which laughed at him and exploited him. I wanted not to be identified with that! . . .

I remember at a movie about Africa, a nervous kind of laughter, and snide, contemptuous remarks about nakedness, kinky hair, blackness, even though they [the kids in the theater] too were black or had kinky hair . . . It made me nervous and uncomfortable, because they were making fun of people who in many respects were our relatives . . .

With this we spin on down to where that sinking feeling leads. We have come past the fact of backwardness, past the charge of inferiority by heritage, past the implications of savagery, and we come finally to what I think is the bottom of most of these wounding memories. This is the shrinking from what is seen as the ultimate badge, and perhaps even the source of the inferiority and the savagery both. It appears again and again in the words and phrases that speckle these recollections: "blackness," "kinky hair," "a black, kinky-haired specimen," "black-complected ugly people with ugly hair," "with an elongated head and prognathous jaw," "fuzzy haired, features on a flat plane," "animalist types." It is in fact the African's blackness, his features, his hair, his very Negroidness itself that rises up out of these pages, looks down from the screen, and smites the child, and inflicts the wound from which the pain never passes. This is the impact of it because, as a great mountain of evidence testifies, the Negro had it borne in upon him, and he took it in and made his own conviction that blackness was ugly, that blackness was evil. And this blackness was African.

So these, in the end, are the key words in this complex history of debasement and self-debasement: *primitive, savage, African, black, evil.* Separately or in different combinations, these are the keys to much that lies hidden in the inner chambers of the mind. They reappear in the openness of life as attitudes and beliefs, cryptic reactions and responses, in the epithets of daily exchange. Some fleeting examples from the interviews:

If a child was very dark and had kinky hair, he would be scorned with, "You look like an African!"

I had an aunt who . . . when the kids got out of hand would say: "You little black Africans" or "You little fuzzy-headed Africans!" She herself was quite light.

To call a kid an African was an insult. It was calling him savage, uncivilized, naked, something to laugh at, a naked black savage with a spear and war paint. It was equivalent to ugliness, everything painful and distasteful associated with Africa. . . . In common talk the term was always derogatory—"You're acting like a wild African."

The worst thing anybody could say to you in addition to calling you "black nigger" was "black African."

In this darting phrase, *black African,* we come, I believe, to the heart of the heart of the matter.

In the American Negro universe the word "black" became the key word of rejection, an insult, a fighting word. Prefixed to any name or obscenity, it multiplied the assault many times. I suggest that every time black was used or perceived this way the word *African* came after it, whether it was actually spoken or not, whether it was there or remained an echo in the mind. For the Africans *were* the blacks, the source of all the blackness, the depths from which all had come and from which all wanted to rise. Africa was the "darkness" they wanted to leave behind in order to rise to the "light" of the white man's world, his religions, philosophies, his ways of life. Hence the social prestige and inherent virtue of the lighter skin acquired from actual kinship with the white man; hence too all the artificial efforts to achieve the same effect by those whose white antecedents did not show plainly enough on their skins and faces or in the hair on their heads. Hence the pride in mixed forebears, the white, the Indian, the "Spanish," in anything but the African. Hence the ambivalences and confusions at the margins of the dominant white society, the self-hatred, the "yearning after whiteness" which, as some Negro writers have tried to show us, shaped so much and sickened so much in Negro life. Hence the whole elaborate structure of caste based on color—and here the measure of the distance from blackness (or from "bad" or "ugly" features or hair) was precisely the measure of the distance from Africa. Even the obscure and turgid controversies over the words "Negro" and "colored" come from this, for they are linked in a host of acknowledged and unacknowledged ways to these attitudes about blackness and beyond the blackness to Africa. Surely it was no accident that the pull back to Africa expressed in the Garvey movement was also an aggressive pull back to blackness, or that the re-emergence of Africa now is having as one effect the re-establishment of some virtue, even beauty, in blackness; the Kwame Nkrumahs and the Tom Mboyas are destroying more than the crudest of the old stereotypes. This is the root of the matter, I believe, for at bottom the Negro's rejection of Africa was his rejection of himself, and this was the principal stuff of which the "aversion" to Africa was made.

# 4. REJECTERS, INQUIRERS, AFFIRMERS

Each person's response to these childhood discoveries of Africa was deeply bound up with the way in which he came to view himself. This view of self, or sense of identity, sometimes emerged clear and strong, fashioned by the individual out of his unique gifts, his particular inheritance, and the conditions of his environment, and hardened by struggle to change his estate; composed as it is, our present panel is filled with impressive examples of this achievement. At the other extreme this self-view is dominated wholly by the white man's image and evaluation of the Negro; this has led to much enfeeblement and human failure. More commonly in between, it is a view of self that remains forever blurred and unsettled, a pattern of chronic ambivalence and uncertainty, almost always deformed by some measure of the anger, shame, or self-hatred that became part of the Negro American's common lot, relieved only by the power for derisive laughter that became part of his common defense.

Each one's response to Africa is part, then, of the larger pattern of what each man or woman is, and that is why, as I now try to group these responses as I found them, I propose to let each person speak as fully as possible for himself. In this way the reader will also appreciate just how complicated these feelings really are, and how wide are those foggy spaces where different attitudes and emotions keep running into one another. I trust that it is clear that the purpose here is to report these different views, not to pass judgment on them. If they are arranged along a scale and given some labels—rejecters, inquirers, affirmers—it is not to establish any order of merit or demerit or to place them in tight and separate compartments, but simply to mark out some of the plain or shadowy differences among them.

## The Rejecters

Most of the members of this panel by far reacted to their early discovery of Africa by trying in one way or another to undiscover it. The common state of indifference or unawareness of Africa was often a true remoteness from the subject, reflecting its low priority among the many other problems of a person growing up as a Negro in American society in all these years past. But it was also often the result of an effort of the mind to thrust it away, to ignore it, to deny or minimize any significant connection or kinship between Africa and oneself, an automatic closing of internal hurtproof doors.

This was a part of the much more inclusive process of denial and self-denial to which so many Negroes, in common with members of other despised minorities, have been driven. If all the inferiority stemmed from Negroness, and Negroness stemmed from blackness, and the ultimate sources of both the blackness and the Negroness lay in Africa, each person could, according to his character and color, seek his own cutoff point. He could try to cease being a Negro. He could downgrade blackness. Most easily of all, he could divorce himself from Africa. Some who were "white" enough did the first, "passing" right out of the Negro community. Some who were not "white" enough but desperately wanted to be succeeded only in ending up among the pathological case histories. In its more viable form this same condition turned up in Negro life as color caste. But there were still many who were too Negro, too healthy, or too intelligent to carry their self-rejection quite so far. They could not or would not deny their identity as Negroes, nor their blackness, perhaps not even that famous "one drop." But they could, with much greater ease and reasonableness, cut themselves off from Africa. And this many of them commonly did.

We find some form of this divorce from Africa in the accounts of at least two-thirds of our present panel of selected individuals. The kinds and degrees of this rejection vary greatly, and although we will try to order these responses by some of these varieties, they will mostly have to emerge by themselves. Let me start with some examples in which the sense of detachment from Africa is most strongly put, where the early recall is dimmest, and where it seems that even any newer interest in the subject still rises reluctantly or not at all. The following quotations are all from interviews. The first is from a scholar:

As a child I remember my mother and father talking about African classmates they had at college, they were brown, Moroccans—not black. Nothing after that until college at Fisk; Africa as a factor in international relations. . . . I can't even remember Africa as a subject in geography at school. I can't call it up. My interest in Africa came late and it is still limited, not only limited, but I have numerous inadequacies on this. When I was working on my lectures and writing, I had to work very hard at it. I have great difficulties in sustaining my interest and retaining knowledge about Africa or any part of it. There is almost none of the sentimental interest I see in some Negroes. It fascinates me, but I don't seem to have it.

Again, from a noted public figure:

I don't have any recollections of first impressions about this. I learned very early about American Negroes going to Africa and founding Liberia, childhood discussions of slavery, in a general way the history of the slave trade, but no formulated picture of contemporary Africa. I suppose I shared the general vague picture Americans had, and I suppose still have: a place by our standards backward, "uncivilized,"—I don't think I varied too much from the stereotype. We were all brought up in the same public schools. I have no sense of any tie between me and Africa. My father and mother did not talk of or identify with Africa; no personal identification. At no time in my career have I been in contact with African problems or leadership. There is a legend in my family that one of our ancestors on my mother's side three or four generations ago was supposed to have been a princess of Madagascar. Heard this in my childhood. It is the one thing I can recall that smacks of any kinship or personal identification linking me to Africa. There was no reading on this in my childhood, and right to high school. Had a high-school teacher once who was interested in the Negro's African heritage. I was interested, but I don't think I had any feeling that I was the kind of person I am because of my African background, or as a mixed-blood product of white ancestry. I have no recollection of rejecting or affirming. I suspect that the African scene was too far

removed from my experience to be a force one way or another. . . .
It has not been central in my thinking, though I am enough of a
chauvinist—if this be chauvinism—to have some special interest in
what a community dominated by persons of Negro blood does.

Note the unusual guarded tightness ("Just geography and the
movies, nothing special") in the following, from a well-known
individual:

[Encountered Africa] in college, studying political science, international affairs, colonial problems. Before that, just geography and
the movies, nothing special. Hollywood stuff. Discovered it the same
way I discovered other parts of the world, the existence of Asia, Europe. I never had any special interest in Africa, never had a feeling
of kinship, except in the same way that a third- or fourth-generation
American may think of his remoter background. I never had any
personal feeling of this. I make no distinction between Africans or
Malayans. . . . The question never really rose with me, not in church
or in school or when I came up in Detroit or in Los Angeles. . . .
As far back as I can go in thinking, my interests and my becoming
aware of the Negro problem were concentrated on the struggle for
the rights of Negroes here as Americans to be identified with American society.

One of the best known of all national Negro figures reflects the
familiar early experience and the onset of recent changes:

In school I read about cannibals. It meant nothing. You didn't
ever associate with them. That was in Pasadena. You would see movies about dark Africa, cannibals, read stories, but all this had no connection to me. I had problems of my own. Maybe this was because
I didn't want to associate myself with Africans. . . . Why? Why I
looked at those man-eaters—nobody ever pointed out any of the good
things—and I didn't want to be a party to that. I never really gave
it much thought, but I have begun to think only recently that this
is probably the reason why I never gave it much thought; that is,
that I didn't want to be party to it. Many Negroes are having just
the feeling that I now have. I never really recall any talk at all
about Africa until here lately it began to loom so large all over the
world. From my mother I got the knowledge that Negroes had come
from Africa, but we never traced any family tree about it and I
didn't associate myself with it.

All the individuals quoted so far have one thing in common: they are all people who have crashed through the "big gate" from the Negro world into the larger white world beyond. There is a certain suggestion in this that the further a person has moved across that threshold, the further he is likely to be from Africa in almost every way. His early encounters were either less sensitively experienced or, more likely, with latter day success, are less sensitively remembered. He is, in any case, less concerned with any African ingredient in his background or individual makeup. He is a man who has established his individuality not only as a "Negro" but as a particular person whose gifts have wrung recognition from society at large. To this extent he has "solved" (if that is the word) the problem of his own individual identity. If he has any problem, it is more likely to be the problem of his continuing identification with Negroes as a group. He is usually a "first" Negro to have achieved this or that distinction. Because of this, he occupies a special place on both sides of the racial line and only most rarely can he manage to ignore this fact. A complicated set of internal and external obligations closes in upon him and if he fails to meet them, a peculiar guilt attaches to his failure, a special visibility attaches itself to all his behavior.

A similar complex of identification and obligation still trails after individuals of other minorities as they rise to distinction; Catholics and Jews both experience it. But members of these groups are now strung out along the further, more open slopes where there is much more space, many more paths to travel outward and upward, where the group barriers are pushed to more distant boundaries, and are, for most people, quite out of sight. Here individuals can and do outdistance the trailing-group tie much more easily than the Negro can. The Negro is a much more conspicuous figure as he steps through that gate out from among his fellows, hemmed in on that last narrow ledge he has just surmounted, or massed in pain and hardship and in plain sight further behind and below him. He carries with him a responsibility not only for himself but to them, and this can sometimes become a burden of anger and despair. But he is likely to be a man already carried by his own gifts too far toward some broader human (or intellectual or artistic or professional) identification to be drawn very willingly backward toward some narrower conception of himself bounded by race or color, much less to a far continent of his remoter origins. He is a particle of proof that the American dream works, and this is where he wants his commitment to stand.

Among these, and other successful men who stand nearer, at, or still just behind that "gate," you often get the most vehement insistence on being *American,* a refusal to entertain any notion of a hyphenated identity like "Afro-American," and a strong resistance to the idea that the attraction of emergent Africa in any way reduces their intentness on achieving successful integration in America. This comes out clearly in the strong words of a public official:

I have no personal affinity in thinking of Africa, though I am unquestionably tied to it many generations back. I think no more of Africa than a fourth- or fifth-generation German thinks of Germany. . . . I don't think my sympathy for the underdog goes to the African any more than it goes to anyone else. I consider myself an American. I am interested in *all* of these foreign problems, but as an American. . . . This goes all the way back to my childhood, missionaries in our church, lectures, collections. . . . There was never any sense of family connection, but we heard lots about it. . . . I gave my dimes and I would have done so for the Eskimos too. There was no unique pressure on us as Negroes, people in white churches were doing the same thing. I think that then, 35 to 40 years ago, as now, we saw ourselves as Americans, not as anything else. We never wanted any association with any nationalist groups, any of the "go-back-to-Africa" movements or the Communist ideas of self-determination for Negroes. All such thoughts were anathema. . . . Today very few of us would seriously consider going to Africa or doing anything more than giving sympathetic support, and this only because if the African gets his place in the sun, the lot of the Negro in the U.S. will be 10 times better.

As we move on back among those who, though in the front rank, are tied more and more closely in with the group as a whole, we find that the tone of rejection becomes sharper, and more of the reasons for it begin to appear. A first example, from the words of a major civil-rights fighter:

It must have been early, perhaps at about five, when I had the problem of not being able to keep on playing with a white boy, and my mother tried to explain the system to me, and told me about slavery; and Africa was mentioned, the slaves from Africa. In school I think it was in the early geography books, a country of jungles, primitiveness, an impression never really corrected. For a long time the American Negro was ashamed of his African heritage and his early American heritage, so he tried to get as far as possible from the discovery of it; tried as far as possible not to identify with Africans. So even a college student grew up with misinterpretations. This was my experience. I definitely did not want to have anything to do with Africa right through high school.

Here, more sharply put, the recollections of a prominent churchman:

As a young boy [it was] all negative; cannibalism, the Sunday-school literature, naked women, heathen, tribal masks. The worst thing anybody could say to you in addition to calling you "black nigger" was "black African." You spent most of your time trying to dissociate yourself from Africa, being ashamed of it. You got this through the churches, through discussion at home, through talk of the racial patterns, lamenting our sad and sorry state, the slaves, and how they got here. Also out of the white newspapers, magazines, books, and the pictures they gave of Africans.

The elements of ancestry, color, Negroidness begin to bulge in knobs along the smoother surfaces of the view a man gives of himself. Three vivid examples:

If a child was very dark and had kinky hair he would be scorned with "You look like an African." . . . *African* was a symbol of inferiority, my family and others always made disparaging, contemptuous remarks about Africans. Anything connected with Africa was inferior. But when these things were said, I didn't have any notion that they included *me*. My ancestors were European, American Indian, and African and my father always stressed our Indian ancestry. He had a huge portrait of a Cherokee Indian, his grandfather. He laid heavy stress on this, that we were not mainly European or African, but Indian. All my uncles looked like Indians . . .

Africa has been a subject of interest to me, its history and the missionary concern, but I have felt no ties, or ever identified it even as ancestral. This was not only a matter of feeling mixed ancestry. I had a friend who was quite dark, who had no identification with Africa either. . . . As a kid I looked on Africa as any American did, a savage, pagan land, needing missionaries—though I quickly got over the idea of thinking of any people as savage. . . . This is a problem, this problem of ancestry—came up quite late. The African background was a truth that you knew, but it had no importance. There is the problem of the mixed blood of the Negro in America. He has so many ancestors, white, Indian, Negro. It was a question never too well known in detail or thought about too much. None of my grandparents were in any way related to Africa. They were American Negroes, not Africans. . . . I was taught the stereotypes about Africans. This was part of Americanization, all Negroes, all Americans were taught thus. *But I wasn't in it.* Nothing led me to resent it. I simply wasn't concerned. These were savages and benighted heathen. Nobody was talking about any of *my* folks! . . .

The movies, pictures of cannibals, stupid, running around half naked with spears. . . . Hardly admirable, looking at uncivilized people, feelings of embarrassment, of identification with these people. I mean embarrassed among my white chums and playmates, because I would feel that these people were my ancestors, not just some natives, always cannibals, always sacrificing a white maiden. There would be great applause when the white hunters came along in time. I would sit there embarrassed by the whole thing, angry. . . . There in the movies were my ancestors. My grandfather would have said it was ridiculous to call them our ancestors. In my family a big point was made of our Indian ancestors. My great grandmother was a Shincook Indian, a big bronze-colored woman with beautiful straight gray hair. . . . At college there were African students. They were the victims of our rabble. We respected their scholarship but we made fun of them. Lincoln [University] was a rough place and the Africans were the butts of many jokes . . .

And every once in awhile these elements break through into plain view:

When I was in school, seeing somebody from Africa was like seeing a white elephant. We had Africans at Tuskegee; people didn't regard them as the same as us. They were strangers whom we looked down on. They didn't have anything to offer. Earlier, in classroom, never anything but just the location of Africa. At home, nothing at all, no talk at all about it. In books there were pictures of black-complected people with ugly-looking hair. They didn't have anything to do with me. I don't react to this. I have no impression of any connection to Africans, just none at all. At Tuskegee I studied history, began to trace things back. But it never did impress me with any idea of connection. It was true as far as race was concerned, but I never got close to it in any way, just some reading about it. I never did consider it seriously. I don't think anybody did. I haven't changed on this. I always think the African is a black person, just as black as you make them. Over here we all got tampered with, so we got different colors. It is easier for a person my color to trace his white ancestors than to trace his Negro ancestry. . . . No attention to Africa at all. Our church takes up a collection for a Negro mission in Africa once a year. This is about the only time I heard of it. . . . I have read about Ghana. I sympathize with it, but that's about all. I have seen some slides and movies, showing the improvements that have been made. I guess we have got to change our way of thinking about Africa.

Some of these individuals reflect a certain shift of view that took place as they matured, not leading them by any means toward a more positive African identification but rather toward a more critical appraisal of what they had been taught to think about Africa and what it implied for them as Negroes. This experience appears in the account of a noted writer and critic:

As I got over these Americanized stereotypes about all peoples, including Africans, I came to resent them with their stories on savagery. I resented Vachel Lindsay's poem *Congo* for what it said about the American Negro. I was reviewing books in *Opportunity* then, books about Africa and Haiti, and I developed a defensive feeling for the human quality of Africans which was not in these books. This was not a sense of identification, but it was a certain tie, because they were all Negroes, and I wanted the Negro character treated more honestly. I tried to read up on the Africa background in order to understand how it figured in the case of the Negro in American life and literature. I read people like Sir Harry Johnson, the explorer, on African character—"short memories, mercurial"—he was much quoted on Africans and these characteristics were applied to the American Negro. I was battling against that kind of thing. It was not proved about the African and certainly had nothing to do with the American Negro.

## The Inquirers

This brings us, on our way from the rejecters toward the affirmers, into a small company of men to whom neither label can quite rightly be attached. They all went through much the same common early experience of discovery of Africa, were exposed to the same images, saw the same pictures on the same screens, and reacted with all or many of the same emotions. Like the rejecters, they generally resisted the notion that there was anything but the most remote kind of kinship between them and Africans. But unlike the rejecters, they did not thrust the whole matter so violently away from them. Like the affirmers, whom we shall shortly meet, they had strong impulses to resist the crushing negativism of the images they were given of their forebears and of themselves. But unlike them, they did not try to do this by transforming all these negatives into positives. Hence we discover them taking attitudes of tentativeness, sometimes of skepticism or outright disbelief, of entering reservations, of waiting to see what more there was to the whole matter. They were still often ambivalent, angry, or guarded; but they were also essentially open, curious, demanding to know more.

The striking thing about these different individuals—and they are very different, indeed, from one another—is the fact that they all went on to become either scholars or journalists. Let me hasten to add at once that this implies no universal equation: there are other scholars and other journalists located at every point in our spectrum. I should perhaps also note that the qualities of mind that led them to take inquiring attitudes are sometimes the same qualities that make men capable of creatively reconstructing the past. But this can be entered here only as a most limited reservation. Each of these particular men has a distinctive style of his own which he has made known to sizable publics of readers and listeners over many years, and it is only in the interest of consistency that I preserve their anonymity in these quotations. Let them appear now for themselves in three examples, beginning with the somewhat transitional views of a scholar:

Frye's geography in the third or fourth grade, horrid pictures of cannibals and savages. Missionaries in the Baptist Church, supporting in the main the initial images from the geographies of wild savage peoples. . . . You began to get other things from Negro history. This was before Carter Woodson or Benjamin Brawley. It must have been Du Bois' *Souls of Black Folk*. My father had no use for missionaries. He thought they were the "least reliable" in the ministry. He respected Du Bois. I think it must have been Du Bois' essays on the slave trade. Anyway, I certainly knew of this before I went off to school. . . . I remember once saying in class that Africans sold some Africans, and having an argument with a teacher who disagreed with me.

I can't remember anything my father ever said about any of this. He was at least three-quarter Negro, from Jamaica. He died when I was seventeen. I had a vague idea of some kind of heritage in Africa. My mother's side was mixed. Her family had a tradition of free ancestors and white slaveowners in Virginia. . . . As far as I was concerned, I had no sense of direct identification. I was not like any of those people. . . . I was to be a minister, the fourth of my family line in that role. My ego was not involved. There was nothing in the climate of being a Negro before I went to high school that made Africa anything but a distant part of my background, with only the most passing suggestion that it might be something meaningful to me. . . . But Negro history interested me. I read Brawley, knew Carter Woodson, who used to come to our house. At Morehouse High School I roomed with an African, Harry Maponyoue, who had tribal marks and spoke rather poor English, but who described tribal life in a way nobody ever had. He taught me an American hymn in his tribal language. I can still recite it. It was rather ridiculous to me, I suppose. But in my college time, Africanism was being promoted as a subject with which Negroes should be familiar. This was stimulated by the Association of Negro Life and History and I began getting interested in it.

A man who became a journalist and then one of the major figures in the civil rights struggle:

There was always some reference to Africa in my home when I was a boy. I was never unaware of Africa. I started to read *Crisis* very early and read Du Bois on Africa and as I grew up I learned more and more about it. . . . Our church, the A.M.E. church in St. Paul, always had a bishop in Africa and here I had very early contact with it. Got the typical missionary viewpoint of people badly needing help, with some warmer overtones because of our special interest and identification. It was different, say, from Lutherans or Episcopalians doing this sort of thing . . .

There was not much in school. The regular geography and history treatment. . . . We got that picture of Africa as a dark continent, savages, uncivilized people . . . that fellow with the bone through his nose. . . . When I was at college at the University of Minnesota [1919–23] we had a South African there; he belonged to our church and Sunday school. He was studying animal husbandry, and went on to study medicine. I got from him a personal image of an African.

I would say I got the notion from my boyhood that Africans were people, different, but not savages. I had no definition of any relationship, though there was the connection of color. I had no sense of it being my homeland, or regarding them as kin, or Africa as the old country. Nothing about ancestry, really, only a color connection, a kind of remote kinship.

You see, you had an ever-present feeling engendered by your own treatment that you got because *you* were "different." So you questioned the popular concept of Africans as given by the movies and ordinary channels of information. You would always question it when somebody described Africans as "ignorant savages." This was not identification—the average Negro certainly did not identify with Africans—but this was my image of them. And then there was Du Bois hammering on Africa, on art, history. . . . I know this had hard going among Negroes for acceptance. Only a few bought it. I did not buy it wholly, but I did not brush it aside. . . . It seemed to me that Negroes in America were rootless, were kept completely in ignorance about their own history and I think Du Bois was making propaganda against this ignorance . . . to offset the depressing propaganda that held Negroes down.

The posture of detached curiosity comes up most clearly in this self-picture by a senior Negro journalist:

When I was a little boy, when I could first read, I had books on Stanley, Livingstone, and things like that. The A.M.E. church began missionary work way back in 1850, so the subject of missionaries in Africa came up in our household. I knew about Africa, the slave trade, Liberia, that American Negroes had founded it. I have followed all the major events affecting Africa for the past 55 years or so. I have had a continuing interest in Africa from as early as I can recall and I am sixty-four now.

I knew I was of African descent. When I first studied geography, about 1902, I remember well that the map of Africa had blank spaces with the word "unknown" and I wondered: Unknown to whom? How about the people who were there? This helped me realize that what you saw in a book depended on the point of view of the writer. They presented the people as they undoubtedly were, naked, carrying spears and shields. I never took umbrage at that. There is nothing more wrong with carrying a spear than with carrying a Colt. The early textbooks I had didn't particularly stress cannibalism, but I never took offense at this idea, because I came to know something of the international character of cannibalism. Most Negroes are too hypersensitive on this sort of thing, taking offense.

For my part, my only identification was the fact that we originally came from Africa and I simply took this for granted and I was always interested in learning about it. I read about how Freetown was founded. I read books by Negroes like George Washington Williams. I heard of Edward W. Blyden, the great Negro historian who went from the Virgin Islands to the United States and then to Sierra Leone. Of course we all knew about Menelik's defeat of the Italian Army in 1896. We knew about the wars of the Zulus in South Africa, and the Boer War. I used to seek information about all these things in the library in Syracuse. I also remember Williams' and Walker's musical comedy *Abyssinia,* about 1905, with the song in it, "My Castle on the Nile." . . .

[The idea of going back to Africa] keeps cropping up all the time, and you still have many Negroes emotionally involved with Africa— Bishop Turner, Chief Sam, then Garvey. I thought the Garvey movement was fanatical. I was of the group that thought the American Negro is American in every way, has been here a long time, is doing pretty well, that the Negro had only a sentimental identity with Africa and there would have been less of this if they went there. . . . You still have a lot of people, especially on the lunatic fringe, with sentimental attachments to Africa.

## The Affirmers

Besides rejection and inquiry there is also, in a substantial minority of our panel, a strong measure of affirmation about Africa. There are more positive emotions about it, more accepting views of it, and these appear in different forms and at different times in the lives of those present.

Right now there is the brand new current of fresh response to newly emergent Africa, with its promise of great transformations and a new standing for the black man in the world's affairs. But going back in time, there are some individuals who came out of their childhood discovery of Africa with the characteristic rejection and withdrawal and carried this view with them until later, in youth or young adulthood, when they came upon people, books, or experiences which caused them to revise their attitudes. A first example, from a noted educator:

> From missionary publications and from visitors in and out of our home, I got a picture of Africa as a land of savage, illiterate people, living in the wilds of jungles, with hardships and handicaps; the dark continent, not a place you would like to go to. In my own family we were very mixed and had white connections. I never thought of Africa as *my* homeland, or part of *my* background. But at high school in Livingstone College, I had J.A.K. Aggrey [the great African teacher and leader] as my teacher for five years. Aggrey was a coal-black person with no mixture at all. He was a noble, intelligent person. . . . Then I was sent to school in Virginia, and there I had an African boy as a roommate and he is now a member of the Ghana Supreme Court. In my early environment, the general idea was of African savages, primitive, and in need of enlightenment. But after these contacts, I didn't look down on Africans.

The account of a noted minister:

> I definitely did not want anything to do with Africa right through high school. But in college I had a classmate and friend from Nigeria who gave me a new appreciation of Africa. We discussed it a great deal and I began to read about it, books by Carter Woodson, articles in the *Journal of Negro History*, the writings of Du Bois, and [I began to see that] the system in the United States and colonialism in Africa were both based on contempt and exploitation, so

there was an identification in the sense that we are all oppressed people, and were also related racially . . .

Or this, from a top figure in Negro journalism:

At first I was ashamed of Africa and of Africans, from the first time I opened a geography and saw Africa represented by a naked African with a headdress, some feathers around his middle, and a spear, witchcraft, disease, the dark continent. But then at Tuskegee, I began to learn about it. I met some African students there and they were not savages. They were strong and alert people and gave me a new appreciation for Africa. There were several teachers who went back and forth and there were always some African guests coming and going. This became part of the whole growing interest I had in black people . . .

An editor:

I didn't connect African inferiority to myself. It didn't bother me until later, when I learned what it meant. Not until I was in high school and at Virginia Union and started reading books by Du Bois, Carter Woodson, Franz Boas, did I realize the other side of this. But I didn't develop any sense of identity with Africans until the 1930's. I connect it with reading Maurice Delafosse's *Afrique Noir*, a history of the African kingdoms of Benin, Timbuctu, and Ghana, and learning that Africans had produced civilizations comparable to those of Europe.

A final example, a woman artist:

I will never forget my third-grade teacher, who one day when the subject of Africans came up, said: "They had nothing to do over there anyway. They just ran around dressed in banana leaves." I took this as a terrible blow. Then of course there is the fact that I am dark, and got discrimination from within the race itself, even among my friends as a child, I would be called "You African!" sometimes jokingly, sometimes as a curse. All through my growing-up years this was how I was received . . . I came to feel a certain deep shame at everything about my being a Negro. I even felt ashamed when spirituals were sung. Then at Hunter College I had a friend, a Jewish girl named Judy, who made me feel different. She took me to museums and made me look at exhibits of African sculpture, and made me begin to learn something about Africa. I came to realize that what I had been feeling ashamed of was slavery, not Africa. And I started seeking to know more about it.

But we are interested most of all at this point in the small number of individuals who say they responded to Africa affirmatively from the beginning, from the time of their childhood, at home and in school. Like all the others, they describe being exposed to the same images of backwardness, savagery, inferiority. Like everyone else, they resented and rejected these images. But unlike the rejecters, who thrust these images away, or the inquirers, who wanted to know more about them, these individuals reached out and grasped Africa for their own. They identified with it. They affirmed their kinship with it. Some examples:

As a child I just resented those pictures. I didn't reason or know much about it, but to see the pictures of the five races and to show *my* picture in that distorted form—I would see it as false and inside of me there was a resentment against these books by white men. We didn't believe it. We believed we were kin to the Africans. They represented our ancestry and we respected our ancestors like all nations do . . .

I remember the pictures in the book, of naked savages with rings in their noses and the most forbidding kinds of facial decorations designed to show them as the lowest stratum of the human family. My brother and myself just didn't believe it. We felt a revulsion and anger. We had been told that *we* came from Africa, and this was a reflection on us. We had been conditioned to racial contrasts and we connected ourselves to these people of the same color who were shown as savages and saw this as part of the propaganda designed to show we were degraded. We learned from our father to accept Africans as our kin and Africa as the homeland of our forebears. We had been taught that the colored world was not without history and past . . .

I think I saw Africa as a place where black people had their country, and that it would be mine too; no particular place, just Africa. As the U.S. is a white man's country, Africa is the black man's country. Blackness must have come in here in some degree, but I don't remember anything impressing me about color solely . . .

Among the members of our panel, there were eleven who

describe this early, positive, accepting view of their ties with Africa. How were they different from all the others? Why did they as children reach for the hot, black coal of Africa as they did?

The beginning of the answer appears in their ages: four are past seventy, three are in their sixties, two are closer to fifty, and only two are under forty. This tells us that most of them are old enough to have been influenced by the beginnings of the movement to regain race pride, to beat back the whips and scorns of time and the white world's contumely, to refute the charges of the Negro's lack of history by re-establishing the racial past and reasserting its greatness. This effort was fueled and nourished by scholars and writers, and it had its guardians and propagandists in a particular class of doughty ministers who forever kept summoning their people to a better sense of their own worth. It is unsurprising, therefore, that of our present group of eleven positive affirmers, four were sons of ministers, and the fifth, brought up in a strong churchgoing home, became a minister himself.

Obviously there have been all kinds of ministers, all kinds of ministers' sons. Various types are sprinkled even through our present panel and reflect shadings of attitude and experience in all its parts. Moreover the church, as we have seen, was the source and communicator of some of the most benighted and lurid images of its people's African kin. But there were two kinds of impact made in some churches that sometimes produced the effects we see in these particular cases.

The first was powerfully evangelical, covering the whole subject of Africa with a thick coat of devoted benevolence, a dedication to black-Christian need denied by white-Christian malevolence:

My father was a minister and I grew up in the church, National Baptist Convention, and I learned everything through the church; met all kinds of people passing through and visiting, and all sorts of things about Africa I gleaned from them. I have always known about Africa. I can't name the beginning. Sometime early I heard the great Negro missionary Sheppard, who told us about the mutilation of people in the Congo. It made an indelible impression on me.

In the humblest Negro church there was a willingness to give in order to send missionaries, an interest in peoples' need of the Gospel and a special interest in Africa because we knew we were descendants of Africans. Myself, I have always known this. I had a school principal who talked to us of the colonial empires and white domination and predicted to us that the people who were doing this would destroy themselves. I was eleven or twelve, and this made a profound impression on me.

The other kind of impact was made by a certain kind of minister, often a black man, but always a strong "race" man, a preacher who made the whole Gospel a vehicle for raising the race not only to Heaven but to some higher place in its own estimation. An example:

At home my father, mother, and grandmother all spoke of Africa. The text that "princes shall come out of Egypt and Ethiopia shall stretch forth her hands to God" is the earliest passage I remember learning from the Bible. It meant that the Negro people wouldn't always be down, that they would come up again. We were always taught that the Egyptians were Negroes and that other Negroes once had power in the world, and that Africans would come up again among the rulers in the world. . . . From when I was a baby at home with mother, we knew we were African. We resented the schoolbooks that made the African a heathen-looking animalist type. The Sunday-school books were better, with pictures of Philip the Eunuch, the Queen of Sheba, the wife of Moses, Negroes in the Old Testament; those old Sunday-school cards, you will find them reproduced in glass in the church I built in Louisville, where we have bronze angels in the windows to make the children know that they have heroes in their color.

Another vivid recollection paints a portrait of the father of a very famous Negro:

My first important recollections about Africa are from my father, who was an A.M.E. minister in Florida. He used to talk of Africa— "And Ethiopia shall stretch forth her hands. . . ." He believed that Christ and Moses were colored, that angels were not white, that the white man was the work of the devil. He was a strong racialist. I heard first of Ethiopia. My father told us the history of Egypt and Ethiopia, of ancestry going back to a dim past, and that this was our ancestry. He was a very black man and very ardent. . . . My brother and I were avid readers of racial literature. The whites had a flood of literature to drown every bit of racial pride and we swam against it. When I was still in school in Jacksonville, I knew about Frederick Douglass and Nat Turner. I was quite precocious because of my father's interests. . . . Then I read Du Bois' *Souls of Black Folk* about when it appeared. I was sixteen or so, and my brother and I gloried in the language of it, the poetry of it . . .

There was quite another source for an early affirmative view of Africa: West Indian origin. There are two individuals in our present group—the two who are in their fifties in age—who were children of families that migrated to the United States about the time of the First World War. This means that they came out of a background which was often much more aggressively race conscious than its American counterpart and were raised in the peculiarly intense atmosphere that produced and was produced by the Garvey movement. One of them, clutching her mother's hand, went to Liberty Hall to hear Marcus Garvey himself, and the second, already a bit older, went despite his more indifferent parents to hear the great man, to take in the excitement, the fun, the high color, and the fine great noise of it. Here are their accounts:

When I was seven, the Garvey movement. My mother was a member of the Universal Negro Improvement Association, and I went to meetings with her and heard it discussed at home. . . . Africa as a homeland was not a new idea. My mother's great-grandmother came from Africa when she was still old enough so that she remembered being brought to the West Indies. I grew up as a little girl with African tales told and retold by my mother. I later found these much resembled popular West African tales. When I was ten, we had a Nigerian student, a Moslem, staying with us. In my growing years there was always some African friend around, seamen, students, always someone from Africa in association with us . . .

I always knew Africa was the land of my ancestors and the origin of my race. My people knew Africans in the West Indies. . . . In school I heard about the Africans, slavery, and so on. But I never thought of Africans as savage. I came from an environment that knew Africans and knew them not to be savage. I never had the classic attitude which saw the African that way. What I learned at home was a bulwark against what was said outside. The outside view embarrassed me. I was embarrassed that I should be equated with that savage on the [movie] screen. I used to get very annoyed in the movies. As a kid I read Aggrey. I also lived only half a block from the Garvey headquarters in Harlem. Had a tremendous experience with Garvey. Have written about it. Living half a block away I couldn't help but be influenced by it. I attended the church of St. Benedict the Moor, a black man, and I would sit there every Sunday, for years and years, and see that statue of that black man.

These two individuals illustrate the fact that the West Indian origin is by no means the whole story. There are others of West Indian background in our panel who appear at quite different points in this spectrum of early attitudes about Africa. And even these two remind us that there are always other sets of reasons that lie beyond the obvious. Sometimes these are still on the surface, like the color of one's skin; and one of these individuals is indeed quite dark skinned, has never been freed of the sense of being an alien in the American environment (including the Negro-American environment), and looks with a complicated passion toward Africa for an end to this special apartness. The second, on the other hand, who happens also to be much lighter skinned, locates himself at quite the other extreme of expectation. With his acceptance of African kinship, he is also a strong believer in and a well-published prophet of successful integration in American society. So it is not a matter of being a West Indian—a little more, perhaps, of being a certain kind of West Indian—but most of all, it is a matter of being a certain kind of person.

This brings us directly to a last group of individuals who had an affirmative view of Africa precisely because each one was a certain kind of person having a particular kind of experience. They were not attached to Africa because they were West Indians, or had read Du Bois in their childhood, or were the sons or daughters of strong raceman preachers, but because of some special aspect of their uniquely individual private lives. A first example:

My father didn't think in a very complimentary way about Africa. He was proud of his Indian background. His mother was a full-blooded Indian, and she had contempt for Negroes, and would speak with contempt to my mother. But my mother was interested in the history of the Negro and I was conditioned from childhood to think of Africa as a land worth knowing. Her grandfather had come from Africa and was proud of his origins. He was a Mohammedan and I had an uncle named Mohammed and his son, my cousin, collected African art objects. They almost deified their African background, and they had a great influence on my mother and on me too. I never thought much about this in the years of my young adulthood, but it gave me the background I needed . . .

In young adulthood this individual married a recent immigrant from Africa, and later, "accidentally," became involved in a life's work relating to Africa.

Or consider these recollections of a well-known educator:

Africa makes me think of my black grandmother who, I heard, did not like my mother because she was brown. My grandmother wanted my father to marry a lighter woman. But I admired her. She was a wonderful old woman who, when emancipation came, farmed for herself, raised her children and sent them to school. Granny, to whom I never talked very much, had a sister, Aunt Mary, also black, though they were both supposed to be Negro-Indian combinations. Aunt Mary talked a lot, both about Indians and Africans. She was a very old lady and it is quite possible that since she was probably born about 1830, her own grandparents had come from Africa. . . . In school I remember the geography, the horrible picture of the African in it. We had it around the house and I discussed it with Aunt Mary. It was insulting, not true. I think this is always with me. It was insulting because I was one of these people described as the "black race" and I knew black people, Aunt Mary, my mother and father, and they were not like that. . . . At Lincoln, I heard Aggrey and he made Africa wonderful. . . . Most students were indifferent to Africa, but some of us formed a group called "Sons of Radical Africa." I had a sense of Africans being my brothers, part of my family, so it became my imperative duty to resent any ill done to them. . . . When I pray and say "Bless me and my folks" I include an old woman I saw in a church in Nigeria who looked just like Granny, and I think of the tunnel I saw where the slaves were brought to be loaded onto ships, where my ancestors were carried out, my blood brothers.

There were, finally, two others who turned up among these positive affirmers, sharing this common view of early experience of Africa across a wide gap of difference in years, settings, and experiences. And it turns out, in one of those suddenly arresting coincidences, that there was something else they had in common: the fathers of each of them had strong race views, were successful in business, had decided to migrate to live freer lives, and had chosen, many years apart, to go to Mexico for this purpose. But these two are writers, and we are about to see how they and a group of their fellow writers have dealt, over a period of time, with this matter of Africa and their ancestors.

# 5. DU BOIS AND AFRICA

Of all the writers of books who helped to shape the thinking of the members of our panel, none was mentioned more often than Du Bois. His name recurred again and again as early memories were summoned up of how each individual discovered his world and the meaning of his place in it as a Negro. Mostly the Du Bois influence was associated with the issues of the struggle for rights in the society, but it was also a reflection of his impact that these issues were linked, much more often than not, with some kind of a rediscovery of Africa or an alteration in attitudes toward it. Here is the way some of these memories came up in our interviews:

I learned of Du Bois at my mother's knee, and she finished in a one-room four-year school in Markham, Virginia, and we were poor people. All the Negro intellectuals of my generation and those born up to 10 or 15 years later were his disciples . . . The international aspect of his thought was very little noticed, however. It was a question of our posture vis-à-vis the whites . . .

I've known of Africa all my life, from Du Bois' *Souls of Black Folk,* from *Crisis.* . . . The way Du Bois presented Africa was beautiful and inspiring. . . .

Du Bois' history of the Negro in the 1920's gave me my first assured knowledge of the history of the Negro in Africa. . . . Du Bois is responsible for [changing attitudes on color] . . . In one of his books he glorified the dark and the brown, used phrases "satin black, golden brown, warm ebony," and people can now find a black girl beautiful, whereas 40 years ago nobody would have . . .

I remember Du Bois from early girlhood . . . Swallowed his work whole. I never thought he could be wrong about anything . . .

I first read Du Bois' *Souls of Black Folk* in my home, and his novel, *The Quest of the Silver Fleece.* . . . He writes, my father

195

would say, but he doesn't lead anybody . . . But my father also felt the evils of oppression and responded to Du Bois' lashing out at discrimination. It was a sort of catharsis; a way of going out and shooting all those white people . . .

It was very seldom a black person would admit he was "black." Du Bois used "black" deliberately to attempt to overcome this.

It seems like I have been aware of Du Bois all my life. I read him first at least 50 years ago . . . I was in high school when I read in *Crisis* about Du Bois' Pan-African Conference in 1919. His name was a household word. His sentiments were those of my family, though my father didn't like Du Bois. He thought he was too cold, too aloof, not human enough with ordinary people.

I remember getting angry when I heard Du Bois speak to a packed house in Louisville in which he kept referring to Christianity as the bringer of all evils through the ages to so many people . . .

You couldn't discuss anything with Du Bois. You had to listen to him. If you challenged him he became indignant and showed it by becoming manifestly discourteous . . .

Du Bois was rude to Arthur Compton at my table and I never invited him again . . .

Du Bois was strapped in by his aristocratic stance. He appealed to the intellectual, but his intellectual quality was really quite low.

I think Du Bois would be very ill at ease in a contemporary discussion by Negro intellectuals about Africa. . . . He was a cocky and proud guy who could not pass on the one hand, or identify with the mass of colored people on the other . . .

These recollections come from some men in their seventies and some in their forties. Some go all the way back to 1903, some only as far back as 1933, but after that they fade, reflecting how Du Bois himself, in his last quarter century, has faded from people's minds. One of our panelists reported:

Three years ago I asked a class of students, "Who is Du Bois?" Nobody knew any more about him other than that he was a "great man." Some didn't know his name at all.

Let us have a look, then, at this man who occupies such a

special niche in the minds of so many older Negroes, a lesser one among the young, and who among whites has remained throughout hardly known at all.

The lifetime of William E. Burghardt Du Bois, the most prolific of all American Negro writers and intellectuals, spans nearly the whole century back to Emancipation. He was born in 1868, had his first book published in 1896, and has been writing continuously ever since. His works include sociological studies, essays and sketches, biography and autobiography, history, novels, and poetry. As editor of several different series of scholarly papers and pamphlets and of several periodicals, he fathered still more words, especially in the volumes of *Crisis,* which he founded in 1910 and edited until 1933, the period of his greatest personal impact on the affairs of Negroes in the United States. Never a successful leader or organizer or even a popular public figure, Du Bois with his words alone scratched deep, life-changing marks on the minds of a whole emergent generation of aspiring Negroes as it came to its youth and maturity in the first three decades of this century.

Du Bois' impact began in 1903 with the publication of *The Souls of Black Folk,* still his most famous and best-remembered book. In it he openly took issue with Booker T. Washington, until then the undisputed and unchallenged leader of American Negroes. Du Bois called upon Negroes to abandon the posture of submissiveness and modest aspiration that Washington counseled them to hold, and instead urged them to stand up to and fight for their rights as men and citizens in the American society. Instead of the limited system of education-for-work that Washington promoted at Tuskegee, Du Bois called upon Negroes to reach for the heights of all learning and to produce that famous "Talented Tenth" to lead Negroes to the full enjoyment of freedom. In 1905 he and a group of cothinkers launched the Niagara movement to promote these aims, and in 1910 he joined with a group of white liberals to found the National Association for the Advancement of Colored People, becoming its research director and the editor of its organ, *Crisis.*

In the columns of *Crisis* for the next 23 years Du Bois made himself the most eloquent tribune of the fight for civil rights and equality of opportunity for Negroes, lashing, arguing, cajoling, pontificating, fighting white injustices with slashing journalism, savage wit, and fierce polemics, and fighting black weaknesses with every weapon he could grasp. He fostered pride in Negro history, Negro achievements, and Negro good looks. He coaxed out artistic talent, ran issues devoted to college graduates, budding writers and artists, and beautiful babies. And ever and always he set forth in his own articles and editorials his own strong views of issues big and small in the Negro's fight for equality. In addition, almost as an extracurricular activity to which even his Negro readers paid scant attention, Du Bois organized between 1919 and 1927 four Pan-African Conferences in an unsuccessful attempt to give world scope to the black man's struggle for freedom from the oppression of the white. But his editorial performance was spectacular enough, pushing *Crisis* from an initial subscription of 10,000 to a top of 104,000, a figure small in looks but large in meaning because it included all Negroes who had set their faces upward and were pushing at the barriers for better education, political freedom, and better economic opportunity. It was a stormy editorship, because Du Bois, a prickly and vain man, was no easy associate. His object was to influence people, not to make friends, and he succeeded to a remarkable degree. Du Bois has written, sometimes sadly but more often complacently, of his special aloofness, and especially his aloofness from any personal contact with whites. From his earliest days he preferred to accept being glassed in—a figure of speech he has himself used. It was a withdrawal he liked to see as proud and austere, but it was really much more like the shrinking of a porcupine inside his armor of rising spines. A biographer will one day pursue this thread of self-separation through all the reams of Du Bois' writing about himself and about the world. It will help explain why, when he reached a time of despair after 30 years' struggle for integration and equality, he reverted to a program of self-imposed isolation for Negroes, a plan for growth-within-the-ghetto that took him all the way back into the shadow of Booker T. Washington.

In the same way, a biographer who seeks to put this man's parts together again will have to see the links and the spaces between his persistent elitism, his delight in elegance and aristocracy, his half-digested Marxism, his belief in power and authority and in a "Talented Tenth" to lead the slower-moving mass, and his slow gravitation toward the international Communist movement, ending in the last decades of his long life in a close embrace—indeed, a marriage—with totalitarian Communist world power. Over most of his active years Du Bois' attitudes toward the Soviet Union and the Communist Party were conditioned, like everything else in his life, by considerations of race. He held the Communist Party in rather scornful disdain most of the time for its gross ineptitude in the "Negro question," but he warmed to the Soviet Union early for its anti-colonialism and for what he believed to be its abdication of the color line. In the 30 years since he left the editorship of *Crisis,* Du Bois moved first for a confused interval toward self-segregation and then more and more steadily into the camp of the Communists. In doing so he drifted into greater and greater isolation from Negroes in general, from most of those who still admired him for the great days of his past, and indeed from any significant contact with American or Western society. It is hardly accidental that Du Bois finally turned for his compensations and realizations to the emergent world of Communist power only when he could begin to see in it the verification of some of his prophecies of doom for the Western white world, the instrument for the defeat on the largest possible scale of the Anglo-Saxon dominators who were always his prime foes. In return, the Communist empire has given Du Bois the eminence and recognition of which he felt deprived in his homeland and even among his fellow Negroes in these last decades of his long life. In 1958–59, Du Bois made a long journey across the Soviet half world from Prague to Peking, and he was showered with honors by Communist universities and leaders in country after country. Responding to encomiums offered on his ninety-first birthday on February 23, 1959, in a speech broadcast over the Peking radio, Du Bois gave his thanks and he said: "In my own country for nearly a century, I have been nothing but a nigger." [1]

Even a thumbnail introduction of W. E. B. Du Bois stretches from paragraphs into pages and thereby illustrates some of the difficulties of our task. He has already been the subject of a first book-length biography [2] which barely begins the task of telling his long story. I want here to try to show how Du Bois has dealt with the particular matter of the Negro relationship to Africa, but this by no means narrows the compass. For Du Bois, uniquely among the writers to be discussed in these pages, made Africa one of the central themes of his thought and his writings. On it he centered some of his most personal and some of his largest dreams. In the re-creation of Africa's past he saw the means of regaining for all Negroes the pride that he clung to so strongly in himself. For the reconstruction of Africa's own present and future he produced his vision of Pan-Africanism in a world of colonies reconquered by the nonwhite races from their white overlords. On these subjects he hammered away at his audience for year after year, re-educating some, stirring a few, but meeting most of the time that deep unresponsiveness to Africa which not even he, alone, could overcome.

Nor in dealing with Du Bois and Africa is it possible to deal any less with Du Bois and race, for, as he has put it himself:

In my life the chief fact has been race—not so much scientific race, as that deep conviction of myriads of men that congenital differences among the main masses of human beings absolutely condition the individual destiny of every member of a group. Into the spiritual provincialism of this belief I have been born and this fact has guided, embittered, illuminated and enshrouded my life.[3]

When Du Bois made the familiar boyhood discovery that to be a Negro in a white-dominated world was to be despised and rejected, his own reaction was to cut himself off for life from all but the most superficial personal contact with white people. But

---

[1] *The New York Times,* Mar. 5, 1959.
[2] Francis L. Broderick, *W. E. B. Du Bois, Negro Leader in a Time of Crisis* (Stanford, 1959).
[3] *Dusk of Dawn,* pp. 139–140.

the problems of whiteness and nonwhiteness were part of some of the deepest issues of human society in times that were, as always, out of joint. Even while holding himself haughtily aloof behind that famous "veil" of which he wrote so often, he could put his gifts, glands, and powers to work to set things right, not for himself (he was above it, he always said) but for all. And this is what he set out to do. All that he has been and done in his life has been aimed to settle the score created by his racial identity and to do so in the largest possible arenas.

No matter what his subject or format, Du Bois has been writing autobiography all his life, and yet he has always managed to brush quickly past those episodes of his childhood that precipitated him into his life's struggle. He was born in Great Barrington, Massachusetts, and grew up there in a fatherless home. He shared the schooltime and playtime of his early years with white boys from the middle-class upper crust of the burgeoning industrial society of that small mill town. His natural impulse was to gravitate toward the top. He says he was in and out of their homes, "except [for] a few immigrant New Yorkers, of whom none of us approved." And again: "I cordially despised the poor Irish and South Germans who slaved in the mills, and annexed the rich and well-to-do as my natural companions. Of such"—he adds self-appreciatively—"is the kingdom of snobs!" His discovery that he in his turn was also despised came, he says, more slowly.

Very gradually—I cannot now distinguish the steps, though here and there I remember a jump or a jolt—but very gradually I found myself assuming quite placidly that I was different from other children. At first I think I connected the difference with a manifest ability to get my lessons rather better than most and to recite with a certain happy, almost taunting, glibness, which brought frowns here and there. Then, slowly, I realized that some folks, a few, even several, actually considered my brown skin a misfortune; once or twice I became painfully aware that some human beings even thought it a crime. I was not for a moment daunted—although, of course, there were some days of secret tears—rather I was spurred to tireless effort. If they beat me at anything, I was grimly determined to make them sweat for it! Once I remember challenging a great, hard farmer-boy to battle, when I knew he could whip me; and he did. But ever after, he was polite.

As time flew I felt not so much disowned and rejected as rather drawn up into higher spaces and made part of a mightier mission. At times I almost pitied my pale companions, who were not of the Lord's anointed and who saw in their dreams no splendid quests of golden fleeces.[4]

Unsurprisingly, it was a girl who brought on the first great climax in the discovery of his Negroness and set him on his way. In a schoolhouse party one day the youngsters were gaily exchanging visiting cards and all was merry until one girl—a newcomer—"peremptorily, with a glance," refused Will Du Bois' card.

Then it dawned upon me with a certain suddenness that I was different from the others; or like, mayhap, in heart and life and longing, but shut out from their world by a vast veil. I had thereafter no desire to tear down that veil, to creep through; I held all beyond it in common contempt, and lived above it in a region of blue sky and great wandering shadows . . .[5]

In another version of this episode, describing his flight from the pettiness of individual slights and insults to the larger shapes of things beyond, he gives it the literal form of a race to a hilltop:

Then I flamed! I lifted my chin and strode off to the mountains, where I viewed the world at my feet and strained my eyes across the shadow of the hills.[6]

His straining eyes began then to see all the other Negroes in America, then all black men everywhere, and before long all the nonwhites in the world. He stretched his view to all the great continental arenas, America, Europe, Asia, Africa, and even, on some of his steeper rhetorical flights, right up into the unwalled and gateless spaces of Heaven itself.

It is difficult to resist a parenthetical pause here to explore the beginning of this process a bit further, for Du Bois offers

[4] *Darkwater: Voices from Within the Veil* (New York, 1920), pp. 11–12.
[5] *The Souls of Black Folk*, p. 2.
[6] *Darkwater*, p. 11.

the biographer a striking example of one of the ways in which intensely personal and powerfully impersonal forces can combine to shape the drives that make a notable life. Erik Erikson, in *Young Man Luther*,[7] has described this process of score settling in a psychoanalytic framework, showing us some of the less obvious underpinnings of Luther's career. Luther became the one to shake and change his world because of a whole complex of historical circumstances which provided the opportunity and a whole set of uniquely individual gifts and drives which led him to seize it when it was offered. Erikson suggests that one of the deepest and most decisive of these drives came from his great outward push from the issue of his relations with his own father to the issue of the Christian's relations with his father, the Pope, and man's relations with his Father, God. The Du Bois story suggests a certain rearrangement of weights and measures in this kind of analytical outline.

A great reformer or world changer who comes out of a dominant group in society may acquire his score to settle in some intensely individual experience in the parental and family setting in his earliest years; the biographer alerted by Erikson will perhaps find such experiences in the lives of men like Franklin Roosevelt or Woodrow Wilson at depths he might otherwise fail to sound. But the world shaker who comes out of a despised caste or class has a score to settle even before he is born, before he has ever opened his eyes or first seen the faces or heard the voices of those first beings who hover over him. It is there in his situation, ready made and waiting for whoever, out of whatever unique combination of personality, history, time, or social circumstance, will seize upon it and meet his own deep need by forcing society to meet the collective need of his fellows. This element is to be found in a Simon Bolivar's mixed blood and the stigma attached to it at the Spanish court, or in a Nehru, stung by his automatic subjection to British assumptions of superiority. The unique life experiences of such men help tell us why they became *the* men who did what they did; but the target for their energies had been there, waiting for them long

[7] (New York, 1959.)

before their fathers and mothers had combined to make them or tried, the one or the other, to break them. Every revolutionist or reformer has had a father to contend with, but that does not mean that all revolutions, all great reforms, have been at bottom against fathers.

In the case of a Negro coming up in American society, a host of common and special features appears in the making of each individual personality. In our present group, consisting almost entirely of men of considerable achievement, it would be a matter of no small interest to try to assemble some of these shaping factors: the presence or absence of a father in the early years, the nature of the father and mother and of their relationship, the special roles of grandparents, uncles and aunts, friends, and even of strangers so often called upon to play the roles of substitute parents. Then there is all that appears in their own adulthoods, the shape of their own life experiences, the making of their own families, the raising of their own children, or their childlessness. Many of these things, to be sure, gave many such men and women their uniquely personal scores to settle; the panel includes some notable examples of this. But it was rare that even these did not become entwined with all the elements of race imposed on each one's pattern of self-discovery and self-assertion—the items of color, of caste, and the great overhanging pressures of the white world. It was perhaps something about this ready-made and common identity, as well as the white world's myopia, that helped form that feeling, expressed by almost every Negro writer, that their Negroness had deprived them of their individuality, glassed them off from the world of men—as Du Bois put it—or made them "invisible"—as Ellison had it. Whether or not this became part of any one man's picture, the big score to settle was nevertheless always there for all of them, awaiting the challenge that some one man, given the gifts and opportunity, might try to solve in the larger areas of life.

Du Bois is hardly to be classed as a world shaker or world changer. Other Negroes have been far greater as leaders and played much larger historic roles. But he did reach for the larger role, and though he failed to grasp it, he did make an impact on men's minds and even perhaps on events. Both in its public and private dimensions his life story offers most of the standard materials for such a case study. He came up in a fatherless home, and he has written much about his grandfather and about his forebears and about his life to suggest all kinds of clues to the course of his development. But except by their own mixtures of racial backgrounds through which they passed on the great tangle of ambivalences and confusions with which the young Du Bois rose to wrestle, none of his forebears, immediate or remote, "made" the issue which guided and enshrouded his life and made him what he was.

Under the towering shadow of his racial subjection, the Negro child generally learned some way of accepting his fate, of turning his hatreds and frustrations upon himself, and in one way or another upon his fellow Negroes. But always out there, beyond himself, his family, his kind, was the great white world to fear and to hate, which he did, and to defy only if he dared. Whatever his sins or failings, or whatever his father's or mother's, they were—or could be seen as—part of the weight of the sins of society so heavily visited upon them all. I am sure that deep analysis of each individual case would eventually unravel all the inner connections, but I notice all the same that up to now in literature written by Negroes and in the autobiographies that have partly unfolded before me in so many of these interviews, it has been only rarely that a father has cast a larger or longer shadow across a youth's life than the larger, longer, more dominating, more threatening and, until now, seemingly unchallengeable figure of the white man. Perhaps we must wait until the age of deprivation passes and this, too, appears more commonly among the gifts of tomorrow's freedom.

Du Bois, then, from his hilltop, linked himself to the whole world of nonwhiteness. In the beginning this meant regaining contact with Negroes. From the isolation of Great Barrington he did not go at first to Harvard, as he had dreamed of doing, but was content enough ("after a twinge, I felt a strange delight") to be deflected to Fisk, where he came into the company of other Negroes.

I was thrilled to be for the first time among so many people of my own color or rather of such various and such extraordinary colors, which I had only glimpsed before, but who it seemed were bound to me by new and exciting and eternal ties. . . . Above all for the first time I saw beautiful girls. At my home among my white school mates there were a few pretty girls; but either they were not entrancing or because I had known them all my life I did not notice them; but at the first dinner I saw opposite me a girl of whom I have often said, no human being could possibly have been as beautiful as she seemed to my young eyes that far-off September night of 1885.[8]

At Fisk he not only related himself to other Negroes and especially to beautiful young Negro girls, but with the same romantic idealism about race he also, for the first time, embraced Africa.

His great-grandmother ("black, little, and lithe") used to "croon a heathen melody" to her children, and the song came down in the family to become "the only one direct cultural connection" Du Bois ever had to his African background as a child. But his upbringing was "not African so much as Dutch and New England," and he came to Africa only after discovering that New England rejected him. He says this clearly:

My African racial feeling was then purely a matter of my own later learning and reaction; my recoil from the assumptions of the whites; my experience in the South at Fisk. But it was none the less real and a large determinant of my life and character. I felt myself African by "race" and by that token was African and an integral member of the group of dark Americans who were called Negroes.[9]

When I interviewed the aged but crisp Du Bois in his Brooklyn home, I pressed him a little to look back down the years all the way to Great Barrington to see what else about Africa might have brushed him in his boyhood. He first again mentioned the African song that had come down in his family. No, he did not remember reading about Africa then, though he devoured everything the Great Barrington library had on its shelves. "The

[8] *Dusk of Dawn*, p. 24.
[9] *Ibid.*, p. 114.

books I remember taking out were books on English history and such. If I had sought books about Africa there, I doubt that I would have found any."

"And in school?" I asked.

"I was tremendously incensed that there was nothing in the textbooks about Africa," he said. "Only pictures of white men, no pictures of colored or black men, and this began to get me curious."

Did he mean, I asked, that no pictures of people accompanied the mentions of Africa in those first textbooks? And here Du Bois came up with his own report of the familiar experience. "We did get pictures of the races of man," he said, "a white man, a Chinese mandarin, and the savage Negro. That was what the class got and it made me especially sensitive. I did not recognize those pictures in the book as being my people.

"Africa," he went on, "was not a major thing in my thought or any part of my experience. My first real acquisition of any of this was at Fisk, where they had the beginnings of an African museum, some pieces like that one up there—" and he pointed to a small carved figure of stone on his mantelpiece. "But Africa still never came to the center of my thought. It was something in the background. There was always a lack of interest, a neglect, a resentment at being classed as Africans when Negroes felt that they were Americans. Interest in Africa did not begin with anyone until after 1880 or so. . . . I did not myself begin actively to study Africa until 1908 or 1910. Franz Boas really influenced me to begin studying this subject and I began really to get into it only after 1915."

Du Bois' tie to Africa remained pure racial romance, whether he related to it as an individual, as a propagandist for the greatness of the Negro's past, or as a geopolitician of race, a dreamer of great dreams of Pan-Africanism as part of a general re-emergence of the world of nonwhites brought together by their common history of slavery, discrimination, and insult. All of this appears together in a single passage in his 1940 autobiography:

As I face Africa, I ask myself: what is it between us that constitutes a tie that I can feel better than I can explain? Africa is of course my fatherland. Yet neither my father nor my father's father ever saw Africa or knew its meaning or cared overmuch for it. My mother's folk were closer and yet their direct connection, in culture and race, became tenuous; still, my tie to Africa is strong. On this vast continent were born and lived a large portion of my direct ancestors going back a thousand years and more. The mark of their heritage is upon me in color and hair . . . But one thing is sure and that is the fact that since the fifteenth century these ancestors of mine and their other descendants have had a common history, have suffered a common disaster, and have one long memory. The actual ties of heritage between the individuals of this group vary with the ancestors that they have in common and many others, Europeans and Semites, perhaps Mongolians, certainly American Indians. But the physical bond is least and the badge of color relatively unimportant save as a badge; the real essence of this kinship is its social heritage of slavery; the discrimination and insult; and this heritage binds together not simply the children of Africa, but extends through yellow Asia and into the South Seas. It is this unity that draws me to Africa.[10]

Du Bois could write that the "physical bond" was "least" and that the "badge of color was relatively unimportant," while nourishing for all his life a near-obsession with color. He was hardly ever able to describe anyone without stress upon it, or to deal with many values far detached from it. On the lighter-brown side himself, he early set his face against the Negro color caste. In his Harvard days he "hotly championed the inclusion of two black schoolmates whose names were not usually on the invitation list to our social affairs." In Europe he turned away the proffered love of a white girl and back home even ended a courtship with a Negro girl who "looked quite white" and therefore might create misunderstandings that would embarrass him. In his writing he began to stress blackness as a positive virtue, and when he did eventually set foot himself in Africa, he positively swooned on its "black bosom."

This journey took place at the end of 1923, and William E. Burghardt Du Bois returned to his ancestral homeland as, of all things, Envoy Extraordinary and Minister Plenipotentiary of

10 *Ibid.*, pp. 116–117.

the President of the United States to the inauguration of the President of Liberia. This episode is described fully and lovingly by Du Bois himself.[11] There is first a sharp and wonderfully revealing vignette of Du Bois on shipboard, a day out of Africa, the land of so many dreams, reading his favorite author. His diary note, full text: "Tomorrow—Africa! Inconceivable! As yet no sight of land, but it was warm and we rigged deck chairs and lay at ease. I have been reading that old novel of mine—it has points. Twice we've wired Liberia. I'm all impatience." Then at the landing, came the nearly orgasmic ecstasy he felt in his role, in the trappings and protocol and the snap of his military escort, the pomp of his reception at the presidential mansion, the bows of the assembled diplomatic corps, and the reading of his address as all respectfully listened. In calling this experience perhaps his greatest hour, Du Bois suddenly shows us a small man, shrunken inside the vestments of his golden words.

He goes on, from the story of the brief spurt of his enjoyment of the sensations of sovereignty, to the gushing, melting passion of joy over his reunion with the land of his black ancestry:

The spell of Africa is upon me. The ancient witchery of her medicine is burning my drowsy, dreamy blood. This is not a country, it is a world, a universe of itself and for itself, a thing Different, Immense, Menacing, Alluring. It is a great black bosom where the spirit longs to die. It is life so burning, so fire encircled that one bursts with terrible soul inflaming life. One longs to leap against the sun and then calls, like some great hand of fate, the slow, silent, crushing power of almighty sleep—of Silence, of immovable Power beyond, within, around. Then comes the calm. The dreamless boat of midday stillness at dusk, at dawn, at noon, always. Things move— black shiny bodies, perfect bodies, bodies of sleek unearthly poise and beauty. Eyes languish, black eyes—slow eyes, lovely and tender eyes in great dark formless faces . . .[12]

Du Bois walked out into the "bush" to visit a village. He wrote:

How shall I describe it? Neither London, nor Paris, nor New York

[11] *Crisis*, Apr. 1924, pp. 248–251; *Dusk of Dawn*, pp. 122–125.
[12] *Crisis*, Apr. 1924, p. 274.

has anything of its delicate precious beauty. It was a town of the Veys and done in cream and pale purples, still, clean, restrained, tiny, complete. It was no selfish place, but the central abode of fire and hospitality, clean-swept for wayfarers. . . . They gave our hands a quick soft grasp and talked easily. Their manners were better than those of Park Lane or Park Avenue. Oh, much better and more natural. They showed us breeding . . . These folk have the leisure of true aristocracy, leisure for thought and courtesy, leisure for sleep and laughter. They have time for their children—such well-trained, beautiful children with perfect, unhidden bodies. . . . Come to Africa and see well-bred and courteous children, playing happily and never sniffling or whining . . .[13]

He never saw a quarrel or fight, "nor met with a single lewd gesture." He saw "no impudent children or smart and overbearing young folk," and found everyone, old and young, uniformly polite and full of deference, tolerance, and affection for each other. And always recurring, his special duet on bodies, one part in tropical rhapsody:

I believe that the African form in color and curve is the beautifulest thing on earth; the face is not so lovely, though often comely with perfect teeth and shining eyes—but the form of the slim limbs, the muscled torso, the deep full breasts! [14]

And the other, in shrill New England tenor:

I have read everywhere that Africa means sexual license. Perhaps it does. Most folk who talk sex frantically have all too seldom revealed their source material. I was in West Africa only two months, but with both eyes wide. I saw children quite naked and women usually naked to the waist—with bare bosom and limbs. And in those sixty days I saw less of sex dalliance and appeal than I see daily on Fifth Avenue. This does not mean much, but it is an interesting fact.[15]

So much of Du Bois is here in this brief African interlude: the elitist gratified by the rituals of power; the man drawn by deep full breasts; the daydreamer won by languor; the poet swooning

---

13 *Dusk of Dawn*, pp. 126–127.
14 *Crisis*, Apr. 1924, p. 273.
15 *Dusk of Dawn*, pp. 127–128.

on Africa's black bosom; the rhapsodist celebrating color, curve, and form; the aristocrat pleased by dignity, deference, order and gentility; the Puritan alert to any nonpoetic license. But never submerged in any of these is Du Bois the race propagandist, always trying to carry his readers with him toward a better opinion of their past and present links to Africa and thereby toward a better opinion of themselves.

To this same end he also took the work done by various scholars and writers in history, art, and archeology to resurrect the African past, and in book after book, alongside his autobiographical fragments, his discourses on race issues and world politics, his exhortations and his polemics, he kept filling in and enlarging the tapestry of the Negro's remoter past, painting in great strokes of majestic achievement and prideful memory. In this work Du Bois was content to try to be the popularizer of the most favorable findings of others. For his own preserve he took the intermingling of world politics, history, and race, and he entered upon it with full zest, wielding his pen like a field-piece, scattering his words like shrapnel over the whole range of the white man's depredations on the nonwhite world. For Du Bois the study of history was the study of the geopolitics of race.

In 1900, barely twenty years after he had raced, hurt, to that Massachusetts hilltop and strained his eyes toward farther horizons, W. E. B. Du Bois wrote one of his famous sentences:

The problem of the twentieth century is the problem of the color line—the relation of the darker to the lighter races of men in Asia and Africa, in America and the islands of the sea.[16]

He had by now taken into his widening view all the black men of America; he had explored their history and something of their present state. He had looked beyond them to the black

---

[16] These words are given here as they appear at the beginning of *The Souls of Black Folk*, first published in 1903. I am indebted to Professor Rayford Logan for a reference to Bishop Alexander Walters', *My Life and Work* (New York, 1917), p. 257, indicating that Du Bois first used this formula in 1900 at a conference in London where the slogan of Pan-Africanism was born.

men of Africa and to all the nonwhites in the rest of the world, and their common plight under the rule of the white master race, and in a deep lunge of intellect and intuition he had developed the issue to its full global dimensions.

When the First World War came, Du Bois saw it as a massive and bloody collision between rivals for the spoils of the earth. The issue was world power, and a major issue in power had become the distribution of colonies in Asia and Africa. Du Bois had already taken half a hold on the Marxist-socialist view which saw the fulcrum of affairs as economic and the main division in society running between exploiters and toilers. But he also saw that white toilers were just as committed as white capitalists to the maintenance of the color line in all its brutishness, indeed often more so, and this kept him for years from coming closer to any of the forms of socialist doctrine professed by white politicians. On the world scene, as anyone could see, the exploiters were white and the toilers nonwhite. Around its world system of strategy, power, and political economy, Europe had draped an elaborate racist ideology, declaring, as Du Bois put it, that it was "the duty of white Europe to divide up the darker world and administer it for Europe's good." This was rationalized by the belief that the "darker peoples are dark in mind as well as in body" and are therefore "born beasts of burden for white folks." For their profitable toil they were to be paid what they— held nearly worthless—were worth. Du Bois wrote:

> Such degrading of men by men is as old as mankind and the invention of no one race or people. Ever have men striven to conceive of their victims as different from the victors, endlessly different, in soul and blood, strength and cunning, race and lineage. It has been left, however, to Europe and to modern days, to discover the eternal world-wide mark of meanness—color! [17]

This marking of the color line gave Du Bois a hard and sometimes twisting path, but it also often lead him to the heart of things:

> This theory of human culture and its aims has worked itself

[17] *Darkwater*, p. 42.

through the warp and woof of our daily thought with a thorough-ness that few realize. Everything great, good, efficient, fair, and hon-orable is "white"; everything mean, bad, blundering, cheating, and dishonorable is "yellow"; a bad taste is "brown"; and the devil is "black." The changes of this theme are continually rung in picture and story, in newspaper heading and moving picture, in sermon and school book, until, of course, the King can do no wrong—a White Man is always right and a Black Man has no rights which a white man is bound to respect. There must come the necessary despisings and hatreds of these savage half-men, this unclean canaille of the world—these dogs of men. All through the world this gospel is preaching. It has its literature, it has its priests, it has its secret prop-aganda and above all—it pays! [18]

Of large events it gave him a much clearer view than most peo-ple had at the time, in 1920, when he wrote these prophetic words:

The World War was primarily the jealous and avaricious struggle for the largest share in exploiting darker races. As such it is and must be but the prelude to the armed and indignant protests of these despised and raped peoples. Today Japan is hammering on the door of justice, China is raising her half-manacled hands to knock next, India is writhing for the freedom to knock, Egypt is sullenly muttering, the Negroes of South and West Africa, of the West Indies, and of the United States are just awakening to their shameful slavery. Is, then, this war the end of wars? Can it be the end, so long as sits enthroned even in the souls of those who cry peace, the despising and robbing of darker peoples? If Europe hugs this delusion, then this is not the end of world war—it is but the beginning! [19]

Better vision, one must add, than a great many people had had (or still have!) now that we have gone through so much that Du Bois so clearly foresaw 40 years ago.

Through his racial window on the world Du Bois saw some things hard and clear, but some were out of focus, others out of sight, and often his view was downright myopic. Like many

[18] *Ibid.,* p. 44.
[19] *Ibid.,* pp. 49–50.

more common men, he built some of his prejudices out of his vanity and out of scanty personal experience. His schooltime in Berlin gave him a curiously affectionate view of culture in Hohenzollern Germany. Because the French showed greater subtlety in applying the color line both at home and in the colonies and showed some greater readiness to recognize merit in black men (even if it was only their merit in serving their white masters or offering up their lives for the metropole in war), Du Bois took a much kindlier view of French whiteness than of most others. He was untiringly proud of his own Dutch and French ancestors, and especially of the suggestion of Huguenot nobility and wealth in the latter. He described himself as being born "with a flood of Negro blood, a strain of French, a bit of Dutch, but, thank God! no 'Anglo-Saxon'!" Du Bois had started out to be a social scientist, to accept the harsh discipline of the truth seeker in the belief that the truth would make men free. But when he felt driven to become a race propagandist, his truth seeking became more selective and his truths more supple. Negroness and blackness not only had to be made acceptable; they had to be romanticized. Race doctrine that was anathema when it was white became eloquent when it was black: "I believe in the Negro race, in the beauty of its genius, the sweetness of its soul . . ." The enslavement of black men by black and brown in the times before the white incursions into Africa became under his pen "the mild domestic slavery of the African tribes and of the Arabs and the Persians." The Moslem slave trade in black Africans was mitigated in his eyes by the thought that it was intended to supply soldiers and servants to a leisure class, not profit-making labor to a "commercial class." [20] And when virtual slavery was found still being practiced in modern Liberia, Du Bois brushed rather lightly over the facts as they were established in 1930 by a League of Nations commission of inquiry.[21]

Du Bois managed mainly not to notice either slavery past

20 *The World and Africa* (New York, 1947), p. 77; *Black Folk Then and Now, An Essay in The History and Society of The Negro Race* (New York, 1939), pp. 130–131.

21 *Ibid.*, p. 292; Cf. Broderick, *W. E. B. Du Bois*, pp. 134–135.

style or wage slavery modern style when they appeared in modern black Liberia. Perhaps the style of his bias will be illustrated best in two widely separated passages from his writings, both about the daughters of rich households. The first is imaginary:

> . . . a lovely British home, with green lawns, appropriate furnishings and a retinue of well-trained servants. Within is a young woman, well-trained and well-dressed, intelligent and high-minded. She is fingering the ivory keys of a grand piano and pondering the problem of her summer vacation . . . her family is not wealthy, but it has a sufficient "independent" income from investments to enjoy life without hard work. How far is such a person responsible for the crimes of colonialism? It will in all probability not occur to her that . . . her income is the result of starvation, theft, and murder, that it involves ignorance, disease, and crime . . . Yet . . . she is content to remain in ignorance of the source of her wealth and its cost in human toil and suffering.[22]

The second household is a real one, a mansion he visited upriver in Liberia:

> A mansion of five generations with a compound of endless native servants and cows under the palm thatches. The daughters of the family wore, on the beautiful black skin of their necks, the exquisite pale gold chains of the Liberian artisan and the slim, black granddaughter of the house had a wide pink ribbon on the thick curls of her dark hair. . . . Double porches one above the other, welcomed us to ease. A native man, gay with Christmas and a dash of gin, danced and sang. . . . Children ran and played. . . . We sat at a long broad table and ate duck, chicken, beef, rice, plantain and collards, cake, tea, water, and Madeira wine . . .[23]

Du Bois might have noted the painful irony of the reproduction of the plantation manor of the old slave days in America. He might have asked whether these daughters, with the pale gold chains on their handsome black necks, had ever paused to think where the gold had come from, or all their comfort and plenty, including the "endless native servants"; and one wonders whether Du Bois would have found their ignorance, like the white girl's, "a colossal crime in itself." But if he did ask, he

[22] *The World and Africa,* pp. 41–42.
[23] *Crisis,* Apr. 1924, p. 250.

does not tell of it, and if he did wonder about it, we do not know, because he does not say.

Du Bois' color astigmatism appears even more strongly in the way he dealt over the years with the phenomenon of Japan. After exulting, like nonwhites all over the world, over Japan's defeat of Russia in 1905, Du Bois had wishfully seen Japan as the striking edge of the colored world against the white. He remained defensive about Japan's transformation into an aggressive imperialist power on its own terms. He saw its predatory assaults on China as part of colored Japan's resistance to the white West. He insisted that Japan's attacks on China were a prelude to a Japanese-Chinese bloc against the white world, and as late as the Manchurian invasion in 1931, he was seeing them as Japan's effort to save China from enslavement by Europe and America.[24] In his 1940 book, *Dusk of Dawn,* Du Bois managed to avoid any mention at all of Japan's ongoing war in China, and in 1947, in *The World and Africa,* he gave this remarkable capsule summary of the events just past: "Japan aroused Asia, and by attacking America thus furnished the one reason, based on race prejudice, which brought America immediately into the war."[25]

Du Bois poured his racial fantasies, his view of the world, his obsession with color, his public judgments and his secret hopes, and some of his own innermost dreams into a novel he called *Dark Princess,* published in 1928. It is one of the most forgotten of his many books, and as a work of literature deserves no other fate. But as a biographical item it is very much worth dwelling upon here for a bit, since it tells us much about our man and about our subject.

His story is of a young American Negro, frustrated by prejudice in his effort to become a doctor, who thereupon quits America for Europe. "I'm through," Matthew Towns writes his mother. "I cannot and will not stand America longer. I'm off." In Berlin he strolls into the Viktoria Café on the Unter der Linden, looking exactly as the young Du Bois himself has been de-

24 Broderick, *W. E. B. Du Bois,* pp. 133–135.
25 *The World and Africa,* p. 14.

scribed in his own Berlin days, wearing a new suit with "his newest dark crimson tie that burned with the red in his smooth dark face; he carried cane and gloves and he had walked into this fashionable café with an air." Here he encounters the Princess, whose color filled his eyes even before the rest of her beauty came into focus:

First and above all came that sense of color: into this world of pale yellowish and pinkish parchment, that absence or negation of color, came, suddenly, a glow of golden brown skin. It was darker than sunlight and gold; it was lighter and livelier than brown. It was a living, glowing crimson, veiled beneath brown flesh. It called for no light and suffered no shadow, but glowed softly of its own inner radiance.

He meets her by knocking down a white American who tries to annoy her. She turns out to be Her Royal Highness the Princess Kautilya of Bwodpur, India, who promptly invites him home for dinner. His fellow guests are a Japanese nobleman, two Indians, two Chinese, an Egyptian and his wife; all richly dressed, all obviously people of high status and importance. Matthew "could not keep his eyes from continually straying sidewise to his hostess. Never had he seen color in human flesh so regally set: the rich and flowing grace of the dress out of which rose so darkly splendid the jeweled flesh."

"You will note, Mr. Towns," she says, "that we represent here much of the Darker World. Indeed, when all our circle is present, we represent all of it, save your world of Black Folk."

The group turns out to be the executive committee of a world movement of the "Darker Peoples." They had just been debating whether to include American or African blacks, some of them questioning the "ability, qualifications, and real possibilities of the black race in Africa or elsewhere." Matthew hotly defends his race and proves its genius and its desire for freedom by suddenly singing the spiritual, "Let My People Go." The Egyptian, who had scornfully questioned the merit of "the black rabble of America," is silenced. "Pan-Africa belongs logically with Pan-Asia," decrees the Princess, "and for that reason Mr.

Towns is welcomed tonight." So Pan-Africa, in the person of Mr. Towns-Du Bois, joins the circle.

Matthew goes back to America and there almost falls prey to utter corruption when the Dark Princess appears to rescue him from this threatened suicide of his soul. He and the Princess then live a brief idyll in a Chicago slum. The Princess tells of her dream of the "substitution of the rule of dark men in the world for the rule of white, because the colored peoples were the noblest and the best bred." Matthew tries to broaden her view, arguing for the admission of "the masses of men of all races who might be the best of men simply imprisoned by poverty and ignorance." Indeed, throughout, Du Bois' hero valiantly tries to keep the broader human mass in view, just as he continues to argue for peaceful means as against violence; he has a hard time on both counts. He must also convince her that black men have their rightful part in the great times to come and were not, as her friends had charged, "only slaves and half-men."

In the end Kautilya's doubts are resolved and she writes Matthew, in language that oddly mingles the accents of Du Bois' global racism and the Communist Party's doctrine, brand new in 1928, of "self-determination in the Black Belt," the idea of a Negro Republic across some part of the American South. Here is Kautilya's message:

You are not free in Chicago or New York. But here in Virginia you are at the edge of a black world. The black belt of the Congo, the Nile, and the Ganges reaches by way of Guiana, Haiti, and Jamaica, like a red arrow, up into the heart of white America. Thus I see a mighty synthesis: you can work in Africa and Asia right here in America if you work in the Black Belt. For a long time I was puzzled ... but now I know. I am exalted, and with my high heart comes illumination. I have been sore bewildered by this mighty America, this ruthless, terrible, intriguing Thing. My home and heart is India. Your heart of hearts is Africa. And now I see through the cloud. You may stand here, Matthew, here, halfway between Maine and Florida, between the Atlantic and the Pacific, with Europe in your face and China at your back; with industry in your right hand and commerce in your left and the Farm beneath your steady feet; and yet be in the Land of the Blacks.

It develops that the Princess has not, as he thought, gone home to India, but to his mother's cabin in Virginia, to have Matthew's baby. He is summoned there by an East Indian courier in rich garb who bows low before him in his South Side tenement room. With her summons comes a prophecy:

The great central committee of Yellow, Brown, and Black is finally to meet. You are a member. The High Command is to be chosen. Ten years of preparation are set. Ten more years of final planning and then five years of intensive struggle. In 1952, the Dark World goes free—whether in Peace and fostering Friendship with all men, or in Blood and Storm—it is for Them—the Pale Masters of today— to say.

Matthew flies back to Virginia and walks up the long path to his mother's cabin, and there standing by the old black tree is the Princess, dressed in her royal robes and great jewels, blood rubies, silk, and gold, and in her arms is their baby, the new Maharajah of Bwodpur. In a wonderful touch that is like a sudden and unexpected chuckle from the author, Matthew's mother produces a local preacher to marry them "to make this little man an hones' chile." So there in the curve of a Virginia hill they are joined with a proper Christian knot, while from among the trees in the forest the royal retinue of Indians hails the pair and the princeling: "King of the Snows of Gaurisankar! Protector of Ganga the Holy! Incarnate Son of the Buddha! Grand Mughal of Utter India! Messenger and Messiah to all the Darker Worlds!"

Once again, much—if not all—of Du Bois appears in his book, his thoughts and fantasies about the world, and his dreams about himself, and about love and about fulfillment. Here are his angers and confusions, his color fixation, his racism, his belief in an aristocracy of talent and, more secretly, in an aristocracy of blood, really only the blood of dark-skinned men. Here too is his dream of liberation, a day of stern justice and reckoning but not—he struggles to believe—of vengeance. He dreams of it not as Armageddon but salvation, the rescue of the white world from self-destruction and the redirection of its energies—under the generous aegis of the new elect—toward true human advancement.[26] He presents it all with but small saving touches of a restraining intelligence and humanity and occasional flickers of prophetic insight. Written in 1928, his prophecy that the "Dark World" would go free by 1952 was not bad, not bad at all.

But in our present context the most striking thing about this whole fanciful construction is the virtual absence from it of *Africa*. It is included as a place name, but the only "African" who actually appears is an Egyptian, who has to be rapped to order for prejudice against black skins. The whole black race gets admitted to the circle of the Darker World only because young Towns-Du Bois, with gloves and cane, rescues a beauteous brown princess from a white American wolf in a Berlin café, and she, Pan-Asia, welcomes him, Pan-Africa, to her side. This singular personification was not an accident nor was it merely a literary convenience, for Pan-Africa was the other shape of Du Bois' dream, and while he dreamed it for Africa's fulfillment, what he really saw in it was his own.

Du Bois was a romantic racist, but through all the ups and downs and twists and turns of his thinking through the years he never got romantic enough to choose the ultimate option of urging Negroes to migrate en masse to Africa. Neither in his

26 Du Bois liked to see himself as a cool human spirit with an icy mind contemplating squirming men from a high lonely seat behind the veil. But he has on occasion allowed himself the luxury of an outburst of good, hot hate, as in these lines from a 1920 poem:

Valiant spoilers of women
And conquerors of unarmed men;
Shameless breeders of bastards,
Drunk with the greed of gold,
Bating their blood-stained hooks
With cant for the souls of the simple;
Bearing the white man's burden
Of liquor and lust and lies . . .
      I hate them, Oh!
      I hate them well,
      I hate them, Christ!
      As I hate hell!
      If I were God,
      I'd sound their knell
      This day!

Who raised the fools to their glory,
But black men of Egypt and Ind,
Ethiopia's sons of the evening,
Indians and yellow Chinese,
Arabian children of morning,
And mongrels of Rome and Greece?
      Ah, well!
And they that raised the boasters
Shall drag them down again . . .
      —*Darkwater*, pp. 53–54.

greatest anger nor in his deepest despair was he ever driven to the notion that there was an answer for Negroes in recrossing the ocean to resettle in the inhospitable homeland of their black ancestors. When he reverted in 1933 to the idea of Negro self-segregation, it never entered his mind that this self-containment would take place anywhere but right here in the United States. Du Bois had the imagination and intelligence to see, long before anyone else, that the meaningful slogan for beleaguered American Negroes as far as Africa was concerned was not *Back to Africa* but *Africa for the Africans,* and this is what he tried to promote with his Pan-African movement. He tried to win both the rulers of the white world and the Negroes of his own world to the self-serving good sense of his idea, and he failed with both.

Du Bois understood that the idea of going Back to Africa had appealed over time "not simply to the inexperienced and the demagogues, but to the prouder and more independent type of Negro . . . tired of begging for justice and recognition." [27] But from times past on down to the "crazy scheme of Marcus Garvey," Du Bois had simply found the idea impracticable. Negroes were not equipped to be pioneers, he patiently explained at the height of the Garvey movement, and in any case, Europe's expansion "made colonies in Africa or elsewhere about the last place where colored folk could seek freedom and equality." To would-be migrants moved by Garvey, Du Bois made sober answers:

No person of middle age or beyond should think of migrating. . . . Young and energetic people who want to migrate to Africa must remember [that] laborers are not needed in Africa . . . Skilled labor . . . is wanted, but even there the difficulties of remunerative work . . . are very great . . .[28]

Or again:

Africa belongs to these Africans. They have not the slightest intention of giving it up to foreigners, white or black . . . They resent the attitude that assures that other folk of any color are coming in to take and rule their land. Liberia, for instance . . . is not going to

[27] *Dusk of Dawn,* p. 195.
[28] *Crisis,* June 1924, p. 57.

allow American Negroes to assume control and to direct her government. Liberia, in her mind, is for Liberians. . . .[29]

No, Du Bois wanted to bend Africa otherwise to his designs. He had come strongly to believe, as we have seen, that the rise of the black man in America was linked with the rise of the non-white all over the world. He had real illusions in 1919 that the rulers of the white world, war weary and even frightened, might see the wisdom of beginning to change their ways. He saw that Japan and China were both seeking new voices for themselves in the postwar world. He thought that as far as the black men were concerned, the American Negro, rising steadily in education and attainment despite all obstacles, had to take the lead. He had to speak for the more slowly awakening masses of Africa, just as his hero did in *Dark Princess,* and, indeed, as Du Bois himself did when in Paris in 1919 he organized his first Pan-African Congress. He tried to bring Africans onto the world scene and to make their voices heard for the first time in the councils of power.

To American Negroes at home he tried to explain what he was up to:

This is not a "separatist" movement. There is no need to think that those who advocate the opening up of Africa for Africans . . . desire to deport any large number of colored Americans to a foreign and, in some respects, inhospitable land. Once for all, let us realize that we are Americans, that we were brought here with the earliest settlers, and that the very sort of civilization from which we came made the complete adoption of Western modes and customs imperative if we were to survive at all. In brief, there is nothing so indigeneous, so completely "made in America" as we. It is as absurd to talk of a return to Africa, merely because that was our home 300 years ago, as it would be to expect the members of the Caucasian race to return to the vastnesses of the Caucasus Mountains from which, it is reputed, they sprang.

. . . The African movement means to us what the Zionist movement must mean to the Jews, the centralization of race effort and the recognition of a racial fount. To help bear the burden of Africa does not mean any lessening of effort in our own problem at home.

29 *Crisis,* July 1924, p. 106.

Rather it means increased interest. For any ebullition of action and feeling that results in an amelioration of the lot of Africa tends to ameliorate the condition of colored peoples throughout the world. And no man liveth to himself.[30]

This was Du Bois in 1919. He got nowhere. His attempt to be sensible about migration was drowned in the din of the Garvey movement and its alarms and diversions. His attempt to give focus to the inner dynamic relating the American Negro to Africa went unnoticed. His words remained without echo until now, more than 40 years later, when they ring in the air all around us.

Du Bois had first heard the word "Pan-African" at a conference he attended in London in 1900. It is odd, yet characteristic of the man, that in his earlier autobiographical work he makes no mention of this meeting. In a later book, in 1947, he refers to it briefly, remarking that here is where the word "Pan-African" first appeared, but even then not mentioning his presence there, perhaps because it was a meeting conceived and called not by him but by a "black West Indian barrister, practicing in London," whom he does not even name.[31] In 1911 Du Bois addressed a Congress of Races, held also in London under the auspices of the Ethical Culture movement. Whatever sequel that might have had was engulfed by the war. When Du Bois suddenly got the chance to go to Europe in 1919, he conceived the notion of trying to dramatize his cause by calling a conference of black men under the slogan of Pan-Africa. As he has recounted in several places,[32] he managed to assemble a Congress of 57 individuals from 15 countries, nine of them African. The Congress appealed to the Versailles Conference to give Africans a chance for free development under international auspices, starting with the African territories taken from Germany. Du Bois says that this was the origin of the mandates system. Du

[30] *Crisis*, Feb. 1919, p. 166.

[31] *The World and Africa*, p. 7. The West Indian barrister was H. Sylvester Williams. *Cf* Walters, *op. cit.*, ch. 2. The conference created an organization of which Du Bois was named as American vice-president.

[32] *Dusk of Dawn*, pp. 260–262, 274–278; *The World and Africa*, pp. 9–12, 235–245.

Bois persisted and managed to assemble a second, larger conference in 1921, a third at Lisbon in 1925 and a fourth token gathering held in New York in 1927. Through almost all of this time Du Bois, to his great embarrassment, saw his Pan-African movement confounded in the world's press (and in many chancelleries) with Marcus Garvey's more flamboyant enterprise. It was, he wrote ruefully, a situation of "comedy and curious social frustration, but . . . real and in a sense tragic." [33] In the face of apathy and even resistance among his American associates and a large measure of indifference abroad, he made a last try to call another conference, this time in Tunis in 1929, but it failed to take place and the Pan-African movement fell into a coma. It was not revived until 1945 when the fifth Pan-African Congress was held at Manchester, England. It was organized by George Padmore, the ex-Communist West Indian writer who became father counselor to the colony of West African nationalist expatriates in London, and one of the most energetic members of that colony, a young man named Kwame Nkrumah. They invited Du Bois to serve as chairman. Nkrumah went on to become leader of the new Ghana and adopted the idea of Pan-Africanism as a central theme in his own vision of the African future. He invited Du Bois to the independence celebration in Accra in 1957, but Du Bois refused to sign the affidavit relating to Communist affiliation that was then part of the passport application, was refused a passport, and therefore did not go. In 1958, when Nkrumah convened the first All-African People's Conference at Accra, he again invited the aged Du Bois to come and witness the fruition of his early dreams. But this time Du Bois, who had received his passport when the affidavit requirement was dropped, was ill in Moscow and sent his wife to Accra to represent him. Opening the conference, Nkrumah paid tribute to Du Bois and to Marcus Garvey, linking their names, in a final ironic twist to this history, as the pioneers who had "fought for African national and racial equality." [34] Du Bois finally did get back to African soil to attend the Ghana Republic Day celebra-

[33] *Dusk of Dawn*, p. 277.
[34] St. Clair Drake, "Pan-Africanism, What Is It?" *Africa Today*, Jan.–Feb. 1959, p. 7.

tions in July 1960. He was much honored as the "father of Pan-Africanism," but he used the occasion mainly to warn Africans against Anglo-American capitalism and to extol the Soviet system. In the fall of 1961 he returned to Ghana, apparently this time to stay, even though by now the Communist empire far more than Africa had become the nonagenarian Du Bois' chosen spiritual home. His last act before leaving the United States was to apply formally for membership in the Communist Party.[35]

When I was finally granted an hour's audience with Dr. Du Bois on a winter day not long before his ninety-second birthday, I knew it would be impossible to re-explore much of all this past, that most of my questions would have to go unasked, that I would be lucky enough to catch a glimpse of how he now saw the future, of how the long story was ending. One wanted this glimpse, even knowing that for a quarter of a century what Du Bois thought had ceased to echo in the thinking of others, that he had passed from behind his famous veil to a new place behind an even more famous curtain.

In his half of a comfortable house in well-to-do Brooklyn Heights, I was shown into Du Bois' study, heavy with his life's accumulation of books, including his own on a long shelf. In spaces on the walls were the parchments of some of his recently acquired honors from Communist institutions in Eastern Europe. Over the mantel hung a portrait of what I took to be one of his prized ancestors, a handsome, fair-skinned patrician-looking man. Du Bois walked in slowly, short but of good carriage, fingering the gold chain across his gray waistcoated middle with a polished Phi Beta Kappa key gleaming upon it. With his small goatee, his high bald crown, his sharp and clear light eyes, his acquiline face, his tone and air of authority, he was the breakfast-table autocrat, only semiretired, calmly scornful of a world too unintelligent to accept the verities of which he was now the venerable guardian. But he was graciously willing to measure them out in quiet and genteel and clean sentences. His politeness, nearly punctilious, gave an odd contrapuntal effect to his

[35] *The New York Times*, Nov. 23, 1961.

words, especially when he was offering up, like verses out of scripture, bits of crude Communist hagiography.

He began by asking me what went on at the Center for International Studies, and when I spoke of its interest in world problems, he tapped his fingertips knowingly together and said: "I suppose this all has to do with investments." It became clear that what he pictured was a roomful of men with top hats, beaked noses, big bellies, and clawed hands grasping great big moneybags, drooling over the outlook for new profits in Asia and Africa. I murmured a small denial and changed the subject, but at first this did not help at all. When we began to discuss the impact of world affairs on Negroes, he said: "There is really no way for the young Negro to get to know about world affairs. All the news here is suppressed and distorted. He has no way of learning what is going on in the Soviet Union or in China." Any young Negro traveling abroad, he went on, is "coached as to what to say. It means that a young man when he goes abroad has to be more or less a traitor to his people. He either keeps his mouth shut abroad or else he lies." When I opened the matter of his early recollections about Africa, he tapped a fat manuscript on the desk before him. "I have dealt with this in a new autobiography I have just finished," he said. "I will offer it for publication here, but I doubt that it will get published. Of course it *will* be published, in Russia, Czechoslovakia, and East Germany." I looked over his head at the shelf of his own works, all issued here over the many years, and I thought that I might ask him if in all the Soviet Union or China he could find such a shelf of books, or even a single volume, written by anyone who was even in small part the critic, opponent, and rebel against the society that Du Bois had been all his life in America. But I pressed on to other things, and although Du Bois has never been a man lightly turned away from his obsessions, we did cover some small patches of new and higher ground, enough to show me that even in this latest and perhaps last of his outlooks an impressive intelligence survives.

It quickly became clear that Du Bois, who had despaired 25 years before of winning through to Negro integration in American life, was now concerned with the effects of integration, seeing its success as already assured. He had leapfrogged ahead to new problems: "The Negro child gets into a school which is integrated, and the chances are nine out of ten that he will have an unsympathetic teacher who won't know or care anything about the history of Negroes. How will he ever get to know anything about it?" He was worried much more by the fear that with growing economic opportunity and well being, Negroes were getting to be just like whites: "Why, most of the Negroes who went to Ghana for the independence celebration or have gone there since have been interested in business and investments, in what money they could make . . . In Ghana there was a flood of Americans, Negro and white, who just wanted to make money. It was the same when Nkrumah was here." And the principal difference from the past was that "the Negro now assumes he has the same chance" as the white man to profit. "This is the sickness of the whole American civilization, money! The insidious thing is that Negroes are taking white Americans as their pattern, to make a life out of buying and selling and become rich, spending for show."

What were the alternatives for the Negro? I asked. Alienation? Migration? Integration?

Du Bois ruled out alienation, and he credited this to the Communist world. "The thing that will stop any new alienation of Negroes from whites will be the attitudes of the Soviet Union and China. The Negro gets more consideration in the Soviet Union and China than he ever got in England or France or elsewhere. You can't have another movement like Garvey's [i.e., against whites] because you would have to include as whites the two hundred million Russians, Czechs, and so on. And now countries that can't get capital on satisfactory terms from the West can turn to the Soviet Union, and eventually to China, and get it at two percent."

Migration? He thought not. "Of course it is true that for a long time many Negroes had come to think that there was no hope of winning equality in the United States and that it was best to get out. But they were disappointed in Liberia and disappointed in Garvey and had to be content with the emphasis, sometimes the overemphasis, on Africa and race pride in books like Carter Woodson's. . . . But there will be no reproduction of any urge to migrate. Negroes now have the chance to go into business, opportunities are opening up. You now have Negro millionaires!"

Integration, then?

"The real question is: after there is no more discrimination based on race and color, what do you do? Where do you go? I have somewhere drawn the analogy of being on a train, and having a fight with my fellow passengers over my treatment on that train while I should be thinking: Where is this train going? We have fought down discrimination. There has been tremendous improvement. Negroes are becoming Americans. But then what are Americans to become?"

Well, what is the prospect, then, and what about Africa?

"I don't know," replied Du Bois. "The Negro is not working it out. He doesn't really see the problem yet. In the next ten to twenty years there will be a change of thought regarding the relationship of the American Negro to Africa and to the world. We used to think that because they were educated, and had some chance, American Negroes would lead Africans to progress. But the chances are now that Africa will lead American Negroes. But into what kind of world? And what kind of world will there be to be led into? I do not know where the American people will decide to move, but I am sure that the organization of Africa will have a decisive effect on what American Negroes will do and think about the future. I don't think they will leave the United States. Negroes will be more and more integrated. There will be more and more intermarriage . . . But this will be a longtime development of a hundred years or more. The question even then is: What culture of Africa and what culture of the American Negro will succeed in surviving? What in general of the culture of the world? The question really is what will all human society be like? We prefer varieties. What will the varieties be? I don't think it is really important for the future of mankind what color skin men will have or what their racial characteristics will be. I don't think the issue of race is central, that the color of skin is the important thing. The Negro has been trying to unmake the situation in which this was important and he should not be drawn back toward it. I don't really care what the racial identity of people will be in the twenty-third century. I don't think the future of 'Negritude' is important. What will be important is what people will be thinking and doing by then."

This was Du Bois, at ninety-two, straining his eyes harder than ever from his lonely hilltop, and now, as at the beginning, glimpsing dreams and ideas far, far away, across a foreground pitted and barred by the grotesque shapes and distortions of the nearby reality. For him these were the enshrouding distortions of racism, and to fight debasement he made himself into a racist, genteel, intelligent and literate, but still a racist. When he came, in his late age, to abandon the racist view—if that indeed is what he has really done—it has been to embrace as more humane the greater inhumanities of Communist totalitarianism. All his life Du Bois scornfully rejected the preachers of pie in the sky, believing that in heaven a man was nothing and had to win his freedom on earth, only in his last years to surrender to those for whom a man's freedom is nothing, neither in heaven nor, most of all, on earth.

Du Bois did not settle the Negro score. It is being settled by the great glacial pressures that do finally move human society. But he did make himself part of those pressures and the "settlement," as it comes, resembles much of what he wanted for black men in America and in Africa, and from this he must gather what satisfaction he can. But Du Bois did not settle his own score either. He wanted recognition, acceptance, eminence, a life among peers. When he was denied, he cut himself off. Today he still stands apart from all except the Communists, who cynically do him honor for his use as a symbol now, especially abroad, and some older Negroes who remember with respect what he did for them in a distant past. It is impossible for me to know whether all of Du Bois' unsatisfied urges and dreams for himself are gratified and realized in the recognition extended to him by the Communist world. He may insist that he sees Communist world power as man's last best hope; it is hard not to imagine that he also sees in it history's means for finally settling the white world's accounts with him and with his fellow nonwhites.

Either way, he helps explain the nature of his failure and leaves one only to guess what a great man he might have become had he been able to set himself resolutely all his life against *all* forms of tyranny over the minds of men.

# 6. FIVE WRITERS AND THEIR ANCESTORS

In the same years that Du Bois was speaking for Pan-Africanism in his cultured tones and Marcus Garvey was raising his loud plebeian clamor for Negroes to go Back to Africa, a school of new Negro poets appeared who also, in their own way, sang of Africa. They were partly influenced by Du Bois—many of their poems first appeared in *Crisis*. Like Du Bois they were romantics, but they were Bohemian poets, not strait-laced geopoliticians. They looked back, not ahead. They preferred their dreams of an idyllic past to his intercontinental visions of the future. They also felt the emotions that surged up around Marcus Garvey, but they were too sophisticated to join his simple-minded followers or take part in his pageantry. Their dreams were much less literal, and their flights of romantic imagination could take them much more swiftly to Africa—and much more safely back to Bohemia again—than the Black Star Line ever would.

## Back to (Literary) Africa

The reaching out to Africa as a "literary homeland" was one of the features of the so-called Negro "Renaissance" of the 1920's, the birthtime of the "New Negro," the emergence of new Negro voices in literature. This outburst of high creativity was a product of the many moods and circumstances of the time. It was part of the world-wide postwar shake-out of hopes and values, part of the response of Negroes in America to the postwar despair, part of their resistance to the re-establishment of the supremely white order of things. It was also part of the larger literary stirrings of the period. Among the many new preoccupations, new modes, new subjects, some white writers had begun to "rediscover" the Negro: Eugene O'Neill *(Emperor Jones)*, Sherwood Anderson *(Dark Laughter)*, DuBose Heyward *(Porgy)*, and Harlem's rediscoverer-in-chief, Carl Van Vechten (*Nigger Heaven*). In various tangible and intangible ways this school of white writing helped open the way for a whole new school of Negro writing about Negroes. Much has been written of the Harlem Bohemia of the time, of the young Negro writers who began to flash, to flicker, and sometimes to shine, the best remembered among them now Countee Cullen, Claude McKay, and Langston Hughes, but also figures like Jean Toomer, who fell so quickly silent, and Wallace Thurman and Rudolph Fisher, who died so soon, and many others now to be found only in the literary histories. Some of these writers discovered the "New Negro" in the postwar turmoil or rediscovered "old" values in the folklore; a few discovered themselves, and all of them discovered Africa. It is this African thread in the pattern that we want here, without quite absenting ourselves from the rest, to trace awhile.

In a way it can be said that what began to take place was a new exchange in the old dialogue of hope and despair. Just a few years earlier, in 1917, the poet and humanist, the gifted James Weldon Johnson, summoning Negroes to face down their adversity, chose these words:

> Far, far the way we have trod
> From heathen kraal and jungle dens
> To freedmen, freemen, sons of God,
> Americans and citizens . . .
> No, stand erect and without fear
> And for our foes let this suffice—
> We've bought a rightful kinship here
> And we have more than paid the price.

But in hardly any time at all the poet esthetes of Harlem were trooping back to the kraals and the jungle dens, going "Back to Africa" in their own way, just like the despairing black masses who lined up behind Garvey to reach the homeland on his steamship line. The poets had an international current of their own to drift in; among other things the world of the white literati had developed a new interest in primitivism, Picasso taking up African sculpture, Gide writing of the Congo, and a great vogue for African naturalism following the award of the 1921 Prix Goncourt to *Batouala,* a novel of African tribal life by René Maran, a Martinique-born Negro. Some of this was in an old tradition; despairing of nobility in modern white civilization, sentimentalists began to look for it in primitive black savagery. But there was also a fascinated reach for the primeval mysteries, the jungle depths, for the abysmal brute, for the Freudian id personified in the naked black man in his natural state and setting. Books about voodooism, wild rites, and magic in the black Caribbean and Africa helped to set this style. So did Vachel Lindsay's poem "The Congo," which he subtitled "A Study of the Negro Race" and the first section of which he called "Their Basic Savagery," illustrating the theme with tom-tom rhythms and bloody doings along the black river. With Brutus Jones, Sterling Brown remarked, O'Neill did move the Negro from comic relief to the tragic center, but did so by relying on "tom-toms, superstition and atavism." Brown remembers "the discovery of Harlem as a new African colony" as cheap faddism:

Wa-wa trumpets, trap drums (doubling for tom-toms) and shapely dancers with bunches of bananas girdling their middles in Bamboo Inns and jungle cabarets nurtured tourists' illusions of "the Congo cutting through the black. . . ."[1]

Much was made of primitive sculpture, and there was ample white patronage for all sorts of alleged Africanisms among Negroes, in poets, in night clubs, and in individual behavior. The idea of the Negro as savage, whether noble or brute, had a peculiarly exploitable appeal, and it was played for all it was worth in the short-lived, high-temperature Harlem Bohemia, in that time when, as Langston Hughes has put it, "the Negro was in vogue."

On the other hand, Alain Locke, the critic-philosopher and chronicler of *The New Negro,* thought that "the current mode of idealizing the primitive and turning toward it in the reaction from the boredom of ultrasophistication" was only the "Caucasian strain in the Negro poet's attitude toward Africa at the

[1] Sterling Brown, "The New Negro in Literature," *The New Negro Thirty Years Afterward,* Howard University (Washington, D.C., 1955), pp. 58–59.

present time," and, fortunately, was "not dominant." He thought he saw in all the ferment "the most sophisticated of all race motives—the conscious and deliberate threading back of the historic sense of group tradition to the cultural backgrounds of Africa." [2]

This was not easy to find. Negroes finding their voices were either trying to express their angry defiance of the wave of lynchings across the country at that time or seeking an escape from it. The most famous and most often-quoted cry of anger was Claude McKay's "If we must die, let it not be like hogs/ Hunted and penned in an inglorious spot . . ." In another poem, called "To The White Fiends," McKay wrote:

> Think you I am not fiend and savage too?
> Think you I could not arm me with a gun
> And shoot down ten of you for every one
> Of my black brothers murdered, burnt by you?
> Be not deceived, for every deed you do
> I could match—out-match: am I not Afric's son,
> Black of that black land where black deeds are done?

Of Africa itself McKay wrote in sorrow and loss:

> The sun sought the dim bed and brought forth light,
> The sciences were sucklings at thy breast;
> When all the world was young in pregnant night,
> Thy slaves toiled at thy monumental best . . .
> Honor and Glory! Arrogance and Fame!
> They went. The darkness swallowed thee again.
> Thou art the harlot, now thy time is done,
> Of all the mighty nations of the sun.

And he yearned in despair in a sonnet he called "Outcast":

> For the dim regions whence my fathers came
> My spirit, bondaged by the body, longs.
> Words felt, but never heard, my lips would frame;
> My soul would sing forgotten jungle songs.
> I would go back to darkness and to peace.
> But the great western world holds me in fee,

---

[2] Alain Locke, "The Negro in American Culture," Calverton ed., *Anthology of American Negro Literature*, p. 264.

And I may never hope for full release
While to its alien gods I bend my knee.
Something in me is lost, forever lost,
Some vital thing has gone out of my heart,
And I must walk the way of life a ghost
Among the sons of earth, a thing apart.

For I was born, far from my native clime,
Under the white man's menace, out of time.

Among our panelists the best-remembered poem of this theme
and of this time was Countee Cullen's "Heritage." Cullen,
writer of romantic lyrics, had used many lines to idealize Africa,
"the dusky dream-lit land" where black men and women had
been kingly and queenly. But in "Heritage" he both dreams
and chides himself for dreaming. It begins:

What is Africa to me:
Copper sun or scarlet sea,
Jungle star or jungle track,
Strong bronzed men, or regal black
Women from whose loins I sprang
When the birds of Eden sang?
*One three centuries removed*
*From the scene his fathers loved,*
*Spicy grove, cinnamon tree,*
*What is Africa to me?*

The italics are Cullen's. He goes on to dream of lying in the
jungle, of "great drums throbbing through the air," of dancing
a lover's dance naked in the rain, of remembering the "quaint,
outlandish, heathen gods," and wishing that the God he did
serve were black. "One three centuries removed," he repeats,
"what is Africa to me?" Because, as Alain Locke observed, his
poem "dramatized the conflict so brilliantly," his readers could
and did take his intent either way; some cited the poem to me
to say that it expressed their feeling of kinship with Africa;
some quoted it to say that to them, as to the poet, Africa was
too far removed to mean anything at all. But the poet is seeing
Africa as a dream to which he can flee from anguish. "Africa?"
he asks, "a book one thumbs/ Listlessly, till slumber comes." In

another poem, "The Shroud of Color," in his dream he flies free:

> Now suddenly a strange wild music smote
> A chord long impotent in me; a note
> Of jungles, primitive and subtle, throbbed
> Against my echoing breast, and tom-toms sobbed
> In every pulse beat of my frame. The din
> A hollow log bound with a python's skin
> Can make wrought every nerve to ecstasy
> And I was wind and sky again, and sea,
> And all sweet things that flourish, being free.[3]

The dreamland Africa of the "Renaissance" poets and the night-club Africa of the Harlem faddists receded, just like the Africa in the dream dreamed by Marcus Garvey. What is remembered now about the Negro writers of the 1920's is not how they languished over Africa but how they asserted themselves in America, as in the memorably wishful words of the 1926 manifesto of Langston Hughes:

> We younger Negro artists who create now intend to express our individual dark-skinned selves without fear or shame. If white people are pleased, we are glad. If they are not, it doesn't matter . . . If colored people are pleased, we are glad. If they are not, their displeasure doesn't matter either.

Langston Hughes has proved to be the hardiest of all these literary figures. He was among those yearning after the ancestral home way back then, and he is helping to exult in its new eminence now. This makes his work the logical place to begin an effort to trace variations on the Africa theme in the works of certain Negro writers as they have appeared in the years from the "Renaissance" of the 1920's until now.

For this purpose I have chosen five writers whose lives overlap each other's by five to ten years, a difference sufficient in each case to mark a passage into another literary—and political—gen-

---

3 For a relevant discussion of Countee Cullen, see J. Saunders Redding, *To Make a Poet Black* (Chapel Hill, N.C., 1939), pp. 108–112. Redding calls Cullen the "Ariel of Negro poets" who could "not beat the tom-tom above a faint whisper." Also see Davis, "The Alien-and-Exile Theme in Countee Cullen's Racial Poems," *Phylon*, 4th quarter, 1953, pp. 390–400.

eration. Only Langston Hughes' writing life spans the whole time; he was born in 1902, the year before Du Bois' *Souls of Black Folk* appeared, published his first poem in 1921, and has been going strong ever since. Richard Wright was born in 1909. His first book appeared in 1936 and *Native Son*, the work for which he is famous, in 1940. Ralph Ellison followed Wright closely enough—he was born in 1914—to share many common experiences with him, but his novel, *Invisible Man,* did not appear until 1952, and remained part of a world that Wright chose to leave. James Baldwin, born in 1924, is wholly the product of a different era. His first work, *Go Tell It On the Mountain,* was published in 1953. Finally, born only yesterday in 1930, Lorraine Hansberry completes the group, not because she has made her way as yet to any solid small summit of her own, but because her play, *A Raisin In the Sun,* was a hit of the 1959 season, because it dramatizes in its freshest form some of the old dilemmas with which we are dealing, and finally because by the very title of her play, taken from one of his poems, she will enable us to end our essay, as it begins now, with Langston Hughes.

## Langston Hughes

Of all the poets in Harlem who sang of Africa in the 1920's, Langston Hughes was the only one who had been there. Perhaps this was why he sometimes sang of Africa in a key different from the rest:

> We cry among the skyscrapers
> As our ancestors
> Cried among the palms in Africa
> Because we are alone,
> It is night,
> And we're afraid.

Or, in a different mood:

> We should have a land of trees
> Bowed down with chattering parrots
> Brilliant as the day
> And not this land where birds are grey.

It was more common to sing about happy Africans long dead, or imaginary Africans who never lived, but Langston Hughes saw himself trying to shake hands with live Africans, now:

> We are related—you and I.
> You from the West Indies,
> I from Kentucky.
> We are related—you and I.
> You from Africa,
> I from these States.
> We are brothers—you and I.

As he tells it, the young poet's trip to Africa happened to him like an odd chance, as unpremeditated as a line of poetry coming unbidden into his head. He had wanted simply to get away, to break from all his young life up to then, and like a lot of young people who had this urge, he tried to do it by going to sea and to any far place he could reach. On his first try he got a job on a freighter tied up among the war-weary discards in the Hudson, going nowhere. He stayed aboard her for a long season, excursioning to Bear Mountain and only a few times back to Harlem. Come spring, he tried again, took the first job offered and only afterward learned that the ship was sailing for Africa. In telling this story in his autobiography, *The Big Sea,* Hughes does not even add an exclamation point to this discovery of his unplanned destination. The exclamations came later. At the moment what mattered was not where he was going but what he was leaving. That night, sailing out of New York, in a scene that can stand forever as an image of youth declaring its manhood, twenty-one-year-old Hughes dumped all his books into the bay and felt that it was like dropping all his burdens, "everything unpleasant and miserable out of my past . . . like throwing a million bricks out of my heart."

Langston Hughes tried to take Africa as he tried to school himself to take most things: casually, on the surface, and wherever possible, with a laugh, even a sad laugh. With Hughes this was more than a device or a literary style; it was a way of functioning, of coping with life. There was so much on the Negro surface, after all, hardly noted by anyone until he came along.

Langston Hughes achieved real uniqueness as a poet by describing the life and people of the Negro ghetto, catching them by their sights and sounds, by some of their sorrows and some of their angers, but mostly by their sardonic humors. He achieved his effect mostly by peeling off a layer of the surface, hardly ever more than a single layer, and then usually leaving what he found there undescribed, for the reader to see and hear if he could. He modeled his emotional patterns on the blues whose rhythms he adopted. This mood, as he explained in a prefatory note to an early volume of his poems, "is almost always despondency, but when they are sung people laugh." In addition to this, Hughes set out to do what few, regardless of race, creed, or color, have succeeded in doing, to earn his living by his writing alone. The result has been a body of work that has given us a rich, varied, and often vivid picture of the tops of a lot of things about Negroes and Negro life in America; rather little at depth about any one person, especially about himself.

Still, even under that single layer, and even in his Africa so briefly glimpsed through young eyes bright with adventure, we do learn something about Hughes if we look hard enough at what he has shown us. The exclamation points about Africa came on that first voyage when Hughes, fresh (he said) from a gay night in a love palace in Las Palmas, kept watching for the first sight of the African coast:

And when finally I saw the dust-green hills in the sunlight, something took hold of me inside. My Africa, Motherland of the Negro peoples! And me a Negro! Africa! The real thing, to be touched and seen, not merely read about in a book.

Dakar was too French and too Mohammedan, but:

. . . farther down the coast it was more like the Africa I had dreamed about—wild and lovely, the people dark and beautiful, the palm trees tall, the sun bright, and the rivers deep. The great Africa of my dreams!

But here, in the Africa of his dreams, the young Hughes almost immediately finds again the heaviest of the burdens that for a heady moment he had imagined dropping with his books into

New York Bay. Here in Africa, where everything was dark and beautiful, we come upon Hughes touching—lightly as always—on one of the central themes of his life:

> There was one thing that hurt me a lot when I talked with the people. The Africans looked at me and would not believe I was a Negro. You see, unfortunately, I am not black.[4]

And this is where Hughes goes back to tell the story of his life, of his family with all its mixtures of bloods and colors, of white great-grandparents, of strains of poets and statesmen and Indian chiefs, Cherokee, Jewish, Scotch, French, and Negro forebears, of his "olive-yellow" mother and his "darker-brown" father, whom he saw once when he was six and not again until he was seventeen. He tells of his wandering life, with his mother, with an aunt, with a stepfather, and with his father who had migrated to Mexico to make his way because there was no color line or Jim Crow there. His father hated "niggers" and "hated himself too, for being a Negro"; he had great contempt for all poor people and valued only money made to keep.

It was while he was bound for Mexico to see his father that Hughes, just out of high school, wrote one of the best known of all his poems, "The Negro Speaks of Rivers." This act of creation came out of a fusing of thoughts about his father, Negroes, himself, slavery, and his ancestors in dim and distant Africa. He was on the train out of St. Louis, he relates, and was feeling badly over his parting from his mother ("my best poems," he adds in a parenthesis, "were all written when I felt the worst. When I was happy, I didn't write anything.") He goes on:

> It came about in this way. All day on the train I had been thinking about my father, and his strange dislike of his own people. I didn't understand it, because I was a Negro, and I liked Negroes very much. . . . Now it was just sunset, and we crossed the Mississippi, slowly, over a long bridge. I looked out the window of the Pullman at the great muddy river flowing down toward the heart of the South, and I began to think what that river, the old Mississippi, had meant

4 *The Big Sea* (New York, 1945), pp. 10–11.

to Negroes in the past . . . how Abraham Lincoln had made a trip down the Mississippi on a raft to New Orleans, and how he had seen slavery at its worst, and had decided within himself that it should be removed from American life. Then I began to think about other rivers in our past—the Congo, and the Niger, and the Nile in Africa—and the thought came to me: "I've known rivers," and I put it down on the back of an envelope I had in my pocket, and within the space of ten or fifteen minutes, as the train gathered speed in the dusk, I had written this poem, which I called "The Negro Speaks of Rivers." [5]

Much of what made up the inner life of Langston Hughes stares out at us from the telling of this story of how he made a poem. He has told us here and elsewhere of some of its separate parts. It is of their inner connections that he has never written.

In Mexico he experienced a great crisis in his hatred for his father. The teen-age boy fell into a deep illness that no doctor could diagnose, much less cure, because Hughes preferred to lie in his expensive hospital bed—his father was paying the bills— and not to tell them what was the matter with him. It was two years after this, following a try at student life at Columbia, a series of odd jobs, and his winter with the dead fleet in the Hudson, that he crossed the sea and saw Africa as he said he had dreamed of it:

A long sandy coastline, gleaming in the sun. Palm trees sky-tall. Rivers darkening the sea's edge with the loam of their deltas. People

---

[5] *Ibid.*, pp. 54–55. The poem, his first to be published outside of his high-school paper, appeared in Du Bois' *Crisis* in June, 1921:

> I've known rivers;
> I've known rivers as ancient as the world and older than the
>                     flow of human blood in human veins.
> My soul has grown deep like the rivers.
> I bathed in the Euphrates when dawns were young.
> I built my hut near the Congo and it lulled me to sleep.
> I looked upon the Nile and raised the Pyramids above it.
> I heard the singing of the Mississippi when Abe Lincoln went down to
>                     New Orleans, and I've seen its muddy bosom turn all golden
>                     in the sunset.
> I've known rivers:
> Ancient, dusky rivers.
> My soul has grown deep like the rivers.

black and beautiful as the night. The bare, pointed breasts of women in the market places. The rippling muscles of men loading palm oil and cocoa beans and mahogany on the ships of the white man's world . . .

It was 1923, and the Africans Hughes met had heard of Marcus Garvey and they "hoped that what they had heard about him was true—that he really would come and unify the black world and free and exalt Africa."

"Our problems in America are very much like yours," I told the Africans, "especially in the South. I am a Negro, too."

But they only laughed at me and shook their heads and said: "You, white man!"

It was the only place in the world where I've ever been called a white man. They looked at my copper-brown skin and straight black hair—like my grandmother's Indian hair, except a little curly—and they said: "You—white man."

One of the laborers aboard, a Kru from Liberia who knew about these things, explained to Hughes that most nonwhites who came to Africa from abroad came to help the white man, whether as missionary or as clerk or helper in colonial governments, "so the Africans call them all *white* men."

"But I am not white," I said.

"You are not black either," the Kru man said simply. "There is a man of my color," and he pointed to George, the pantryman, who protested loudly.

"Don't point at me," George said. "I'm from Lexington, Kentucky, U.S.A. And no African blood nowhere."

"You black," said the Kru man.

"I can part my hair," said George, "and it ain't nappy."

But to tell the truth, George shaved a part in his hair every other week, since the comb wouldn't work. The Kru man knew this, so they both laughed loudly, for George's face was as African as Africa.

And then Langston Hughes adds this astonishing parenthesis:

(Yet dark as he was George always referred to himself as brown-skin, and it was not until years later, when a dark-skinned minister in New Jersey denounced me to his congregation for using the word *black* to describe him in a newspaper article, that I realized that

most dark Negroes in America do not like the word *black* at all.
They prefer to be referred to as *brownskin,* or at the most as *dark-brownskin*—no matter how dark they really are.)[6]

In this remarkable statement Langston Hughes, the poet whose
appeal and repute was based on his sensitive awareness of the
common mores of Negroes, asks his readers to believe that until
the late 1920's he had no idea that Negroes had any special feelings about the word *black.* We are asked to imagine a youthful
Hughes—the same one who wrote *Weary Blues* and *Fine Clothes
to the Jew*—equipped with a selective soundproofing device
which kept out all Negro talk of blackness but let in all the
other words and sounds and feelings out of which he made his
poems. Whether this is what Hughes really remembered about
himself when he wrote these words (in 1945), or whether he was
deliberately "misremembering," the effect is much the same: it
reveals a block so deep and so important that one's first impulse
is to step away from it. But his statement is so extravagantly
absurd that it becomes a revelation in itself; Hughes the writer
is violently signaling that Hughes the man had some superspe-
cial feelings himself on this subject of blackness. This becomes
even clearer as we go on, because this curious little parenthesis
is sandwiched in between the story of how Africans had called
him a "white man" and the story of a golden-skinned boy who
came aboard at one port looking for reading matter in English.
He was the son, he told Hughes, of an African woman and an Englishman who had gone back to England. Now he and his mother
were ignored by the whites and shunned by the blacks. "Was it
true," the boy wanted to know, "that in America the black people were friendly to the mulatto people?" Hughes later had a
letter from the boy but never answered it "because I have a way
of not answering letters when I don't know what to say." Instead Hughes wrote of the encounter in a short story called
"African Morning." He says he had always been "intrigued"
with this problem of mixed blood which was, he added, "a minor
problem." On this minor problem he also wrote "several other
short stories"; a poem called "Mulatto" about which he says,

6 *Ibid.,* pp. 102–104.

"I worked harder on that poem than on any other that I have
ever written"; and a play, also called *Mulatto,* which ran successfully on Broadway.

Langston Hughes never did write a poem about Africans calling him "a white man." Instead he wrote many poems about
being black, black, black.

> I am a Negro:
>     Black as the night is black,
>     Black like the depths of my Africa.

In "Dream Variation":

>         To fling my arms wide
>         In the face of the sun,
>         Dance! Whirl! Whirl!
>         Till the quick day is done.
>         Rest at pale evening . . .
>         A tall slim tree . . .
>         Night coming tenderly
>             Black like me.

Again in "Me and My Song," a poem 80 words long, the word
black appears nine times. A sample:

>     Black
>     As the gentle night,
>     Black as the kind and quiet night,
>     Black as the deep and productive earth,
>     Body
>     Out of Africa,
>     Strong and black . . .
>     Kind
>     As the black night
>     My song
>     From the dark lips
>     Of Africa . . .
>     Beautiful
>     As the black night . . .
>     Black
>     Out of Africa,
>     Me and my song.

Hughes had also joined in the popular poetic pastime of beating the tom-toms:

> The low beating of the tomtoms
> The slow beating of the tomtoms,
> Low . . . slow
> Slow . . . low
> Stirs your blood . . .

But in the end he was badly tripped himself by the vogue for primitivism and the noble-savage idea. When the bright "Renaissance" was fading into the gay depression, Hughes had got himself a patron, a rich old lady who lived on Park Avenue. She fed him well, sent him around town in her chauffeured limousine, and generally made his life comfortable and pleasant so that he could write "beautiful things." But one day he wrote a crude and angry poem contrasting the lushness of the newly opened Waldorf Astoria with the toil and growing deprivation outside. His benefactor did not like it at all. She wanted him to write out of his simple primitive soul, and poor Hughes did not know how.

She wanted me to be primitive, and know and feel the intuitions of the primitive. But, unfortunately, I did not feel the rhythms of the primitive surging through me, and so I could not live and write as though I did. I was only an American Negro—who had loved the surface of Africa and the rhythms of Africa—but I was not Africa. I was Chicago and Kansas City and Broadway and Harlem. And I was not what she wanted me to be.[7]

His parting from his patron threw Hughes into the second great emotional crisis of his life. As he had in Mexico in the crisis of his hatred for his father, he now again fell violently ill. It was a complicated shame and anger he felt, and an even more complicated loss. What he did was to go home to Cleveland, to his own mother, who had always demanded much of him and given him little. In Cleveland he took to the bed which his mother and stepfather vacated for him and stayed sick until he had spent what was left of his Park Avenue money, mostly on

7 *Ibid.*, p. 325.

doctors who did not know what was wrong and could do nothing for him.

Hughes was, in truth, "not Africa" at all. Africa had become another one of the world's places he had liked and left. During the next ten years he circled the world and saw much of its busy surface—Russia, China, Japan, Spain. In a second volume of his autobiography chronicling these travels up to 1938,[8] nowhere in all the pages filled with the sights he had seen and the names endlessly dropping does he again revert to the subject of Africa except in one or two incidental mentions. His notions about Africa remained mostly locked away among his old poems and old thoughts, and he did not bring them out and dust them off until recent years when new Negro and world interest in Africa rose so sharply. Then he revived them all, full of their drum-beats and ancestral memories and sad yearning, and wrote some new ones in the new mood and made them all part of "The Poetry of Jazz," a sequence of readings that he performs for large audiences, reciting to the accompaniment of beating drums. His new tone on Africa sounds like this:

> Africa,
> Sleepy giant,
> You've been resting awhile.
> Now I see the thunder
> And the lightning
> In your smile.
>
> Now I see
> The storm clouds
> In your waking eyes:
> The thunder,
> The wonder
> And the new
> Surprise.
>
> Your every step reveals
> The new stride
> In your thighs.

8 *I Wonder As I Wander* (New York, 1956).

"Big roll," says the direction to the accompanying drummer, as this poem ends.

## Richard Wright

Unlike Langston Hughes, Richard Wright never beat any tom-toms, never yearned after a dead past, or sentimentalized about a primitive present. Nor does it appear that any of his particular personal problems were wrapped up in the shades of color, in what it means to be light, not dark, tan, not brown, brown, not black. There is no mystique about blackness in Wright's pages. His mystiques are ideological and about these he tries to be as explicit as he can. He was not a man to touch a deep matter and, like Hughes, after brushing it lightly with a short poem, dance away until another day. Wright wrestled long and hard with the problems of world society and never found the art of fiction adequate to his need. Even in *Native Son,* the novel on which his fame mainly rests, he gave over 15 pages at the end to the courtroom summation in which Bigger Thomas' lawyer explains the sociology of Bigger's crime. Wright published twelve books, of which only three are novels, one short stories, and one an autobiography. The bulk of his work has been reportage, lectures, and essays, earnest and urgent explanations, exclamations, and exhortations. One of these books, *Black Power,* is the story of Wright's trip to Africa, to what was still the Gold Coast, in 1953. From this book we learn that Wright, like Langston Hughes, went through an experience of rejection and repulsion in Africa, though it was of quite a different kind. It is this experience that will concern us here. But to begin to see the individual Wright in Africa we have to try to see where the politician-ideologist Wright located Africa in his own larger setting.

As he constantly reminded his readers, Richard Wright spent twelve years, from 1932 to 1944, in the Communist Party. The cost of this experience was heavy. Though the Communist gods failed him, they did make him over sufficiently in their image to turn him into more of a political being than an artist. It was mainly to win back his identity as an artist that Wright, by his own account,[9] finally broke from the Communist grip. But he did not do so before they had more than half shaped him permanently in their ideological mold. The effects kept appearing in many of his ideas and in much of his writing in the years after he struck out on his own. But Wright not only left the Communist movement in which he had lived so long; soon afterward the native son also quit his native land to live in exile in France. Thus Wright left all his familiar places and chose to live, intellectually and physically, in limbo. Now anyone who tries to be heard from limbo has to shout loudly, and whether in these conditions Wright could grow or wither as an artist was a question that was cut off unanswered by his death in 1961. Except for a few bravely whistling passages,[10] he did not try—as far as we yet know —to deal with the stuff of his life in exile. In his third and last-published (1958) novel, *The Long Dream,* Wright went back to the Mississippi setting of his early years where his own apartness from the world began. A few topical references (e.g., to the Korean war) fix the time in the mid-1950's, but Wright unfolds his story as if it were happening a full generation earlier, never referring to the changes in the larger society which have made Mississippi part of a shrinking last stronghold of the white-supremacy system. At the end, when his protagonist finally leaves there, Wright has him board a train in his deep Southern town, then picks him up soaring over the land, never allowing us to see him set foot for an instant in any of the places where so much has changed since Wright went away. He has him continue instead, aloft in his plane, straight on across the sea bound for . . . Paris.

On the other hand, besides being a gifted writer, Richard Wright was also an honest and serious man who clung hard to the idea of some larger commonwealth for human society than the tribe, the nation, or the race. From his French exile he rest-

---

[9] *The God That Failed,* Richard Crossman, ed. (New York, 1950).

[10] "I'm a rootless man, but I'm neither psychologically distraught or in any wise disturbed because of it. Personally I do not hanker after, and seem not to need, as many emotional attachments, sustaining roots, or idealistic allegiances as most people. I declare unabashedly that I like and even cherish the state of abandonment, of aloneness; it does not bother me . . ." *White Man, Listen!,* (New York, 1957), p. 17.

lessly wandered to far corners in search of this larger identity. His thoughts on these matters appear in books like *The Color Curtain*, the story of his journey to the Bandung Conference in 1955, and *White Man, Listen!* a collection of lectures given in Europe between 1950 and 1956. In these works Wright is often strident and naïve and stretches some of his points until they snap. Too often, also, he seems to see himself as the first to discover what many before him have seen and said about the history of the West in Asia and Africa and about the emergent Asian and African elites. But even if he was not Balboa looking out over this turbulent sea, Wright brought special perceptions and emotions to bear upon his discoveries. They took him swiftly, unhindered by too much encumbering knowledge, to the sharp edges of many an Asian-African dilemma.

On the place of traditional cultures in the changing scene, about which so much loose talk passes, Wright sees clearly, for example, that the West was "irrevocably triumphant in its destruction of [the old] culture" of the lands it despoiled, and that in the very act of spoilation, "white Europeans set off a more deep-going and sudden revolution in Asia and Africa than had ever obtained in all the history of Europe." [11] The present task is one of total reorganization of all aspects of life and culture in these countries, and in this process Wright sees, with deep apprehension, the surviving power among these peoples of "race and religion, two of the most powerful and irrational forces in human nature." [12] In the matter of race, Wright sees dark and dangerous crevices ahead and illustrates with an anecdote about being served out of turn, ahead of a white American, by an Indonesian official:

Well, there it was . . . I was a member of the master race! I'm not proud of it. It took no intelligence, no courage. . . . It was racism. And I thought of all the times in the American South when I had had to wait until the whites had been served before I could be served. . . . All you have to do in a situation like that is relax and let your base instincts flow. And it's so easy, so natural, you don't have to think; you just push that face that is of an offensive color out of your mind

11 *The Color Curtain* (New York, 1956), p. 73; *White Man, Listen!*, p. 95.
12 *The Color Curtain*, p. 140.

and forget about it. You are inflicting an emotional wound that might last for years . . . but why worry about that! You are safe; there are thousands around you of your color, and if the man who's been offended should object, what the hell can he do? . . . That was how the whites had felt about it when they had had all the power . . . and now I saw that same process reversed. Will Asians and Africans, being as human as white men, take over this vicious pattern of identification when they become, as they will, masters of this earth? Racism is an evil thing and breeds its own kind.[13]

Wright described himself as being "numbed and appalled" by Asian and African religion:

The teeming religions gripping the minds and consciousness of Asians and Africans offend me. I can conceive of no identification with such mystical visions of life that freeze millions in static degradation, no matter how emotionally satisfying such degradation seems to those who wallow in it.[14]

He ponders uneasily over what could happen in the world if these outlooks ever became welded to the techniques and power instruments of the twentieth century. These countries will not progress, he argues, "until such religious rationalizations have been swept from men's minds," and the world will not be safe until the narrow "secular and rational base of thought and feeling" developed in the West fuses successfully with the similar base that, "shaky and delicate as yet, exists also in the elite of Asia and Africa."

And those two bases of Eastern and Western rationalism must become one! And quickly, or else the tenuous Asian-African secular, rational attitudes will become flooded, drowned in irrational tides of racial and religious passions.[15]

So here was Richard Wright, unwilling to lean on desiccated tradition and rejecting all superstition (in which he included all religion, from Anabaptism to Zoroastrianism) and everything else that he thought hobbled the free human mind. He looked, in his own way, for new reaches of the human spirit. He did not

13 *Ibid.*, pp. 114–115.
14 *White Man, Listen!*, p. 80.
15 *The Color Curtain*, p. 219.

want an identity made up of what he saw as the useless baggage
of the past, and in his own past he saw little that he wanted to
carry forward with him at all. This was his pain and trouble, and
this is what drove him apart not only from most of the white
world but also from much of the nonwhite world as well, because
in both worlds most men still reach back for the buttressing
comfort of tradition, even when it is hollow. This was the lonely
man who in 1953 journeyed to Africa, wondering what he would
find there that would link him to Africans in a common legacy
from the ancestral past.

Richard Wright went to the Gold Coast four years before it
became the independent state of Ghana. Nkrumah was already
"Leader of Government Business," but the British were still in
control. The new shape of things was present in outline but as
yet had little substance. In his account of this journey [16] Wright
has much to say about Gold Coast politics and Nkrumah's politics. He ends by urging Nkrumah to be "hard," to "militarize"
his people for the leap, in one generation, out of the past. "Our
people must be made to walk, forced draft, into the twentieth
century!" But such views are not unique to Wright and are
in any case another subject. For our purposes here we will bypass
Wright's thinking about the politics of Africa and pick up instead the thread of his reactions to Africans; his painful exploration of the real or imagined elements of kinship between him
and the Africans among whom he came as a black American
stranger. This was in fact the principal theme that raced through
his mind at the outset when it was first suggested to him that he
go to Africa:

I heard them, but my mind and feelings were racing along another and hidden track. Africa! Being of African descent, would I
be able to feel and know something about Africa on the basis of
a common "racial" heritage? Africa was a vast continent full of "my
people." . . . Or had three hundred years imposed a psychological
distance between me and the "racial stock" from which I had

[16] *Black Power, A Record of Reactions in a Land of Pathos* (New York, 1954).
All following quotations from Wright are from this source, until otherwise
indicated.

sprung? . . . My emotions seemed to be touching a dark and dank wall . . . Am I African? Had some of my ancestors sold their relatives to white men? What would my feelings be when I looked into the black face of an African, feeling that maybe his great-great-great-grandfather had sold my great-great-great-grandfather into slavery? Was there something in Africa that my feelings could latch onto to make all of this dark past clear and meaningful? Would the Africans regard me as a lost brother who had returned? . . . According to popular notions of "race" there ought to be something of "me" down there in Africa. Some vestige, some heritage, some vague but definite ancestral reality that would serve as a key to unlock the hearts and feelings of the Africans whom I'd meet . . . But I could not feel anything African about myself, and I wonder, "What does being *African* mean?"

The meeting between Richard Wright and Africa produced something less than love at first sight. At first sight what did strike him—as it has other Negroes—was the fact that "the whole of life that met the eyes was black"; but instead of being enthralled by it, Wright was full of the grim thought that these were the people whose so-and-so ancestors had sold *his* ancestors down the river and across the sea into slavery. In his first minutes ashore he was exchanging hostilities on this score with the second African he met, a clerk in a store who pressed Wright to explain why he did not know where in Africa his ancestors had lived. "You know," he said "softly" to the startled clerk, "you fellows who sold us and the white men who bought us didn't keep any records." It is characteristic of Wright that of all the possible reasons for avowed or unavowed Negro constraint toward Africans, this should be the one to float free and first at the top of his mind. He brings it up again several times during his stay, and when, just before leaving, he makes the pilgrimage to the great grim castles from which the slaves had been fed out to the ships riding offshore, again this is first among the images in his mind. At Christianborg Castle he tries to imagine a decked-out chief leading his prisoners into the castle to be sold, but "my mind refused to function." At Elmina Castle he looked into the slave dungeons through the slits from neighboring rooms where "African chiefs would hide themselves while their captives were being bid for by Europeans." Wright thinks of this as a principal source for American Negro alienation from Africans, but only once in all my interviews did anyone even mention this particular view of Africans as guilty participants in the historic crimes of enslavement. Whatever else it might prove to be at more obscure depths, this thought is at least part of an effort to be evenhandedly honest. In Wright it is also a defense against sentimentality, or worse, racism.

Actually as a "raceman," or more correctly an "antiraceman," Wright confronted Africa with all sorts of harsh and complicated questions in his mind. But he reacted at the same time at several different levels. He reacted also, to begin with, as a Western man, a man of Paris, New York, Chicago, a comer to Africa from a different world, a different century. As he rode into town from the shorefront where he landed, "the kaleidoscope of sea, jungle, nudity, mud huts, and crowded market places induced in me . . . a protest against what I saw . . . [not] against Africa or its people [but] against the unsettled feeling engendered by the strangeness of a completely different order of life . . . a world whose laws I did not know . . . faces whose reactions were riddles to me." Wright not only felt the familiar revulsion of the Western man at the sights and smells of non-Western backwardness and poverty; he was also overcome by a strong sense of its impenetrability. "Faced with the absolute otherness and inaccessibility of this new world, I was prey to a vague sense of mind panic, an oppressive burden of alertness which I could not shake off." It was not merely that the lack of modern sanitation assailed his Western-style fastidiousness; it was more the lack of modern thinking that assailed his Western-style intelligence. For Wright reacted most of all as a rationalist who had put his faith in the power of the mind to conquer ignorance and violence. He made a positively heroic effort to explore and understand African religious notions and superstitions as he came upon them, trying to discuss them with ordinary people and with intellectuals, trying to make sense out of what he could find to read about the matter. Going by his own rules, he tried to banish the thought that this was all "irrational" and to get at "the underlying assumptions of the African beliefs." He dived in, and then had to "come up for air, to take a deep breath," and while he came up musing with the thought that the African's religious dreams might be better suited to his old ways, might indeed be "the staunchest kind of reality," his strong sense of history told him that this could not ever be the stuff of life in the twentieth-century world that the white man had irrevocably made over in his image. It appalled him to find that belief in juju or magic was by no means confined to the uneducated. He ran into it even in Nkrumah's anteroom, where the chief minister's secretary warned him not to underestimate its power.

At the end of his journey Wright wrote to Nkrumah that he had "felt an odd kind of at-homeness, a solidarity that stemmed not from ties of blood or race, or from my being of African descent," but from "the deep hope and suffering imbedded in the lives of your people, from the hard facts of oppression . . ." Again, Wright is trying to be as truthful as he can. But by his own account he never did get to feel at home at all in the Gold Coast. He left the country as he had come, full of his broad, general bonds of political solidarity and sympathy, but still a stranger. He was confounded by what he saw of the psychological and cultural havoc wreaked by the whites, especially by their missionaries. But he was also shaken by what he discovered about the nature of surviving African culture. Wright was at home in none of this, either with any part of the society or with individuals. As he traveled about, questing, probing, asking, he never did find it easy to open channels of communication with Africans. On this score, in fact, he delivers some whopping generalizations:

I found the African an oblique, hard-to-know man who seems to take a kind of childish pride in trying to create a state of bewilderment in the minds of strangers.

Or again:

I found that the African almost invariably underestimated the person with whom he was dealing; he always placed too much confidence in an evasive reply, thinking that if he denied something, then that something ceased to exist. It was childlike.

His most qualified statement:

Most of the Africans I've met have been, despite the ready laughter, highly reserved and suspicious men . . .

He found the attitude of distrust to be universal:

I could feel [the] distrust of me; it came from no specific cause; it was general. I was a stranger, a foreigner, and, therefore, must be spoken to cautiously, with weighed words. Distrust was in full operation before any objective event had occurred to justify it. A stranger confronting an African and feeling this distrust would begin to react to it and he'd feel himself becoming defensively distrustful himself. Distrust bred distrust; he'd begin to watch for evasion; he'd begin to question a flattering phrase . . . In the end what had begun as a stranger's apprehension of the African's wariness would terminate in a distrust created out of nowhere, conjured up out of nothing. This fear, this suspicion of nothing in particular came to be the most predictable hallmark of the African mentality that I met in all the Gold Coast, from the Prime Minister down to the humblest "mammy" selling *kenke* on the street corners.

Wright thought for awhile that "this chronic distrust arose from their centuries-long exploitation by Europeans," but after he had wandered farther, especially into the Ashanti country to the north, he came to think that the "African's doubt of strangers" was "lodged deep in the heart of African culture." He thought he discovered its source deep in the patterns of fear and guilt that he found in the ancestor worship and blood sacrifices that dominated traditional African beliefs. "Men whose hearts are swamped by such compounded emotional problems," he concluded, "must needs be always at war with reality. Distrust is the essence of such a life."

Restlessly, Wright took his questions to all sorts of people. He was relieved to find a quality of relative directness in one of the Gold Coast's leading intellectuals, author of a work he'd consulted on the country's religion. But he was left again at a loss when this man assured him that if he would stay longer in Africa he would come to *feel* his race.

"*What?*"
"You'll feel it," he assured me. "It'll all come *back* to you."

"What'll come back?"

"The knowledge of your race . . ."

. . . I knew that I'd never feel an identification with Africans on a "racial" basis. "I doubt that," I said softly.

Again and again Wright remarks that his blackness, his African descent, did not help him at all in achieving communication with Africans. After being caught up one day in a funeral procession and trying to learn what it meant, he wrote: "I had understood nothing. I was black and they were black, but my blackness did not help me." He found it the same with young black officials, with young nationalists, with Nkrumah himself. Something of their nature as he found it, or something about his unrelenting inquisitiveness, or both together, threw up a barrier that baffled him. "I'm of African descent and I'm in the midst of Africans, yet I cannot tell what they are thinking and feeling."

But in this matter of kinship linking Africans and American Negroes, Wright did have one experience that pulled him up sharply and again left him baffled in the end. On one of his first days in Accra he rode around town with Nkrumah. Crowds gathered around their car, shouting and singing their greetings to the leader, the women dancing, "a sort of weaving, circular motion with their bodies, a kind of queer shuffling dance . . ."

And then I remembered: I'd seen these same snakelike, veering dances before . . . Where? Oh, God, yes, in America, in storefront churches, in Holy Roller tabernacles, in God's Temples, in unpainted wooden prayer-meeting houses in the plantations of the Deep South . . . And here I was seeing it all again against a background of a surging nationalistic political movement. How could that be? . . . What I was now looking at in this powerfully improvised dance of these women, I'd seen before in America. How was that possible?

He had always rejected the ideas of "some American anthropologists" about "what they had quaintly chosen to call 'African survivals,' a phrase which they had coined to account for exactly what I had observed."

I understood why so many American Negroes were eager to disclaim any relationship with Africa . . . first, it was a natural part of his assimilation of Americanism; second, so long had Africa been described as something shameful, barbaric, a land in which one went about naked, a land in which his ancestors had sold their kith and kin as slaves—so long had he heard all this that he wanted to disassociate himself in his mind from all such realities.

The bafflement evoked in me by this new reality did not spring from any desire to disclaim kinship with Africa, or from any shame of being of African descent. My problem was how to account for this "survival" of Africa in America when I stoutly denied the mystic influence of "race," when I was as certain as I was of being alive that it was only, by and large, in the concrete social frame of reference in which men lived that one could account for men being what they were . . . that "racial" qualities were but myths of prejudiced minds . . . I sighed. This was a truly big problem . . .

Wright kept churning this matter in his mind and finally produced a lumpy sort of answer: where he was free to do so, the transplanted African adapted to his new environment and, like any other human being, changed to meet its demands; but where he was barred from fitting himself fully into his new setting, he retained some of his "basic and primal attitudes toward life, including "his basically poetic apprehension of existence." This does not appear to shed much light on the question of "African survivals," but the episode does sharpen our picture of Richard Wright. For he also tells us that instead of making him feel any closer to Africans, the sight of the dancing women had made him feel his apartness all the more:

. . . This African dance today was as astonishing and dumbfounding to me as it had been when I'd seen it in America. Never in my life had I been able to dance more than a few elementary steps and the carrying even of the simplest tune had always been beyond me. So, what had bewildered me about Negro dance expression in the United States now bewildered me in the same way in Africa.

Here perhaps is the ultimate clue to Richard Wright's experience in Africa, indeed to his experience anywhere. For Wright reacted to Africa not only as a Western man, a rationalist, a twentieth-century man, an American Negro, but also as a man whose chosen life style was outsiderness, the source of his chief pains and anxieties and also of his chief satisfactions. Unlike Langston Hughes, Wright does not feel "outside" merely because he is neither wholly white nor wholly black. But more like Du Bois, in his mind's eye he sees himself standing out in the open spaces of history that time has not yet filled; his limbo again. In Africa Wright, already separated by so much from the Europeans, found himself also apart from Africans, because Europeans and Africans alike carried with them too much of the burden of the past that he wanted to see left behind.

Three years later, at a conference of black artists and writers in Paris, convened under the mystic aura of the concept of *negritude,* Wright was described (in an account by James Baldwin) as being claimed as a spokesman both by American Negroes and by Africans; but when it came his turn to speak, Wright could only speak for himself. He had been listening to the proceedings with a troubled ear. He was both a black man and a Westerner, he said, and this made for painful contradictions. "I see both worlds from another, and third, point of view." [17] This meant that while he shared the black man's rejection of the white world's power and prejudices, he also insisted upon recognizing that Europe, though seeking its own selfish ends and acting quite blindly, had also freed Africans from the "rot" of their past, and that this was a good thing. For the American Negroes who were trying to establish contact with the Africans at the conference this was, at the very least, tactless, and they were embarrassed by it. As for the Africans, most of them were either politically intent on using their sticks to beat all white beasts, including the American, or they were deep in the dark pool of *negritude,* trying to recreate a racial mystique as the basis for making the unique African presence known, at last, to the world. The result was that both for Americans and Africans, Wright succeeded only in making alien noises. This left him where he always chose to be, outside.

17 James Baldwin, "Princes and Powers," *Encounter,* Jan. 1957, p. 58.

But Wright's experience did bring the subject of Africa back
into his thinking about the problems of American Negroes and
their endless effort to identify themselves. All of Wright's books
had been about the shaping of Negro identities, including his
own. But the thought of Africa in this connection had not come
to the top before this, neither in the life of Bigger Thomas, nor
in his own early years, as told in *Black Boy,* nor in his 1953
novel, *The Outsider.* It appears for the first time in Wright's
fiction in *The Long Dream,* published in 1958, blowing in on
wisps of talk among four teen-age boys in a small Mississippi
town. One of them is the son of a strong raceman type who
thinks Negroes ought to acquire as *African* the identity denied
them as *American.* He brings the matter to his friends, and they
try it out on Fishbelly:

"Fish, you want to go to *Africa?*"
Fishbelly blinked, looking from black face to black face.
"Hunh? To *Africa?*" Fishbelly asked. "*What for?*"
Zeke and Tony stomped their feet with glee. Sam scowled.
"*I told you.*" Zeke screamed triumphantly.
"Fish, you sure looked funny when you heard that word 'Africa.' "
Tom whooped.
"But who's going to Africa?" Fishbelly asked, seeking the point of
the debate.
"Nobody but damn fools!" said Zeke emphatically.
"Nobody but fatheads!" Tony growled.
"You niggers don't know nothing!" Sam railed at Zeke and Tony.
"Who's a nigger?" Zeke asked, fists clenched . . .
"A nigger's a black man who don't know who he *is,*" Sam made
the accusation general.

Sam goes on to charge them with wanting to be *white,* and when
the others indignantly deny it, he taxes them with trying to
straighten their hair, "like white folks' hair." But it is not to
make it look *white* but to look *nice,* the boys answer. Sam sneers
back that this is because *white* folks think straight hair is *nice,*
and the others scream that he is lying. Sam then makes Fishbelly
admit that if he went back far enough, he had to agree that his
folks had come from Africa:

"Okay, they came from Africa." Fishbelly tried to cover up his hesitancy. . . . Sam now fired his climactic question.

"Now, just stand there and tell me, what *is* you?"

Before Fishbelly could reply, Zeke and Tony set up a chant:

"Fishbelly's a African! Fishbelly's a African!"

Sam then tries to prove to the confused and uncomfortable Fishbelly that if he was no longer African he certainly could not say he was American:

"All I know about Africa's what I read in the geography book at school," Fishbelly numbled, unwilling to commit himself.

"Sam wants us to git naked and run wild and eat with our hands and live in mud huts!" Zeke ridiculed . . .

"Okay," Sam agreed sarcastically. "Nobody wants to go to Africa. Awright. Who wants to go to America? . . ."

"We awready in America, you fool!"

"Aw, naw you ain't," Sam cried hotly. "You niggers ain't *nowhere*. You ain't in Africa, 'cause the white man took you out. And you ain't in America. . . . You can't live like no American, 'cause you ain't no American. And you ain't African neither! So what is you? Nothing! *Just nothing!*"

Wright had gone to Africa to find out, among other things, whether a black man who was *nothing* could become *something* there. He had come away knowing that Africans were on the way to becoming *something,* but he did not know what, and he was not sure he liked it. As for black Americans, Wright had no word. As we have already remarked, his novel ends with the boy Fishbelly leaping, in a sentence or two, from Mississipi to France. There is no hint that there is an answer for Fishbelly in France or in Africa. But neither is there any hint that Fishbelly carried any word to Paris that might have brought Richard Wright back to America to see if any new answers were forming here. Unless there is some new light on the matter in the papers he left behind him, we will never know.

## Ralph Ellison

"Richard Wright," said Ralph Ellison, had "a passion for ideology and [was] fascinated by power. I have no desire to

manipulate power. I want to write imaginative books." The
books Ellison wants to write are books that will come out of
the American Negro's own culture and as works of art become
part of the culture of man. He has made it his problem to identify that culture and preserve it in literature, while Wright's
problem, he said, was that he "cut his ties to American Negroes"
and [was] more concerned wth world politics and world sociology. "People who want to write sociology," Ellison has written,
"should not write a novel."

Like Wright, Ellison rejects racial mysticism, and he also
strongly rejects the idea that there is any significant kinship between American Negroes and Africans. But unlike Wright, Ellison feels this so strongly that he has not even allowed himself
any curiosity about the matter. He was offered a trip to Africa
in 1955 but turned it down. "I said I had no interest in it," he
told me, "no special emotional attachment to the place. I don't
read much on Africa nowadays. It is just a part of the bigger
world picture to me."

At the time we talked, events in Africa had already begun to
make a visible impact among Negroes, but Ellison had remained
quite unimpressed by it. In years past, he remarked, "Negroes
either repeated all the very negative clichés, or else laughed at
Africa, or, in some cases, related to it as a homeland." As an
example of the latter type he mentioned the black nationalists,
like the character Ras the Exhorter in *The Invisible Man*, and
he also remembered that he had felt involved in the Ethiopian
war. "Back in the 1930's I was for Ethiopia too, of course, but I
did not identify with the Ethiopians as people. I remember
being amused when Haile Selassie denied any identity with
American Negroes." At the present time, Ellison went on, the
rise of nationalism in Africa has made many Negroes feel good.
"The man on the street might say now that Africa is justifying
Garvey. He might say: 'They said Garvey was a boob, but look
now, just watch, they'll go right on to South Africa and kick
those crackers out of there.' There is a lot of this pride, predicting things, putting the bad mouth on the whites, now that
things are finally moving in Africa." Middle-class Negroes might
share this pride to some extent, but Ellison said he did not know

much about middle-class Negroes. As for intellectuals, he was contemptuous. He thought that there was a lot of "fakery" in some of the new organizations springing up to exploit the new feeling about Africa and he scornfully referred to a certain well-known Negro intellectual who "had taken to wearing African robes at Alabama State."

Ellison himself had been unable to respond in any direct way to Africans, and the experience had been mutual. "The Africans I've met in Paris and Rome have seen me as an alien. They see most American Negroes this way. I never really got into contact. I won't have anything to do with racial approaches to culture." His only point of contact, he said, was an interest in African art. He had read Malraux's new interpretations of it and gone to some exhibitions, but that was all. Not having any political interests like Wright's, and believing that the African origins had only the most remote place in the making of a distinctively American Negro culture, Ellison has not written at all on the subject, alluding to it only in glancing remarks in some of his essays. Hence what I report here on the way in which Ellison sees Africa (as well as himself) comes out of a long day's talk during which he freely and generously and with cool candor answered a great many questions.

As we spoke of Wright and other Negro writers who have chosen to live as expatriates in Europe, Ellison showed me a clipping from *Time* in which he had been included among the exiles because he had just spent two years in Rome on a fellowship. In a letter to the editor sharply correcting the report Ellison said: "While I sympathize with those Negro Americans whose disgust with the racial absurdities of American life leads them to live elsewhere, my own needs—both as citizen and as artist—make the gesture of exile seem mere petulance." He said he thought for a writer the key question was where he could work well, adding that Faulkner did all right in Mississippi and Hemingway and Henry James in Europe, while "Richard Wright wrote better in Chicago and Brooklyn than he did in Paris." As for himself: "Personally I am too vindictively American, too full of hate for the hateful aspects of this country, and too possessed by the things I love here to be too long away."

Ralph Ellison came up just behind Richard Wright—he is five years younger—and for a few years in the 1930's they traveled together in the orbit of the Communist movement, with Wright serving as a help and an inspiration to the younger man. But Ellison had come up by a different path, from Oklahoma via Tuskegee, and out of a life that eventually shaped him into a different kind of writer. Like Wright, Ellison had lost his father at an early age, but to death, not desertion. His father had been a construction foreman, served in the Army in the Philippines and the Orient, had read widely, and had named his son after Ralph Waldo Emerson. Ellison's mother was a strong-minded woman who worked as a servant in a white home, but also helped canvass Negro voters for Eugene Debs' Socialist Party and was in touch with "liberal whites who tried to keep Oklahoma from becoming like Texas, but failed." His mother bought her two sons a phonograph and records, electrical sets and chemical sets, and a toy typewriter, and told them the world would get to be a better place if they fought to change it. Oklahoma was Jim Crow, and "you knew about the villainies of white people, yet in Oklahoma it was possible to realize that it was not a blanket thing . . . We had some violence, there was fighting between Negro and white boys, but it was not too deeply fixed in the traditions or psychology of people." Ellison's mother had encouraged him to read, and at Tuskegee he "blundered onto T. S. Eliot's *Wasteland* and started to follow up all the footnotes, reading all those books . . ." Ellison came to New York, then, not as Wright had come to Chicago, out of a seared childhood and with a parched mind. He did not come escaping, but seeking, and this difference laid its mark on their preoccupations and their work as writers. Wright became the restless ideologue, pulling away from the near, small things, and looking for the large solutions, while Ellison, as he began to write *The Invisible Man,* asked himself: "Could you present the Negro in his universal aspects and not keep your imagination in the leash of sociology? How do you do this and have it understood?"

In trying to think his way through to expressing what he believes to be a distinctive American Negro culture, Ellison has little or no thought at all of any African influence on this culture, past or present, or on himself. "I have great difficulty associating myself with Africa," Ellison said. "I suppose this is because so many people insist that I have a special tie to it that I could never discover in any concrete way. I mean the sociologists, Negro friends of mine who are trying to find some sort of past beyond the previous condition of servitude. I have always felt very Western. I can't find that in Africa in any way. I think now of Ghana, new countries, their problems, their need to bridge the gap between tribal patterns and the needs of modern government and life."

As we began to talk of his awarenesses of Africa and began to move back in time, all the familiar experiences quickly turned up in his memories. He brought them in and flicked them away: "the usual crap" in geography class, "the African villain in jungle movies." By his account these had simply rolled off his hard surfaces:

"As a small boy, I remember the Garvey movement. We had some enthusiasts out there in Oklahoma. People wanted to go to Africa. The people I knew thought this was very amusing, going back to a place they had never been. The other association I can remember was in geography class, the usual crap, Africans as lazy people, living in the sun. I always knew we were partially descended from African slave stock. I knew that Negroes were black and that blacks came from Africa . . . There were expressions, the fist, for example, was called 'African soupbone.' No"—he dismissed my question shortly—"I don't think this was an allusion to cannibalism.

"You ran into the African villain in jungle movies," he went on. "I suppose that like all other kids I identified with the white heroes. I have no vivid memories of them or the feelings they aroused. I don't remember being repelled. You might have related to the blacks in some way, but you identified with the hero, not with the villains. I do remember a Negro named Noel Johnson who always played Indian roles, and all Indians, of course, were villains. We always went for him, though, and when they would be coming after him, the kids in the movie would shout: 'Look out, Noel, here they come after you!' "

In his reading, Ellison came across it quite incidentally, as in Countee Cullen's poem "Heritage." At the time, 1931, he said, "I felt it to be artificial and alien. I was reading all these people very intensely and I felt something missing in them that I ran into in Eliot, the folk tradition they had and didn't know what to do with." This was at Tuskegee where "we had African princes walking around the campus. There was a girl from Sierra Leone and West Indians—we tended to link them all together. The sense of the alien was strong. It was not antagonism but a matter of totally different cultural backgrounds. I didn't share much of the interest in these people . . . Usually I thought them quite British. I had no cultural identification with them. I rejected any notion of a link, just as I later rejected Herskovits' ideas [about African cultural survivals]. Lorenzo Turner on African survivals in American speech interested me. But I did not—and I do not—feel a lack in my cultural heritage as an American Negro. I think a lot of time is wasted trying to find a substitute in Africa. Who was it that saw Americans as 'a people without a history but with a new synthesis'? The thing to do is to exploit the meaning of the life you have."

In *The Invisible Man* the African theme appears only in the person of Ras the Exhorter, leader of the ultraracist black nationalists in Harlem, patterned on one of several successors to Marcus Garvey in the Harlem of the 1930's. In Ellison's novel, Ras, a West Indian black man, contests the streets of Harlem with the Communists. During a fracas caused by Ras' attempt to break up a Communist street meeting, Ras, knife in hand, makes a passionate appeal to a black Communist:

"You *my* brother, mahn. Brothers are the same color; how the hell you call these white men *brother?* . . . Brothers the same color. We sons of Mama Africa, you done forgot? You black. BLACK! You—*Godahm*, mahn!" he said, swinging the knife for emphasis. "You got bahd *hair*. You got thick *lips!* They say you stink! They hate you, mahn. You African. AFRICAN! Why you with them?"

The two Communists, one of them Ellison's protagonist, listen fascinated despite themselves as Ras tells them the only allies to seek were not white men but black and yellow and brown allies, and that the white men would only betray and betray and betray them in the end. "This man's full of pus," says Ellison's hero as he pulls his friend away, "black pus." At the novel's end, in the wild and bloody rage of a Harlem riot, Ras the Ex-horter appears on a black horse in the midst of his followers, dressed "in the costume of an Abyssinian chieftain, a fur cap upon his head, his arm bearing a shield, a cape made of the skin of some animal around his shoulders." Ras confronts Ellison's hero on the dark street just as he has come to realize the perfidy involved in bringing on the bloodshed. He tries to reason with Ras, he wants to say, "Look, we're all black folks together . . ." But Ras is blood mad and they fight, and it is in fleeing from Ras the Destroyer that Ellison's hero descends into the deep cellar where he begins to re-order everything he has learned in his life. His principal discovery seems to be that not only the black man but every man shares the common plight: "None of us seems to know who he is or where he's going." He ultimately decides that he must shake off the "old skin," leave it in the hole behind him, and re-emerge into a world of "infinite possi-bilities"—"a good phrase and a good view of life and a man shouldn't accept any other."

Thus while Richard Wright wandered over the world hold-ing fast to his outsiderness, Ellison clung hard to his home ground and began trying to reach for a new sense of Negro *insiderness,* for a distinctive cultural personality that asserted its legitimacy within the American society and, for that matter, within the total human culture. Ellison is trying to look beyond the threshold of the conquest of civil rights and equality of status for Negroes, and asks himself: What does the Negro be-come when he has shed his second-classness? "What part of Negro life has been foisted on us by Jim Crow and must be got-ten rid of? What part of Negro life, expression, culture do we want to keep? We will need more true self-consciousness. I don't know what values, what new tragic sense must emerge. What happens to the values of folk life, of church life? Up to now it has been a matter of throwing things off. But now we have to get conscious of what we do not want to throw off." Ellison be-lieves that the Negro identity of the future will be shaped out of the unique Negro folk tradition. He believes this can be preserved—though he is not sure how—and that the Negro is not struggling to become free simply in order to disappear.

"To the question, *What am I?*," Ellison said, "I answer that I am a Negro American. That means far more than something racial. It does not mean race, it means something cultural, that I am a man who shares a dual culture. For me, the Negro is a member of an America-bound cultural group with its own idiom, its own psychology, growing out of its preoccupations with certain problems for hundreds of years, out of all its history. The American Negro stock is *here,* a synthesis of various African cultures, then of slavery, and of all the experience of Negroes since."

Of all these ingredients the African is the least: "The African content of American Negro life is more fanciful than actual," Ellison said, and this is why he has such a minimum interest in it. He thinks that it is the novelist's business to translate the unique Negro experience into literature. "As long as Negroes are confused as to how they relate to American culture," he said, "they will be confused about their relationship to places like Africa."

## James Baldwin

What would you say, I asked James Baldwin, if a man from Mars appeared suddenly before you and asked: "What are you?" Baldwin looked at the question quizzically. "At the time I left the country in 1948," he said, "I would have answered your man from Mars by saying: 'I am a writer'—with an edge in my voice while thinking: I am a nigger, you green bastard. Now I think I'd say to him: 'I'm a writer with a lot of work to do and wondering if I can do it.' "

Both Richard Wright and Ralph Ellison had something to do with this change in Baldwin's concept of himself over this space of years. In 1948 Baldwin was twenty-four years old, born and grown in Harlem, already full of knowing he had to write and already full of bile and desperation. He followed Richard Wright's example and left this country for France. "I knew I would die if I stayed here," he said, "that I would never be a writer." In 1952 Baldwin came back to America for a brief visit, and while he was here he met Ralph Ellison. He came away from that encounter with the impression of a tough-minded man who already took it for granted that great changes had come and that it was time for a Negro writer to learn a new job, "to help Negroes destroy their habits of mind of inferiority, those crushing habits, to become men and women, not to use 'black' as a crutch, but to get past it, to become a person with no special privilege and no special handicap." Baldwin went back to exile with habits of mind and handicaps of his own to overcome, but with this new idea also turning slowly within him. As he thought and wrote searchingly about the problems of his identity, as a man, as a man with African ancestors, as a Negro, an American, a writer, Baldwin was already beginning to look around him with a fresh eye, though it was some time before he was able to bring what he saw into focus. When he finally did so—it took another six years—new emotions of assertion of self had displaced his hatred for whites, and Baldwin came home.

"I began to be oppressed in Europe by the American colony talking about how awful America was," Baldwin said. "It made no sense, it made me mad. There in France, with its own injustice and corruption, the Algerian thing, people just as small-minded as everywhere else. It just wasn't *that* much better! Sitting on a café terrace and trying to explain Little Rock made me feel as though I was letting the best years of my life go to nothing." Baldwin looked critically at Richard Wright whom, he said, he "admired and liked" but "who has gotten caught between his habits of rage and what is going on in the world, so he doesn't understand it very well. He is frightened by the Africans he knows in Paris who have such different attitudes than he has, and by the things which have happened in America, depriving him of his role of being the celebrated victim." [18] Through a long and painful process Baldwin came anew to an old conclusion: "You have to go far away to find out that

18 For Baldwin's thoughts about Wright after the latter's death, see "Alas, Poor Richard," *Nobody Knows My Name*, pp. 181–215.

you never do get far away." He also came to realize: "I couldn't get to *know* France. The key to my experience was *here,* in America. Everything I could deal with was *here.*" From a pile of papers, Baldwin pulled out an article he had just written that was to have appeared that very week in the strikebound *New York Times Book Review,*[19] in which he reviewed his rediscovery of his identity as an American:

For even the most incorrigible maverick had to be born somewhere. He may leave the group which produced him—or he may be forced to—but nothing will efface his origins, the marks of which he carries with him everywhere. I think it is important to know this and even find it a matter for rejoicing, as the strongest people do, regardless of their station. On this acceptance, literally, the life of a writer depends.

Baldwin could not come to this acceptance easily. He had much to weigh, including some acutely important personal considerations. But one day in the tenth year of his exile he finally chose to quit Wright's path for Ellison's in order, ultimately, to find his own. He wrote:

This is a personal day, a terrible day, the day to which his entire sojourn has been tending. It is the day he realizes that there are no untroubled countries in this fearfully troubled world, that if he has been preparing himself for anything in Europe, he has been preparing himself—for America. In short, the freedom that the American writer finds in Europe brings him full circle back to himself, with the responsibility for his development where it always was: in his own hands.

So Baldwin came back from exile, after ten years, and went on a journey of discovery to the American South, which he had never seen. "That was when I realized what tremendous things were happening," he told me, "and that I did have a role to play; that I was part of it, could work for it." Baldwin looked away. "I can't be happy here," he said, "but I can work here."

[19] It appeared in the issue of Jan. 25, 1959, and was republished in *Nobody Knows My Name* (pp. 3–12) under the title "Discovery of What It Means To Be An American."

In James Baldwin's story of himself and his rediscoveries we come upon Africa at several different levels and in several different guises. It appears most directly in the persons of the Africans he met in Paris during the years of his exile. Baldwin found them difficult to get on with, difficult to talk to, and he had a sense of a great gulf of difference between them and himself. In a 1950 essay [20] he describes this difference:

The African before him has endured privation, injustice, medieval cruelty; but the African has not yet endured the utter alienation of himself from his people and his past. His mother did not sing "Sometimes I Feel Like A Motherless Child," and he has not, all his life long, ached for acceptance in a culture which pronounced straight hair and white skin the only acceptable beauty. They face each other, the Negro and the African, over a gulf of three hundred years —an alienation too vast to be conquered in an evening's goodwill . . .

In our talk about these matters Baldwin added these details:

I think these Africans admired whites more than I did, and thought the white world was worth getting into. I thought they were naive. They liked American things, cigarettes, clothes. I suppose they frightened me. They illustrated all the things I had been running away from. All my clothes were dark. I would run from wearing bright clothes. They went around in outrageous getups. They were terribly goodnatured, but did not seem to have, really, any understanding of the world or of how society is put together. I say this of the students, not of people like [the West African poet] Senghor . . . Senghor frightened me because of his extraordinary way of being civilized and primitive at the same time. . . . This frightened me. I thought this meant sooner or later a great clash between myself and someone like that. I was committed to Western society in a way he could not be . . . All discussions were on politics. You could never get into anything else. They disgusted me, I think. They thought I had money, but I didn't. Maybe I was insufficiently intransigent against America. I couldn't really hate America the way they did. They hated America, were full of racial stories, held their attitudes largely on racial grounds. Politically, they knew very little about it. Whenever I was with an African, we would both be uneasy. On what

level to talk? The terms of our life were so different, we almost
needed a dictionary to talk. . . .

At quite a different level, as he searched out the terms of his
elusive identity, Baldwin for a long time saw Africa as the blank
and empty backdrop of his past. It was the edge of the world
over which he dropped, he thought, into nothingness as he
backed away, an unwanted and unsharing alien, from the rich
and busy world of non-African culture:

> . . . I was a kind of bastard of the West; when I followed the line
> of my past I did not find myself in Europe but in Africa. And this
> meant that in some subtle way, in a really profound way, I brought
> to Shakespeare, Bach, Rembrandt, to the stones of Paris, to the cathe-
> dral at Chartres, and to the Empire State Building a special attitude.
> These were not really my creations; they did not contain my history;
> I might search in them in vain forever for any reflection of myself.
> I was an interloper; this was not my heritage. At the same time I
> had no other heritage which I could possibly hope to use—I had cer-
> tainly been unfitted for the jungle or the tribe. I would have to ap-
> propriate these white centuries, I would have to make them mine—I
> would have to accept my special attitude, my special place in this
> scheme—otherwise I would have no place in *any* scheme.[21]

At one time Baldwin went (to work and to recover from a
"species of breakdown") to a tiny village in Switzerland where
he was the first black man any of the villagers had ever seen.
The children ran after him calling "Neger! Neger!" and
touched his hair or tried to see if his color came off when they
rubbed it. He told them he came from America, but they did
not really believe it because they knew that "black men come
from Africa." The village made an annual pre-Lenten collection to "buy" African natives into Christ's grace. Two village
children blackened their faces, put horsehair wigs on their
blond heads, and solicited money for the missionaries in Africa.
Baldwin was proudly informed that the last year they had
raised enough to "buy" six or eight Africans out of hell's grasp.
Baldwin tried vainly to imagine "white men arriving for the
first time in an African village" and the astonishment with

21 *Ibid.*, p. 7.

which the black villagers might exclaim over the white men's hair and skin.

But there is a great difference between the first white man to be seen by Africans and being the first black man to be seen by whites. The white man takes the astonishment as tribute, for he arrives to conquer and convert the natives, whose inferiority in relation to himself is not even to be questioned; whereas I, without a thought of conquest, find myself among a people whose culture controls me, has even, in a sense, created me, people who have cost me more in anguish and rage than they will ever know . . . The astonishment with which I might have greeted them, should they have stumbled into my African village a few hundred years ago, might have rejoiced their hearts. But the astonishment with which they greet me can only poison mine.[22]

Baldwin saw the villagers possessing "an authority which I shall never have" and saw himself as a latecomer without right to any part of everything they have inherited—in which Baldwin included the whole of Western culture. Once again, he divorced himself from Chartres and the Empire State Building:

For this village, even were it incomparably more remote and incredibly more primitive, is the West, the West onto which I have been so strangely grafted. These people cannot be, from the point of view of power, strangers anywhere in the world; they have made the modern world, even if they do not know it. The most illiterate among them is related in a way that I am not, to Dante, Shakespeare, Michaelangelo, Aeschylus, Da Vinci, Rembrandt, and Racine; the cathedral at Chartres says something to them which it cannot say to me, as indeed would the Empire State Building, should anyone here ever see it. Out of their hymns and dances come Beethoven and Bach. Go back a few centuries and they are in their full glory—but I am in Africa, watching the conquerors arrive.[23]

These were the matters that Baldwin eventually resolved by coming around to a clearer view of American culture and a more inclusive view of human culture and his place in it. He came to see, for one thing, that his sense of lostness, far from distinguishing him from white Americans, made him kin with

22 *Ibid.*, pp. 163–164.
23 *Ibid.*, p. 165.

them, that they were just as lost and alienated as he was, and that "this depthless alienation from oneself and one's people is, in sum, the American experience." Baldwin also settled the problem of his sense of divorcement from the stream of culture. "No matter where our fathers had been born," he wrote in the same *Times* article quoted earlier, "or what they had endured, the fact of Europe had formed us both, was part of our identity, part of our inheritance." This discovery helped Baldwin to stop thinking that he had no share of Chartres, Beethoven, or the Empire State Building. In fact, by the time we talked of this he had forgotten he had ever cut himself off from these monuments of human achievement and was struck anew to discover how far he had come since he had unhappily walked the streets of that village in the Swiss Alps. He had stopped seeing himself as waiting, emptyhanded and empty minded, for the white conqueror in Africa while Western man created his glories. Now he saw that in all time all people had exchanged and appropriated cultures, and in doing so reshaped them. "Henry James said somewhere," Baldwin said, "that a novelist has to be someone on whom nothing is lost. When you've taken it in, it is yours!" Baldwin had come to see with great liberating excitement that the world was his if he made it so: "All that has ever been done in the world speaks to a basic human experience that is constant. What the Greeks did, what the people did who built Chartres, what they were all doing is what *I* am doing now, coming up with something out of human experience, plunging into that great sea where there are no barriers at all, of race or of any other kind."

Thus Baldwin regained a sense of American identity by realizing that it is the search for an identity that makes all Americans kin, and he won his way through to share in Rembrandt and Bach by striking out boldly from his remote African shore and making his own path through the great sea of the common human experience. But while this did begin to settle Baldwin's problem of cultural identity and brought him back home for a fresh beginning, it did not mean that he left Africa abandoned behind him. On the contrary, Baldwin still carries something of Africa within him at a deeper and much more obscure level than we have yet explored, continuing to haunt and bedevil his search for an understanding of who and what he is.

As anyone can know who reads Baldwin's novel *Go Tell It On The Mountain* or the title essay of *Notes Of A Native Son*, his father—or more correctly his stepfather [24]—was the most important person in his young life. As anyone can also know by reading his second novel, *Giovanni's Room*, or his more recent *Another Country*, Baldwin is deeply preoccupied with the problems of homosexuality. Baldwin himself has linked these two concerns, for to the hero of *Giovanni's Room* he gave his stepfather's name. And through all of this, not always visible or traceable, runs a dark little African thread.

Twice in *Notes Of A Native Son* Baldwin associates Africa with his stepfather. At one point he tells of thinking of his father as he was being told how the Swiss children, blackfaced and with wigs on their blond hair, collected money to "buy" black Africans for Christ. The second time, in the fuller account of the man he called his father, he makes the association more directly:

Handsome, proud . . . he looked to me, as I grew older, like pictures I had seen of African tribal chieftains; he really should have been naked, with war paint on and barbaric mementos, standing among spears. He could be chilling in the pulpit and indescribably cruel in his personal life and he was certainly the most bitter man I have ever met; yet it must be said that there was something else in him . . . It had something to do with his blackness, I think—he was very black—with his blackness and his beauty, and with the fact that he knew he was black but did not know that he was beautiful . . .[25]

[24] In *Go Tell It On The Mountain* (New York, 1953), Baldwin's hero is brought, the infant son of another man, into her May-December marriage with the preacher; an angry man full of hate who becomes the principal influence in the boy's life. In the autobiographical essay in *Notes Of A Native Son*, Baldwin writes of such a man as his actual father. It seemed reasonable to think that the literalness of the essay was exact; that in the novel Baldwin had used his license to deny blood kinship with the man he came to hate so mortally. But *my* literalness was simple-minded; the fictional version was the true one.

[25] *Ibid.*, p. 87.

When we talked of Africa and carried it back in time, much more appeared about the link in Baldwin's mind between his father and Africa. Africa, he said first, made him think of: "A very black man, much blacker than me, naked, very romantic, very banal, sweat, something very sensual, very free, something very mysterious. Africa's mental and emotional structure," he added, "is hard for me to imagine. It intrigues me. Also frightens me."

There was certainly nothing about Africa before he went to school, he first said, but then went on:

But there is something vague tied up with the image of my father before I ever went to school, seeing his face over my mother's shoulder. What this has to do with Africa I don't know, but somehow my first association with Africa comes through him. I compared the people in my father's church to African savages. This was because of my relation to my father . . . I was ten or twelve. The church and my father were synonymous. Music and dancing, again sweat, out of the jungle. It was contemptible because it appeared to be savage. But this was also my image of my father. I guess I was hipped on being American, and the things they did seemed so common, so vulgar. My image of myself was of not having anything to do with my father or anything my father represented.

Baldwin then talked about going to the movies:

I hardly ever went, but every once in awhile I did see savages. There was something painful, sort of embarrassing about it. I suppose it was because that savage was black like me and was making a fool of himself in front of the whole white world which laughed at him and exploited him. I wanted not to be identified with that. I know the general attitude about Africans was uneasy contempt, embarrassment, a little fear. I think also of Stepin Fetchit rolling his eyes. African savages did that too. "You're acting like a nigger," you were told if you rolled your eyes, if your nails were not brushed, or you used bad language. These attitudes about Africans did not become explicit.

Again he returned to the subject of his father:

"I don't know when Africa came in first. It *must* have been from my father. My associations . . ." Baldwin stopped for a long moment. "My father thought of himself as a king," he went on, "and he would have said something like we were descended from kings in Africa." There was another agitated silence. Then he talked of a clash that had taken place between himself and his father over a white schoolteacher who had been kind to him—he tells this story also in *Notes Of A Native Son*—and the deep way in which the issue of blackness and his father and the church and Africa got all mixed up in his mind. "When I joined the church at fourteen . . ." he began, and stopped again. "This gets very complicated. In church I imagined myself as an African boy, dancing as I might have danced thousands of years ago. It really was a mystical experience and did something permanent to my sense of time . . . But I wasn't in the least prepared to deal with Africa. I gave a kind of lip service to it as the land of my forebears, and tried to find out things about it, mainly through the sculpture . . . But I don't know where any of this left me or my father or the church . . ."

Then we moved away from this territory toward the more open spaces where other people were reacting to Africa, and Baldwin described the man-in-the-street reaction to Africa in this way:

A few years ago he would have laughed and said: "A bunch of funky Negroes." Funky has to do with the odor of sweat, I think. I don't know what he'd say now, but he wouldn't say that. He might say: "They're showing; they're doing all right." I'd be astonished if anybody reacted to newsreels or movies of Africans the way I did. Now there is pride. The shot of Nkrumah getting off his plane has an effect on all the other images. It takes a certain sting out of those pictures of the African savage. I am presumably not talking about myself now, but of others, like my baby sister who's fifteen.

We talked of the "new" Africa and the "new" Negro reaction to it, and then at the end Baldwin said:

I want to go to Africa one of these days. I think there is a great deal I can discover about myself there. There is something beautiful about it. I want to find out. It is at the gateway of the modern world, and I could help be a guide. I've been there; I know some of the goat tracks. I might also find that part of me I had to bury when I grew up, the capacity for joy, of the sense, and something almost dead, real good-naturedness. I think they still believe in miracles there and I want to see it.

## Lorraine Hansberry

James Baldwin was six years old when the depression set in, but by the time Lorraine Hansberry was six the depression was nearly over. This was a divide great enough in itself to mark off two quite different generations. But the difference between the two is marked by more than time, for Lorraine Hansberry came of a comfortably situated family, and though she knew what life was like for most people on Chicago's South Side, in the department of economic well-being her pangs were all vicarious. Miss Hansberry, born in 1930, is old enough to have footholds of memory back in the world of pre-1945. She remembers newsreels about Italy's invasion of Ethiopia and the strong feelings in her home over that event. She was nine when Europe went to war in Poland and eleven when Pearl Harbor was bombed, and she remembers her father's ambivalent emotions over the conflict between the nonwhite Japanese and the white Americans. Her adult years did not begin until after that war ended. When she came from two years in college in Wisconsin to make her way in New York, it was 1950. All of this makes Lorraine Hansberry old enough to feel some share in the experience of her elders, but leaves her young enough to accept the present climate of great change as her natural environment. She is also so new as a writer that her hit play of 1959, *A Raisin In the Sun*, was the first and only work of hers that anybody knew. It is precisely because of her youth and her newness, and the way in which the subject of Africa appears in her play, that Lorraine Hansberry turns up here at the end of our progression of Negro writers and our scrutiny of the ways in which they have dealt with the matter of their African ancestors.

Lorraine Hansberry took the title of her play from a line by Langston Hughes: "What happens to a dream deferred?/ Does it dry up/ Like a raisin in the sun?" Her success was the winning of a dream that originally came upon her in her young girlhood when she first read the poetry of Langston Hughes and others. Much of this poetry, as we have seen, was about Africa, and on this subject too, curiously enough, Miss Hansberry also in a way completes a circle begun by Hughes. In a new and much more realistic setting, she also has had a vision of a romantic reunion between Negro American and black African. But her vision is shaped by new times, new outlooks. It is no longer a wispy literary yearning after a lost primitivism, nor does she beat it out on synthetic tom-toms. Nor is it any longer a matter of going Back to Africa as the ultimate option of despair in America. In Lorraine Hansberry's time it has become a matter of choice between new freedoms now in the grasp of black men, both African and American.

This idea appears only glancingly in *A Raisin In the Sun,* going largely unnoticed by raving critics and applauding audiences alike. The play is about the drive of the members of a poor Negro family to better their estate. Against this strong and sober central theme, the subtheme of Africa appears only in incidental passages and is used mainly to lighten the play's main emotional burdens. The action turns on the use to be made of the insurance money of the hard-working father who has just died, the son's ill-judged and costly effort to get ahead quickly, and the mother's intentness on lifting them out of the black slums. The daughter of the family, oddly named Beneatha, is the real symbol of its passage from lower-classness; she is already at the university and wants to become a doctor. She has two beaus, one the son of a successful Negro businessman, the other an African, a student from Nigeria. On these two the author's biases are laid with a heavy hand, for the rich man's son is presented as a well-advanced case of bourgeois American decay who offers the girl a future of mink coats and Cadillacs. The Nigerian, by heavy contrast, brings a new look and a new sound to the African theme in American Negro life. He is the most literate, the most self-possessed, the most sophisticated, most purposive, I-know-where-I'm-going character in the play. He offers the girl a life of dedication, work, and self-realization in emergent Africa.

The imminent arrival of this young African brings on this colloquy between mother and daughter: [26]

MAMA. I don't think I never met no African before.

BENEATHA. Well, do me a favor and don't ask him a lot of ignorant questions about Africans. I mean, do they wear clothes and all that—

MAMA. Well, now, I guess if you think we so ignorant 'round here maybe you shouldn't bring your friends here.

BENEATHA. It's just that people ask such crazy things. All anyone seems to know about it when it comes to Africa is Tarzan—

MAMA. [*Indignantly*] Why should I know anything about Africa?

When the young African, also oddly named as Asagai (which sounds more like the Zulu word *assegai,* a sawed-off spear, than like a Nigerian name), finally appears, Mama acquits herself, as always, with dignity. He comes bearing a Nigerian robe as a gift for the girl. He teasingly reminds her that she had first approached him at school to say: "I want very much to talk with you. About Africa. You see, Mr. Asagai, I am looking for my *identity!*" It is clear that this is no joking matter to the girl, and it becomes even less so when he gently but sharply reproves her for "mutilating" her hair by trying to straighten it. She hotly denies that she is "assimilationist," which is one of Miss Hansberry's favorite words.

In a later scene, Beneatha appears in her Nigerian robe and headdress. She flicks off the "assimilationist junk" on the radio and goes into what she imagines to be a Nigerian tribal dance. Brother Walter comes in drunk, full of the angers and confusions arising out of the main business of the play. He enters into her mood. "And Ethiopia shall stretch forth her hands again!" he shouts, and together they go into a wild and noisy and hilarious caper punctuated by what are supposed to be African shouts. Walter leaps on the table and begins to address his imaginary tribesmen, summoning them to battle. In the stage directions we discover that he is seeing himself as "a great chief, a descendant of Chaka," the great Zulu chief—and the

[26] All quotations from the play are from the published text, *A Raisin In the Sun* (New York, 1959).

creator, incidentally, of the weapon called the *assegai*. It is hard to tell from the text how seriously the author intended all this to be taken; the night I saw the play it convulsed the house with laughter. At its height George, the rich man's son, walks in. Walter holds forth his hand: "Black brother!" he cries. George looks amazed and disgusted. "Black brother, hell!" he says, and demands that Beneatha go in at once and change to go out. She accuses him of being "ashamed of his heritage," and when she is asked to explain, she goes on:

BENEATHA. It means someone who is willing to give up his culture and submerge himself completely in the dominant, and in this case, oppressive culture!
GEORGE. Oh dear, dear, dear! Here we go! A lecture on the African past! On our great West African Heritage! In one second we will hear all about the great Ashanti empires, the great Songhay civilizations, and the great sculpture of Benin—and some poetry in the Bantu—and the whole monologue will end with the word *heritage!* [*Nastily*] Let's face it, baby, your heritage is nothing but a bunch of raggedy-assed spirituals and some grass huts!

Beneatha retorts that he is slandering the people who were "the first to smelt iron on the face of the earth" and who "were performing surgical operations when the English . . . were still tattooing themselves with blue dragons!" But she changes all the same and dutifully goes out with George.

The last act also opens on a relieving bit about Africa. The main action of the play has just come to climax, Walter has stupidly lost the money, and Beneatha sits in crushed defeat and despair, when young Mr. Asagai again appears. He tries to comfort her with philosophy, and she turns on him in anger, predicting that things will be just as bad in Africa when the black man takes over. He retorts that for better or worse it will be the black man's own fate, determined by himself. Then abruptly he invites her to come home with him. At first she misunderstands.

ASAGAI. I mean across the ocean, home—to Africa.
BENEATHA. To—to Nigeria?
ASAGAI. Yes! [*Smiling and lifting his arms playfully*] Three hun-

dred years later, the African prince rose up out of the seas and swept
the maiden back across the middle passage over which her ancestors
had come—

BENEATHA. [*Unable to play*] Nigeria?

ASAGAI. Nigeria. Home. [*Coming to her with genuine romantic
flippancy*] I will show you our mountains and our stars; and give
you cool drinks from gourds and teach you the old songs and the
ways of our people—and, in time, we will pretend that you have
only been away for a day . . .

Beneatha is shaken and confused by all that has been happening
and wants time to think. Asagai, gently and sweetly understanding, looks back at her from the door. "How often I have looked
at you and said, 'Ah—so this is what the New World hath finally
wrought . . .'" and makes a graceful exit.

In the play's last moments, the main issue happily resolved,
again after a scene of the highest tension, the unresolved subject of Africa reappears to help break the strain. To make talk
to cut in on the insupportable emotion of the moment, Beneatha announces that Asagai had asked her to marry him.
Mama is barely able to hear what she says.

BENEATHA. [*Girlishly and unreasonably trying to pursue the conversation*] To go to Africa, Mama—be a doctor in Africa . . .

MAMA. [*Distracted*] Yes, baby.

WALTER. Africa! What he want you to go to Africa for?

BENEATHA. To practice there—

WALTER. Girl, if you don't get them silly ideas out of your head!
You better marry yourself a man with some loot . . .

And the two of them go out, still arguing, George versus Asagai,
as their voices fade away, leaving the issue—America or Africa—
hanging in the air, rustling and sounding there after they'd
gone, like the theme of another play to come.

In *A Raisin In the Sun* the new shape of the African idea in
the American Negro universe made its first appearance, I believe, in any play or story of wide public notice. If it appeared
only incidentally as a secondary theme to a much more moving
main story, this too was appropriate, since this was just about

where the subject of Africa stood in the thinking of Negroes at the time the play was produced. The play's audiences were moved by its dramatization of an American problem, by the classic figure of the strong mother, by the son's struggle to find his manhood, by the endurance of the son's wife, and by the fresh forthrightness of the daughter. But few, it seemed, were quite ready to tune in on the new sounds and sights of Africa that also came into view in Miss Hansberry's play. They will no doubt reappear at higher and stronger levels as time goes on and will be counterposed to something more substantial than Miss Hansberry's idea of decadent bourgeois affluence in America. Still, she opened the subject to a new and higher visibility than it had yet enjoyed, and I found, when I sought her out to talk about it, that she was grateful to have someone notice it. She was being praised so highly for creating "real" people in the play that hardly anybody had given her credit, she said ruefully, for also trying to deal symbolically with some important ideas.

These ideas, I found as we talked on, had been assembled out of a series of sources and exposures going back to her childhood and were sometimes expressed in a string of broad generalizations somewhat eclectically tied together. Thus Miss Hansberry described herself as "a strong Negro nationalist" who also believed that all peoples and cultures must eventually merge in a common humanity. "It will be a great day when people merge biologically and in culture," she said, "but until that day, oppressed peoples must express themselves," and this has to be done by stressing one's special identity. "I want all to assimilate in all," she said at one point, "but now one must identify." It sometimes seemed during our conversation that a kind of shape-as-you-go quality had been imposed on Miss Hansberry's thinking by the need, in her sudden celebrity, to answer a lot of questions about herself that she had never been asked before or, for that matter, asked herself. Because she had so successfully created some "real" people on the stage, she was having the wonderful but rather unseating experience of discovering that her opinions about all sorts of things had become important overnight. Inevitably some of her opinions and perhaps some memories had to be put together on the spur of the moment. But Lorraine Hansberry was not only a polite and decent young woman trying hard to keep her balance in the storm of a Broadway success. She was also a bright and thoughtful person, and almost every thread of her thought did lead back to some significant life experience.

Talking about the changes in the world, she described how sometime after the Second World War she had begun to feel not so much a member of an American minority as of a "world majority" of oppressed people who were beginning to throw off the systems that oppressed them. "As a fairly self-conscious Negro," she said, "I began to feel this kinship, the feeling from the past summed up in 'aren't we all miserable?' passing to a new and happier feeling: 'Aren't we all moving ahead!'" For herself, she thought, this was not a change, "just a logical progression. Why ever since I was three years old," she exclaimed, "I knew that somebody somewhere was doing something to hurt black and brown peoples. Little as I was I remember the newsreels of the Ethiopian war and the feeling of outrage in our Negro community. Fighters with spears and our people in a passion over it; my mother attacking the Pope blessing the Italian troops going off to slay Ethiopians. When the Pope died that was the thought of him that came to my mind. I didn't know a thing about Spain but I certainly did know about Ethiopia. I didn't know about Hitler, but I certainly did know about Leopold cutting off the hands of the people in the Congo. Japan's war in China? Vague, very vague. I don't remember people talking about it. In 1941, though, many people saw the Japanese as a colored nation, and this affected their feelings, certainly in Chicago, and this was reflected even in my own home. But we just expected that things would change. We had been saying for a long time: 'Ethiopia will stretch forth her hands!' This always meant that *they* were going to pay for all this one day."

Miss Hansberry said she remembered the verse about Ethiopia's hands "because I am the granddaughter of an African Methodist Episcopal minister." She was also the daughter of a strong-minded man who evidently devoted himself with considerable success to winning just the kind of bourgeois affluence she deprecates in her play. Besides being a well-to-do business-man and a power in the Chicago Negro community, her father was also a strongly race-conscious man. "My father was a student of history," said Miss Hansberry, "and we were always taught pride in our Negro heritage." Her father gave her a strong sense of the positive virtue of Negroness but these all had to do, she remembers, with Negroes in America. "It was all in terms of the United States," she said, "nothing in particular about Af-rica." At the same time, her family also had certain prejudices about color. "My people had the stereotyped attitudes," she said. "They thought blacker people were less attractive, and we were a dark-skinned family! Nowadays nobody would admit ever having such feelings. We assumed, of course, that *our* color was the marking-off point . . . The prejudices in my family were very, very complicated. We were never proud of its atti-tudes." Some combination of these factors, involving attitudes about Africa and color, doubtless had something to do with the odd fact that by her own account Lorraine Hansberry had never even heard about Marcus Garvey until after she came to New York in 1950. But little Lorraine took in a great deal about Africa nonetheless. Her father's house "was full of books," and when she was about nine she started reading the Negro poets and got some of her first and more enduring images of Africa from their lines, so much so that when I first asked her what came to her mind when she thought of Africa she instantly said:

"Beautiful mountains, plateaus, beautiful dark people." And these pictures came, she added, "from the poets I grew up read-ing, Langston Hughes, Countee Cullen, Warren Cuney. I was deeply influenced by them and their images of Africa were marvelous and beautiful."

Out in the hard world of the Chicago South Side, in its schools and on its streets, Lorraine had ample opportunity to summon up the resources of pride she had acquired from her father and from Langston Hughes' poetry. She ran into all the familiar hateful images, and she fought them back with all she had:

In school in the lower grades, primitive peoples, hot, animals, mostly negative, how good it was we were saved from this terrible past. Most of the kids reflected this. To call a kid an African was an insult. It was calling him savage, uncivilized, naked, something to laugh at. A naked black savage with a spear and war paint. It was equivalent to ugliness. Everything distasteful and painful was associated with Africa. This came from school, from the movies, and from our own people who accepted this. In common talk, the term was always derogatory—"You are acting like a wild African!" This meant heathen, unchristian. Most children absorbed this and acquired a deep shame of their African past. But I resented what I saw in the movies and I resented the teachers who couldn't give a more positive view. This too was mainly about our own American Negro past. We were very sensitive to such things as how the slavery issue was discussed, even in grade school. I resented all of it. I was very unique in that I extended this [resentment] to the African thing too. The others didn't do this, but I made the connection . . . I really don't know why this was so, but I was very aware, and even when kids said "You look like an African" as a form of insult, this hurt me, it brought me pain. At the movies when one white man was holding off thousands of Africans with a gun, all the kids were with the hero, but I was with the Africans. When I was thirteen or fourteen I was more sophisticated. I had begun to read Carter Woodson. My brothers and I talked about Hannibal; we had passion, if not information, and we thought Africa was a great thing in the world . . .

Lorraine Hansberry, then, got her early defensive race consciousness from her father and her romantic view of Africa quite largely from the poems of Langston Hughes. These two influences in her young life were further linked by a curiously arresting set of coincidences that I mark here because of their obvious relevance not only to our grasp of these two individual writers but also to our general subject. I can do so, however, only in scantiest outline, for they involve the two fathers about whom neither writer has yet told us quite enough.[27] Lorraine Hansberry's father and Langston Hughes' father were evidently

[27] My information about Hughes' father comes entirely out of Hughes' autobiographical volume, *The Big Sea*. I know about Hansberry Senior only what Miss Hansberry herself told me. Essentially the same details appear in the autobiographical account she gave of herself in the *New Yorker*, May 9, 1959.

in many ways very similar men, both hard-driving and ambitious and intent on wealth and recognition. As the reader will recall from our brief account of Hughes, his father quite early in his life quit the United States because it did not allow a Negro to be a man and migrated to Mexico, where he made his fortune in business. Lorraine's father made *his* fortune here, in Chicago, after coming up emptyhanded out of Mississippi. He fought personally to wring recognition of Negro rights out of the white world. At his own expense he carried a restricted-covenants case right up to the Supreme Court, and he won. But he finally came to the despairing conclusion, like Hughes' father and others before him, that the United States was no place for a self-respecting black man to live out his life, and he decided to migrate. It was not Africa, however, that he had in view. As Miss Hansberry's own account intimates, her father had something less than a romantic view of Africa. Remember, she had never even heard of Marcus Garvey in her father's race-conscious home—the only version of Back to Africa that had ever reached her, she told me, was Senator Bilbo's race-baiting bill in Congress to ship all Negroes back where they came from —and there were also the elder Hansberry's views about blackness. These views and attitudes were somehow linked, but we will not ever know their inwardness unless Miss Hansberry one day chooses to explain why her father's color attitudes were so "very, very complicated." In any case, when he planned to migrate, the elder Hansberry fixed his eye not on Africa, but like the elder Hughes some 40 years before, on Mexico. In 1945 he took the step, actually bought a house in a Mexico City suburb, and put Lorraine and her sister in school there. But he had waited too long. Within a short time Mr. Hansberry died, and the family returned to the United States.

Her brothers, Lorraine Hansberry told me, have been moved to follow in their father's path, but they now see West Africa, not Mexico, as a more promising land since they have been able to develop business interests there. But Lorraine herself chose quite differently. Like Langston Hughes in a far-gone year, she decided that she was *not* Africa, or Mexico, but Chicago and New York. She went even further and by marrying a non-Negro added to her vision of the far future the ultimate end of all troubling race distinctions. At the same time she has clung hard in her near view to a strong insistence on racial and national identifications. She thinks it an absurd idea that persons of African descent should return to Africa because of that; Africans have their own national identities, and American Negroes have —or must now shape—their own. And this, again, is the rub. Here Lorraine Hansberry in her turn arrives, behind Ralph Ellison and James Baldwin, at the new edge of time and with them looks out over the same confusions: as he emerges from his second-classness, what does the American Negro become? And in this process of new becoming, what is he to Africa, and what is Africa to him? "I don't know about the future," answered Lorraine Hansberry, "or what role Africa will have in it. One thing, though, the shame about Africa among Negroes is actively disintegrating. I don't think this change should be so difficult. Most people are glad to replace a negative view with an affirmative view."

# 7. SOMETHING NEW OUT OF AFRICA

What came new out of Africa in the late 1950's for a great many Negro Americans was indeed the chance for the first time to identify in a positive way with the continent of their black ancestors. Instead of looking away from it, many began to look at it. In place of indifference, rejection, and shame, they began to feel a rise of interest, acceptance, and pride. This change began to set in with the approach of independence in Ghana and the appearance of Kwame Nkrumah as the first new African world figure, followed in a quick few years by the great swarm of new African states and the coming of other African black men to places of power. What came out of these events was not only the spectacle of white power fallen or falling, but the new and even more gratifying image of black men acquiring dignity and commanding attention and respect. Africa became visible, and black men moved into positions where they could be seen by all and where the white world at last had to take account of their presence. This in itself was enough to establish *something* where—it had seemed for so long—there had been *nothing,* a quickening sense of importance where there had been that deadening feeling of insignificance, Africa offered the Negro American a new place not only in the here and now but also in history; a new link to his past and the part played by his forebears in the unfolding story of man. The African emergence dramatized in these peculiarly personal ways the new leverage in world affairs working on the affairs of the Negro in America.

These new sensations started up at many different points and varied greatly in shape and intensity in different individuals and among different layers of people. They began to show themselves in a new rush of written and spoken communication about Africa and in outcroppings of many kinds of new behavior and experiences: crowds roaring welcomes to visiting

African leaders on parade in the big cities; the elect discovering the feel of red carpet beneath their feet as they more and more commonly joined in social events honoring Africans at the Waldorf, at the delegations and embassies, or at the White House; leaders forming the American Negro Leadership Conference on Africa, adopting resolutions on matters of American policy in Africa and being received at the White House to present their views to the President; intellectuals forming the American Society of African Culture to promote the new mutual rediscovery on a high cultural plane, others forming organizations to enjoy the new opportunities on many other planes (Americans of African Ancestry, Afro-American Cultural Society, Friends of Ghana, African Heritage, etc.); nationalist and chauvinist groups enjoying the spur of having their prophecies of the rising of the black man coming true at last and winning national and international visibility by their demonstration at the United Nations in February 1961 during the great and passionate confusions surrounding the murder of Patrice Lumumba in the Congo; ordinary folk reading about these things or following the heavy budget of news from Africa in their newspapers, by radio, or watching on their television screens the reappearance of Kenyatta in Kenya, Luthuli accepting a Nobel Prize in Stockholm, a great sudden flow of documentary reports by word and film of country after country in Africa, and dignitaries or interviewers facing a succession of newly distinguished African visitors, Mboya, Touré, Nyerere, Balewa, Senghor, Houphouet-Boigny—all of this in a great flood dislodging a mass of old images of Africa that still filled most minds, undercutting old emotions and fixed ideas, and creating a floating tangle of old and new ideas out of which a new order of things would not quickly be made.

This great jumble of new impulses, sensations, moods, and experiences remains in constant motion. It can hardly be seen whole or even easily caught in part. Great numbers of people are passing from one set of notions and emotions to another, and each one makes this passage in his own unique way, traveling with his own special mixture of what he brings to these exposures and what he takes from them. Of all this I can here make only a modest report, a series of glimpses and vignettes which suggest how the matter was seen by certain individuals at certain moments. These glimpses are of value, I believe, partly because of the identity of these individuals and because the moments in which we catch them here all fell at various times between 1958 and 1961 when these impacts were at their newest and the changes only beginning to show. The first cluster of these vignettes is drawn from the interviews I conducted in the United States during this time, and the second from conversations with Negroes I encountered in West Africa during the summer of 1960.

## As Seen From Afar

The range of views begins with a very small number which believed that the Negro "man in the street" still had no interest in Africa at all. Two examples:

He would say: "What've I got to do with Africa or Africans?" He's as removed from interest in Africa as the white man in the street is from interest in Rumania!

I think the man in the street has the same ideas I have about it, no interest, too far away from his own problems, getting a living, housing, desegregation.

Others felt a clear sense of change taking place:

Now he's interested in finding out about it. Two years ago he would have said: "I couldn't care less." Four years ago he would have shown a rejection of Africa and anything it stood for, including black people and Negroid characteristics.

A few years ago, if asked about Africans, he would have laughed and said: "A funky bunch of niggers!" Now there is pride.

A considerable majority, however, already saw this change in views as an emphatic shift to the affirmative side.

Many Negroes are still ashamed of being identified with Africa, but I've heard men on the street corner right here on 135th Street say that they can hold their heads up higher since Nkrumah and Azikiwe came up.

I would expect the man in the street to say: "It's wonderful!" I'd expect him to know the names of the important places and the names of some of the leaders. This has all happened since Ghana's independence. It would not have been so, much more than five years ago.

It's changing and exploding, a new and revived interest in Africa. The Negro never could escape being thought of, consciously or unconsciously, as a relative of Africans. He now can at least be proud of what is happening there and get increased status for himself by identifying with it.

I heard an uneducated woman say: "Those Africans standing up there in the UN, they make me proud!"

A query about the "black bourgeois" response to the African emergence brought some answers that strongly reflected Franklin Frazier's characterization of that upper economic group, e.g.:

This type of Negro is not too emotionally involved, not at all wrought up about it. He is too caught up in the Cadillac-mink-coat culture.

Africa has become quite fashionable lately; Many have become interested because of money-making opportunities out there.

Just a few years ago, Africa would have been the last place in the world people would have thought to go to; now it's a tourist spot.

But Professor Frazier himself, when we talked about this, put the matter on quite a different level:

I believe that in a way the African is helping the Negro to find his world. With independent states in Africa, there is greater recognition of Negroes here. As Negroes in America increasingly accept an identification with Africa, it will mean something different to them from what it meant in the past.

Africa was already coming to mean something strongly different to many of these individuals. Its emergence in world affairs, its importance in politics, its mere presence in the day's news, had already begun to make this difference. There were many examples of the feeling that what was good for the African in Africa was going to be good for the Negro in America. Here is how the matter was put by the editor of a major Negro weekly:

We are giving more and more emphasis to what is taking place in Africa. Ghana's independence was the starting point of this . . . This is all good news for the Negro because it gives him a sense of pride. I feel that if the African is successful in winning respect for the African personality, he will help me in terms of my own status. If he fails, I am inclined to believe I fail along with him. I share in the disdain with which black people are regarded. If black people any-where in the world make a significant impact and thereby win respect and status, I share in some of it.

A New York editor:

I am happy and proud when Africans reach their potential, be-cause I believe this will automatically help me. The African in the next 25 years will do more to ease the stigma of color than the American Negro has done in the past 99 years he has been free . . . What they do in remote Africa has a direct bearing on me . . . the feeling that they are fighting there, and we are fighting here, and someday in the never-never they will and we will win and then things will be great.

A government official:

Africa provides me today with a kind of proud identification with ancestors. It can cause you to swell with pride just to see an African on the podium of the UN, Africans who have to be consulted in the decision-making process in the world. The kind of pride other peo-ples have had, of being recognized. It gives the Negro American something outside of himself and this little world of discrimination. He gains some kind of feeling of importance. When a Negro wants to go somewhere to feel that he can be somebody, he doesn't go to Paris anymore, he goes to Ghana.

A Southern businessman:

I think I am getting a new respect for the African, reorienting myself entirely. You see pictures of the prime ministers in *Time* magazine, face to face. I declare, you never expected anything like this. The Southern papers never carried pictures like that. We are getting a better feeling of kinship. Instead of thinking of Nkrumah as an African, I think of him as another Negro . . . Events have given me a new appreciation of Africa. I am now overcoming the rejection which made me recoil from it.

A leader of a major Negro organization:

It is the feeling of importance. The average Negro sees that the whole world is forced to recognize and readjust its attitudes toward the colored world; the rising black man is the theme of his thinking . . . The enthusiasm about Ghana has tended to submerge that kind of irritation [we used to feel]. Now everything African is welcome. Ghana independence parties were held everywhere. For the first time American Negroes found those robes admirable instead of quaint or embarrassing.

Finally, a senior Negro leader:

There is a new feeling that Africa is becoming a great force and the Negro in America takes pride in this. This is more than a bandwagon interest. It has an element of a reach for survival. So long as there is an Africa, this assures the Negro his historic continuity, his place in history.

These were all responses to Africa in the large and from afar, with Ghana still standing in the foreground as a symbol for the whole. They came, moreover, in the first flush of the emergence and reflected the fine first glow of the ideas of *freedom* and *independence* not yet complicated by the development of authoritarian politics or the confusion over the events in the Congo, and only to a limited extent by actual contact with Africans. But by this time a growing number of Negroes had gone to Africa to have a look for themselves—of those I interviewed 30 had already done so—and had begun to experience more directly the adjustment of their old views to the new actualities. During the summer of 1960 in West Africa I met Negroes who had begun to see and feel many new and complicating dimensions in this process of rediscovery. Here, in a series of vignettes caught in a moment of time, is the way this swiftly moving and changing experience appeared to some of them.

## As Seen in West Africa

One of the first American Negroes I met was a young but highly qualified professional who had come out on a three-year contract to teach in his special field. I asked him why he had taken this job, and he said, "I came to Africa because I was looking for a place to be comfortable. I thought I might feel easier here, feel more free, just settle down and do a job and be myself." He shook his head at my unasked question. "No," he said. "I haven't."

Practically all the American Negroes I met in West Africa had come to the ancestral continent with some form of the same idea in their minds. They had come looking for freedom from racism and prejudice, or at least for a racial situation that counted them in instead of out—that provided solace and a sense of identity in a world where everyone was black. They had also looked for a chance to share in the new pride of achievement stemming from the black man's reassertion of himself and his "African personality." In West Africa in that summer of 1960, the Negro pilgrim could find some of this, often enough of it to give him a great new store of satisfactions. But the individuals I spoke to found that it did not last long, hardly past the first flush of the sensation of being in a place where the white man is not master. In almost every case that I encountered, the Negro pilgrim found himself not free at all, more than ever without solace and a sense of identity, fighting new patterns of prejudice, and suffering the pangs of a new kind of outsiderness. He had thought he was alien in America, but he discovered that he was much more alien in Africa. Whether he liked it or not, he found that he was American, and that in Africa he became an American in exile.

Most of the Negroes one met in West Africa were travelers, come like everyone else to have a look at the boiling and bubbling turmoil of the African emergence. Some of these were notables—guests at the frequent celebrations, delegates to the innumerable conferences, members of advisory commissions—and others more ordinary folk, such as a fast-moving, exuberant Chicago schoolteacher I met at various places who was spending her savings on a swift tour of the continent, all by herself, just to have a look, "so I can tell the children in my classes what it is really like." A much smaller number of the Negroes had come out on particular jobs—scholars, teachers, technical specialists on contract for one, three, or five years to various African institutions. Then there were the Negroes scattered through the official American establishments; at that time one was an ambassador (he has since been replaced), and others regular embassy staff members, cultural attachés, information officers, members of technical-aid missions—perhaps a dozen in all.

Besides these temporary sojourners there was a still smaller group of longer-term or even permanent expatriates who had come to try to make new lives for themselves in Africa. Leaving aside the Negro Americans who live in Liberia, with its history of special links with America, it was made up of individuals varying greatly in activity and outlook. A few were businessmen who came, scored, and stayed. The successful ones lived as expatriate businessmen have usually lived abroad, sending their children home to school and getting back themselves for occasional visits, regarding themselves as *in* but not *of* the country of their chosen residence. A second and rather larger group of expatriates with rather more permanent commitments consisted of the two or three dozen young women who had married Africans, usually as a result of campus romances in America, and had come to Africa to live. Finally, in the smallest numbers of all—I met only two and heard of only two or three others—there were migrants who had left America because they were no longer willing or able to bear life here as Negroes and who were committed to permanent exile. One of the two I met was a young woman who had become a Liberian through naturalization and then a Ghanaian by marriage. She was, incidentally, the only American Negro I met in West Africa who had given up her American citizenship.

Here and there in the several countries I visited I met individuals in each of these situations and listened long and hard to some of them, in certain cases pursuing our subject in extended interviews. This was, let me emphasize, no sample survey but a series of conversations with individuals as I encountered them or sought them out. The total population of Negro Americans at that time and in those places was, however, quite small, and my inquiry included a substantial proportion of the whole. I had extended interviews with 16 individuals out of a roughly estimated total of 50 permanent or semipermanent residents in the countries I visited (not counting Liberia), the great bulk of them in Ghana. To these I add interviews with 11 young Negroes whose experience I shared in connection with my study of the summer work-camp operation, Crossroads Africa.[1] Finally there were the briefer and more casual observations and conversations involving perhaps a dozen other Negro travelers I met at various places.

The forms of their experiences and the details varied greatly. Focus, intention, and expectation differed and gave different weights to the emotional content, and it obviously made a great difference whether a person was a traveler, a sojourner for a time, or someone who thought he might want to stay in Africa for good. But with only one possible exception, all those I met were making much the same discovery. It was perhaps best put by a young man who had come to Africa to see if there was any relief there from the anger he carried in his heart against America and the whole world of white men: "I came to Africa feeling like a brother, but there I was, I was not a brother. I was not Senegalese, or Nigerian or Ghanaian. I was American, an American Negro from an Anglo-Saxon culture, or as much of it as filtered down to me, determining what I am, what I think, what I feel. I could come back, and color might not be a problem, but I would always be an outsider coming in. It would be true of any outsider, and true of me. It's the way anybody looks at a stranger."

The young professional who had come out to teach because he was "looking for a place to be comfortable" had been very successful at home, a man who was among the first in his field and in his particular job. But he was weary of "being special," weary of always fighting, always being vigilant. In his college days he

---

1 See *Emergent Americans*, especially pages 81–87.

had met some Nigerian students who impressed him by their air of dedication to something larger than themselves. So when the chance came to him to teach in his field in Africa for a few years, he took it up. "I was greeted with 'Welcome, brother, you've been through a hard time'—that sort of feeling," he told me. "I did not like being patronized this way. I also found that the air of dedication was deceiving. It is the same old rat race here that it is everywhere else." He also found that being an American did not only mean, if you were a Negro, that you were a victim of discrimination. It also meant that you were used to telephones that worked and to telephone conversations that worked too; that is, appointments that were kept, promises that were carried out, or decisions that were remembered the next day. "It's ridiculous, but I had never before realized how much of my life had nothing to do with the race problem at all," he said. "I mean just the way you do everything you do, what you mean when you say something, and how you understand what the other fellow means. I simply cannot function the way they do here. I like things put straight and got out of the way. Nothing is done that way here. Nothing is fixed. Do you realize what it means to have to bargain about the price of the bread you buy every day?" But there was a sharper and deeper edge to his feelings than mere impatience with slow or inefficient African ways. When he invited me to his home that evening to take potluck with him and his wife, I discovered that they were servantless, having fired their "steward" only the day before. In their long recital of their experience with him it became clear that they had fired him only because he was incompetent, dishonest and unresponsive, and not because the unfamiliar sensation of having a servant made them uncomfortable or uncertain. The breaking point came when, after one of their final expostulations with him, he argued back that he was held in contempt by his friends and fellow stewards because he was working for them and they were not white. This was the real reason they let him go.

The subject of relations with servants came up quite often in these encounters. Indeed one of the more ironic experiences that any onetime dweller in old empires can have in West Africa these days is to listen to members of a new generation of American expatriates talking about their servants—the humor and irritations of dealing with them, and what there was to learn from them about African mores, habits, and character. There was even an echo of old China days when I dined one evening in the home of a white American who had been raised in China. "There is just no comparison," my hostess sighed, "no comparison at all between these African servants and those wonderful Chinese servants we had!" Thus the ironies in all the talk about servants cut several ways and made a crisscrossing design of their own among the swiftly changing relationships of our time.

It was not only that these were Americans, white or Negro, who would probably not have servants at home; this was largely true in the old days too. Nor was it that they were likely to have ideas of equality and dignity that did not fit with the master-servant relationship; this was also true of some in the past. But in the past it was possible for many expatriates to be drawn quite easily into conformity with the established order of things —the colonial system was one big master-servant relationship, after all—and even to begin taking to the habit of mastery with increasing relish. Today, as everyone knows except the Portuguese, colonialism is dead or dying. Some of its behavior patterns survive among the older expatriate hands and are still seized upon by a few of the uglier newcomers. But, generally speaking, everyone nowadays is called upon to be as democratic and equal as possible, and Americans are more self-conscious about this than any other people, including the Russians. Hence it comes as an embarrassing shock—especially to the American determined not to be ugly—that the "new" democracy is for him to practice, while his hosts, the upper crust of the newly emancipated people, treat their own servants, and all other inferior orders, with remarkable contempt. In West Africa, as in most of Asia, there are few things uglier than an upper bureaucrat's bearing toward a middle bureaucrat, or a middle bureaucrat's bearing toward a lower, or the bearing of any of them toward any menials in their service.

"They treat them horribly!" exclaimed a dismayed young

woman, a Negro traveler who had enjoyed all of her journey until she stayed for a few days in the home of some African friends. "The servants need force, they tell you, and even say they are not human and you don't have to worry about them. They feed them scraps from the table, they yell at them and call them names. I would try to be nice to the servants, but my hosts never liked this." This behavior on the part of Africans was peculiarly shocking to anyone who had idealized the African struggle for freedom, or who was naïve enough to think that only whites treated blacks with disrespect. "I run into this quite a bit," observed an American Negro who is now a permanent resident in Africa. "In the attitude of the policemen toward the people, for example, and the customs officers at the border. There is the attitude toward servants and also the attitude among the servants—the attitude of the steward toward the 'small boy,' of the cook toward the steward. The same in the government bureaucracy—obsequious to the higher; nasty to the lower. This does not exist among us. But here, unfortunately, it is very common; you get it right through the society."

There is an even more mordant aspect to the matter. Hardly any scorn is more justified than that felt by Negroes for whites in America who say they "know" Negroes because they have had them for servants or workhands all their lives. Yet I met Negroes in West Africa who "knew" all sorts of things about Africans—things they had gleaned almost exclusively from their servants.

The experience of American girls who have married Africans and gone to Africa to live is still another subject impatiently awaiting its author. It is hard to know just how many such marriages there are now; I was told at that time that in the city of Accra alone there were about a dozen. As more and more African students come to the United States, there will be more and more of them. In the eyes of the African the educated American Negro girl is a great prize. By marrying such a girl he is often making a major bid to complete his passage from his own traditional culture to the new world of modernism and change. American girls are attracted to these romances for different reasons—Lorraine Hansberry showed us one of them in *A Raisin in the Sun*—but one of the most poignant is the groping of the dark Negro girl for the regard and acceptance that are still so commonly withheld from her in American Negro society. Wherever these marriages begin, however, they soon, I was told, run into rough going. The American wives of Ghanaians in Accra were described to me by other Negro residents and by two of their own number as a group of unhappy and frustrated women who spend much of their time sharing their complaints and trying to console each other.

The complaints vary, but living conditions are large among them. While some of the husbands manage to do well with the professions they acquired abroad, most of them have to be satisfied with jobs that give them a standard of living miles above that of the lowly African laborer but still not so high for a girl raised in modest, or even poor, circumstances in Harlem or on Chicago's South Side. Even where there is not actual poverty, or what seems to be poverty, there are the hurdles of differences in habit, taste, and diet; there are the complexities of marketing and bargaining; and there are the deeply engrossing problems of ordinary sanitation. Although these are not necessarily great differences, they are not often easy to manage. But much more painful, it appears, are the problems of American girls married to husbands who often have rather un-American ideas about the status of women. "In Africa," one of these wives told me, "even when they are Christians, they do not understand that a wife can talk up to her husband and that she has a right to be heard by her husband. They just don't understand this!" There was also some discussion of the peculiarly nettling combination of male jealousy, resulting in strict control of the behavior of the wife, and a much more relaxed view of the permissible behavior of the husband. This is of course not uniquely African, but in the African setting it is often bound up with some profoundly different customs and attitudes. In certain groups, for example, child spacing is achieved by an imposed continence until well after the child is weaned—sometimes a matter of two years, or even more. In this period the wife is restricted and the husband definitely is not. This may lead, as anyone can readily see, to serious problems in an American girl's marriage.

What these girls have to cope with in their husbands is the familiar but always difficult pattern of contradictions and ambivalences in the ways of a human being in motion between two cultures. Only very rarely does such a person succeed in shedding all the old ways and adopting all the new. However far he does go in one direction, he is still tied by a thousand bonds of upbringing, habit, and family to the customs and practices of the culture in which he was raised. These conflicts can sometimes be gracefully reconciled (I visited one remarkable couple, a Nigerian and his English wife building and running a school together), but usually they are not—especially not in an intercultural marriage involving an American girl, with her ideas of her own rights and dignity. African cultures have not assigned many rights or much dignity to women. They are the hewers and the drawers of the society; in fact they appear to do all the great volume of work that the men have been able to avoid doing. African traditional culture is also still quite largely polygamous, and this is an issue about which emergent African men are going to hear more and more from emergent African women. I was not told of any American girl who was confronted with another wife to share her husband and her home. One assumes—or hopes—that this is one issue that is settled before marriage, and that an African taking an American wife knows he is committing himself to a single wife. In any case, there are other problems, and they are quite formidable enough.

Often much worse than the matter of the husband's relations with other women is the matter of the wife's relations with her husband's family. Even in modern and Christian families, the girl's problem of adjustment can be overwhelming. Here is part of the story of a woman of great beauty and great force of character who had accompanied her husband to Ghana strongly determined to make a success of her new life. In the beginning it was simply wonderful:

It was even better than I had thought it would be. The people were so warm and welcoming. It was almost a little too much, both from the family and from strangers. First, they liked me because I was dark. I was almost as black as my husband, and my mother-in-law thought I was scrumptious. I was *real* black. "You brought one of our own back!" she cried to her son that first day. "Not like the others, who brought back such light girls." And my hair was bushy and kinky. My mother had always kept telling me that it was *good* to be black, but all my life I heard so many ugly things . . . When I came here, it was so different! Here my blackness was my greatest asset. "She's one of us," everybody said.

Then, about three months after we came, a brother and a cousin of my husband's came to live in our house. They have been in the house more than a year now. They burn out the lights, they never keep clean, they mess up the kitchen and the toilets. They have dirty habits. One goes to college and one works, and the brother got married and brought his wife to the house. They are rude. They don't respect me. They feel that they are entitled to a share of whatever my husband has. My husband sees their point of view and he sees mine, but he protects them against me. He wants me to be patient. I mustn't expect them to have my attitudes, he says.

I finally asked them to leave. They went to my husband, and he put the whole thing off. They insisted, and he agreed they could stay, but he did not tell me that this was what he had agreed. Then, one night, he said to me: "Put locks on the door and then they'll see you mean it." So I put locks on the door, but his brother just pulled them off. We had a big scene. My husband began to speak in Twi to my sister-in-law. I demanded that he speak English, so I could understand what was going on. But he didn't. He just left the room. My sister-in-law smiled, and her husband said, "We'll show you how we treat *strangers!*" That's what I really was, a *stranger*. I went after my husband and tried to get it straight with him. "You've left me to fight them," I said. "You've let your sister-in-law feel triumphant over me; you don't know where to stand, you don't know where your loyalties are!" My sister-in-law had gone to her room and locked herself in. I wanted my husband to face her. But she wouldn't come out. I was really wild. I tried to break down the door. I demanded a showdown. I wanted to force him to tell them that he stood on my side. "You must have known I wouldn't stand for this!" I said. "If you wanted someone to take this sort of thing, then you should have picked someone else, not me!" I really went way up and began to throw dishes. Then I began to pack. I told him I could go, I could get out and make my way by myself, and right here in Ghana, too, if I wanted to.

"Would you?" I asked.

She smiled and shook her head. "No," she said. "I don't want to break this marriage. I love him intensely. I can't believe he will fall back into the old pattern. Why should he have picked someone like me and then just fallen back? No, it will work, you'll see, just the way I want it." [2]

On first arriving almost anywhere in West Africa now, an American Negro visitor feels a tingling thrill to see black men everywhere, black men doing all the jobs, lowly *and* high, right up to the black men who now sit in the seats of power, occupy the palaces, and whiz through town in their limousines. It is like a dream he never thought could come true except up in the sky where that pie is. He feels a great relieving pleasure wash over him at the loss of conspicuousness in a black crowd. "It gave me a sort of joy," said a young man from the Midwest. "On the streets, the billboards with black faces, and, most of all, that great sea of black faces that day I went to the stadium." Yet almost at once this young man's sensation became mixed. He did not want to get quite so lost, and, more particularly, he did not want anybody to mistake him for an African:

I will confess that sometimes I resented the fact that I was mistaken for an African [he told me]. Like going into a bank and not getting received there like an American—I mean sometimes getting special attention. This would just come as a flash in the mind. When you were mistaken for an African, you did not get that kind of service, even from Africans. Walking the street as a black man, I was just part of the crowd. But never once did I want to be an African. Why was this? I would ask myself. It was a pleasure to me not to stand out in a place, the way you do whenever you walk into a room full of white people. You don't want that kind of special attention drawn to you. In Africa I enjoyed not having this special place. But I didn't want to be mistaken for an African. When I walked into that bank, I wanted special service as an American, I put on a robe once, and sandals, but I really wanted to be seen not as an African but as an American wearing this apparel. I wanted to be understood to be an American. I can't explain this contradiction.

[2] For a much grimmer picture of problems involved in such American-African marriages, see Ida Lewis, "Americans and Africans—Another Kind of Mixed Marriages," New York *Amsterdam News*, June 3, 10, 17, 1961.

As a Negro, you are always pushing so many things away. Maybe I have never really faced up to it. In Africa, I wanted to get lost in that black sea as a black man, but I did not want to get lost as an American in an African culture. In America the Negro is conspicuous but also is not seen as an individual. I am not *me;* I'm some kind of "Negro." In Africa I was not conspicuous, and could be taken more as an individual, but I wanted to be taken as an American individual, not an African.

There was another reaction some of the Negro visitors had as they moved among these busy masses of black men so newly free of their white masters. It was a certain stab: Here were these Africans, who one had always thought were so far behind, now seeming to run so far ahead. Thereafter the reactions would divide: some of the visitors would go on feeling left behind by the Africans, and would bow their heads lower and lower as they ran into African views on this subject; others would begin to discover virtues in their own American identity that they had never suspected were there. After awhile some actually would come to the point of saying, as one man said to me, "Please don't misunderstand, but I find myself thinking: Thank God for slavery! It got me out of this and made me what I am instead!"

In most places the Negro visitor is still likely to get a hearty first greeting: "Welcome, brother! When will *all* our brothers come home?" There is a lot of this, but the subject of the original departure remains oddly guarded. I was told that Africans do not much like to talk about it. Few Negroes seem to have given much thought to the fact that black Africans had a good deal to do with the capture and sale of the slaves. As we have previously noted, when the late Richard Wright first came to that coast eight years before he bridled at the first African he met, seeing him as the great-great-great-grandson of that so-and-so who sold his great-great-great-grandfather into slavery. The Negro pilgrim today can visit some of the places where such sales were made. Until recently Kwame Nkrumah occupied one of them as his official residence—Christiansborg Castle, right on the sea at Accra. But the old slave dungeons and passages here have long since been sealed off. Ninety miles up the

Ghanaian coast, at Elmina Castle, there is more to see. To be sure, the descriptive leaflet studiously omits any mention of the castle's role as an entrepôt in the slave trade. You are given its dates, an account of its successive Portuguese, Dutch, and British occupants, and a description of its present use as a police-training barracks. But here you can walk into the dungeons and crouch your way through the passages, look through the slits where the chiefs watched their "catch" being sold to the white traders, and follow the stone path to the slithering rocks from which the slaves were run out to the ships beyond the breakers. The pilgrim looks out over the water and into the dimness of that past and thinks his thoughts. The African policeman who acts as guide gives no sign of appreciating the emotions involved. He even seems to think the visitor has come to see the police barracks, and not a place that his ancestors may have passed through as naked slaves so long ago. The Negro pilgrim who stands here can think with pride and wonder of the strength and resilience that his ancestors must have had to survive their ordeal, and the great power to endure, to sorrow, and to win that has been handed on down to him. I have one friend who stood here and felt the great burden of shame for her slave past finally lift from her shoulders. She realized that it was to her black ancestors that she owed her powerful instinct to fight for life against all adversities, and with this she at last put to rest the obscure shame she had felt all her life in the belief that as a descendant of slaves she was somehow less than other people.

But now, at any rate, the returning Negro pilgrim is greeted like a long-lost brother. Sometimes—usually in the remoter areas or among the less sophisticated people—this is a genuine, open-hearted welcome, full of admiring wonderment at the strange brother who has been far away and has become something remarkable, different, educated, successful, and, like all Americans, rich. Among the more sophisticated Africans and in the main centers the Negro pilgrim also finds a welcome up to a certain point. A good part of his feeling of welcome has simply to do with the fact that he finds himself at last in a place where he can go anywhere, anywhere at all, and feel blessedly free of that everlasting fear of humiliation, restriction, and exclusion. This is no small thing, and the enjoyment of the sensation can last a long time. Some visitors never get beyond it, and they cherish the experience. ("Two whole months," said one. "For the first time in my life, two whole months without incidents or insults.")

On occasion this welcome was more active. Kwame Nkrumah and some other African politicians had a definite interest in the link to a politically important American minority, and both in Accra and in the United States, whenever he has come here, Nkrumah has made much of the relationship. On his first return to the United States as Ghana's Prime Minister, Nkrumah shook a crowd at the armory in Harlem with a passionate appeal to race brotherhood. Prominent Negro Americans were invited to the independence celebrations in 1957 and again to the Republic Day ceremonies in 1960. He hailed successful Negro athletes and performers, and all Negro notables who came to Accra could be sure of high-level hospitality on the cocktail-and-dinner-party circuit. The same has been true in Lagos and some of the other new African capitals.

But it did not take long for the Negro pilgrim who stayed on long enough to get past the first friendly greetings to discover the limits of this warmth and this welcome. As Richard Wright learned on his journey in 1953, the stranger among Africans finds his path studded with difficulty, pain, and sometimes even danger. Wright was accused of blundering, of not knowing how to appreciate and get along with Africans, of probing too hard and in the wrong places. It is certainly true that some Negro Americans have managed to get along better in West Africa than Wright did, but it is also true that they have done this by settling for much less than he was ready to settle for, and by not asking the questions he insistently asked. Most of the Negro Americans I met in West Africa in 1960 resembled Wright's stranger a good deal more than they did Nkrumah's brother. They were finding this out in a host of ways, some that barely pierced the surface of their feelings, some that cut deep.

It is painful for a black American to be rejected by black

Africans, but it is both painful and unbearably ironic for him to be rejected, along with white Americans, by black Europeans. Among the new men of power in West Africa are some black Africans who are more British than the British, more French than the French. Indeed, long before they dreamed of becoming free Africans—that happened only recently—many of these men mainly aspired to become black Englishmen or black Frenchmen. This was a stratum of people common to all colonial societies, relatively few in number but extremely important because of their education and training, occupying lower rungs of the bureaucratic, business, and educational systems prior to independence, and in most countries moving into positions of high authority immediately afterward. Out of this group came some who helped bring the nationalist movements into being, some who wrestled with the deeper dilemmas of the transition from traditional to modern cultures. But among them were a great many who took over from their colonial masters their own version of the externals of the higher orders of life, language, food and drink habits, ways of buying, selling, worshiping, running schools and operating a bureaucracy, and usually also many of their assorted little and big snobbisms. They hated their masters but wanted also to be as much like them as possible. This too was part of the legacy they carried with them into the places of power. Hence the American who goes to Africa still not uncommonly meets in Africans a kind of low-grade copy of a variety of low-grade prejudice he used to meet in certain types of Englishmen and Frenchmen. According to this view, "Americans" are brash, loud, pushy, vulgar, materialistic, without culture or sophistication, wit or knowledge. The West African who is so disposed applies this prejudice to all Americans without regard to race, creed, or color. No matter how alienated he may feel from his own society at home, the Negro American in Africa usually finds it no easier than the white American to keep his hackles down when this sort of thing comes up.

A well-known Negro social scientist in a visiting post at a West African university was not invited to the home of a single one of his African colleagues during his first nine months there, and in two years he was invited out in this circle only two or three times. When I saw him, near the end of his stay, he was still pondering the matter in some perplexity, unable to decide what kind of snobbism had been at work—British, academic, conservative, or plain African. Another Negro, serving on the staff of a United States embassy, recalled with some retrospective amusement how on his first contacts with local government officials he had had to face down remarks like "You gross Americans . . ." A young Negro in Senegal spent a whole summer finding his way through the personal, political, racial, and cultural haze of his relations with some Senegalese students. "At bottom, I think they felt I was a barbarian because I wasn't French," he told me. "It was a schizophrenic sort of thing. They were African Frenchmen looking down on me, an American, just as they looked down on any English-speaking African. They were always talking about culture, and I finally realized that by culture they meant *French culture!*"

Besides being amusing or annoying, this snobbism is often also damaging. Entrenched British and French attitudes about American education still govern in much of West Africa—attitudes that were built up in the past partly out of real (if deluded) convictions held by the Europeans, partly out of the wish to keep young Africans from being infected by American ideas. Until quite recently, Africans who managed to get to America and earn degrees, even as medical doctors, had a hard time getting posts from African superiors trained by the British or the French. Americans have met with the same kind of rebuff. An American Negro girl who is a trained nurse was not accepted at a hospital in Accra and was working in the city as a secretary. Another Negro, a man who had left America for good, was refused a teaching job because the local authorities would not recognize his degree. This pattern has been breaking down of course. Nkrumah himself was educated in America; thousands of African students are flocking to American colleges, or trying to, somewhat to the dismay of the older group of European-trained officials; and American teachers, Peace Corps volunteers, and other specialists are making it hard for the old prejudices to survive. But meanwhile the Negro American is not likely to be overcome with warmth toward those of his African kin who

throw European aspersions on his hard-won American education. It is often an odd sensation for him to feel defensively
American, but he comes to it, and in matters that go still deeper.

Negroes come to Africa questing for something they call "acceptance." What they seek may not be findable by anyone anywhere; certainly they do not find it in Africa. "The Negro who
comes here has to have the right attitude," said one of the older
hands among the American Negroes in West Africa. "He has to
know he is not going to be able to run for President here either.
He won't get into the political arena, or even into the educational arena, until they shake off the British heritage, while in
business it will depend on how he operates." In other words, in
Africa, as in certain other parts of the world that Negroes are
acquainted with, they can get along all right if they know their
place. As for business, it is true that there were a few Negro
sharpshooters who came to Africa to make a killing among the
brothers. Some of the people who knew Nkrumah when he was
a student in America came rushing over, and one or two of them
had to be rushed out. Africans—some of whom are becoming
pretty good sharpshooters themselves—keep saying they will welcome Negro entrepreneurs and specialists, and a few of those
who have come have made places for themselves, but the way is
not open or easy or free to all comers. "They have no intention of
seeing people with better backgrounds and education come in
here and take over," said a young man who regards himself as a
"permanent settler" in Africa. "They don't want to let any outsider get ahead faster than Africans do." But it is not often as
aspiring politicians or ambitious money-makers that the pil-
grims come; the "acceptance" they want is acceptance as human beings—something to do with full freedom to be what they
are and become what they can. Here, among those who come to
Africa seeking this, we begin to encounter the more truly
wounding discoveries of their strangerhood.

For one thing, the confusion over the name to go by follows
the Negro to Africa, where he finds that some Africans, like so
many American Negroes, reject the term "Negro," thinking of
it as representing something lowly, unworthy, and associated

with the stigma of slavery.[3] When it occurs, this African rejection is clearly part of an assertion of African superiority over Negro Americans. To the Negro American who has made his peace with the term "Negro," who only yesterday thought himself superior to the African and whose ego is at best in a fragile condition, this comes as a blow not lightly taken.

Another blow is hidden in still another kind of terminological confusion. We have already reported Langston Hughes' confusion when he was called "white" by Africans, and how it was explained to him that this term was based not so much on color as on identification in dress, language, and background with the European. In the Twi language, for example, the word *oburoni* apparently is used for both "stranger" and "white," and even my scrumptiously black friend, whose marriage story was told a few pages back, was, to her bewilderment, called "white lady" by the marketwomen in Accra. It sounds simple enough, but there is a confusion here that, followed far enough, can take us— as I hope some of our previous chapters have shown—into some of the deepest inwardnesses of this encounter. Let only a few examples suggest how these episodes touched some of the most sensitive areas of Negro-American experience:

The light-skinned Negroes who had trouble convincing Africans that they were Negroes. One young man, nearly desperate, said he wanted to hang a sign around his neck proclaiming the fact.

The tan American girl in Guinea who found that Guineans believe in race purity, that you have to be black to belong to the accepted group, and that "some hold the mulatto to be inferior, lower than the black."

[3] At the 1961 meeting of the American Society of African Culture, a Negro American speaker at one session denied that this was so and cited examples of Africans using the term "Negro." At the same meeting but at another session Sheikh Kaluta A. Abedi, Mayor of Dar Es Salaam, Tanganyika, told the audience that "the term 'Negro' is rather detested in Africa, and we prefer to call the African-American *African*-Americans, not Negroes." *Summary Report,* Fourth Annual Meeting, American Society of African Culture, June 1961, p. 3. What this illustrated was simply that differences and confusions over this issue prevail in Africa as well as in America.

The dark-skinned American who was asked: "Are all American Negroes as light as you?" This "shocked me very much, because I've always thought of myself as fairly dark."

The very dark American girl who found that for a summer Africa was "one place I could be accepted without conditions." As she explained it, "American Negroes never think of themselves as black, always think of themselves in terms of white people—this or that is what is most 'white' about me, my features or color or whatever. Now I think of myself as *black*. It's given me more respect for myself."

"Why do you Negroes want to be *white*?" demanded a group of Senegalese students as they bore down on two young American Negroes. "But we don't," the Negroes replied. "Then why do Negroes put grease on their hair? Why do they sell skin bleaching?" The young Negroes tried to explain—to tell who did this sort of thing and who didn't, and how it came about—but it was hard; it was hard to explain the whole business of being a Negro in America.

There is a deep pool of mutual ignorance and miscomprehension between Africans and American Negroes, and it is easily stirred up. Some of the stirrings come from a long way down. Until the day before yesterday, American Negroes generally considered themselves superior to Africans. As we have seen, they rejected the thought of their kinship with Africans, wanted no association with them, even used the word "African" as an expletive to suggest wild or barbarous or ignorant or wicked ways. The sources of this feeling lay in the great obscure tangle of the Negro's struggle for acceptance in America, his lack of footing in any non-American past, his racial mixture, his effort to escape the lowliness universally associated in the dominant white world with blackness, Negroidness—with, in short, being African. Thus Negroes usually saw Africans only as benighted and backward creatures who had never been able to come out of the jungle. Some Negro missionaries went to Africa to "save" them, but for more than a hundred years efforts made by benevolent or malevolent whites to send American Negroes back to

Africa as colonists had little success. All but a few Negroes scornfully rejected the idea. Those who did go back and founded the Republic of Liberia did not exactly make a record calculated to arouse pride and a feeling of association among many Negroes in America. The small sprinkling of Africans who began to come to American schools—especially American Negro schools—were looked upon as either barbarians or ex-barbarians who had become snobbish Europeans. At Negro schools they were made to feel this prejudice most explicitly and painfully; they were isolated, made the butts of harsh jokes, and generally left to huddle among themselves and nurse their countercontempt and counterprejudice against their American "brothers." They found that, as foreigners enjoying different accents and British passports (no Africans came from French territories until quite recently), they could often gain admission to places where Negroes were forbidden to go—movies, restaurants, and the like, even in the South—and they often did so, sneering back at the Negro for his lack of status in his own country. Some of Africa's new leaders went through this American experience: Nkrumah; Nnamdi Azikiwe, now Governor General of Nigeria; and others less well known. It is against a background of such memories that they now proffer their "Welcome, brother!" In the new relationships created by African independence this welcome has its limits.

These have begun to appear even in Liberia, the one country in Africa where American Negroes have had certain ties—where they have been looked upon as more successful elder cousins, and where, as helpers and supporters and as doers of good works, they have enjoyed status and prestige. The descendants of the Negro colonists from America who founded Liberia, in 1822, held fast to their American connections. Since they faced hostile tribes in the interior, rapacious Europeans on their borders, and indifferent whites in America, American Negroes were through almost all their history their only friends anywhere—and, indeed, there were not too many of them. Only a very few Negroes in America appreciated either the regard or the dependence of the Liberians, the rest being generally embarrassed by the Liberian performance. Nevertheless, those Negroes—mainly in the churches—who did interest themselves in Liberia's problems maintained the thin bonds through the years, helping to establish and staff churches and schools. The Americo-Liberians sent their sons and daughters to American Negro schools and married them to Americans whenever they could. An American Negro whom I met in Monrovia described the position in these words: "Psychologically, they feel here that they are a part of the American Negro group. They use the word 'home' in this way. One speaks of a ship coming from 'home.' They have always looked for their American brothers to join them here. The churches are all closely connected to fellow churches in the United States. In this society, girls born and raised in the United States are the highest prestige group, higher on the marriage scale than Liberian women. Girls born here of parents who came from the United States are the second-best group as marriage partners. No president of Liberia has been the son of two parents born in Africa; at least one has always been American born."

This is almost enough in itself—without going into the complex history of Negro-Liberian relationships—to suggest the simmering jealousies and the rancors of dependence that must lie deep in the Liberians' feelings about American Negroes. Now, suddenly, great events are conspiring to free them of this dependence. Africa is waking up. White America wants African friends and is beginning to spend money in Liberia—real money, not the dribble of dimes and quarters that could come from earnest but poor American Negro churchgoers. And beyond white America lies white Russia, which also might be interested in helping Liberia if America should not move fast enough. There is now indeed a faction of growing power in Liberian government that wants to open negotiations with Moscow and begin to derive the advantages to be gained by "neutrality" in a world of contending benefactors. There is no place in this big time for the small-time American Negro benefactor who has been around all these years to serve as Liberia's only rich uncle. "Now there has been a reaction of feeling against Negroes," said the Negro observer in Monrovia whom I have already quoted. "People here feel that Liberia has been in the backwash of Africa, and some of them think this is because they have allowed the United States to be represented here all this time by American Negroes. Now they want roads and harbors, they want what the other countries are getting, and they think the answer is to get American whites and Europeans in here."

This change in the Liberian climate was signaled by the rumors that flew about in mid-1959, when the post of American Ambassador to Liberia was filled for the first time by a white diplomat. Traditionally this had been the one post in the world reserved for some politically deserving or otherwise distinguished Negro. But now, it was reported, the Liberians were seeing this as a sign of their second-classness and had demanded that Monrovia be graced by a representative of the United States who was white. These reports were denied by Liberians, but a white ambassador, a regular foreign-service officer, was duly named to the post.

The issue of appointment of Negroes to diplomatic posts in Africa, incidentally, had already become at this time the object of many mixed feelings and attitudes—one of the new complexities arising out of the new situation. The Liberian appointment in 1959 followed the sending of a white career officer to Ghana in 1957 after Nkrumah had been widely reported to have indicated to Washington that he preferred not to have a Negro as ambassador from the United States. This attitude was not a new one; it had risen a decade or so earlier in relation to the new states in Asia. Premier U Nu of Burma was said to have told the United States Government then: "When you have sent Negroes to London, Paris, and Rome, then send them to us." No Negro was ever sent as ambassador to any Asian country, but in 1959 President Eisenhower did appoint a Negro, John Morrow, to be Ambassador to Guinea. When Morrow resigned in 1961 with the change of administration, he was replaced by a white envoy. Whether this was at the instance of the Guinean

Government the available record did not show, but E. R. Braithwaite, who traveled to Guinea early that year, quotes a high Guinean official on the subject:

. . . We cannot be expected to entertain the highest regard for a black ambassador when we know that in many parts of his own country he would be refused hotel accommodation and other facilities merely because of the color of his skin. And when he speaks to us on matters of importance, we cannot be sure that he speaks on behalf of all America. It therefore follows that America must quickly introduce changes to equate the status of her black citizens with that of her white citizens or keep the black ones out of international-representative office.[4]

This attitude on the part of some African nationalists was plainly nettling to American Negroes for its implication that Negroes were "second class" and that "first-class" recognition had to come only in a white skin. On the one hand, this attitude on the part of Africans nourished and encouraged whatever surviving prejudice and discrimination still governed appointments to government jobs. On the other hand, it underlined the extent to which the real issue was not the status of Negro Americans in Africa but their status in America. The basic issue had to be the demand for equal opportunity for Negroes to be appointed to all government posts everywhere, that Negroes, like other qualified Americans, should find places throughout government service, including places in Africa, and that only such a general distribution would reflect the true advance of Negroes to equal status in a more truly open and plural American society. There was never any getting away from this fundamental fact: equal had to be made to mean *equal,* not *separate* or *special.*

But progress in this direction was still painfully slow. Until now Negroes had been all but totally excluded from such opportunities. Not until now had the government itself moved to try to correct this state of affairs, and it obviously was going to take a good deal of correcting. Some new or more flexible government agencies like the Peace Corps and the various

4 *A Kind of Homecoming* (Englewood Cliffs, N.J., 1962), p. 35.

aid missions were sending more and more Negroes to posts all around the world. In the diplomatic service this new recruitment was much less rapid. At the ambassadorial level, President Kennedy named Clifford Wharton, the only Negro so far to reach senior rank as a career officer, to be Ambassador to Norway and Mercer Cook of Howard University to the Republic of Niger and, early in 1963, Carl Rowan to Finland. At the lower levels of the diplomatic service, the systematic exclusions of the past made rapid retrieval even more difficult. To a group especially convened in the summer of 1961 to help it recruit more Negroes more rapidly, the State Department reported that of 3,732 Foreign Service officers only 17 were Negroes; of 1,140 reserve officers only 3 were Negroes; of 3,527 members of the secretarial and clerical staff only 38 were Negroes. Attracting qualified recruits had become a major task for the department.[5] To redress this condition was going to take more time, time that was so unconscionably long for Negroes and yet could still seem so short to whites who did not know how late it was.

Some Negroes anxious to speed up the slow process argued that Africa should be seen as a place for extending "special" opportunities for appointment of Negroes to posts at all levels. This was in effect an argument not for changing but for enlarging to all of Africa the ghetto status previously limited to Liberia and Haiti. It also had to be based to some extent on the notion that Negroes had some special assets for work in Africa that whites lacked, or some special measure of acceptability to Africans that whites could not enjoy. Some Negroes did indeed feel that because they were "black" they could communicate with Africans more freely and easily than white Americans could.[6] That this might be true of some Negroes and some Afri-

[5] New York *Amsterdam News*, Aug. 26, 1961.

[6] E.g., Joseph C. Kennedy wrote that during a year's research work conducted chiefly in villages in West Africa he was usually taken for "white" or "European" and recognized as an American Negro only by more educated persons. But he was received courteously everywhere and felt that his identification as a Negro made him more trustfully received and won greater credence for his answers to questions about the race situation in the United States. "From my experience [he wrote] I am convinced that . . . [there is] a skin-color affinity and bond of

cans in some places hardly made it, however, the basis for a general rule applying automatically to all Negroes and to all Africans; nor could it justify making Africa a "special" preserve for Negro Americans. Whether there is a "skin-color affinity" arising out of the mysteries of *negritude* as a bond between Africans and Negro Americans is at least a moot point. If, on the other hand, the alleged "affinity" is based upon a person's alienation as an American and his reach for a new identity in African terms, it becomes still another kind of matter. Assuming that such an "affinity" could be established on this basis, it would be reasonable to ask why this would qualify such an individual for a job in which he represented the United States. These were, after all, posts in which American interests were being served, and it could not be assumed that American interests and those of any or all of the new African governments would coincide at all times. No government can be expected to tolerate divided loyalties in its servants, and this would apply just as much to Africa-minded Negroes in Africa as it would, say, to Zionist-minded Jews in Israel. Negroes had to appear representing the United States in Africa not because they were Negroes or had any special affinity to Africans but because they were qualified Americans. And this was the rub for many Negroes who at this moment in time were simultaneously discovering the "new" facts of their association with Africa and resolving the equivocal facts of their identity as Americans. This had to do with much more than filling this or that job; it had to do with some of the most fundamental aspects of the Negro American's redefinition of his place and his commitments in his new world.

It was precisely here where he often just now felt weakest—in his sense of himself, of his place, and his future in American society—that the Negro pilgrim in Africa often found himself under the most direct assault.

The African nationalist, in his new freedom from white control, now feels himself to be his own man in his own land and

warmth that draws the African and the American Negro together." "The American Negro's Key Role in Africa," *The New York Times Magazine*, Feb. 4, 1962.

is full of self-pride. The American Negro, on the other hand, is still struggling to achieve equality of status within a plural but white-dominated society, and that struggle goes slowly and painfully, is punctuated by Little Rocks and snarling New Orleans women, by unpunished murders, and extended by seemingly immovable white supremacists in the South and by smugly self-deceiving whites in the North. In this situation the Negro is an embattled man, and the African, swelling with self-congratulation and enjoying a certain malice, drives his point home. Examples:

"Why don't you American Negroes stop singing spirituals and playing banjos, and get out into the streets and fight for your rights?"

"You Negroes are fools, imitating the white Americans. Isn't it high time you set out to be what you are—*black men, Africans?*"

"Why don't you Negroes stand up and fight for your freedom, *the way we did?*"

Such questions came, certainly not from all Africans or even from all African nationalists, but generally only from those caught up in their own brands of ultrachauvinism; those who for a great variety of personal or political reasons felt defensive or resentful of America and Americans and peculiarly free to vent their feelings on Americans who were black.[7] But the American Negro who had these sneering questions thrown at him tended to feel vulnerable, so vulnerable that most of the

[7] To quote Braithwaite's Guinean friend again: "Black Americans . . . are not much better than the white ones. I hear that they want to identify with us Africans and that they've started all kinds of organizations which claim to reflect their African heritage. Very good, provided they maintain the distance between America and Africa and are sensible enough to understand that a black skin does not make everyone an African. I've seen them here and in other places and been rather sorry for some of them when I observed their disillusionment with us . . . Do you know, quite often I meet black Americans in Africa and by God, they're so American in everything they do and say, that they don't seem to realize it, and we Africans find it most irritating because of the common factor— our black skins . . . Maybe one day we Africans will become as familiar with air-conditioning and labor-saving devices and department stores so that we'll develop a few more factors in common with our American cousins." *A Kind of Homecoming*, pp. 22–23.

time he accepted his guilt as charged. More often than not, he
was too oppressed by anger, despair, confusion, and self-hatred
to give full self-respecting value to his own heritage of struggle
in America. Because of his burden of self-rejection, he would
not know or else would profoundly underrate his history. The
truth is that the Negro's heritage of struggle in America is by
far the longer, is filled with more men who suffered and fought,
and is adorned by a vastly greater number of remarkable
leaders, tribunes, and fighters than one can easily discover in
the short histories of the West African nationalist movements
now so suddenly crowned with power. But here in the fresh
glow of African independence, newly shining in that summer
of 1960, it rarely occurred to any of these individuals to ask
the African: "Tell me, my friend, tell me about *your* struggle
to be free." No question could be more unwelcome to all but
a handful of West African nationalists because the plain fact
is that the great bulk of the new West African politics came
into being to *receive* power, not to *struggle* for it. This was
not likely to become a popular or a widely acknowledged
truth among West Africans, who were much too busy building up new mythologies to hide it from their view and would
recoil angrily from any such threat of exposure. Where any
such exchange did take place, the effect was rarely relaxing or
clarifying.

On the other hand, any attempt by the Negro American to
explain his situation would generally only result in reinforcing
the African's prejudices. This is how one young American
woman described the views of her Ghanaian husband and his
friends:

The Ghanaians feel that Negroes in America are stupid to keep
on begging for something, while if they had the right frame of mind,
they would come back here and really try to work for Africa. But
no, they think the Negroes would rather go on begging favors from
the white man through the NAACP and that sort of thing. That's
what my husband says. He has no sympathy for American Negroes
and doesn't want them to come here. I won't say he looks down on
them. He just feels they're stupid. Well, yes, I guess that *is* looking
down on them, isn't it? All I can say is that if a Negro who believes

in this fighting for civil rights to become part of white America comes over here, he just won't be accepted here, that's all.

But even if you were a Negro who had abandoned the struggle in America and had come to Africa to make a fresh start among your African brothers, it seemed that you were not accepted very warmly either. There were at that time few such individuals. Among those I met in Africa there were several who indeed felt very alienated from America but still had come to Africa in a tentative, seeking way. But in Ghana I did meet one young man who had left America for good, he said, some eight years before and had been struggling ever since to get a feeling of being "inside" with Africans. He had not succeeded in doing so. He said:

When I first came, I couldn't get my college degree accepted. It almost made a patriot out of me, I was so mad. An American college degree is actually much better than any degree from Cambridge or Oxford in the things that people need here. But I couldn't get into the educational system or the civil service here. I married an African girl and that helped; it made some difference. As far as jobs went, I certainly remained outside. But I have begun to get a certain superficial warm welcome in many circles. I'm invited around though I don't have a very busy social life. When I first arrived here, an old lady said to me, "What took you so long to come back?" Ordinary Ghanaians do often have a sentimental attachment to American Negroes. But upper-class people immediately add to this: "Watch out, we don't want outsiders coming in and taking over." Still, I stay in Africa. I left the United States both rejected and rejecting. On the whole, I think it may be more satisfactory for me here, since I grew up on a fence, partially accepted, partially rejected, and I know this is the way an exile feels anywhere. It was the same in the United States. It is the same here.[8]

8 After the appearance of this passage in a magazine article, this individual wrote me not to contest what it reported of his experience in Africa but to protest being described as one who had "abandoned" the struggle for first-classness in America. What he had done, he said, was simply to transfer to Africa his effort to promote the cause of the "Gandhian or nonviolent way of life." He wrote: "I distinctly remember the main point of my exposition being that there was a greater opportunity for a society with the values I believed in developing in Africa, with all its drawbacks and imperfections, than in an America which had gone so far down the road of materialism and power madness." One month

But most of the Negroes I met in West Africa during that summer were not ready to give up their fight against second-classness in America simply to accept second-classness in Africa. Nor was this only a matter of being a Negro, an American, or an outsider. In much of West Africa, it already took no profound discernment to see that however sweet it might be to be relieved of the power of the white man, the new power of the black man did not yet smell much like freedom—certainly not like the freedom to which the American has learned to aspire. So, stung by the African's scorn and rejection, by his stubborn refusal to accept the American Negro's *bona fides,* many a visitor found himself cast in an exasperating role: an alienated Negro American passionately defending segregationist America against the attacks of a national-chauvinist African. This was the summer odyssey of one young American who, like so many others, had come to find out whether in Africa he might have the chance he felt he would never get at home. His story:

As hard as I could ever push it, I could never really think of myself as an American, not ever. When I was in Japan and Korea with the Army, I always thought of myself just as Negro, not even as hyphenated Negro-American, just Negro. But what I have found is that you might get rid of the color problem, but you get into something else. You know, in the beginning I had exactly the same experience Richard Wright had in Indonesia. I got called up in front of a line of Europeans and got waited on first. This was discrimination in reverse, and I have to say I enjoyed the sensation, even though I began to feel guilty about enjoying it. By the end of the summer, I'd thought a lot about it, and I just wanted to get away from there. I had to see that I could never become Nigerian, or any other kind of African, never really become part of it. I could not run away.

---

after he wrote these lines the cabinet minister for whom he worked was forced to resign and fled the country for fear of imprisonment or worse. Scores of critics and opponents of Nkrumah were being jailed at the time, and a special court was empowered to impose the death penalty for "political offenses." Other cabinet ministers were later ousted amid charges of corruption and a scandal caused when the wife of one of them bought a gold bed in London to use in their sumptuous new mansion in Accra. Nkrumah was now known as the *Osagyefo,* meaning "The Redeemer." Amid these outbreaks of power madness and materialism my correspondent himself left Ghana.

Maybe the truth is that as an American Negro I have no place to go at all. Maybe that is the situation.

When the African students talked about American Negroes' wanting to be white, I had to agree this was true. They also said we hadn't done enough to push for equality, that we should get guns, if necessary, and go out onto the streets. But they hadn't done this, either, I reminded them. I tried to trace for them the development of what had been done.

There was one fellow, a most articulate Marxist type. He kept attacking American Negroes, how American Negroes weren't doing any of the things Africans were doing in Africa. We finally had a real run-in one day, when we were tired and irritated. He said something, and I found myself defending America, the whole thing, in a way I could never have imagined myself doing. I said yes, there was Little Rock on one side, and a lot of things on the other side, people pushing and fighting; all sorts of things can happen and do happen. As I was talking, I found myself being pinned against the wall. They kept coming back at me with "You try to be white!" And that is true. I realized I was defending something I wasn't even sure I wanted to be defending. But I think at that moment I began to understand. Here I was defending this thing. But it was because I knew there were other sides to it. As big a racist as I am—and I am a racist—I could see that they would only hear of Little Rock and New Orleans, and would never hear of the lunch counters integrated in Nashville. They wouldn't hear it even if you told them about it! I said to myself, All right, but I'm going to see that they hear all sides, hear *our* side. I don't know if they ever believed anything I tried to tell them.

---

❈

---

## PART FOUR

# NEGROES
# AND
# AMERICA

# 1. *THE KEEPING OF THE DREAM*

In rediscovering their African origins Negroes are not regaining their identity as long-lost Africans but are reshaping their identity as Americans. This is a complicated and difficult matter for all the reasons we have seen that lie imbedded in the Negro-American experience. It is also complicated and difficult because being *American* is itself not so much a condition as a process whose nature is still imprecisely defined and whose ultimate shape no one clearly sees. Nevertheless, like so many other people who have become members of the American society, Negroes have to blend their unique character as a group with the common character they share as Americans. Between these two identifications there has been up to now a deep and mutually deforming split. Negroes have had to fight fiercely for the most elementary part of their share of the common American holding—their equality of rights as citizens. The exclusions and denials that were their lot for so long dominated the shaping of their unique character while laming—as with a shriveled limb—the common American identity itself. Now this system of exclusion is coming to an end, or is at least being sweepingly revised. The Negro group identity based upon it is becoming obsolete, and some kind of new group identity must somehow take shape out of the old elements and the new circumstances. Like the restoration of sight or the use of a paralyzed limb, this change in Negroes must at the same time profoundly alter the American organism of which they will now become a more normally functioning part.

To try to see Negroes going through this great transition is to see a confused melee of people at many different points: in motion physically and psychologically; pushing in and out of ghettos, in and out of blind alleys; trying to cope with old foes and old problems while facing new pressures and new demands and new circumstances. There is no way of simplifying these complexities or of catching them whole except perhaps as the artist might. Still, as Ralph Ellison said, the struggle for first-class citizenship for Negroes is but the first paragraph of the first chapter of a long story that has yet to unfold. Sluggishly or swiftly, now or soon, painfully but irresistibly, Negroes are moving up and out of the conditions of their second-classness, and this upward motion brings them face to face with new questions about themselves: What new transforming combinations are to come out of the changing conditions of life? What is to be made now of the Negro's uniqueness as Negro in the changing pattern of his identity as American? Out of the ghetto and beyond the veil, what are to be the new meanings of being Negro in America?

Negroes bring to this experience their own distinctive character, their peculiar history, and the drives and conditions of their present circumstances. But for all their uniqueness, the matter is hardly unique to them. The same or similar questions have come up out of many of the same patterns of separateness, alienation, assimilation, and integration of many groups that have gone through—or are still going through—the business of trying to fit themselves into some kind of an American whole. With all their many differences in kind, time, place, and process, and with all their varieties of intensity, irony, and agony, the questions now so belatedly and sharply posed for Negroes have in one form or another faced Irishmen, Jews, Italians, Poles and Ukrainians, Chinese, Japanese, and Mexicans. They have been long present for American Indians and have much more recently come into the lives of other groups whose status in the American society has been going through significant changes: Puerto Ricans, Hawaiians in all their shades and mixes, and even Alaskan Eskimos. For what we are dealing with here is the problem of American pluralism, the working out of the pattern of the many separatenesses within an American effort to create an open society embracing all measures of assimilation and of sustained differences on the basis of a shared common culture, a shared set of institutions, and a shared set of rights and opportunities.

The gap between this American dream and the American reality has closed so far only at relatively few places. The American society is still composed of many hierarchies and systems of mutual exclusion. At various times different groups of peoples have made their way onto the great common ground at varying rates and have achieved various measures of assimilation, absorption, and acceptance by the society as a whole. At the same time each group has preserved some of its separateness and elaborate structures of prejudice and discrimination have continued to exist. Thus each new breakthrough is a notable event: a Jew reaches the Supreme Court, an Italian reaches the Cabinet, and most spectacularly, an Irish Catholic reaches the Presidency. In general it can be said that separate group identities based primarily on national origins have yielded most readily to the homogenizing process of Americanization. Hyphenated nationality groups persist and still celebrate a calendar of national days in a bright array of costumes to the piping of all sorts of music. Some special food habits persist among members of each national tribe while a few cuisines—like the Chinese and the Italian—have been naturalized by an intelligently appreciative general public. But for the great mass of Americans the principal surviving evidence of national origins is mostly to be found in the names they go by, the characteristic American conglomeration that turns up so dramatically on almost any ballot, roster, or casualty list. In some places the grouping of these names on the ballot still reflects group association, or at least special appeal to national groups, and their inclusion or exclusion from some membership lists may still often indicate some surviving local snobbery. But, much more largely, the distinctive identity and separateness based on national origin become more or less shadowy reminiscence within a few generations and in many cases fade away altogether. By contrast, religious differences are made of much stronger stuff and retain the power of great separateness within the society long after the different national origins have blurred or dissolved. Where we have come in this matter was dramatized both in strong and positive aspects in the presidential campaign of 1960. There are many who fear that the approaching end of Protestant dominance in America is bringing with it paradoxically not less but more religious divisiveness.[1] But while religious differences still govern many kinds of exclusion in American life, they are hardly as many or as damaging as exclusions based on differences of "race." In the gradual making of an open plural American society the barriers of nationality have stood lower than the barriers of religion, and the barriers of religion have stood lower than the barriers of race, which have stood highest and hardest and longest of all.

These barriers barred entry for Negroes into the great common world of American life until just now. Only a few much smaller groups also seen as racially distinct—the Chinese, Japanese, and Mexicans—and the Jews, with their peculiarly equivocal mix of ethnic and religious separateness, have shared in any degree the kind of exclusion and rejection which was the central burden of Negro-American experience. Members of all these groups are still the objects of more or less virulent prejudice and discrimination. All of them have only quite recently achieved a partial and still-fragile measure of inclusion. But for Negroes the breakthroughs into the open spaces of the nation's life are only just beginning. They have remained submerged, staying at the bottom, as James Baldwin has wryly observed, "because it's the only way everyone in America will know where the bottom is." The openings in the American society which were there for every successive immigrant group for more than a century were never there for Negroes. The new urban

---

[1] The growing sense among Catholics that they need no longer maintain their defensive stance as a minority subject to discrimination is perhaps well illustrated by this news report: "Cardinal Cushing bluntly accused 4,000 Catholic nurses meeting in Boston . . . of living in a ghettolike past because their Protestant counterparts were not included in the four-day program . . . 'The whole lot of Catholic councils for professional people, youngsters, lay men and women need to be modernized,' he said. 'We have no need of these organizations if it's going to mean only Catholics getting together. We don't want to live in a ghetto.' " Boston *Globe*, June 8, 1962. A recent study by two Jewish writers suggested that the closer the culture moves toward a religious pluralism, the greater the tendency of Protestants, Catholics, and Jews to separate themselves behind the walls of "a triple ghetto." The authors say: "Evidence abounds that while the legal walls of racial and religious segregation are tumbling down in the United States, the walls of self-segregation are springing up." E. J. Lipman and Albert Vorspan, eds., *A Tale of Ten Cities* (New York, 1962), p. 339.

politics, largely created by the great immigrant masses, occasionally gave some voters the chance to vote more than once but never systematically prevented any body of citizens from voting at all. A crudely growing society often bent its legalities out of shape, but only people across the racial barrier, e.g., Negroes, Chinese and Japanese, were subjected to mob violence or were systematically deprived of due process because of their "race." Yankees despised Irishmen and Irishmen despised Italians and Polacks, and they all despised Jews; great whole subworlds with their own tribal systems, dialects, and codes of relationship were built up around these assorted mutual antipathies and prejudices. But members of these groups were never successfully denied access to all the public rights and places open to all citizens, or the eventual freedom to push out into wider living spaces where they might still live under certain handicaps and disabilities but where they could at least live tolerably and work to better their estate. Most of these groups came into American life in the time of the sweatshops in the cities and varieties of labor peonage in the mills and mines. But when these workers finally organized themselves into trade unions to fight for better conditions of life, they rigidly excluded Negroes from their trades and from their unions. They made it all but impossible for Negroes to acquire the skills and therefore the jobs that would help them rise. They left Negroes to live as they could at the bottom, at the lowest levels of unskilled toil, or by whatever ways they could devise of living better by living off each other inside their ghettos.

The Negro became the most estranged, rejected, and alienated member of the American society—the man out of the whole American process. His circle intersected the fewest of the others along the narrowest arcs and barely even touched the great open center at any point. Inside his physical and psychological pale he concentrated mainly on surviving; he had to learn to live in a human setting hardly more hospitable than the natural environment in which his African kin had to learn how to survive. He managed it partly by devices of accommodation and partly by abrasive resistance. Deep inside he lived as he could; at the outer gates he pushed and fought and performed prodigies of counterassertion, pushing out and being pushed back again. This went on and on until only yesterday when, as he pushed with increasing force, the battered and quivering gates in front of him began to collapse, brought down finally by winds that had begun to blow in hard from far away. Outside that gate waited no easy ascent, no goal clearly in view, but a steep cliff still separating yesterday from today, a future for which he still had to fight step by step and which now faces him in a blur.

Appearing over these fallen and falling barriers is a figure being called the "New Negro." This is a recurring term meaning essentially a newly militant, newly self-assertive Negro who will no longer submit to the humiliations of the past. There have been such Negroes in every generation, and there is nothing really "new" about them at all. What is new is that today's "New Negroes" are appearing in a situation where for the first time the odds are with them; their newness, their militancy, and their self-assertion are at last bound to pay off. The new world is finally coming, but it is coming differently for different people. There is more than one kind of "newness," more than one way of seeing the new situation, putting the new questions, seeking the new answers.

If an artist were to try to catch a picture of Negro Americans caught at this moment as on a wide mural, he would put at the forward end the young men and women, mostly students at Negro colleges in the South, who began writing their own climatic chapter to this history only in 1960 when they launched the sit-in movement. By this they carried the challenge beyond the legal structure of segregation to the whole pattern of customary behavior in the established white order. Just behind, pushing these young people ahead, he would paint in the plain men and women of Montgomery, Alabama, who walked to and from work for a year in 1955–56 rather than continue to ride in segregated seats in the buses. By their act they shook up the entire Negro population of the country and directly inspired the subsequent turn to mass action, the sit-ins, boycotts, and picketing which have since been changing so much of the hitherto immutable "way of life" South and North. Here would come the young adults who have led the way into the white

universities of the South, the "new" young Negro with the
brawny spirit represented by James Meredith of Mississippi.
Here too would come the children who have been walking the
gauntlet into their desegregated classes, and their parents, led
by the little-sung plaintiffs in the court cases that made these
first great breakthroughs possible, and the NAACP lawyers and
their supporting organizers and workers who fought those cases
up through the courts as a climax to a fight that had gone on
for more than half a century. After them would come the new
young ministers in the old Negro churches, a whole new species
come to replace those who in a past time could only preach endurance. All together they still make a painfully thin vanguard
of people who are where they are because a still smaller but still
more persistent band of predecessors fought to open the roads
they have traveled—all of them carrying a tremendous weight of
commitment, not only pushing against a great and resistant society in front of them but also pulling a great and sluggish mass
behind them. These are the people who believe that there is a
self-respecting status for them to win in the American society
and that they are at last winning it. Because they believe this is
so, the young Negro novelist Julian Mayfield, who does not believe it, has called these Negroes in sad and bitter words, "the
last defenders of the American dream."

## 2. THE LOSING OF THE DREAM

Victory comes in sight, but it comes late and it comes slowly. It comes, moreover, not because the democratic creed, much less the Christian, is triumphing at last but because the white world is forced to change its ways out of fear for itself. I remember the late Franklin Frazier, a few weeks after the 1954 school decision, putting it in his own bald and bitter way—I edit only slightly: "The white man is scared down to his bowels, so it's be-kind-to-Negroes decade at last." The victory approaches so late and for so many "wrong reasons" that for many it begins to bear the visage of defeat. More, it comes here and not there, for some but not for others, enough to end forever the old submission but not enough to assure a new freedom. The changes bring on resistance from the racists, and racist resistance brings on fresh episodes of violence, and the fresh violence strains to breaking the patience of people already strained beyond all reasonableness. Every gain is partial, and some hand is always there to try to take away what some other hand has "given." A reluctant or timid white liberalism clings to "gradualism" in a situation where slowness has become failure. The longer the process stretches out, the more stubborn the resistance within pockets of the white society, the more the issue gets wrapped up in the nation's embattlement for survival as a power in the world, the greater the disarray and disorientation, the greater the cynicism rising hard and ugly, especially among young Negroes who emerge to find the fruit of the struggle rotten. Instead of a relieving sense of achievement with every advance, in some a new kind of despair rises side by side with hope, often in the breast of the same person, bringing with it a new uprush of alienation: If I am really never going to get *in*, a man says to himself, then let me get the hell *out*.

There is surely no easy way *in* for the great mass of Negroes still trapped in their poverty. They have moved by the millions to escape it, from South to North, from country to city. But they have moved from rural to urban slums, into a process of decay and change which opens no early prospect of betterment for them. The economy as a whole is not growing fast enough to provide the expansion and multiplied opportunities that these masses of people need; the dead weight of even 4 to 5 percent permanent unemployment in the system keeps them down at the bottom. The economy is moving, furthermore, toward automation which will narrow still further the opportunities open to labor with the lowest order of skills, again primarily Negroes. They will find themselves counted out as skilled and better-paid workers just as they are beginning, in painfully slow numbers and against grim obstacles both in industry and the unions, to find their way in. The solution for them is wrapped up in some of the most difficult and complex problems of the whole society, and it will not come swiftly, surely not swiftly enough to transform the lives of these trapped millions. They express their hopelessness and their alienation in all the ways familiar to the life of poverty: apathy, squalor, ignorance, degradation, crime. The energies and tensions that are generated find a few outlets in hoodlumism and violence; in the ghettos they break out into periodic explosions of targetless wrath. More recently they have taken the form of direct attack on authority, attacks by street crowds on policemen, always the prime symbol and too often in the black slums the actual perpetrators of the white world's violence and injustice against the black man.

Around the edges of this dispossessed mass there has always been a fringe of cults to which people could turn to appease their despair. Two generations ago they turned in great numbers first to Marcus Garvey's dream promise of escape to Africa and then to Father Divine's offer of a nearby heaven. Although today's emergent Africa is much more real than Garvey's, it is a striking fact that the desperate poor have stayed with the religious cults and that the most newly successful of these is Elijah Muhammad's Black Muslim movement, which is oriented not toward ancestral Africa but toward a vaguely neo-Islamic or pseudo-Islamic tradition which has been present for a long time as a distinct strand in Negro cultism. Turning to a "Moorish" or "Arab" identity became one way not only to escape in fantasy from the oppressions of the white world but also to escape from being Negro. In the tiny cultlets out of which Muhammad's movement grew, the nakedness of the Negro could be covered with flowing robes, the nothingness of his past filled with the history of Islam, the emptiness of his life filled with a new content of dreams which had not been made or imposed upon him by the white man. At the far outer edges of Negro life such cults have long competed with the far more successful appeal of evangelical Christianity, but only in the last few years with the break in the power and prestige of the white world has such a cult been able to become more than an insignificant flutter at the fringe. Elijah Muhammad's movement lived a fitful life for thirty years or more in Detroit and Chicago but only in the last decade has become a national organization credited with anywhere from 100,000 to 250,000 members, with temples in some 40 cities, and with an influence among urban Negro masses well out of proportion to their actual numbers.[1]

The Muslims represent the current most extreme form of wanting *out*—out of America, out of the white world altogether. They recruit their members from among the lowly and in the prisons with a doctrine that declares the white man to be the devil himself doomed for his evil deeds. They demand total separation for themselves, asking for land to be carved out of the territory of the United States on which they would make a fresh start as the nation of black men chosen by God to embody virtue on earth. The Muslims call on the Negro American to cease being both "Negro" and "American." They reject the term "Negro" as the badge of subjection and seek to rid themselves of everything else that has come to them out of the white man's culture, including not only the names acquired out of slavery, as we have already remarked, but many of the other more bitter fruits of degradation and poverty. Muslim converts are "made over"—they abandon crime, dope, alcohol, prostitu-

[1] For a detailed description see Lincoln, *The Black Muslims in America*. For earlier cults see Fauset, *Black Gods of the Metropolis*.

tion. They acquire new habits of life, a new view of themselves and of their blackness, a new kind of militant self-respect which many other Negroes look upon with fascinated envy. Like Marcus Garvey's, Muhammad's appeal is essentially to racial pride and separateness. His passionately violent indictment of the white world carries the ring of truth to almost any listening Negro, and his defiant rejection of the white society brings an involuntary inward assenting response from many who are otherwise not at all ready to accept the melancholy suggestion that their only road to regeneration lies in black racism and in a total flight from the social reality.

But there are Negroes who are no longer caught on the deep undersides of the society who do not have to flee quite so far from reality in order to express their moods of despair and their impulse to escape. One finds them among the newly arriving youth, now often schooled up to the higher degrees, but no longer schooled in that peculiar quality of endurance that their elders acquired as a matter of course; or youths from whom the new opportunities demand more than they can give as individuals standing on their own, who cannot bear the frustrations of failure or rejection which might no longer be due to the fact that they are Negroes. From among these comes a new fringe of pseudoradicals who retreat either into beat apathy or into a new brand of racial nationalism which gives them the chance to dream of either migrating to the new Africa or, preferably, of waiting right here to welcome the triumphant onrush of the newly rising tide of color in the world. But a certain despair rises also now not only among youthful newcomers but, far more poignantly, in older men weary of having to continue a struggle that they thought, for a brief time in the 1950's, might really be coming to an end at last. Here, spread thinly but meaningfully along these several different layers of the population, one comes upon the feeling that effective integration for Negroes in the American society is unlikely, impossible, or even no longer desirable. Many of those who share this mood also begin to feel, just like the Black Muslims, that they want *out*.

The young radicals are still but a tiny handful. The demonstrators at the United Nations at the time of the death of Patrice Lumumba in February 1961 brought some of them into the larger public view for the first time. That demonstration actually mustered only some 200 persons divided into several competing groups. When newspaper reporters went hastily looking to see where this "new" Negro radicalism came from, they found—besides the Black Muslims, who took no part in the demonstration—a mass of groups and grouplets which by their own claims had at the largest 400 members and at the smallest 25, and added up to a grand total of under 2,000.[2] Some of these were the heirs of the defunct Garvey movement but others were new organizations created by younger newcomers to the scene. Some of these latter were "new" only partly in the sense that they brought a greater literacy and a somewhat more sophisticated tone to the little fringelet of black nationalism that had always been there. They were "new" most of all because, unlike the black nationalists of Garvey's time and spirit, they now had the great emotional overhead of change in America and change in Africa to feed upon. Unlike the lowly and more benighted, they do not need the dream world of Garvey or an Elijah Muhammad into which they can release their frustrations and angers. They usually deprecate the fantasies and the racism of the extremists, but they do not repudiate them. "Muhammad preaches black supremacy," one of the leaders of the Lumumba demonstration said to me in a conversation, "and I don't think there is any race supremacy, but I don't think we can give up any weapon. If we have to extol the virtues of being black, then let's do it!" Again, unlike their less fortunate counterparts in the slum streets, they do not have to strike blindly at white authority by throwing rocks or bottles at policemen on the beat. Out in the turbulently changing world they find all kinds of surrogates to deal their blows for them at the authority and prestige of hated white America, new heroes with whom to identify, hostility with which to associate themselves, struggles for "freedom" which they can join from afar.

Unlike so many of the radicalized and alienated youth of the

2 *The New York Times*, Mar. 1, 1961.

1930's who looked for political and social solutions, very few of
these young people become supporters of the Communist movement. They do not join Khrushchev, they simply cheer him on
when it suits them. They subscribe vaguely, as do most of the
African nationalists, to "socialism," but they have no real commitment to any political or social ideology. Most of them know,
moreover, what Negroes learned of old, that the Communists
are politicians intent upon putting the issues of race at the service of their politics, whereas the black nationalist is much more
intent upon putting whatever politics comes to hand at the
service of race. Russian power may be the best and biggest instrument at hand for dealing out retribution to America, but
it is still, for all that, white power. In the Communist world the
affinities of the new black nationalists move rather toward the
Chinese, who can be seen more and more as the most passionate
and unswerving of America's foes precisely because their challenge is of the newly risen nonwhite against the white, and it
is addressed not only to America but to Russia as well. (Half-a-
dozen years before American political pundits began to specu-
late seriously about this possibility, a Negro newspaperman I
knew was contemptuously brushing aside the immediacies of
the Russian-American power struggle and predicting that the
Russians and Americans would make common cause against
China long before they would collide with each other.) But Mao
Tse-tung is only one of a whole gallery of newcomers. The
world is dotted now with the newly arisen dealing stinging
blows at Western white men. The wreath passed in a few years
from Nasser to Nkrumah to Sekou Touré to Lumumba—moving from one to the other as each of these new figures reached
his own small peak of defiant cleavage from the white West—
and above all to Castro, whose success in defying and embarrassing American colossus made him a hero not only to these few
pseudoradicals but to much larger numbers of Negroes ready
to cheer any challenger of white American power. Great crowds
turned out to greet the white Cuban Castro when, in pursuit
of his own shrewd exploitation of the racial tensions in the
United States, he came to Harlem while attending the United
Nations General Assembly session in 1960. Members of the

Negro upper crust were invited to enjoy Castro's hospitality in Cuba, and not a few went in the initial period. "I very strongly doubt," wrote James Baldwin, "that any Negro youth now approaching maturity and with the whole vast world before him is willing, say, to settle for Jim Crow in Miami when he can . . . feast at the welcome table in Havana. And he need not, to prefer Havana, [be] pro-Communist or for that matter pro-Cuban or pro-Castro . . . He need merely prefer not to be treated as a second-class citizen." [3]

Only a few of these new alienates have carried their alienation to the point of leaving the country. But a few have, and while some still flee—as Richard Wright and James Baldwin and others did in the past—to the traditional expatriate refuges in Europe, the new world offers new asylums now and the younger crop of migrants have other choices; a few have gone to Cuba, some have gone to Africa. Their numbers are negligibly small— the best guesses in the summer of 1962 ran to a top of a few dozen—but they illustrate the fact that emergent Africa can and does play at least two roles for emergent Negro Americans. For the far greater numbers who are moving purposefully into the era of more successful integration in the American society, it offers the added ingredient of a more realistic and more self-respecting view of their African origins and the chance of a new kind of relationship to Africa as it is now. At the same time, to those Negroes who either do not expect or do not want to become more successfully integrated Americans, it offers an alternative, a choice of a place to go. This choice includes taking on all the limitations, risks and pains of exile but it is still a choice far more real than it could ever be when Africa was still part of the white man's world. The leader of one of these new organizations said: "We are primarily interested in the African liberation struggle. We do not participate in Freedom Rides or sit-ins or anything like that. We do not foster the struggle here. Our job is to win American Negro awareness of the African struggle." Then he added: "I am thinking of going to Africa myself to stay, and if I do, I will give up my American citizenship. That

3 "A Negro Assays the Negro Mood," *The New York Times Magazine*, Mar. 12, 1961.

won't be hard. There has to be another way in the world. The United States just doesn't have it. There must be another way, and I expect to find it in Africa."

These young alienates are but few in number compared to the young Negroes who are fighting to break down the surviving barriers or to grasp hard the whole new world of chances opening to them in schools, business, and in government. They are likely to be fleeing from failures far more individual and personal than social and political, from fears that lie in them rather than in their situation, from a freedom they find terribly threatening. But even so, like the Muslims, they have a symptomatic importance of uncertain extent; they express openly and violently moods and feelings that are felt much more widely but are repressed, rationalized, or deflected. Frustrated Negroes are not the only ones, after all, who fear that Western white society is plunging toward some unimaginable hell, but Negroes in America do have their peculiarly equivocal status to resolve in their minds as they contemplate these prospects. Negroes of every estate have at one time or another exulted when some outside force has dealt white America a blow, have seen the Japanese, the Russians, or the Afro-Asians at the UN as acting somehow for *us* against *them,* and at every crisis in our history for half a century they have had to steady themselves with reminders about which, after all, was which. The deep and abiding identification of Negroes with America that has been maintained despite these feelings has had to persist in the face of the society's deep and abiding refusal to identify itself with Negroes. This has been cause enough in itself for despair to overcome not merely angry young men but mature and thoughtful and courageous men and women who have given the best of their lives to better themselves, the Negro's estate in America, and the position of America itself in the world. Some of the best of men have been assailed by the impulse to give up, to withdraw, to seek an *out;* listen to James Weldon Johnson writing thirty years ago:

There come times when the most persistent integrationist becomes an isolationist, when he curses the white world and consigns it to hell. This tendency toward isolation is strong because it springs from a deep-seated natural desire—a desire for respite from the unremitting grueling struggle; for a place in which refuge might be taken. We are again and again confronted by this . . . [4]

More than one man who, like James Weldon Johnson, had fought the hard fight all his life has been confronted by this same despairing fatigue in the years since the school decision of 1954. They dared hope that the long struggle had come at that point to its climax. In a way, of course, it had; it finally committed the Federal government and the nation to a fundamental change in its racial behavior. But what followed was not immediate compliance but temporizing, resistance, the flouting of legality, compromise, and the seeming settlement of the "moderates" for token desegregation—7 percent in the Southern and border states eight years after the court's ruling, hardly a comforting measure of the rate of change for Negroes in the society as a whole. Faced again with appeals for "patience" from "moderates" who equated fighters for civil rights with the defenders of white racism as "fanatics on both sides," many a stalwart man began to feel tired. Here is how one of the more prominent among them sounded in a conversation early in 1962:

These last three or four years have left big question marks in my mind, making me wonder. I'm talking about the willingness to settle for tokenism which has eroded the whole business of compliance [i.e., with court-ordered desegregation]. There is some evidence that Negro organizations and leadership are getting fatigued, falling into the trap of moderation. Some of the criticism of the NAACP reflects the impatience of the folk Negro and the more articulate working-class Negro, and the impatience of some younger middle-class Negroes against this trend . . .

This is all related to the increase of temporizing, like President Kennedy deciding to postpone civil rights legislation or holding off the housing order. Other things are considered more important. It is made secondary. Personally, I have become an "extremist" on this. I think the only issue with higher priority than racial justice is the issue of world and national survival. But I think these issues are one

4 James Weldon Johnson, *Negro Americans, What Now?* (New York, 1934), p. 13.

and the same. It fascinates me to see how this society can behave as it does. With the dominance of temporizing moderation, you get an erosion of moral strength. You get moral dry rot instead. If we accept the fraud of moderation on the racial issue, it corrodes and erodes our moral potential, and the moral strength allegedly inherent in the democratic system is really all we have got to go on in facing a formidable adversary in the world. Any weakening of this is a weakening of the whole. This is the dry rot. Either you cut it out or you won't have a tree very long.

He went on to say that he felt a deepening discouragement in others as well as in himself:

I think it is pervasive, the pro-Castro business and so on, and frankly, I don't know where it will stop. There is a disturbing and common appearance of this among some of our most successful Negroes. They try to use the symbols of success as a substitute, hiding their feelings under conspicuous consumption or other superficial things. But when such a man stops and thinks, he finds a deep and horrible despair over what it means to be a partial human being. Maybe only a physically handicapped person comes close to knowing what this feeling is, but he does not have a social and legal conspiracy all around him to make him feel unwanted. You can be enormously successful, but still not feel respected in the crucial aspects of your being, still always looking over your shoulder, always having to catch the nuance . . .

There was a long pause and then, musingly, he went on:

One of my best friends, an extremely successful man, bought a home for himself in Jamaica recently. I have felt the pull of this myself. It's a feeling of escape, sure, but one hopes not into nothingness. Thurgood Marshall once said to me: "You get awfully tired trying to save white folks' souls!" Myself, I'm tired of being a prisoner of the idiocy of American racism. I now sometimes find myself flirting with the idea of just getting out it.[5]

[5] In a story called "Reena" (in *Harper's*, October 1962) Paule Marshall has a tired and defeated woman say: "The most important plan right now is Africa. I've already started saving the fare. . . . I must see it, get close to it because I can never lose the sense of being a displaced person here in America because of my color." James Meredith, of the University of Mississippi, who had previously told interviewers of receiving invitations "to study in Ghana, Nigeria, Senegal and many other countries," wrote in a magazine article (*Saturday Evening Post*, Nov. 10, 1962): "If I can't live in Mississippi, I very definitely will leave the country."

It is too soon to know whether the disoriented cultists among the poor, the angry young men among the better-off, or the tired older men among the fighters for civil rights are some of the last casualties before a final victory or harbingers of greater defeats to come. But however they may tip the measures of hope and despair in the process of change, the change itself will obviously continue to take place. It will move with forces larger than individual or group emotions, depending upon the further path of the American economy toward growth or decay, the further evolution of the world's emerging countries toward open or closed societies, the further movement of the world's larger politics toward a less warlike kind of peace or toward some final kind of war. The room for optimism in all these matters is not spacious. But wherever these many intersecting lines may lead— short of apocalyptic catastrophe—Negro Americans of every condition and estate will still have to be redefining themselves and fitting themselves into new places in the society in the years to come. Over this prospect itself—let alone over some of the larger surrounding issues—hangs a great cloud of questions which not even the pace of our times will quickly burn away.

# 3. *TOWARD SOMEBODINESS*

Three quarters of a century ago when W. E. B. Du Bois at age seventeen moved out of the rejecting white world into a closed Negro world, he exulted self-appeasingly: "A new loyalty and allegiance replaced my Americanism; henceforward I was a Negro." Many Negroes listened eagerly to Du Bois for as long as he summoned them to fight to assert their Americanism; none would follow him when he eventually cut himself off from it. If now these unreconciled strivings are to be reconciled at last—if some measure of successful integration does finally offer the Negro a more tolerable life as an *American*—where will it leave him as *Negro?*

The goal of "integration," like "freedom" for the anticolonialists, stands like a great shining blur down at the far end of the struggle road, drawing and inspiring all who fight for it, but becoming not clearer but blurrier the closer one gets to it. Each of these terms has a sufficiently clear and immediate political content; just as "freedom" in the colonial context means the end of alien rule, "integration" plainly enough means the free and open access by Negroes to the common rights of all citizens. But what then? In the ex-colonies freedom from alien rule has marked only the beginning of the struggle for freedom. Here the conquest of civil rights carries us toward those vague and shadowy places where all the new questions about the future of the Negro group identity wait for us.

One view is that there will not be any Negro group identity at all, that with integration Negroes will eventually disappear as a distinct group in the population. From some people this view comes burdened with the whole past and cloaked in despair. Here is how one doughty but very tired old man put it:

> I don't think the Negro has any future in the United States as an identifiable community. He will be increasingly absorbed. I don't

343

believe the Negro will ever be accepted in America so long as he is a dark man. If he is not too dark, he may at best reach the position of the Jew. In some communities, the Negro professional man is already accepted much as the Jew is accepted. I see where the Gallup poll showed that 38 percent would vote for a Negro as President. If this is so, they are thinking of somebody like Ralph Bunche. They are not thinking of a black man. I think color makes the difference increasingly. White people in the North are getting readier to accept those Negroes who approach them in physical type. They need to forget or ignore a person's Negro ancestry. We are not going to wipe out the stigma of Negro ancestry. Taboos shift, but only a little, and these taboos make the stigma. In ordinary society a man might say: "My grandfather was an Italian or a Yugoslav." Nobody is ever going to get up and say: "My grandfather was a Negro," unless it is obvious and he cannot avoid it. When the Negro gets light enough, he will simply pass into the other world.

It is not difficult to recognize in these weary words the residue of self-rejection which is the Negro's heaviest legacy from his past. It gives to the prospect of integration the cast of an ironic outcome. A great many Negroes who for so long desperately wished away their Negroness, like the counterpart Jews who wanted to shed their Jewishness, were trying to become part of a world that so utterly rejected them that it reduced Negroes to subhuman status and managed to annihilate six million Jews in a single holocaust. A few could escape by "assimilating" or "passing," i.e., by simply disappearing into the majority mass, but the greater number could not or would not disappear. Their answer had to be sought in integration, which was the promise of equality of status. But integration, with a jeering kind of irony, can seem to be offering little more than the same option to disappear; by getting rid of the *disability* of being Negro (or Jewish), one can try at last to cease being *Negro* without stealth or shame. Something of this ambivalent confusion hung over the efforts made in recent years by some Negro organizations to drop the word "Negro" from their names, like the National Negro Business League, the National Council of Negro Women (which actually voted to drop "Negro" and then voted it right back again) and the Colored Methodist Episcopal

Church which did in fact change "Colored" to "Christian." [1]

These moves were made in a hopefully or wishfully integrationist spirit, but they could not entirely divest themselves of the quality of stealthy escape, a gnawing sense of a loss of dignity even in an act seemingly designed to help regain it. What this strongly suggests is that wherever integration leads a man, he is going to have to carry with him the memory and the meaning of whence he came. If integration implies society's acceptance of a man, it also implies his acceptance of himself, including the name he bears, the color and physical characteristics he carries, the nation to which he belongs, the origins and history out of which he comes. Such conditions of individual and social health may lie dimly far ahead, if, indeed, they lie anywhere except in the dreams which reaching men allow themselves to have. We will have to wait to see, meanwhile, what the new circumstances do to the old patterns of rejection and self-rejection, what the new sortings of minority and majority will be like, what new shapes will be assumed by the old absurdities, what new reasons will be generated for some people not to want to be what they are.

There is of course a view, held in a much more matter-of-fact way by many, that the Negro will simply blend into the society as all sorts of other groups of people have done in the past, surviving only as a strand or a cast in the common design. This is not a radical miscegenationist view but an acceptance of a process already long underway. Much of this blending has already taken place. As a physical type the Negro American in his greater numbers today is the product of generations of assimilation in its most literal form. This in turn is part of a largely blind and much more inclusive evolutionary process that has been going on for a long time and will continue in one way or another whatever (or almost whatever) else goes on meanwhile. These views about total assimilation invite speculation about the prospects of the more remote future, but the timetable does not seem to be pressing these prospects upon us with any unpostponable haste. "Passing" will no doubt continue at the in-

[1] E. Franklin Frazier, "The Negro Middle Class and Desegregation," *Social Problems,* Apr. 1957, pp. 298–299.

creasingly nebulous frontier between "Negro" and "white," and there will probably be more intermarriage between the two in the time to come than hitherto. But neither one of these long-term likelihoods settles the nearer-by question of the new group identity of Negroes or the new location of Negroes as a group in the American society. Total physical assimilation may take place, but if it does it will take time—not an eon but not just a generation or two either—more time, in any case, than we are concerned with here.

But the extent of physical blending that has already taken place, combined with three centuries of total absorption and involvement in the American culture, have made for total assimilation of another kind which is not a matter for the remote future but is already part of our lives now. This is what sharply distinguishes Negro Americans from Africans and from any other people of whole or partial African ancestry. Negro Americans have shared markedly less of the goods and riches of the American culture they helped to make, but they have shared in everything else, including the ancestries of all other Americans, and in all aspects of the culture, its styles of thought and behavior, its attitudes, expectations, customs, and, with particular effect, in its arts. In morality and politics Negroes became the most critical bearers of the unique and most cherished features of the American identity, even if they did have to do so, up to now, by negation and failure. What Negroes have wanted and needed was not to cease being Negroes, but to cease being "Negroes": i.e., the possessors of an identity marked by their skin and their features which automatically and inescapably condemned them to total disability for life. They want to shed this crippling identity and to become free to move out as individuals onto the great common ground where all other Americans move, to cease having to struggle for simple access to the most elementary rights due them as members of the American society, to begin to discover at last what else besides repression life might hold for them, and what they might hold for it. This is what Negroes have meant and mean now by integration. It simply means being included in everything that everybody else is included in. The rest would be up to the free interplay of society, group, and individual, for this is what the American society ideally offers and must finally offer in fact to all its members: free scope for individuals to develop by their own gifts and for groups to exist within the society by their own vitality and by the needs they serve. This is the open society; this is pluralism.

But an integrated open society implies total freedom of movement across all lines. Successful integration of this kind unquestionably threatens the existence of closed parochial groups; the open society is the foe of all tribes. The groups that cherish their separateness do not fear it idly. The attractive power of the society at large is enormous for members of minority or excluded groups who feel stifled in their physical or psychological ghettos and whose struggle to be free is precisely the struggle to move beyond the narrownesses of the group to some larger coherence. Every despised and rejected group produces its own defensively ingrown values and institutions in which some of its members are glad to live their entire lives but which others find to be intolerable shackles. They want to live in a wider universe, not only without parochial barriers but without frontiers limiting aspiration or creation. The former become defenders of the inner way; the latter push out in search of the larger community. There have been many Jews of the latter sort wherever the society has allowed to all Jews a sufficient *Lebensraum*—an area large enough in which to live and achieve all the elementary goals of life, some decent well-being, without feeling hemmed in. The barriers that remain at the outer rim of such an area are for most people so distant and remote (e.g., becoming President of the United States) or so trivial (not getting into certain clubs or being admitted to certain resorts) that they do not impinge upon or restrict the ordinary rights and decencies of life. In these conditions the group continues to perform vital functions for its members. It provides institutions to defend the rights already enjoyed and, where required, to struggle to extend them. It provides a community that meets most of the ordinary demands most people make on their social life, religious, charitable, "cultural," or personal. It is, finally, the refuge and the asylum, the bosom on which the groupman rests most easily.

One of the advantages of this condition is the freedom it gives the individual to move out if he chooses to wherever his own bents take him and where, without "passing" and still wearing the identifying badges of his origin, he no longer functions primarily as a member of his tribe. No one thinks of Eugene O'Neill as an *Irish* writer, or of Frank Sinatra as an *Italian* singer, or of Felix Frankfurter as a *Jewish* judge, even though their identities remain perfectly visible and on appropriate occasion are duly acknowledged. Negroes being where they still are in our society, one still thinks of Marian Anderson as a *Negro* soprano, Ralph Bunche as a *Negro* public figure, Jackie Robinson as a *Negro* ballplayer. For the same reason of newness and uniqueness of his achievement, John F. Kennedy will still carry in many people's minds the automatic label *Irish Catholic*, but this is no longer by far his primary label or principal distinction. When the Andersons, Bunches, and Robinsons come to wear their group identity as incidentally as the Kennedys, Lehmans, or La Guardias, it will mean that Negroes will have moved at last into an area where life, if not wholly without restrictions, has become more than tolerable. That is still a long way off. But that is why now, despite continuing virulent anti-Semitism and persistent prejudice and exclusion affecting Jews in various quarters of American life, so many thoughtful Negroes, when asked to project their hopes for Negro status in America 25 years hence, say: "If all goes for the best, when that time comes, Negroes will stand in American society about where Jews stand now."

But what Negroes, like Jews, must now discover is how much of the cement that holds them together as a group has been pounded out of the stuff of their oppression over the centuries. Will the cracking of their bonds also crack their group ties? Or is there something else that gives vitality and power of survival to their group existence and places its distinctive mark on what new shape evolution offers? Jews who fear for the survival of their group identity in a free and open society invoke the ethics of their fathers, the universals of their religion, or the defensive parochialisms of a new small nation state. What will a new Negro-American group identity base itself upon? Upon some

surviving measure of rejection under which every recognizably
Negro face will remain a badge of apartness? Or some new
distinction coming up out of the new place and new share in the
community at large in the years to come? Upon the shared history and folk tradition of the long time of oppression, and if so,
how maintained from generation to generation? On institutions
that will survive the process of integration and preserve their
separateness, and if so, which ones, and surviving on what basis?
On color and physical characteristics, and if so, what color and
what characteristics? On some new form of mutually prideful
association with contemporary Africa or involvement in the
shaping of a modern African culture? Or in the contrary circumstances of new alienation, or some African alternative as a way
out of American hopelessness? Or some new racial *mystique,*
like *negritude,* summoned up by black French Caribbean poets
as a desperate counter to the powerful *mystiques* of whiteness?
It is questions like these that wait for Negro Americans just beyond their ghetto gates.

These questions, and all that has been described in these
pages, suggest only some small part of the complex turmoil that
is only beginning now as Negroes in greater and greater numbers shed the burdens of *nobodiness* and take on the new demands and new burdens of what Martin Luther King calls
*somebodiness.* All the elements of identity we have touched
upon—name, color, nationality, origins—and many others that
lie beyond them will have to acquire new shape and new content. All the choices—alienation, assimilation, integration—will
have to be redefined. Out of the recombining of all of these elements in a new environment, a new Negro group identity will
begin to be formed, and so too will the new shape of the American society.

# SELECTED BIBLIOGRAPHY

———————————— ❀ ————————————

*Africa and the American Negro: Addresses and Proceedings of the Congress on Africa, Dec. 13–15, 1895,* Gammon Theological Seminary, Atlanta, Ga., 1896.

Ahmann, Mathew H., ed., *The New Negro,* Notre Dame, Ind., 1961.

Allen, Samuel, "Negritude: Agreement and Disagreement," Paper presented at Third Annual AMSAC Conference, New York, June 1960.

*American Negro Leadership Conference on Africa, Resolutions,* Harriman, New York, Nov. 23–25, 1962.

Aptheker, Herbert, "Consciousness of Negro Nationality: An Historical Survey," *Political Affairs,* June 1949.

Arendt, Hannah, *The Origins of Totalitarianism,* New York, 1958.

Aron, Birgit, "The Garvey Movement: Shadow and Substance," *Phylon,* 4th Quarter, 1947.

Bacote, C. A., "Some Aspects of Negro Life in Georgia, 1880–1908," *Journal of Negro History,* July 1958.

—— "Negro Proscriptions, Protests, and Proposed Solutions in Georgia," unpub. ms.

Baldwin, James, *Go Tell it on the Mountain,* New York, 1953.

—— *Notes of a Native Son,* Boston, 1955.

—— *Nobody Knows My Name,* New York, 1961.

—— "A Negro Assays the Negro Mood," *The New York Times* Magazine, Mar. 12, 1961.

—— "Letter from a Region in My Mind," *New Yorker,* Nov. 17, 1962.

Bardolph, Richard, *The Negro Vanguard,* New York, 1959.

Bell, Howard H., "A Survey of the Negro Convention Movement, 1830–1861," unpub. thesis, Northwestern University, 1953.

—— "The American Moral Reform Society, 1836–1841," *Journal of Negro Education,* winter 1958.

—— "Negro Emigration Movement, 1849–1854, A Phase of Negro Nationalism," *Phylon*, 2nd Quarter, 1959.

Bettelheim, Bruno, "Individual and Mass Behavior in Extreme Situations," *Journal of Abnormal and Social Psychology*, Oct. 1943.

Bovell, Gilbert Balfour, "Psychological Considerations of Color Conflicts Among Negroes," *Psychoanalytic Review*, Oct. 1943.

Bowen, J. W. E., "Who Are We? Africans, Afro-Americans, Colored People, Negroes, or American Negroes?" *The Voice of the Negro*, Jan. 1906.

Braithwaite, E. R., *A Kind of Homecoming*, Englewood Cliffs, N.J., 1962.

Brenman, Margaret, "The Relationship Between Minority-Group Membership and Group Identification in a Group of Urban Middle Class Girls," *Journal of Social Psychology*, SPSSI Bulletin, 11, 1940.

Brisbane, Robert Hughes, Jr., "His Excellency the Provisional President of Africa," *Phylon*, 3rd Quarter, 1949.

—— "The Rise of Protest Movements Among Negroes Since 1900," unpub. thesis, Harvard University, 1949.

Broderick, Francis L., *W. E. B. Du Bois, Negro Leader in a Time of Crisis*, Stanford, 1959.

Brown, Sterling, *The Negro in American Fiction*, Washington, D.C., 1937.

—— Davis, Arthur, and Lee, Ulysses, eds., *The Negro Caravan*, New York, 1941.

—— "The New Negro In Literature," *The New Negro Thirty Years Afterward*, Washington, D.C., 1955.

Bunche, Ralph, *World View on Race*, Washington, D.C., 1936.

Calverton, V. F., ed., *Anthology of American Negro Literature*, New York, 1929.

Carpenter, Marie Elizabeth, *The Treatment of the Negro in American History School Textbooks*, Menasha, Wis., 1941.

Clark, K. B. and M. K., "The Development of Self and the Emergence of Racial Identification in Negro Preschool Children," *Journal of Social Psychology*, 10:1939.

—— "Skin Color as a Factor in Racial Identification," *Journal of Social Psychology*, Feb. 1940.

Coleman, James, *Nigeria—Background to Nationalism*, Berkeley and Los Angeles, 1958.

*Commission on Civil Rights Report*, 5 vols., Washington, D.C., 1961.

Cook, Mercer, "The Aspirations of Negritude," *New Leader*, Oct. 24, 1960.

Cronon, Edmund David, *Black Moses, The Story of Marcus Garvey and the Universal Negro Improvement Association*, Madison, Wis., 1955.

Crummell, Alexander, *Africa and America, Addresses and Discourses*, Springfield, Mass., 1891.

Cruse, Harold W., "Negro Nationalism's New Wave," *New Leader*, Mar. 19, 1962.

—— "An Afro-American's Cultural Views," *Présence Africaine*, Dec. 1957–Jan. 1958.

—— "Racial Integration and Negritude, A Philosophical View," paper presented at Third Annual Conference, American Society of African Culture, 1960.

Cullen, Countee, *On These I Stand*, New York, 1947.

Davis, Allison and Dollard, John, *Children of Bondage*, Washington, D.C., 1940.

Davis, Arthur P., "The Alien-and-Exile Theme in Countee Cullen's Racial Poems," *Phylon*, 4th Quarter, 1953.

—— "Integration and Race Literature," *Phylon*, 1st Quarter, 1956.

Davis, John A., *et al.*, "Foreign Reactions to American Racial Problems," unpub. ms., American Information Committee on Race and Caste, New York, 1955.

—— ed., *Africa Seen By American Negroes*, Paris, 1958.

Drake, St. Clair and Cayton, Horace R., *Black Metropolis, A Study of Negro Life in a Northern City*, New York, 1945.

Drake, St. Clair, "Pan Africanism, What Is It?" *Africa Today*, Jan.–Feb. 1959.

Du Bois, W. E. B., *The Souls of Black Folk, Essays and Sketches*, New York, 1953 (original pub. Chicago, 1903).

—— *Quest of the Silver Fleece*, Chicago, Ill., 1911.

—— "Reconstruction and Africa," *Crisis*, Feb. 1919.

—— *Darkwater: Voices From Within the Veil*, New York, 1920.

—— "On Migrating to Africa," *Crisis*, June 1924.

—— *Dark Princess: A Romance*, New York, 1928.

—— "Liberia, the League, and the United States," *Foreign Affairs*, July 1933, reprinted in *Africa As Seen By American Negroes*, pp. 329–345.

—— "On Being Ashamed of Oneself," *Crisis*, Sept. 1933.

—— *Black Folk Then and Now, An Essay in the History and Society of the Negro Race*, New York, 1939.

—— *Dusk of Dawn*, New York, 1940.

—— *Color and Democracy*, New York, 1945.

—— *The World and Africa*, New York, 1947.

Ellison, Ralph, *Invisible Man*, New York, 1952.

Elkins, Stanley M., *Slavery, A Problem in American Institutional and Intellectual Life*, Chicago, Ill., 1959.

Essien-Udom, E. E., *Black Nationalism*, Chicago, Ill., 1962.

Fanon, Franz, *Peau Blanc, Masques Noirs*, Paris, 1952.

Fauset, Arthur H., *Black Gods of the Metropolis*, Philadelphia, Pa., 1944.

Ferris, William H., *The African Abroad*, 2 vols., New Haven, Conn., 1913.

Fisher, Miles Mark, *Negro Slave Songs in the United States*, Ithaca, N.Y., 1953.

Foner, Philip S., ed., *The Life and Writings of Frederick Douglass*, 4 vols., New York, 1950.

Franklin, John Hope, *From Slavery to Freedom*, New York, 1947.

Frazier, E. Franklin, "All God's Chillun Got Eyes," *Crisis*, Apr. 1925.

—— "Garvey: A Mass Leader," *Nation*, Aug. 1926.

—— "The Garvey Movement," *Opportunity*, Nov. 1926.

—— *The Negro Family*, New York, 1939.

—— *Negro Youth at the Crossways, Their Personality Development in the Middle States*, Washington, D.C., 1940.

—— *The Negro in the United States*, New York, 1949.

—— *Black Bourgeoisie*, Glencoe, Ill., 1957.

—— "The Negro Middle Class and Desegregation," *Social Problems*, Apr. 1957.

Gibson, Charles H., "Concerning Color," *Psychoanalytic Review*, Oct. 1931.

Glicksberg, Charles I., "Negro Americans and the African Dream," *Phylon*, 4th Quarter, 1947.

—— "Psychoanalysis and the Negro Problem," *Phylon*, 1st Quarter, 1956.

Hansberry, Lorraine, *A Raisin in the Sun*, New York, 1959.

Harr, Wilber Christian, "The Negro as an American Protestant Missionary in Africa," unpub. thesis, University of Chicago Divinity School, 1945.

Haynes, George Edmund, "Americans Look at Africa," *Journal of Negro Education*, winter 1958.

Herskovits, Melville J., *The Myth of the Negro Past*, New York, 1941.

Himes, Chester, *The Third Generation*, New York, 1954.

Hofstadter, Richard, *Social Darwinism in American Thought*, Boston, 1955.

Howlett, Jacques, "Présence Africaine 1947–1958," *Journal of Negro History*, Apr. 1958.

Huggins, W. N. and Jackson, J. G., *A Guide to Studies in African History*, New York, 1934.

Hughes, Langston, *Fine Clothes to the Jew*, New York, 1929.

—— *The Dream Keeper*, New York, 1932.

—— *The Big Sea*, New York, 1945.

—— *Simple Speaks His Mind*, New York, 1950.

—— *I Wonder as I Wander*, New York, 1956.

—— *The Best of Simple*, New York, 1961.

*Intergroup Relations in Teaching Materials*, A Survey and Appraisal, American Council on Education, Report of the Committee on the Study of Teaching Materials in Intergroup Relations, Washington, D.C., 1949.

Isaacs, Harold R., *Two-Thirds of the World, Problems of a New Approach to the Peoples of Asia, Africa, and Latin America*, Washington, D.C., 1950.

—— "The Political and Psychological Context of Point Four," *Annals of the American Academy of Political and Social Science*, July 1950.

—— "Asia's Multiple Revolution: The Dimensions of the Crisis," *Saturday Review*, Aug. 4, 1951.

—— "Western Man and the African Crisis," *Saturday Review*, May 2, 1953.

—— "South African Apartheid and the United Nations," *United Asia* (Bombay), Feb. 1953.

—— *Scratches on Our Minds: American Images of China and India,* New York, 1958.

—— "World Affairs and U.S. Race Relations: A Note on Little Rock," *Public Opinion Quarterly,* fall 1958.

—— *Emergent Americans: A Report on Crossroads Africa,* New York, 1961.

Ivy, James W., "The Semantics of Being Negro in the Americas," written for the Second Congress of Negro Writers and Artists, Rome, Mar.–Apr. 1959, pub. in French under the title "Le Fait d'Etre Nègre dans les Amériques," *Présence Africaine,* Fev.–Mai 1959.

Jabavu, Noni, *Drawn in Color: African Contrasts,* New York, 1962 (London, 1960).

Johnson, Charles S., *Growing Up in the Black Belt,* Washington, D.C., 1941.

Johnson, James Weldon, *The Autobiography of an Ex-Coloured Man,* New York, 1928 (orig. pub. 1912).

—— *Negro Americans, What Now?* (New York, 1934).

Kardiner, Abram and Ovesey, Lionel, *The Mark of Oppression,* New York, 1951.

Kennedy, Joseph C., "The American Negro's Key Role in Africa," *The New York Times* Magazine, Feb. 4, 1962.

King, Martin Luther, *Stride Toward Freedom,* New York, 1958.

—— "The Case Against 'Tokenism,' " *The New York Times* Magazine, Aug. 5, 1962.

Klineberg, Otto, ed., *Characteristics of the American Negro,* New York, 1944.

Legum, Colin, *Pan-Africanism,* London and Dunow, 1962.

Levin, Harry, *The Power of Blackness,* New York, 1958.

Lewin, Kurt, *Resolving Social Conflicts,* New York, 1948.

Lewis, Wyndham, *Paleface,* London, 1929.

Lincoln, C. Eric, *The Black Muslims in America,* Boston, 1961.

Locke, Alain, ed., *The New Negro,* New York, 1925.

—— "The Negro in American Culture," Calverton, ed., *Anthology of American Negro Literature.*

—— "Who and What Is 'Negro,' " *Opportunity,* April–March, 1942, pp. 36–41, 83–87.

Logan, Rayford W., ed., *What the Negro Wants,* Chapel Hill, N.C., 1944.

—— *The Negro and the Post-War World: A Primer,* Washington, D.C., 1945.

—— *The Negro in American Life and Thought, The Nadir, 1877–1901,* New York, 1954.

—— "The American Negro's View of Africa," *Africa As Seen by American Negroes,* pp. 217–228.

Mannoni, O., *Prospero and Caliban,* New York, 1950.

Mayfield, Julian, *The Grand Parade,* New York, 1961.

McKay, Claude, *Harlem: Negro Metropolis,* New York, 1940.
—— *Selected Poems of Claude McKay,* New York, 1953.
Mehlinger, Louis R., "The Attitude of the Free Negro Toward African Colonization," *Journal of Negro History,* July 1916.
Meier, August, "The Emergence of Negro Nationalism," *Midwest Journal,* winter 1951–52, summer 1952.
Mencken, H. L., *The American Language,* Suppl. One, New York, 1945, pp. 618–637.
—— "Designations for Colored Folk," *American Speech,* Oct. 1944.
Miller, Kelly, "Negroes or Colored People," *Opportunity,* May 1937, pp. 142–146.
Moore, Richard B., *The Name "Negro": Its Origins and Its Evil Use,* New York, 1960.
Mphahlele, Ezekiel, *The African Image,* London, 1962.
Murray, Pauli, *Proud Shoes,* New York, 1956.
Myers, Henry J. and Yochelson, Leon, "Color Denial in the Negro," *Psychiatry,* Feb. 1948.
Myrdal, Gunnar, *An American Dilemma,* New York, 1944.
*Nationalism, Colonialism and the United States, One Minute to Twelve.* Forum sponsored by the Liberation Committee for Africa, New York, June 2, 1961.
*The New Negro Thirty Years Afterward,* Howard University, Washington, D.C., 1935. (Papers by: Sterling A. Brown, Charles S. Johnson, E. Franklin Frazier, Rayford Logan, Arthur H. Fauset, and others.)
Nkrumah, Kwame, *Ghana,* New York, 1957.
Ottley, Roi, *New World A-Coming,* Boston, 1943.
—— *No Green Pastures,* New York, 1952.
Ponton, M. M., *Life and Times of Henry M. Turner,* Atlanta, Ga., 1917.
*Psychiatric Aspects of School Desegregation,* Report No. 37, Group for the Advancement of Psychiatry, New York, May 1957.
Record, Wilson, *The Negro and the Communist Party,* Chapel Hill, N.C. 1951.
—— "The Negro Intellectual and Negro Nationalism," *Social Forces,* Oct. 1954–May 1955.
—— "Extremist Movements Among American Negroes," *Phylon,* 1st Quarter, 1956.
—— "Changing Patterns of Intra-Racial Differentiation Among American Negroes," pub. in German in *Sociologus,* fall 1959.
Reddick, Lawrence D., "Racial Attitudes in the South's American History Textbooks," unpub. M.A. thesis, Fisk University, 1933.
Redding, J. Saunders, *To Make the Poet Black,* Chapel Hill, N.C., 1939.
—— *Stranger and Alone,* New York, 1950.
—— *No Day of Triumph,* New York, 1950.
—— *They Came in Chains,* New York, 1950.
—— *On Being Negro in America,* New York, 1951.

Reid, Ira De A., "Negro Movements and Messiahs, 1900–1949," *Phylon,* 4th Quarter, 1949.

Robeson, Eslanda Goode, *African Journey,* New York, 1945.

Robinson, James H., *Road Without Turning,* New York, 1950.

Rose, Arnold and Caroline, *America Divided,* New York, 1953.

Rudwick, Elliott M., "W. E. B. Du Bois in the Role of *Crisis* Editor," *Journal of Negro History,* July 1958.

—— *W. E. B. Du Bois, A Study in Minority Group Leadership,* Philadelphia, Pa. 1960.

Russell, Bodine T., "What are the Policies, Practices, and Attitudes of the Foreign Mission Boards in North America With Reference to the Sending of American Negroes as Foreign Missionaries?" unpub. M.A. thesis, Presbyterian College of Christian Education, 1945.

Schuyler, George, *Slaves Today: A Story of Liberia,* New York, 1931.

Schoell, Frank L., "La Question Des Noirs Aux États-Unis," Selections translated by Jessie Fauset, *Crisis,* June 1924.

*Selected Papers Presented at the AMSAC Conference of Negro Writers,* Feb. 28, and Mar. 1, 1959. (Papers by: Saunders Redding, Samuel W. Allen, John H. Clarke, Julian Mayfield, Lorraine Hansberry, and others.)

Shepperson, George, "Education Sponsors Freedom—The Story of John Chilembwe," *Negro History Bulletin,* Jan. 1952.

—— and Price, Thomas, *Independent Africa—John Chilembwe and the Origins, Setting, and Significance of the Nyasaland Native Rising of 1951,* Edinburgh, 1958.

—— "Notes on Negro American Influences on the Emergence of African Nationalism," *Journal of African History,* I:2, 1960.

Stoddard, Lothrop, *The Rising Tide of Color,* New York, 1920.

*Summary Report, Fourth Annual Meeting,* American Society of African Culture, June 1961.

Sutherland, Robert L., *Color, Class and Personality,* Washington, D.C., 1942.

*The Race Question in Modern Science,* UNESCO, New York, 1956.

Thompson, Era Bell, *Africa, Land of My Fathers,* New York, 1954.

Thorpe, Earl E., "Africa in the Thought of Negro Americans," *Negro History Bulletin,* Oct. 1959.

Thurman, Wallace, *The Blacker the Berry,* New York, 1929.

Turner, Bishop Henry McNeal, "The American Negro and the Fatherland," *Addresses and Proceedings of the Congress on Africa, Dec. 13–15, 1895.*

Turner, Lorenzo D., "African Survivals in the New World with Special Emphasis on the Arts," *Africa Seen by American Negroes* (Paris, 1958).

Warner, W. Lloyd, Junker, Buford H., and Adams, Walter A., *Color and Human Nature,* Washington, D.C., 1941.

Washington, Booker T., *The Future of the American Negro,* Boston, 1899.

Weaver, Edward K., "Racial Sensitivity Among Negro Children," *Phylon*, 1st Quarter, 1956.

Welles, Sumner, *Time of Decision*, New York, 1944.

Wesley, Charles H., "The Reconstruction of History," *Journal of Negro History*, Oct. 1935.

White, Walter, *Flight*, New York, 1926.

—— *A Rising Wind*, New York, 1945.

Wilkins, Roy, "The Negro Wants Free Equality," Logan, ed., *What the Negro Wants*.

Woodson, Carter G., *The African Background Outlined; or Handbook for the Study of the Negro*, Washington, D.C., 1936.

Work, Monroe N., "The Passing Tradition and The African Civilization," *Journal of Negro History*, Jan. 1916.

Wright, Richard, *Native Son*, New York, 1940.

—— *Black Boy*, New York, 1945.

—— Essay in, Richard Crossman, ed., *The God That Failed*, New York, 1950.

—— *The Outsider*, New York, 1953.

—— *Black Power, A Record of Reactions in a Land of Pathos*, New York, 1954.

—— *The Color Curtain*, New York, 1956.

—— *White Man, Listen!*, New York, 1957.

—— *The Long Dream*, New York, 1958.

Zalinger, Alvin D., "The West African Student and American Race Relations," paper presented at 2nd Annual Conference, American Society of African Culture, June 1959.

# INDEX

Abedi, Kaluta A. (mayor of Dar Es Salaam), 310n
Abyssinian, name used by Negroes, 149, 153n
Acheson, Dean, 19
Adams, W. A., 82
Adowa (Ethiopia), battle of, 122, 147, 150, 151, 185
Africa, as pictured in geography books, movies, etc., *see* Africans; as reported by the press, 147, 179; in books or reading material in Negro homes, 146-47, 179, 184
African Baptist Church, 66
African Heritage (organization), 289
African Lodge of Masons, 66
African Methodist Episcopal Church, 66, 125, 127, 184, 190, 283
Africanism, survivals in American Negro culture, 107, 108, 109-11, 156, 157, 223, 256-57, 262, 264, 265, 267
Africans, as pictured in American geography textbooks, 128, 161-69, 179, 183, 184, 185, 190, 193, 207, 260, 264; as pictured in books, 181, 188; as portrayed in movies, 169-70, 176, 180, 184, 192, 264, 275, 285; as presented in school, 187, 285; as a subject in geography, 175, 176, 207
Afro-American Cultural Society, 289
Aggrey, James A. K., 148, 186, 192, 193
Alabama, University of, 9
All-African People's Congress of 1958, 142, 224
American Colonization Society, 67, 115, 117, 119. *See also* Liberia, founding of
American Negro Leadership Conference on Africa, 289
American Society of African Culture, 289, 310n

American Youth Commission, Studies on Negro youth, 82, 156
Americans of African Ancestry (organization), 289
*Amsterdam News* (newspaper), 19n, 65n, 93n, 96n, 303n, 316n
Anderson, Marian, 58, 348
Anderson, Sherwood, 231
Anti-Semitism, 348. *See also* Jews
Aptheker, Herbert, 99n
Arendt, Hannah, 99
Arkansas *Gazette* (newspaper), 11n
Association for the Study of Negro Life and History, 106, 183
Atlanta University, 132
Atlantic Charter of 1941, 42
Attucks, Crispus, 116
Azikiwe, Nnamdi, 31, 290, 312

Back to Africa, 67, 99, 100, 114-23, 133-46, 150, 155, 178, 185, 231, 232, 278, 286, 287, 311, 335, 338; DuBois' version of, 221; missionary purposes of, 114, 121, 123, 124. *See also* African Colonization Society, Marcus Garvey, Liberia
Bacote, C. A., 120n
Bailey, Pearl, 94
Baldwin, James, 59, 62, 98, 237, 258 and n, 267-77, 287, 328, 338; born, 237; exile in France, 267-68, 270; on Africa, 274-77; return from exile, 269
Balewa, Abubakar, 289
*Les Ballets Africaines*, 77n
Baltimore *Afro-American* (newspaper), 70, 92
Bandung (Indonesia) Conference of 1955, 249
Barker, Curtis H., 75n
Belafonte, Harry, 94

359

Bell, Howard H., 3n, 66n, 68n, 112n, 118n

Berlin Conference of the Powers (1884), 33, 122

Bethune, Mrs. Mary McLeod, 91-92, 149

Bettelheim, Bruno, 73 and n

Bible, 74, 75, 76, 123, 125

Bigger Thomas (fictional character), 58, 247, 259

Bilbo, Senator Theodore, 140, 286

Black Cross Nurses, 136. See also Marcus Garvey

Black Muslims, 30 and n, 63, 100, 333, 334, 335, 336, 339

Black Nationalism, 63, 99 and n, 134n, 261, 265-66, 282, 289, 335, 336, 337. See also Black Muslims, Marcus Garvey, Elijah Muhammed

Black Star Line of Ghana, 142

Black Star Steamship Line, 133, 139, 143, 231. See also Marcus Garvey

Blake, William, 77-78

Blyden, Edward W., 123, 185

Boas, Franz, 187, 207

Boer War, 185

Bolivar, Simon, 203

Booth, Joseph, 125

Booth, Maud Ballington, 80n

Bovell, Gilbert Balfour, 83n

Boston Massacre, 116

Bowen, J. W. E., 64

Bowles, Chester, 18

Braithwaite, E. R., 315, 318n

Brawley, Benjamin, 183

Brenman, Margaret, 157 and n

Brisbane, R. H., Jr., 29n, 134n

Brod, Max, 73n

Broderick, Francis L., 200n, 214n, 216n

Brown Fellowship Society of Charleston (S.C.) (1790), 68, 81

Brown, Sterling, 233 and n

Bunche, Ralph, 112, 142, 344, 348


Calverton, V. F., 39n

Castro, Fidel, 338, 341; trip to U.S. in 1960, 337

Catholics, 177, 327, 328n, 348

Census Bureau, census of 1790, 66;

attempts to measure African ancestry, 108

Center for International Studies (M.I.T.), 226

Chaucer, Geoffrey, 76

Chiang Kai-shek, 34

Chief Sam, 185

Chilembwe, John, 125

Chinese, Communists, 24, 337; Exclusion from U.S., 24; Revolution of 1911, 35; Revolution of 1925-27, 36

Chinese Exclusion Act (1924), 24

Christian, Christianity, 8, 12n, 33, 42, 106, 114, 118, 121, 122, 123, 124, 125, 127, 128, 156, 167, 189, 196, 203, 219, 300, 301, 332, 334, 345. See also Missionaries

Churchill, Winston, 42

Civil Rights Act of 1875, 120

Civil Rights Commission (U.S.), report for 1961, 47 and n

Civil Rights legislation, see Fair Employment, Housing, etc.

Civil War (U.S.), 32, 33, 115, 118

Clark, K. B., 158n

Clark, M. K., 158n

Cold War, 6, 50, 337

Color caste, 68, 74, 80-96, 137, 138, 141, 143, 149, 156, 171, 174, 195, 204, 208, 247; Garvey's influence on, 145; in marriage, 88, 90-93. See also Color, symbolic use of

Color, symbolic use of, 74-80, 158, 161, 170, 171, 172, 195, 213

Colored Methodist Episcopal Church, 344-45

Communism, Communist Party, 12, 13, 26, 27, 30, 41, 100, 178, 199, 218, 224, 225, 226, 229, 247-48, 263, 265, 337, 338; Chinese, 24, 337; International, 30; issue of the Ethiopian war, 150-52; "People's Fronts," 26. See also Marx, Marxism

Compton, Arthur, 196

Conant, James, 32

Congress Movement in India, 36

Congress of Industrial Organizations, 41

Congress of Races (1911), 223

Convention of Colored Citizens of America (1830), 66

Cook, Mercer, 316
Cosmos Club, 20
*Crisis* (magazine), 41, 43, 63n, 132, 146, 184, 195, 196, 197, 209n, 210n, 215n, 221n, 222n, 223n, 231, 241n
Cronon, Edmund David, 134n, 153n
Crossman, Richard, 248n
Crossroads Africa (student exchange project), 26n, 296
Crummell, Alexander, 73, 112, 129-30
Cuffee, Paul, 117
Cullen, Countee, 58, 99n, 146, 232, 235, 236n, 265, 284
Cumberbatch, William H., 63n
Cuney, Warren, 284
Cushing, Richard F. (Cardinal), 328n


Dandridge, Dorothy, 94
Darwinism, 33
Davis, Allison, 82-83, 156
Davis, Arthur P., 99n, 236n
Davis, John A., 3n, 9n, 109n, 113n
Debs, Eugene V., 263
Delafosse, Maurice, 187
Delany, Martin R., 3, 81, 117-18, 120
Dewey, Thomas E., 19
Diplomats, African and Asians, in racial incidents in U.S., 16ff.; Negroes as, 314-17
Dixon, Thomas, 168n
Dr. Dolittle Stories, 79 and n, 80
Dollard, John, 82-83, 156
Douglass, Frederick, 58, 69, 81, 118-19, 165, 191
Drake, St. Clair, 224n
DuBois, W. E. B., 30, 34 and n, 35, 41, 57, 58, 70, 87, 97-98, 106, 112, 130n, 131, 132, 137, 139, 141, 183, 184, 186, 187, 191, 192, 195-230, 231, 237, 240n, 258, 343; Africa in the writings of, 200; attending inauguration of President of Liberia, 208-09; attitudes toward Communism, 199, 212, 226, 227, 229; birth, 201; early interest in Africa, 207-09; editor of *Crisis*, 41, 132, 197, 198; founding the NAACP, 132, 197; in Africa, 209-10, 224-25; membership in Communist Party, 225; on color caste, 208; on migration, 227; opinion of Marcus Garvey, 221; organizing Pan-African conferences, 198, 223, 224; Pan-Africanism, 138, 146, 150, 200, 205, 207, 211n, 217-18, 220, 221; racism, 211, 219, 220, 229; student at Fisk, 205-07; "Talented Tenth," 197; trip through Communist bloc nations, 199-200; version of Back to Africa, 221, 222
Dulles, John Foster, 14
Dunbar, Paul Laurence, 58


*Ebony* (magazine), 96n, 143n
Eckford, Elizabeth, 11n
Eisenhower, Dwight D., 10, 12, 16, 19, 45, 46, 314
Eliot, T. S., 263
Ellison, Ralph, 23, 204, 237, 260-67, 268, 269, 287, 326; born, 237; on Africa, 261-62, 264; on Communism, 263; on the Ethiopian War, 261; student at Tuskegee, 263, 265
Emancipation, 7, 193, 197; Proclamation, 4, 23
Erikson, Erik, 58, 203
Essien-Udom, E. U., 99n
Ethical Culture (organization), 223
Ethiopian, name used by Negroes, 62, 63, 70, 149, 165
Ethiopian Peace Movement (organization), 150
Ethiopian War, 36, 149-53, 261, 277, 283; Help Ethiopia Movement, 153n

Fair Employment laws, 46
Fair Employment Practices Commission, 47
Fanon, Franz, 82n
Father Divine, 40, 145, 333
Faubus, Orval, 10, 11, 12
Faulkner, William, 262
Fauset, Arthur H., 63n, 334n
Ferris, William H., 72-73 and n
Fisher, Miles Mark, 115n
Fisher, Rudolph, 232
Fisk University, 132, 148, 175, 205-07
Fitzgerald, Ella, 58
Fitzhugh, Davis, 11n
Foner, Philip S., 69n

Fortune, T. Thomas, 35, 64, 69
Frankfurter, Felix, 348
Franklin, John Hope, 40n, 150, 151
Frazier, E. Franklin, 38n, 63n, 68n, 82, 87 and n, 88 and n, 109n, 110 and n, 139, 143, 156, 157, 291, 332, 345n
Free African Society, 66, 116
Freedom Rides, 15, 16, 19, 338
*Freedom's Journal* (newspaper), 117
Friends of Ghana (organization), 289
Frost, Robert, 98

Gandhi, Mohandas K., 36, 52, 320n
Garrison, William Lloyd, 118
Garvey, Amy Jacques, 143n
Garvey, Marcus, 40, 132, 133-45, 149, 185, 191, 192, 221, 224, 231, 232, 236, 242, 261, 265, 284, 286, 333, 335, 336; attacks on NAACP, 137; color chauvinism, 87, 88, 133, 136, 137, 141; conviction of using the mails to defraud, 133; death, 133; deportation, 133; imprisoned, 139; in London, 150, 153; influence on color caste of, 145; pardoned, 133; read by Nkrumah, 142; reaction of American Negroes to, 133ff.
Garvey movement, 70, 99n, 133-45, 150, 157, 172, 191, 223, 224, 227, 264. *See also* Back to Africa, Universal Negro Improvement Association
Georgia state legislature, 120
Gibson, Charles H., 83n
Gide, André, 232
Glicksberg, Charles I., 158n
Goldman, Emma, 99n
"gradualism," 132, 332
Grant, Madison, 138
Griswold, A. Whitney, 27n
Gude, E. W., 75n
Gunther, John, 131

Hair straightening, 74, 93, 94, 96 and n, 259, 279, 311
Handy, James A., 121
Handy, W. C., 58
Hansberry, Lorraine, 237, 277-87, 300; born, 237; on Africa, 278-81, 284-85, 287; on color caste, 284

Harr, Wilber Christian, 124n
Harvard University, 132
Hawthorne, Nathaniel, 77
Hemingway, Ernest, 262
Herskovits, Melville J., 108, 157; on African survivals in American Negro culture, 109-10 and ns, 265
Heyward, DuBose, 231
Hicks, James, 153
Hines, Chester, 85
Hitler, Adolf, 26, 42, 51, 151, 283
Hofstadter, Richard, 33 and n, 34n
Horne, Lena, 92, 94
Houphouet-Boigny, Felix, 289
Housing Discrimination laws, 47
Houston, Charles, 46
Howard University, 30n, 38, 60, 64, 93, 94, 111, 140, 148, 153, 169, 316
Huggins, W. N., 64n
Hughes, Langston, 83, 85, 89-90, 100, 146, 232, 233, 236, 237-46, 247, 258, 277, 278, 284, 285, 310; born, 237; on blackness, 242-44; student at Columbia, 241; trip to Africa, 238-40
Hunter College, 187
Huxley, T. H., 33

Indonesia, insurrection in 1927, 36
Ivy, James W., 63n, 64-65, 82n

Jabavu, Nona, 82n
Jackson, J. G., 64n
James, Henry, 98, 262, 273
Jefferson, Thomas, 22
Jews, 11n, 39, 42, 73, 101, 151, 177, 222, 317, 326, 327, 328 and n, 329, 344, 347, 348
Johnson, Charles S., 82, 87 and n, 156 and n
Johnson, Sir Harry, 181
Johnson, James Weldon, 82, 138, 232, 339, 340
Johnson, Noel, 264
Junker, B. H., 82

Kardiner, Abram, 87n, 157n
Kennedy, John F., 16, 17, 19, 20, 46, 316, 340, 348

Kennedy, Joseph C., 316n
Kennedy, Robert, 18, 19, 20, 46
Kenyatta, Jomo, 165, 289
Khrushchev, Nikita, 337
King, Martin Luther, 51, 52, 54, 349
Korean War, 46, 53, 248
Klineberg, Otto, 157n
Ku Klux Klan, 40, 135, 138

La Guardia, Fiorello, 348
Langston, J. Mercer, 100
Lehman, Herbert H., 348
League of Nations, 152; Covenant, 27; investigation of slavery in Liberia, 130, 214
Leopold (King of Belgium), 147, 148, 283
Levin, Harry, 75n, 77
Lewin, Kurt, 73n
Lewis, Ida, 303n
Lewisohn, Ludwig, 73n
Liberia, 112, 122, 124, 126, 128, 129-32, 142, 215, 312-14; American Negroes' attitudes toward, 130, 131; American Negroes in, 117, 120, 130-32, 295, 313, 314; founding of, 67, 115, 129, 175, 185; slavery in, 130
Lincoln, Abraham, 22, 68-69, 241
Lincoln, C. Eric, 30n, 63n, 100n, 334n
Lincoln University, 148, 180, 193
Lindsay, Vachel, 181, 233
Lipman, E. J., 328n
Little Rock (Ark.), School Desegregation Crisis, 9-13, 19, 268, 318, 322. See also Orval Faubus
Litvinov, Maxim, 152
Livingstone College, 148
Locke, Alain, 233, 234n, 235
Lofting, Hugh, see Dr. Dolittle stories
Logan, Rayford W., 13 and n, 32 and n, 112, 119, 120n, 126, 211n
Lucy, Autherine, 9
Lumumba, Patrice, 337; U.N. demonstrations regarding, 289, 336
Luther, Martin, 203
Luthuli, Albert John, receiving Nobel Peace Prize, 289
Lynching, 9, 14, 28, 38, 39, 40, 135, 234; of Chinese, in the American West, 24, 33

Macmillan, Harold, 28
Makeba, Miriam, 96n
Malraux, André, 262
Manchuria, Japan's invasion of, 151, 216, 283
Mao Tse-tung, 337
Maran, René, 233
Marshall, Paule, 341n
Marshall, Thurgood, 341
Marx, Marxism, 27, 36, 199, 212, 322. See also Communism, Communist Party
Maryland state legislature, 17
Massachusetts Institute of Technology, 50
"Massive Resistance," 15, 47
Mayfield, Julian, 59, 331
Mboya, Tom, 172, 289
McCabe, Edwin P., 119
McKay, Claude, 143 and n, 144, 152n, 153n, 232, 234
Mehlinger, Louis R., 112, 115n, 118n
Meier, August, 99n, 117n
Melville, Herman, 77
Mencken, H. L., 64, 69n
Meredith, James, 15, 331, 341n
Metropolitan Club, 20
Migration, 100, 119, 338; DuBois on, 227-28; of Negroes to Africa, see Back to Africa; of Negroes to Liberia, see Liberia; of Negroes within the U.S., 38, 41, 45, 47, 119, 135, 333
Miller, Kelly, 38, 39n, 60, 64 and n, 69, 73
Milton, John, 74, 76
Minnesota, University of, 184
Missionaries, in Africa, 106, 123-29, 146, 169, 178, 180, 183, 186; in the Baptist church, 12, 183; Negroes in Africa as, 124-29, 148, 181, 184, 185, 189, 311; willingness of Negroes to support, 123, 124, 126, 129, 190
Mississippi, University of, 15
Montgomery (Ala.) bus boycott, 9, 51, 52, 53, 330
Moore, Richard B., 63n
Morehouse College, 148
Morrow, John, 314
Moton, Robert, 149
Movies, Africans portrayed in, 169-70,

176, 192, 264, 275, 285. *See also* Africans

Muhammed, Elijah, 30, 333, 334, 335, 336. *See also* Black Muslims

Murray, Pauli, 85-86

Murrow, Edward R., 15

Myers, Henry J., 158n

Myrdal, Gunnar, 74n, 83n, 109n, 110, 142, 157

Name to go by, 62-71, 309

Nasser, Gamal Abdel, 337

National Association for the Advancement of Colored People, 19n, 35, 40, 43, 46, 70, 74n, 132, 137, 319, 331, 340; founding, 197

National Baptist Convention, 189

National Council of Negro Women, 91, 344

National Negro Business League, 344

Nazi extermination camps, 73

*Negritude*, 101, 229, 258, 317, 349

Negro Convention Movement, 112n

Negro nationalism, *see* Black Nationalism

Negro "Renaissance," 40, 231, 245

*Negro World* (newspaper) 133. *See also* Marcus Garvey

Negroes in Africa, 293-322

Negroes in diplomatic posts, 314-17

Negro stereotypes in literature, 58, 62, 116. *See also* individual characters as Uncle Tom, Sambo, etc.

Nehru, Jawaharlal, 203

New Deal, 41

New Orleans (La.), School Desegregation Crisis, 15, 19, 318, 322

*New York Age* (newspaper), 35 and n, 64, 69n

New York State Commission on Human Rights, 93n

"Niagara movement," 35, 132

Nixon, Richard M., 19

Nkrumah, Kwame, 14, 30, 31, 95, 96, 142n, 172, 227, 251, 254, 256, 276, 288, 290, 292, 304, 306, 308, 309, 312, 314, 321n, 337; Pan-Africanism, 224; reader of Marcus Garvey, 142

Nyasaland, uprising in 1915, 125

Nyerere, Julius, 289

O'Neill, Eugene, 231, 233, 348

Ottley, Roi, 29n, 65n, 143n

Ovesey, Lionel, 87n, 157n

Padmore, George, 30, 31, 224

Pan-African, Congress of 1919, 138, 196, 222, 223; Conferences of 1919-27, 198, 224; Congress of 1945, 224

Pan-Africanism, 101, 138, 146, 150, 200, 205, 207, 211n, 217-18, 220, 221, 223, 224, 231. *See also* W. E. B. DuBois

Parker, Mack, 14

"Passing," 73, 174, 196, 344, 345

Peace Corps (U.S.), 308, 315

Picasso, Pablo, 232

Pittsburgh *Courier* (newspaper), 64, 151

Poe, Edgar Allan, 77

Poitier, Sidney, 94, 165

Ponton, M. M., 121n

Porter, Mrs. Dorothy, 111-12

Presidential campaign of 1960, 327

Price, Thomas, 125n

Primus, Pearl, 92

Public Accommodations laws, 17, 47. *See also* Diplomats, in racial incidents in U.S.

Randolph, A. Philip, 41, 43, 47, 58, 137-38, 139

Reconstruction, 46, 81, 119, 120

Record, Wilson, 99n, 100n, 134n, 152n

Redding, J. Saunders, 85, 99n, 115n, 167n, 236n

Revolutionary War (U.S.), 25

Riff war, 36

Robinson, Jackie, 165, 348

Rogers, J. A., 151

Roosevelt, Franklin D., 42, 47, 91, 203

Rowan, Carl, 20, 168n, 316

Royal African Legions, 136. *See also* Marcus Garvey

Rusk, Dean, 18, 19

Russell, Bodine T., 124n

Russian Revolution of 1917, 36

Russo-Japanese War, 29, 34, 35 and n, 216; peace treaty, 35

Russwurm, John B., 117

Sambo (fictional character), 58, 62, 116
Sandburg, Carl, 68, 69n
Schomburg, Arthur, 147
School Desegregation, Clinton (Tenn.),
  9; Little Rock (Ark.), 9-13, 19, 268,
  318, 322; New Orleans (La.), 15, 19,
  318, 322; Virginia, 15. *See also* U.S.
  Supreme Court
Schuyler, George, 64, 130n
Scottsboro (Tenn.) Case, 26
Selassie, Haile, 150, 151, 152, 153, 261
Senghor, Leopold, 270, 289
Shepperson, George, 113n, 125n, 148n
Shirley, George, 96n
Sierra Leone, settlement of American
  Negroes in, 117, 185
Simple (fictional character), 58
Sinatra, Frank, 348
Singleton, Moses ("Pap"), 119
Sit-ins, 15, 45, 322, 330, 338
Skin whitening, 74, 92, 94, 96n, 311
Slavery, 7, 32, 33, 57, 67, 68, 111, 112,
  118, 123, 157, 166, 168, 175, 179, 188,
  191, 193, 208, 215, 240, 241, 252-53,
  257, 285, 304, 305, 310, 334; associa-
  tion with Africa of, 160; in Africa,
  214; in Liberia, 130, 214; slave trade,
  65, 175, 183, 185, 304-05. *See also*
  Emancipation
Small, John Bryant (Bishop), 129
Smuts, Jan Christian, 43
Smyth, J. C., 105-06, 155
Socialism, Socialist Party, 36, 263
Spanish Civil War, 151
Spencer, Herbert, 33
Sputniks, 11
Stanley-Livingstone story, Negro aware-
  ness of, 146-47, 184
Stepin Fetchit (fictional character), 62,
  275
Stevenson, Adlai E., 19
Stoddard, Lothrop, 138
Sumner, Charles, 3

Tagore, Rabindranath, 25
Tarkington, Booth, 167n
Thompson, E. S. Whitney, 163n
Thorpe, Earl E., 113n, 115n
Thurman, Wallace, 83-85, 232
Till, Emmett, 9

Tillman, Seth P., 27n
Token integration, 10, 47, 340
Toomer, Jean, 232
Touré, Sekou, 165, 289, 337
Truman, Harry S., 19 and n, 45
Turner, Henry McNeal (Bishop), 112,
  120-22, 125, 185
Turner, Lorenzo D., 109n, 265
Turner, Nat, 191
Tuskegee Institute, 15, 148, 149, 181,
  187, 197, 263, 265

Uncle Tom, 58, 62, 116
United Nations, 289, 291, 292, 336, 339;
  Charter, 13; General Assembly, 337
Universal Negro Improvement Associa-
  tion, 70, 133, 134n, 144, 191. *See also*
  Marcus Garvey
U.S. Armed Forces, desegregation, 45;
  Negroes in, 40, 41, 43, 50, 51, 135
U.S. Cabinet, 20, 327
U.S. Civil Rights Commission, 47 and
  n
U.S. Congress, 24, 40, 46; legislation,
  46, 47
U.S. Constitution, Amendments, 32
U.S. Courts, 10, 44, 46
U.S. Declaration of Independence, 25
U.S. Department of State, 17, 18 and n,
  19, 316
U.S. Foreign Service, 316
U.S. Information Agency, 15
U.S. Presidency, 327
U.S. Senate, 3; Armed Services Com-
  mittee, 46
U.S. Supreme Court, 20, 46, 120, 286,
  327; Brown v. Topeka 1954, 46, 47,
  340. *See also* School Desegregation
U Nu, 314

Van Vechten, Carl, 232
Versailles Conference, 27, 223
Verspan, Albert, 328n
Virginia Union, 187
Voice of America, 48
*Voice of the Negro, The* (newspaper),
  64 and n

Walters, Alexander (Bishop), 211n,
  223n

Warner, W. Lloyd, 82, 87, 156
Washington, Booker T., 58, 70, 132, 198; disagreement with DuBois, 197; on migration to Africa, 122-23
Weatherford, W. D., 110n
Weaver, Edward K., 158 and n
Weaver, George, 20
Welles, Sumner, 4 and n
West Indians, 40, 84, 86, 129, 132, 133, 137, 139, 141, 143, 144, 191, 192, 213, 223, 224, 265. See also Garvey Movement
Wharton, Clifford, 316
Wheatley, Phyllis, 58
White, Poppy Cannon, 96n
White, Walter, 28, 29n, 43, 44n, 74n
Wilkins, Roy, 43 and n, 48; editor of Crisis, 43
Williams, George Washington, 112, 185
Williams, H. Sylvester, 223n
Willkie, Wendell, 19

Wilson, James, 14
Wilson, Woodrow, 27, 38, 39n, 203
Wofford, Harris, 18
Woodson, Carter G., 106, 110, 112, 118n, 146, 183, 186, 187, 228, 285
Work, Monroe, 112
World War I, 4, 26, 36, 37, 38, 52, 88, 132, 135, 148, 191, 212, 213, 223; migrations of Negroes during, 38
World War II, 4, 9, 28, 29, 37, 42, 43, 51, 52, 277, 283; migrations of Negroes during, 41
Wright, Richard, 58, 113, 237, 247-60, 261, 262, 263, 266, 267, 268, 269, 304, 306, 321, 338; and Communism, 247-48; born, 237; exile in France, 248; on racism, 249-50, 257-60; trip to Africa, 247, 251-58

Yochelson, Leon, 158n

## DATE DUE

| | |
|---|---|
| | |
| | |
| | |
| | |
| | |
| | |
| | |
| | |
| | |
| | |
| | |
| | |
| | |
| | |
| | |

GAYLORD                                    PRINTED IN U.S.A.